The University Libraries at Penn State
and the Penn State University Press, through the
Office of Digital Scholarly Publishing, produced
this volume to preserve the informational content
of the original. This reprint edition was created
by means of digital technology and is printed on
paper that complies with the permanent Paper
Standard issued by the National Information
Standards Organization (z39.48-1984).

2008

Limited Edition, No. 196

A GUIDE BOOK OF
ART, ARCHITECTURE, AND
HISTORIC INTERESTS IN
PENNSYLVANIA

READING THE DECLARATION OF INDEPENDENCE
Painted by Edwin A. Abbey. © *M. G. Abbey*
From a Copley Print, © *Curtis and Cameron, Publishers, Boston*

A GUIDE BOOK OF ART, ARCHITECTURE, AND HISTORIC INTERESTS IN PENNSYLVANIA

EDITED BY

A. MARGARETTA ARCHAMBAULT

ILLUSTRATED

PHILADELPHIA
THE JOHN C. WINSTON COMPANY
1924

Copyright, 1924, by
THE JOHN C. WINSTON COMPANY

All rights reserved

PRINTED IN THE U. S. A.

17838 -

STATE FEDERATION OF PENNSYLVANIA WOMEN

President
MRS. JOHN B. HAMME

Art Committee for the Guide Book

MISS A. MARGARETTA ARCHAMBAULT, Chairman	Philadelphia
MRS. ROSS BARROWS	Lock Haven
MRS. EARL BARNES	Philadelphia
MISS MARY S. GARRETSON	Pittsburgh
MRS. ETHEL HERRON HAYES	Monongahela
MISS ALICE HENRY	Pittsburgh
MRS. ROBERT MCKELVY	Titusville
MISS IRENE B. MARTIN	Allentown
MISS SARAH R. PAISTE	West Chester
MRS. JOHN G. READING	Williamsport
MRS. WALTER KING SHARPE	Chambersburg
MRS. ANDREW THOMPSON	Honesdale

HAIL! PENNSYLVANIA

Hail! Pennsylvania,
  Noble and strong!
To thee with loyal hearts
  We raise our song.
Swelling to heaven, loud
  Our praises ring;
Hail! Pennsylvania,
  Of thee we sing!

Majesty as a crown
  Rests on thy brow;
Pride, Honor, Glory, Love,
  Before thee bow.
Ne'er can thy spirit die,
  Thy walls decay;
Hail! Pennsylvania,
  For thee we pray.

Hail! Pennsylvania,
  Guide of our youth!
Lead thou thy children on
  To light and truth;
Thee when death summons us,
  Others shall praise,
Hail! Pennsylvania,
  Through endless days!
          Edgar M. Dilley, U. of P., 1897.

Lo, sons of no mean Commonwealth,   *
*   *   *   *   *   *   *
We exultant speak the name of State,
Proclaim the great "experiment" that wrought,
As if by necromance 'mong doubting men,
Fruition sure—beyond his ardent thought,
Yet hidden in very heart of Penn!
And bear the message, flash it sea to sea,
Who freedom serve must of themselves be free!
          Harvey Maitland Watts.

THE PLAN OF THE BOOK

This Guide Book of Art, Architecture, and Historic Interests in Pennsylvania, commenced by advice of Mrs. Edward Biddle of Carlisle, and fostered by Mrs. Samuel Semple of Titusville, during their presidency of the "State Federation of Pennsylvania Women," for the use of tourists, is arranged chronologically, beginning with the counties first formed; towns in each county follow each other in location as closely as possible. Works of good art in the state have been catalogued, together with a story of most interesting pioneer history, that each one of the sixty-seven counties should have a chapter in the book; those that have no art have the Indian trails and thrilling experiences of our first brave pathfinders.

Serious effort has been made to have all the information verified; in some instances, two or three counties have made the same claims for various historic firsts, which have here been given their proper record, through consultation with the State Historians at Harrisburg. To keep the book small, facts are scarcely more than outlined; further information about them may be obtained from the bibliography of this book.

The chapter of each county was written by a most responsible person, who lived there, judges, clergymen, historians, and a few by officers of the women's clubs, thus giving inside knowledge that a stranger could never get. All dry-as-dust statistics are omitted, and only that which is of prominent interest is given.

THE PLAN OF THE BOOK

Authorities consulted have differed, and mistakes will occur; there will be sins of omission and commission in the work, according to the point of view of the reader; but they are few in comparison with the wealth of real information brought together within this cover.

To the many earnest helpers who have given their knowledge, time and patience in obtaining and sending these reports, warmest thanks and sincere appreciation are heartily given; all honor is due to them. We would like to give their names, but some have asked that they be withheld and it is thought best to do so with all.

A. MARGARETTA ARCHAMBAULT, Editor.
Philadelphia, June 15, 1917.

ADDENDA

This book, finished for publication in 1917, was placed in the vaults of the Historical Society of Pennsylvania, as all money was needed for our soldiers. The present committee, appointed by Mrs. Hamme, has decided to publish the work as compiled in 1917, and not delay it by trying to bring the sixty-seven counties up to date. Conditions have been so unfavorable for new construction, since the war, that little has been done. The population of towns, however, has been advanced to the 1920 statistics.

A. M. ARCHAMBAULT.
Philadelphia, June 30, 1924.

TABLE OF CONTENTS

	PAGE
STATE FEDERATION OF PENNSYLVANIA WOMEN	v
HAIL! PENNSYLVANIA	vi
THE PLAN OF THE BOOK	vii
PHILADELPHIA HISTORIC FIRSTS	1

CHAPTER
I.	THE COMMONWEALTH, OR STATE OF PENNSYLVANIA (PENN'S WOODS)	24
II.	BUCKS COUNTY	161
III.	CHESTER COUNTY	175
IV.	LANCASTER COUNTY	183
V.	YORK COUNTY	193
VI.	CUMBERLAND COUNTY	201
VII.	NORTHAMPTON COUNTY	207
VIII.	BERKS COUNTY	215
IX.	BEDFORD COUNTY	223
X.	NORTHUMBERLAND COUNTY	227
XI.	WESTMORELAND COUNTY	231
XII.	WASHINGTON COUNTY	235
XIII.	FAYETTE COUNTY	241
XIV.	FRANKLIN COUNTY	247
XV.	MONTGOMERY COUNTY	253
XVI.	DAUPHIN COUNTY	271
XVII.	LUZERNE COUNTY	277
XVIII.	HUNTINGDON COUNTY	285
XIX.	ALLEGHENY COUNTY	289
XX.	MIFFLIN COUNTY	301
XXI.	DELAWARE COUNTY	307
XXII.	LYCOMING COUNTY	319
XXIII.	SOMERSET COUNTY	323
XXIV.	GREENE COUNTY	327
XXV.	WAYNE COUNTY	331
XXVI.	ADAMS COUNTY	337
XXVII.	CENTER COUNTY	341
XXVIII.	BEAVER COUNTY	347
XXIX.	CRAWFORD COUNTY	351

TABLE OF CONTENTS

CHAPTER		PAGE
XXX.	ERIE COUNTY	355
XXXI.	VENANGO COUNTY	363
XXXII.	WARREN COUNTY	367
XXXIII.	BUTLER COUNTY	371
XXXIV.	MERCER COUNTY	375
XXXV.	ARMSTRONG COUNTY	379
XXXVI.	INDIANA COUNTY	381
XXXVII.	CAMBRIA COUNTY	385
XXXVIII.	CLEARFIELD COUNTY	391
XXXIX.	TIOGA COUNTY	395
XL.	MCKEAN COUNTY	399
XLI.	POTTER COUNTY	403
XLII.	JEFFERSON COUNTY	407
XLIII.	SUSQUEHANNA COUNTY	409
XLIV.	BRADFORD COUNTY	413
XLV.	SCHUYLKILL COUNTY	419
XLVI.	LEHIGH COUNTY	425
XLVII.	LEBANON COUNTY	429
XLVIII.	UNION COUNTY	433
XLIX.	COLUMBIA COUNTY	437
L.	PIKE COUNTY	439
LI.	PERRY COUNTY	443
LII.	JUNIATA COUNTY	445
LIII.	MONROE COUNTY	449
LIV.	CLARION COUNTY	453
LV.	CLINTON COUNTY	455
LVI.	WYOMING COUNTY	461
LVII.	CARBON COUNTY	463
LVIII.	ELK COUNTY	469
LIX.	BLAIR COUNTY	473
LX.	SULLIVAN COUNTY	477
LXI.	FOREST COUNTY	481
LXII.	LAWRENCE COUNTY	485
LXIII.	FULTON COUNTY	489
LXIV.	MONTOUR COUNTY	493
LXV.	SNYDER COUNTY	495
LXVI.	CAMERON COUNTY	501
LXVII.	LACKAWANNA COUNTY	505
BIBLIOGRAPHY		509

ILLUSTRATIONS

READING THE DECLARATION OF INDEPENDENCE. .*Frontispiece*

	PAGE
FOURTH OF JULY IN CENTER SQUARE, PHILADELPHIA.	28
JOHN MARSHALL, CHIEF JUSTICE OF THE UNITED STATES, 1808–1835, PHILADELPHIA	32
BENJAMIN FRANKLIN, PHILADELPHIA	34
CAPTAIN NICHOLAS BIDDLE, PHIADLEPHIA	52
A QUIET HOUR, PHILADELPHIA	58
THE TRAGIC MUSE, PHILADELPHIA	66
BISHOP WILLIAM WHITE, PHILADELPHIA	86
THE DUCK GIRL, PHILADELPHIA	112
GEORGE WASHINGTON, PHILADELPHIA	116
BRONZE TABLET IN BOULDER, CHESTER COUNTY	176
BAYARD TAYLOR MONUMENT, LONGWOOD, CHESTER COUNTY	180
MAIN BUILDING, FRANKLIN AND MARSHALL COLLEGE, LANCASTER, LANCASTER COUNTY	186
CAVALRY STATUE, ERECTED IN 1904, CENTER SQUARE, HANOVER, YORK COUNTY	198
DICKINSON COLLEGE, "OLD WEST," CARLISLE, CUMBERLAND COUNTY	204
THE JAIL AT READING, BERKS COUNTY	216
TRINITY CHURCH, READING, BUILT IN 1791, BERKS COUNTY	220
THE VICTOR, FRANKLIN COUNTY	250
PERKIOMEN BRIDGE, BUILT IN 1798, COLLEGEVILLE, MONTGOMERY COUNTY	256
THE JOY AND BURDEN OF LIFE, DAUPHIN COUNTY	274
GALLERY OF THE SCUPTURE HALL, CARNEGIE INSTITUTE, PITTSBURGH, ALLEGHENY COUNTY	292
THE CROWNING OF LABOR, ALLEGHENY COUNTY	296
THE BLOCK HOUSE, PITTSBURGH, ALLEGHENY COUNTY	298
OLD STONE ARCH ON JACK'S CREEK, MIFFLIN COUNTY	304
ALFRED O. DESHING MEMORIAL ART GALLERY, CHESTER, DELAWARE COUNTY	310
LYCOMING CREEK NEAR WILLIAMSPORT, LYCOMING COUNTY	320

ILLUSTRATIONS

STEPPING STONES, KIMBERLY RIVER, SOMERSET COUNTY	324
RIVERSIDE PARK, IRVING CLIFF, HONESDALE, WAYNE COUNTY	334
OLD PITTSBURGH AND PHILADELPHIA PIKE, ADAMS COUNTY	338
COURT HOUSE AND GOVERNOR CURTIN MEMORIAL, BELLEFONTE, CENTER COUNTY	344
DRAKE MONUMENT WITH STATUE OF THE DRILLER, TITUSVILLE, CRAWFORD COUNTY	354
WASHINGTON STATUE, ERIE COUNTY	358
IRON FURNACE, OIL CITY AND VICINITY, VENANGO COUNTY	366
VINEYARD HILL, BUTLER COUNTY	377
MURAL PAINTING IN THE DOME OF MERCER COUNTY COURT HOUSE, MERCER COUNTY	376
THE DEVIL'S ELBOW, EAST OF INDIANA, INDIANA COUNTY	382
MONUMENT TO THE UNKNOWN DEAD OF THE JOHNSTOWN FLOOD, CAMBRIA COUNTY	386
THE GAP BELOW JOHNSTOWN, CAMBRIA COUNTY	388
ANTIQUE CAPITAL, CHESTER PLACE, WELLSBORO, TIOGA COUNTY	396
KINZUA BRIDGE, MCKEAN COUNTY	400
ON THE SINNEMAHONING CREEK, POTTER COUNTY	404
DEFENSE OF THE FLAG, BRADFORD COUNTY	416
HENRY CLAY IRON MONUMENT, POTTSVILLE, SCHUYLKILL COUNTY	422
ZION REFORMED CHURCH, ALLENTOWN, SCHUYLKILL COUNTY	426
THE OLDEST CANAL TUNNEL IN THE UNITED STATES, LEBANON COUNTY	430
SAWKILL FALLS, MILFORD, PIKE COUNTY	442
THE SUSQUEHANNA TRAIL, CLINTON COUNTY	456
ST. MARK'S PROTESTANT EPISCOPAL CHURCH, MAUCH CHUNK, CARBON COUNTY	466

MAPS

	PAGE
PHILADELPHIA COUNTY	25
COLONIAL WALKS No. 1	27
COLONIAL WALKS No. 2	36
GERMANTOWN	146
BUCKS COUNTY	162
CHESTER COUNTY	174
LANCASTER COUNTY	184
YORK COUNTY	192
CUMBERLAND COUNTY	200
NORTHAMPTON COUNTY	208
BERKS COUNTY	214
BEDFORD COUNTY	222
NORTHUMBERLAND COUNTY	226
WESTMORELAND COUNTY	232
WASHINGTON COUNTY	236
FAYETTE COUNTY	242
FRANKLIN COUNTY	246
MONTGOMERY COUNTY	254
DAUPHIN COUNTY	272
LUZERNE COUNTY	278
HUNTINGDON COUNTY	284
ALLEGHENY COUNTY	290
MIFFLIN COUNTY	302
DELAWARE COUNTY	306
LYCOMING COUNTY	318
SOMERSET COUNTY	322
GREENE COUNTY	328
WAYNE COUNTY	332
ADAMS COUNTY	336
CENTER COUNTY	342
BEAVER COUNTY	346
CRAWFORD COUNTY	350
ERIE COUNTY	356
VENANGO COUNTY	364
WARREN COUNTY	368
BUTLER COUNTY	370

MAPS

	PAGE
MERCER COUNTY	376
ARMSTRONG COUNTY	378
INDIANA COUNTY	382
CAMBRIA COUNTY	386
CLEARFIELD COUNTY	390
TIOGA COUNTY	394
MCKEAN COUNTY	400
POTTER COUNTY	402
JEFFERSON COUNTY	406
SUSQUEHANNA COUNTY	410
BRADFORD COUNTY	412
SCHUYLKILL COUNTY	418
LEHIGH COUNTY	424
LEBANON COUNTY	430
UNION COUNTY	434
COLUMBIA COUNTY	436
PIKE COUNTY	440
PERRY COUNTY	444
JUNIATA COUNTY	446
MONROE COUNTY	448
CLARION COUNTY	452
CLINTON COUNTY	456
WYOMING COUNTY	460
CARBON COUNTY	464
ELK COUNTY	468
BLAIR COUNTY	472
SULLIVAN COUNTY	478
FOREST COUNTY	480
LAWRENCE COUNTY	484
FULTON COUNTY	490
MONTOUR COUNTY	492
SNYDER COUNTY	496
CAMERON COUNTY	500
LACKAWANNA COUNTY	504

PHILADELPHIA HISTORIC FIRSTS

THE first parks in North America provided for the pleasure of the people were dedicated by William Penn at the settlement of Philadelphia in 1682. They were the North Eastern, South Eastern, North Western, South Western, and Centre Squares, now known respectively as Franklin, Washington, Logan, Rittenhouse, and Penn Squares.

In a letter dated 1683, William Penn alludes to the glass-house of the Free Society of Traders. Soon after this a glass-house was erected at Frankford by English Friends.

The first almanac printed in America was "Kalendarium Pennsilvaniense, or, America's Messinger. Being an Almanack for the Year of Grace, 1686." It was edited by Samuel Atkins, and published by William Bradford, 1685.

The first paper mill in America was built by William Rittenhouse, on the banks of the Wissahickon Creek, in the year 1690.

"A new Primmer or Methodical Direction to attain the True Spelling, Reading and Writing of English." This was the first American school textbook; though it was published in New York in 1698, its author was Francis Daniel Pastorius, founder of Germantown.

The first presbytery of the Presbyterian Church in the United States was formed in Philadelphia in 1705. It was composed of seven ministers, and included Philadelphia, Maryland, Delaware, and the Eastern shore of Virginia.

The first botanical garden in America was started in 1705 by Dr. Christopher Witt, at the southeast corner of Germantown Avenue and High Street. John Bartram began his famous gardens in 1728 at Gray's Ferry on the Schuylkill River.

The first Mennonite Church in America was erected in Germantown, at Germantown Avenue and Herman Street, the first service being held therein, May 23, 1708.

The first institution in America for the care of the poor was the Friends' Almshouse, established in Philadelphia in 1713.

First municipal care of the poor in the United States was begun by the City of Philadelphia in a rented building September 1, 1713; the first building was erected in 1731.

The first Dunkard (Tunker) Church in America was formed in Germantown, December 25, 1723, at Germantown Avenue and Upsal Street. The first love-feast celebrated in this country was observed by them the same evening.

The first association for the benefit of workers (or labor organization) in America was the "Carpenters' Company," established in Philadelphia, in 1724.

The first mariner's quadrant, invented by Thomas Godfrey, a glazier, of Nineteenth Street and Church Lane, Germantown, was made in 1730. First used in Delaware Bay by Joshua Fisher.

In 1727 a literary society was formed here by Franklin and eleven associates. This was the famous "Junto," and from it originated the Library Company of Philadelphia, the first library of a public nature in America. The instrument of association was dated

PHILADELPHIA FIRSTS

July 1, 1731, and the charter granted by the proprietary May 3, 1742.

The first club in America organized as a dining and fishing club was the "Colony in Schuylkill," 1732. The name was afterwards changed to the "State in Schuylkill."

The first German newspaper in America was *Die Philadelphische Zeitung*, published by Benjamin Franklin, May 6, 1732. There were but two numbers issued.

The first type made in America was made by Christopher Saur, the Germantown printer, in 1735.

The first volunteer fire company in America, "The Union Fire Company," was founded by Franklin and four associates, December 7, 1736. It lasted for eighty-four years.

February 13, 1741, *The American Magazine, or a Monthly View of the Political State of the British Colonies*, was published by Andrew Bradford. This was the first magazine published in America. Three days later, February 16, 1741, Franklin issued *The General Magazine and Historical Chronicle for all the British Plantations in America*.

The first German Bible printed in America was by Christopher Saur, in Germantown, 1743. Saur also published the New Testament in German. He issued seven editions in the years 1745, 1747, 1748, 1751.

The first institution in America devoted to science and learning was the "American Philosophical Society," organized in 1743. By Articles of Agreement, dated January 2, 1769, there took place a union between this society and "The American Society for Promoting and Propagating Useful Knowledge, held at Philadelphia," the latter an outgrowth of the famous "Junto" established by Franklin and his associates in 1727. From the date of union until the present time but one society has existed, known as the "American Philosophical Society."

The first lightning rod was placed upon the home of its inventor, Benjamin Franklin, at 141 (now 325) Market Street, in 1749.

In December, 1749, certain Scotchmen living in Philadelphia organized the "St. Andrew's Society at Philadelphia in Pensilvania." The object of the society was the relief of poor and distressed Scotsmen. It was the first organization of the kind in this country.

The first hospital in America was "The Pennsylvania Hospital," chartered by Assembly of Pennsylvania, May 11, 1751.

The first American work on botany was by John Bartram and was published in 1751. Its title was "Observations on the Inhabitants, Climate, Soil, Divers Productions, Animals, etc., made in his travels from Pennsylvania to Onondaga, Oswego, and the Lake Ontario."

The first fire insurance company in America was the "Philadelphia Contributionship for the Insurance of Houses from Loss by Fire." It was organized April 13, 1752, and twelve directors chosen at that time, who held their first meeting May 11, 1752. At this meeting was adopted the well-known seal which has given the company its nickname of "Hand-in-Hand."

The first expedition fitted out in the United States for Arctic exploration and the discovery of a north-

PHILADELPHIA FIRSTS 5

west passage, sailed from Philadelphia on the schooner *Argo*, Captain Charles Swaine, March 8, 1753.

The first cartoon published in America was the famous snake divided into eight parts, representing the colonies: New England, New York, New Jersey, Pennsylvania, Maryland, Virginia, North Carolina, and South Carolina, and bore the motto, "Join or die." It was published by Benjamin Franklin in "The Pennsylvania Gazette," May 9, 1754, and was called forth by the massacres of colonists in the French and Indian wars.

The first life insurance company in this country was the "Presbyterian Ministers' Fund of Philadelphia," founded in 1759.

The first mention of Shakespeare (discovered to date, April, 1916) in any American work occurs in "Science, A Poem," by Francis Hopkinson. Published by William Dunlap in Philadelphia, 1762.

The first night school in America was opened in the Germantown Academy, October 14, 1762. The sessions were from 6.00 p. m. to 9.00 p. m., each scholar to find his own candle and pay 2 shillings 6 pence for firewood; the compensation was 10 shillings per quarter.

The first observatory erected in this America was on South Street near Front, and was built for Mason and Dixon in 1763.

The first religious magazine in America was the "Geistliches Magazine," published by Christopher Sauer in 1764.

The first medical school in America was begun by the University of Pennsylvania, May 3, 1765. The first medical commencement was held June 21, 1768, when ten students were given degrees.

"Captains of Ships Charitable Club" was instituted July 4, 1765, and incorporated February 4, 1770, as "The Society for the Relief of Poor and Distressed Masters of Ships, their Widows and Children." This was the first society of its kind organized in America.

The first permanent theatre in America was the "Southwark Theatre," erected at South and Leithgow Streets, Philadelphia. It was opened by David Douglass, November 21, 1766.

The first American play was "The Prince of Parthia," by Thomas Godfrey, Jr., a young Philadelphia poet, and the son of the inventor of the mariner's quadrant. It was produced at the Southwark Theatre, April 23, 1767.

The first American publication on pedagogy was "A Simple and Thoroughly Prepared School-Management," by Christopher Dock, "the pious schoolmaster of Skippack." It was published in Germantown by Christopher Saur, 1770.

"The Pennsylvania Packet; and the General Advertiser," was first issued October 28, 1771. This was a weekly publication printed by John Dunlap. In 1784, Dunlap had taken as his partner David C. Claypoole, and on Tuesday, September 21, 1784, they issued "The Pennsylvania Packet, and Daily Advertiser." This was the first daily newspaper published in America.

The first active protest against the importation of tea, on account of the obnoxious tax, occurred in Philadelphia (not Boston) in 1773. An immense meeting was held in the State House Yard October 16, 1773.

PHILADELPHIA FIRSTS

Under date of November 27, 1773, a broadside was issued warning against an attempt to land any of the objectionable article. On Christmas Day the ship *Polly*, Captain Ayres, reached Chester. Captain Ayres was brought to Philadelphia and informed of the situation. On December 27th he started on his return trip to England, taking his cargo of tea with him. The people of Boston held their tea party December 16, 1773, and cast the tea into the harbor, thus entailing a heavy loss upon the innocent merchants.

"The Garden of the Soul: Or, a Manual of Spiritual Exercises and Instructions for Christians who (living in the World) aspire to Devotion." London; Printed. Philadelphia: Re-printed, by Joseph Cruikshank, on Market Street, between Second and Third Streets (1774). This was the first Roman Catholic prayer book printed in English in America.

"The Society for Promoting the Abolition of Slavery" was founded in Philadelphia in 1774. It was the first society in the country formed for this purpose. It was reorganized February 10, 1784, as the "Pennsylvania Society for Promoting the Abolition of Slavery and for the Relief of Free Negroes Unlawfully held in Bondage, and for Improving the Condition of the African Race."

The earliest mention of the manufacture of carpets in this country is that of William Calverly of Loxley's Court, date supposed to be 1774.

The first joint-stock company formed for the manufacture of cotton was the "United Company of Philadelphia for Promoting American Manufactures." The first general meeting was held February 22, 1775, and

Dr. Benjamin Rush was elected president. This is believed to be the first joint-stock company for any kind of manufactures in this country.

The first piano made in the United States was in 1776, by John Behrent, Jr., joiner, on Third Street below Brown.

The first United States flag is believed to have been made in Philadelphia in 1777.

In 1780 was the first abolition act of America providing slavery be abolished in Pennsylvania.

July 17, 1780, the "Pennsylvania Bank" opened for business. This was the first bank in the United States, and existed until 1784. "The President, Directors, and Company of the Bank of North America" was chartered by the Continental Congress, December 31, 1781. This bank is still in existence and is the only bank in the United States operating under the National Banking Act which is not required to carry the word "National" in its official title.

The first Bible in English produced by an American press was the work of Robert Aitken, the Philadelphia printer, in 1782. It was issued in two volumes. On the back of the title page of the first volume of the copy in the British Museum is this note, in the handwriting of Robert Aitken: "The first copy of the first edition of the Bible ever printed in America in the English language, is presented to Ebenezer Hazard, Esq., by the Editor."

The "Philadelphia Society for Promoting Agriculture," formed in 1785 and incorporated in February, 1809, was the first agricultural organization in this country. Its membership was limited to farmers only.

PHILADELPHIA FIRSTS

The first General Convention of the Protestant Episcopal Church in the United States was held in Christ Church, Philadelphia, September 27 to October 7, 1785. There were present delegates from seven states, and it was at this convention that the Church was organized in America, and the changes made in the Prayer Book necessary for its use in the new nation. Rev. William White, D.D., was chosen president of the convention.

The first free dispensary in the United States devoted to the relief of the sick and suffering was the Philadelphia Dispensary, founded January, 1786. It was opened in Strawberry Alley, April 12, 1786. It is still in existence, and is located at 127 South Fifth Street.

First steamboat in the world was built by John Fitch, a Philadelphian. The boat was successfully operated on the Delaware River, July 26, 1786. Another boat, 80 feet long, was built, and on October 12, 1788, successfully made the trip from Philadelphia to Burlington, carrying thirty passengers.

The first "College of Physicians" in America was formed in Philadelphia, January 2, 1787.

The first Roman Catholic Church for Germans was organized in Philadelphia in 1787. Ground for a building was purchased at the northwest corner of Sixth and Spruce Streets. Articles of incorporation were granted October 4, 1788, under the title of "The Trustees of the German Religious Society of Roman Catholics, called the Church of the Holy Trinity in the City of Philadelphia."

The first medical library in the United States was

established in connection with the College of Physicians in Philadelphia, in April, 1788.

"The Free African Society" was founded April 12, 1788, by Absalom Jones and Richard Allen, two negro clergymen of Philadelphia. The "African Church," the first church in America exclusively for and controlled entirely by negroes, was built by this Society, and opened for public worship July 17, 1794. It was incorporated March 28, 1796, as "The Minister, Church Wardens and Vestrymen of the African Episcopal Church of St. Thomas, in the City of Philadelphia."

In 1789, Lucian's "Dialogues," first Greek book printed in America, was by Joseph James at Philadelphia.

The Philadelphia Stock Exchange, the first in America, originated in 1790, in a building at the southwest corner of Front and Market Streets, known as the "London Coffee House." It was known as the "Philadelphia Board of Brokers" until the 8th of December, 1875, when it was changed to its present name, "The Philadelphia Stock Exchange."

The first law school in America was opened by the University of Pennsylvania, December 15, 1790, President Washington and the members of his cabinet taking part in the exercises.

Turkish and Axminster carpets were first made in this country in 1791, by William Peter Sprague, in the Northern Liberties.

First Bank of the United States, was established in Philadelphia, February 25, 1791.

The first patents for machines for threshing grain in

the world were awarded to Samuel Mulliken, of Philadelphia, March 11, 1791.

In 1791, Charles Willson Peale established a drawing school, which was succeeded in 1794 by "The Columbianum," also established by Charles Willson Peale. This was the first society in the United States for the promotion of the fine arts.

The first canal in the United States was the "Schuylkill and Susquehanna Navigation Company," chartered here in 1791. There were 2000 shares of stock at two hundred dollars per share, and the officers were Robert Morris, president; Timothy Matlack, secretary; and Tench Francis, treasurer.

The first United States Mint was built in Philadelphia, at what is now 37 and 39 North Seventh Street. The corner stone was laid July 31, 1792, and the first coins, consisting of dimes, half-dimes and cents, were struck in October of the same year. David Rittenhouse, a Philadelphian, was the first director.

The first company organized in America to do a marine insurance business was the "Insurance Company of North America," organized March, 1792, though it did not receive a charter until April 14, 1794. In spite of the fact that the granting of the charter was delayed, the company commenced doing business immediately after its organization in 1792, and there is recorded the payment of the first loss June 10, 1793, and the first dividend on its stock was paid in January, 1794.

"The Philadelphia and Lancaster Turnpike Company," the first constructed in the United States. The organization of the company was effected in 1792, under authority granted by the Legislature. The road was completed in May, 1796. The first regular stage left Lancaster at five o'clock in the evening, and reached Philadelphia at five o'clock the next morning, bringing ten passengers. The original officers of the company were William Bingham, president; William Moore Smith, secretary; and Tench Francis, treasurer.

The first successful balloon ascension in America was made from the old jail yard at the southeast corner of Sixth and Walnut Streets, January 9, 1793, by the French aëronaut, J. P. Blanchard.

Sulphuric acid (oil of vitriol) was first made in America by John Harrison in 1793. He was also the first to attempt to produce nitric acid.

"The Female Society for the Relief of the Distressed" was the first society organized in this country for the temporary assistance of the distressed. It was formed in November, 1793; and the first meeting was held in the house of Isaac Parrish, at the southeast corner of Second Street and Pewterplatter Alley.

Ice cream was first made in this country by Peter Bossu, a Frenchman, who settled in Philadelphia in 1794. The first advertisement of ice cream appears in *The Aurora* for July 22, 1800.

The first printing press made in America was constructed by Adam Ramage, in 1795.

"The United States Gazetteer," the first in this country, was compiled by Joseph Scott, and printed by Bailey at 116 Market Street, Philadelphia, in the year 1795.

The "First American Edition" of Shakespeare's

complete works was issued in Philadelphia in 1795, by Bioren and Madan.

To "Ambroise & Company," Mulberry Street (now Arch Street), between Eighth and Ninth, belongs the honor of being the first in America to manufacture inflammable gas and exhibit the effect of gas light. This exhibition took place in August, 1796, in connection with a pyrotechnic display.

Philadelphia introduced the first municipal water works in America, using a steam pump. Ground was broken March 12, 1799; the first brick was laid May 2, 1799; the first pipe (which was of wood) was put in place June 18, 1799; and the same day was begun the foundation of the engine house in Centre Square. The first water was sent through the pipes January 27, 1801.

The first person to make "artificial mineral water," or soda water, in America, was John Hart, a Philadelphia druggist. He did this about the beginning of the Nineteenth century (exact date not known), at the suggestion of Dr. Physick, to imitate waters found in certain mineral springs.

The first United States Navy Yard was established in Philadelphia in 1800. It occupied about twelve acres and extended from Prime Street (now Washington Avenue) to Wharton Street, and from Front Street to the Delaware River. In 1875 it was moved to League Island and the old property sold.

The first frigate of the United States Navy, the *Philadelphia*, was built in 1800, by Joshua Humphreys, near Washington Avenue.

The first mercurials made in the United States were

produced in 1801 by Dr. Adam Seybert, a druggist, whose shop was at 168 North Second Street.

The oxy-hydrogen blowpipe was invented in 1801, by Professor Robert Hare of Philadelphia.

Charles Eneu Johnson, in 1804, produced the first printing ink made in America. His firm is still in business and is known as Charles Eneu Johnson & Company.

The first land steam carriage, or automobile, in the world was invented by Oliver Evans, in 1804. The Eruktor Amphibolis, a machine for cleaning docks, mounted on a wagon, was propelled along Market Street, from Centre Square to the Schuylkill River. At the river a stern wheel was attached and the vessel launched; the machine was navigated by steam on the Schuylkill and Delaware rivers, and was used to deepen the docks.

In 1804, Samuel Wetherill and his son, Samuel, Jr., erected a white lead manufactory at the northwest corner of Broad and Chestnut Streets, and it was here that the first white lead in this country was produced. English manufacturers were so opposed to this industry being established in the United States that they sent an emissary to this country, who destroyed the works by fire. They were rebuilt in 1808 at Twelfth and Cherry Streets, and in 1847 moved to West Philadelphia on the banks of the Schuylkill, where the business is still carried on by the fifth succeeding generation.

The first commission house in the United States for the sale of American manufactures was established in Philadelphia, in 1805, by Elijah Waring.

The first institution in the United States for the

teaching of art was the "Pennsylvania Academy of the Fine Arts." The Articles of Agreement were signed December 26, 1805, by seventy-one citizens. George Clymer was chosen president. The charter was granted March 28, 1806, and it was opened to the public in 1807.

The first orphan society in the United States was the "Roman Catholic Society of St. Joseph for Educating and Maintaining Poor Orphan Children." It was organized by Rev. Leonard Neale, in 1806, and received a charter the following year.

The first riveted hose for fire use in the United States was made in Philadelphia in 1808.

"American Ornithology" was the work of Alexander Wilson, a resident of Philadelphia. Eight volumes were issued, the first in September, 1808. It was published in Philadelphia by Bradford, and was the first book upon ornithology published in this country.

The first American shot was made in Philadelphia, two towers being completed at practically the same time. The advertisements appear under the following dates:

  Bishop & Sparks, October 20, 1808.
  Paul Beck, October 27, 1808.

The first Bible Society in America was instituted December 12, 1808, and was incorporated January 30, 1810, as the "Bible Society of Philadelphia." By an amendment to the charter, dated March 7, 1840, the name was changed to the "Pennsylvania Bible Society," which name has been retained to the present day.

The first cotton goods printed from engraved cylinders in the United States were produced near Germantown in 1809 by Thorp, Siddall & Co., from cylinders brought from England.

The first experimental railroad track in the United States was constructed by Somerville, a Scotch millwright, for Thomas Leiper of Philadelphia, and laid down in the yard of the Bull's Head Tavern, on Second Street above Callowhill, in the Northern Liberties. It was sixty-four feet in length. The test was made July 31, 1809, and was so successful that Leiper had a railroad constructed at his quarries on Crum Creek, in Delaware County, September, 1809. This was the first practical railroad built in the United States.

First institution in the United States chartered to do a trust business was the "Pennsylvania Company for Insurances on Lives and Granting Annuities." Application for charter made January, 1810; refused by the House of Representatives, but finally granted March 10, 1812.

The first chemical society in America was the "Columbian Chemical Society," formed in Philadelphia in 1811.

The first soup society in America was the "Northern Soup Society," on Fourth Street above Brown, formed January, 1817.

The "Academy of Natural Sciences" was the first of its kind in the United States. It was organized January 25, 1812, by John Speakman, Jacob Gilliams, and four others. The society was incorporated by the Pennsylvania Legislature, March 24, 1817.

The first lithograph published in the United States was a portrait of Rev. Abner Kneeland, by Bass Otis, in 1818.

PHILADELPHIA FIRSTS

John Farr, a chemist of Philadelphia, in 1818 introduced into this country the manufacture of Seidlitz powders. He associated with him in business Abram Kunzi, and as Farr & Kunzi, located on Arch Street near Twelfth, they manufactured the first quinine in the United States. This firm, by various steps, has become a part of the Powers-Weightman-Rosengarten Company.

First savings bank, the "Philadelphia Saving Fund Society," commenced business December 2, 1816. Chartered February 25, 1819.

The first church in the world for seamen was erected in Philadelphia about 1820, under the leadership of Rev. Robert Eastburn. It was known as the "Mariner's Bethel."

The "Philadelphia Law Library," first in the United States, was established in 1821, under the auspices of "The Society for the Promotion of Legal Knowledge and Forensic Eloquence."

The "Philadelphia College of Pharmacy" was the first institution of its kind in the world. The organization meeting was held in Carpenters' Hall, February 23, 1821. Instruction was begun in the fall of the same year, with Charles Marshall as president of the institution. The charter was granted March 30, 1822.

The first engraved cylinders for calico printing made in the United States were made in Philadelphia, in 1822, by David H. Mason and Matthew W. Baldwin.

In 1827, William Ellis Tucker, of Philadelphia, was the first in America to manufacture porcelain and chinaware. In 1831 he started the first American queensware factory.

The Pennsylvania Horticultural Society, the first of its kind in America, was organized at a meeting held in the hall of the Franklin Institute, Seventh Street below Market, November 24, 1827. It was incorporated March 23, 1831.

The first one-cent newspaper in the country was *The Cent*, published in 1830, by Dr. Christopher Columbus Conwell, at Second and Dock Streets, Philadelphia.

The first building and loan association in the United States was the "Oxford Provident and Building Association," organized in Frankford in 1831. The officers were Isaac Whitelock, president; Isaac Shallcross, secretary; and Samuel Pilling, treasurer.

In 1832, George D. Rosengarten made the first morphine in the United States.

The first public high school in the United States was established in Philadelphia in 1836. The first building was erected in 1837-38 on Juniper Street fronting on Penn Square, now occupied by the Wanamaker Store. The school was opened October 26, 1838, when a class of sixty-three pupils was admitted.

The first daguerreotype portrait in America was made in Philadelphia by Robert Cornelius, November, 1839, at 710 Chestnut. (Portrait of himself.)

The first homeopathic medical college in the world, the "North American College of Homeopathic Medicine," was organized in Allentown, Pa., in 1835. The second was the "Homeopathic Medical College of Philadelphia," organized in 1848. The next in order was the "Washington Medical College of Philadelphia," chartered May 2, 1853. This last named institution changed its name, July 17, 1867, to the "Hahne-

PHILADELPHIA FIRSTS

mann Medical College of Philadelphia." The first of these institutions lasted a very short time; and by act of Legislature, dated April 2, 1869, the second and third were united under the title of the "Hahnemann Medical College of Pennsylvania." This institution can thus claim to be the oldest of its kind in the world, and though not technically the first, it is practically so.

The first American grand opera, "Leonora," was composed by William H. Fry, a Philadelphian; the words were written by his brother, Joseph R. Fry. It was produced at the Chestnut Street Theatre, June 4, 1845, by Pratt & Wemyss.

The first free college for orphan boys in the United States was established in Philadelphia under the will of Stephen Girard. Girard College was opened January 1, 1848, with a class of one hundred boys.

The first comic weekly in America was *The John Donkey*, edited by Thomas Dunn English and G. G. Foster. Illustrated by F. O. C. Darley and Henry L. Stephens. Published in Philadelphia by G. B. Zieber & Company, 1848.

"The Woman's Medical College of Pennsylvania" is the oldest college in the world organized to train women in the medical profession. It was incorporated March 11, 1850.

The Spring Garden Institute, the first of the mechanics institutes in the United States, was chartered April 12, 1851. The corner-stone of the building was laid July 8, 1851, and the building was dedicated November 12, 1852.

The first English translation of the Hebrew Bible published in America was the result of eighteen years' work of Rev. Isaac Leeser. It was published in Philadelphia in 1854.

The first Republican National Convention met in Musical Fund Hall, June 18, 1856, with Henry S. Lane, of Indiana, as Chairman. John C. Fremont was nominated for president of the United States, and William L. Dayton, of New Jersey, for vice-president.

The process of sugar-coating pills was begun in 1856 by William R. Warner & Co., manufacturing chemists of Philadelphia. This was done in a pan suspended by a chain over a charcoal fire. The original pan is still preserved by the firm.

The first society in America distinctively devoted to numismatic research was the "Numismatic Society," organized in Philadelphia, December 27, 1857, by seven men. It received its charter February 19, 1858. On March 23, 1865, the name was changed to "The Numismatic and Antiquarian Society."

The "Zoölogical Society" was incorporated in 1859; and in Fairmount Park, north of the Spring Garden Water Works, began the first zoölogical garden in the United States. They later moved across the river to their present site, and the new buildings and grounds were opened to the public July 1, 1874.

April 8, 1861, John Wanamaker opened a men's clothing store at Sixth and Market Streets. Fifteen years later, 1876, having been removed to Thirteenth and Market Streets, it had "six departments for the outfitting of men and boys." On March 12, 1877, it was resolved into a general store having sixteen departments covering all classes of dry goods. This is believed to have been the first "department store" in the United

States, probably in the world. This same store, in 1865, made the first announcements of the "one price system," and that anything sold could be brought back for refund of money. The Wanamaker store at Thirteenth and Market Streets was lighted by electricity on the night after Christmas, 1878, being the first store ever so lighted.

First bank chartered under the National Banking Act, the "First National Bank of Philadelphia," June 20, 1863. The first "National Currency" was issued by this bank.

The first Stock Exchange Clearing House in the United States was established here in August, 1870.

The first organization in the world for the insurance of real estate titles was "The Real Estate Title Insurance Company of Philadelphia," chartered March 28, 1876. By an amendment to the charter, under date of December 3, 1881, the title was changed to "The Real Estate Title Insurance and Trust Company of Philadelphia."

The first international fair held in this country was the Centennial Exhibition held in Philadelphia, May 10 to November 10, 1876. It is the only fair of its kind that has paid its own expenses, and received no appropriation from Congress.

Philadelphia is known as the city of the Easter lily. It was brought from Bermuda in 1879 by Mrs. Mary Rogers, who propagated it until in three years there were 100 specimens; then William K. Harris, a florist, Fifty-sixth Street and Springfield Avenue, introduced it in both Philadelphia and New York.

The Philadelphia Bourse, the first and, as yet, the

only one in the United States, was chartered June 25, 1891, and completed and opened for business October 1, 1895.

The "Wistar Institute of Anatomy," founded in 1892, by General Isaac Wistar, and connected with the University of Pennsylvania, is the first anatomical and neurological institute established in the United States.

Philadelphia was the first city to inaugurate a service by pneumatic tubes for the general carriage of first-class mail. A six-inch tube connecting the Bourse station with the Central Post Office at Ninth Street was put in service February 17, 1893, and is still in operation. Eight-inch tubes have been used in lines since installed, and have a capacity of 7,200,000 letters per day each way.

The first concrete arch highway bridge in the United States was built in 1893 by the City of Philadelphia at Pine Road over the Pennypack Creek.

The first institution established in the United States for the advancement of business and trade in all branches, both domestic and foreign, was the "Commercial Museum." It was projected by Dr. William P. Wilson, and established by ordinance of Philadelphia City Council, approved June 15, 1894.

The first successful electric automobile was designed and built by two Philadelphians, Henry G. Morris and Pedro G. Salom. It was patented August 31, 1894.

The first hospital train sent out during the Spanish War, for the relief of the fever-stricken soldiers in the mobilization camps, was sent by the University of Pennsylvania, and the soldiers were brought to and

PHILADELPHIA FIRSTS

treated in the Hospital of that institution. This train left Philadelphia August 17, 1898.

The first Automatic Restaurant (Automat) in America was opened June 9, 1902, at 818 Chestnut Street, Philadelphia, by the Horn & Hardart Baking Co.

I
THE COMMOMWEALTH, OR STATE OF PENNSYLVANIA (PENN'S WOODS)

WITH a royal grant for 40,000 square miles of land in the New World, William Penn, thirty-eight years old, came up the Delaware River in 1682 and landed at the Blue Anchor Inn, built by the Swedes in 1636. The state now covers 45,126 square miles.

No eastern state contains forests of such varied and abundant timber, or extensive mineral deposits. According to official reports of the state geologist, one and one-third billion dollars' worth of mineral products were taken from below ground in 1916; of these coal is the greatest wealth producer, over $1,000,000,000 annually, the production being nearly one-half that of the entire United States; the supply is still ample and new fields are being opened. Over $100,000,000 in coke; and more than $42,000,000 in its by-products. Petroleum counts for $26,000,000. Gold, silver, platinum, and asbestos are found in small quantities. Natural gas has been used in this state for manufacturing purposes since 1874. This is the greatest manufacturing region in the world, and has the richest agricultural land in the United States. Pennsylvania stands first among the states in the Union in the number of towns over 5000 in population, making it a remarkable selling market. PHILADELPHIA, the chief city, and third in population, 1,823,779, in the United

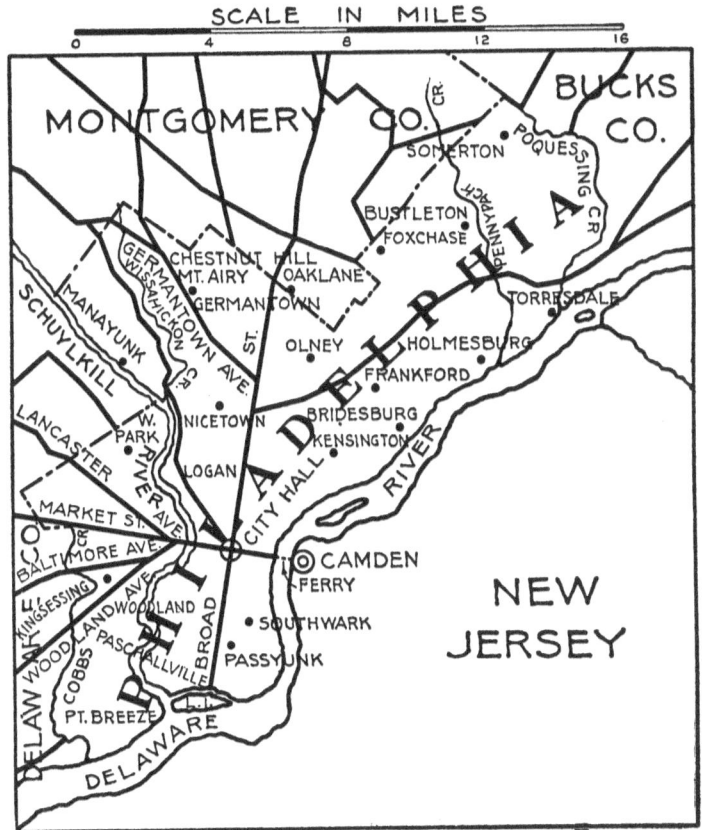

Philadelphia County

States, is on the site of a village of the Lenni Lenape or Delaware Indians, called Coaquanarck. Through William Penn's liberal policy to early settlers, and later being the seat of government of the United States, many national institutions were originated here, and many more historical buildings are here than in any other city in America. It comprises the whole of Philadelphia County, and has a distinctive character of its own, reminiscent of the old Quaker life, which is given in this book in two Colonial Walks; the Revolutionary Period is given in automobile routes, framed on Washington's itinerary; and modern institutions, many of them continuing from colonial times, are in chapters, schools, galleries and museums, hospitals, libraries, music, churches. Philadelphia was the leader in the fight for "Liberty of Conscience."

The obvious picturesqueness of Philadelphia is in the Pennsylvania Hospital, Independence Hall, Christ Church, Old Swedes', St. Peter's. Down in lower Spruce Street and neighboring streets are beautiful colonial houses, stately doorways, decorative ironwork, dormer windows, great gables, facing each other at street corners in harmonious proportions. In not another town were the old streets so well worth keeping unchanged. The early Friends, when they left England, packed up, with their "Liberty of Conscience," the love of beauty in architecture and the money to pay for it. In a fine period of English architecture, they got good English architects—Wren is said to have been of the number—to design, not only their public buildings, but their private houses; and carried over in their personal baggage, paneling, carvings, ironwork, furni-

THE COMMONWEALTH 27

ture and the various details they were not likely to procure in Philadelphia.

Long straight lines of streets give the town serenity and repose.

1. Independence Hall. 2. Independence Square. 3. Philosophical Society. 4. U.S. Custom House. 5. Carpenters' Hall. 6. Bank of North America. 7. Christ Church. 8. Site St. George and the Dragon Inn. 9. Betsey Ross House. 10. Friends' Meeting House. 11. St. George's M. E. Church. 12. St. John's Lutheran Church. 13. Christ Church Burial Ground. 14. Free Quaker Building. 15. Fort Rittenhouse. 16. Mikveh Israel Synagogue. 17. First U. S. Mint. 18. Site Robert Morris Residence. 19. Site President Washington's Residence. 20. Site Pennsylvania National Bank. 21. Franklin Institute.

COLONIAL PHILADELPHIA, WALK NO. 1

The Quaker City; Penn's "Green country towne."

Start at the STATE HOUSE, called INDEPENDENCE HALL in 1776; open free 9 A. M. to 4 P. M.; south side of Chestnut Street between Fifth and Sixth. The most interesting building historically in the United States. Architect, Andrew Hamilton, speaker in the Assembly; Georgian, brick; erected for the Province of Pennsylvania as a Colonial State House. Tower has wooden cupola built in 1828, containing clock and bell, presented to the City by Henry Seybert, in 1876.

First occupied by the Assembly in 1735. Second Continental Congress met here May 10, 1775. George Washington was chosen Commander in Chief of the Continental Army June 15, 1775. Declaration of Independence approved July 4, 1776. Articles of Confederation and perpetual union between the States were adopted and signed July 9, 1778. Constitution of the United States of America, long the pride of Americans, and the model for friends of freedom throughout the world, was formed and signed September 17, 1787.

Lafayette was received here in 1824.

The body of Abraham Lincoln rested in state, April 22–24, 1865.

Second National Encampment, Grand Army of the Republic, January, 1868, when annual Memorial Day, May 30, was instituted by Major General John A. Logan. It was observed the same year by posts of the Grand Army of the Republic and the public.

The Liberty Bell was rung July 8, 1776, in celebration of the Declaration of Independence; inscription on bell, "Proclaim liberty throughout all the land, unto all the inhabitants thereof" (Leviticus xxv : 10). It was hung in the tower in 1755, and it was cracked while being tolled for the death of Chief Justice John Marshall July 8, 1835; not rung since 1843.

Portraits of the Signers of the Declaration of Independence, painted chiefly by Charles Willson Peale, and his portrait of Washington are here. Benjamin West's

FOURTH OF JULY IN CENTER SQUARE, PHILADELPHIA
Painted by John D. Krimmel
Courtesy of the Pennsylvania Academy of the Fine Arts

THE COMMONWEALTH 29

painting, "Penn's Treaty with the Indians"; a large collection of portraits of Pennsylvania men notable in the government of the Commonwealth; and a collection of forty-five small historic portraits in pastel by James Sharples. On Chestnut Street front is a marble statue of Washington; sculptor, J. A. Bailey; erected in 1869 by contributions of the public-school children of Philadelphia.

The building was renovated and restored in 1897 to its early appearance. Small buildings connecting west, contain colonial relics; east, Revolutionary relics. West, open porch leads to CONGRESS HALL, corner of Sixth Street, built in 1789 for Court House of Philadelphia County; Georgian, occupied by the Federal Congress, 1790–1800, after necessary alterations by Major L'Enfant. First floor, House of Representatives; second floor, Senate Chamber; gallery added in 1795. Here Washington was inaugurated President, second term, March 4, 1793; and John Adams, second President of the United States, in 1797. National Currency was established. First National Bank founded. Army and Navy organized. Jay's Treaty determining relations with England considered and ratified. Official announcement of Washington's death in 1799 was made, and resolution offered by Chief Justice John Marshall, to pay honor to the man "First in war, first in peace, first in the hearts of his countrymen."

Contains sculptures in wood by William Rush; statue of Washington carved in 1815; also eagle on globe, portrait of Michael Hillegas, first Treasurer of the United States until 1789, and other paintings.

Building restored 1896, through the Pennsylvania

Society, Colonial Dames of America; architect, William Ziegler.

Corner of Fifth Street, SUPREME COURT HOUSE, or the old CITY HALL, built in 1789. Second floor occupied by the First Supreme Court of the United States, 1791-1800. Mayor's Office until 1896. Later headquarters Boy Scouts and Grand Army of the Republic. Now restored to first appearance; museum, Colonial and American Indian collections, paintings.

In 1783, STATE HOUSE YARD was improved, elms planted, walks laid out, and seats placed. Contains statue of Commodore Barry. 104 South Fifth Street, in State House Yard, the American Philosophical Society, built 1789, brick, Georgian; originated in "The Junto," formed by Benjamin Franklin 1727. See Historic Institutions.

Southeast corner of Fifth and Chestnut Streets, site residence of William Moore Smith, son of first provost of the University of Pennsylvania. Washington's portrait was painted here by Gilbert Stuart.

Northeast corner of Fifth and Sansom Streets, site Philadelphia Library 1790-1830.

427 Chestnut Street, site of Lawrence mansion, Howe's headquarters, 1777-78.

421 Chestnut Street, site of United States Hotel. Charles Dickens stayed here March, 1842, first visit to America.

South side of Chestnut Street, below Fifth, United States Custom House; marble, classic; Doric portico; built 1819; architect, John Haviland.

Northwest corner of Fourth and Chestnut Streets, Provident Life and Trust Company, of Philadelphia,

THE COMMONWEALTH

modern; contains oil portraits of the directors; among the artists represented are Bernard Uhle, Cecilia Beaux, and Thomas Eakins.

Southeast corner of Fourth and Chestnut Streets, site of Friends meeting-house in 1701, later site of Mathew Carey's book store in 1800.

320 Chestnut Street, head of Carpenters' Court. CARPENTERS' HALL; open free daily 9 A. M. to 3 P. M., Saturdays to 12.30 P. M.; Georgian, brick; built, 1770 for use of the Carpenters' Company, founded in 1724.

307 Chestnut Street, Bank of North America; founded in 1781 on the same ground; oldest and first bank, chartered by Congress, in the United States. Through Robert Morris, the first president, victory was made possible to Washington and the Continental Army. Contains portrait of Robert Morris.

Third Street above Chestnut; Post Office in 1713; later Judd's Hotel during war of 1812.

27 South Third Street, site United States Post Office, 1792.

250 Chestnut Street, site first United States Treasury, 1798.

243 Chestnut Street, site of residence of Governor Thomas Lloyd in 1684, appointed by William Penn.

Letitia Street, west side above Chestnut, east of Second; site of Letitia House, William Penn's residence, moved to Fairmount Park.

Southeast corner of Second and Black Horse Alley, above Chestnut Street, site Bradford House and printing office, used for colonial Post Office, 1728; Andrew Bradford, postmaster; in 1719 he published the first newspaper in Pennsylvania, *The Mercury*, a weekly, second in America.

Southwest corner of Front and Market Streets, site of London Coffee House, in 1754, where, in 1780, Robert Morris met with others to consider the establishment of the first bank. Horses, slaves, and cattle were sold here.

About 221-23 North Water Street, site Stephen Girard's last residence.

111 Spring Street, west of Front, above Race, said to have been residence of Benjamin Franklin 1723-26; brick, three stories and attic; still standing.

Jones's Alley, above Market Street, west from 14 North Front Street, site Robert Grace's residence, where the "Junto Club" met in 1727.

110 Market Street, site Robert Aitken's Printing Office in 1782; he printed the first English Bible in America.

Southwest corner of Second and Market Streets, site Friends' first meeting-house, 1695-1808, on land donated by George Fox, founder of the Society.

Middle of Market Street, at Second, facing east, site of old Court House, built 1710; used as town hall and seat of the Legislature until the State House was built in 1735. Acceptance of the United States Constitution was here proclaimed to the people December 13, 1787; shown in large painting by Birch, made in 1829, now in City Hall, Broad and Market Streets.

25 North Second Street, office *Peter Porcupine's Gazette*, edited by William Cobbett, a keen satirist.

CHRIST CHURCH, west side of Second Street, north of Market, built 1695. (See Churches.)

JOHN MARSHALL, CHIEF JUSTICE OF THE
UNITED STATES, 1808–1835
From the original in the possession of the Law Association of
Philadelphia
Painted by Henry Inman

200 Arch Street, site Saint George and the Dragon Inn, built 1700, kept by Nicholas Scull, member Franklin's "Junto," in 1727; sheriff in 1744; he published a map of the city in 1750. Oldest Inn building standing; from 1791–93 it was kept by John Inskeep, Mayor of Philadelphia, 1800–05. Stage coaches for New York and Baltimore left here regularly.

No. 239 Arch Street, BETSY ROSS HOUSE, two-story, brick, marked by tablet; now property of American Flag House and Betsy Ross Memorial Association. She made the first flag adopted by the United States, from pencil drawing by Washington, who with Robert Morris and George Ross, called on her to give the commission; the flag was accepted by Congress June 14, 1777, and is now one of the oldest flags in the world, older than those of France, Spain, Germany, Russia, Italy, and Austria. John Paul Jones was first to fly the new flag. Betsy Ross lived to be eighty-four, dying in 1836; she is buried in Mount Moriah Cemetery, where a flag continously flies over her grave, instituted by the Sons of Veterans. Flag Day was first inaugurated in Philadelphia, 1893.

226 Race Street, site First Moravian Church, 1742–1856.

267 Race Street, site residence of Benjamin Franklin about 1749.

325 Market Street, site residence of Benjamin Franklin, where he first invented the lightning rod, about 1749–50; in 1752, first lightning rod used in the world was set up by Franklin, southeast corner of Second and Race Streets.

229 North Fourth Street, Saint George's, oldest

Methodist Church in the world, used continuously for worship; dedicated November 24, 1769.

Fourth Street above Race, St. Augustine's Roman Catholic Church, 1796; destroyed in the riot of 1844; rebuilt in 1846.

Old St. John's Church, Race Street between Fifth and Sixth; first English Luthern Church in America, built 1806.

Southeast corner of Fourth and Cherry Streets, site Zion Luthern Church (German), built 1766; in 1790 its organ was considered the finest in America.

Northeast corner of Fourth and Arch Streets, James Russell Lowell stayed here with his bride in 1845.

Southeast corner of Fourth and Arch Streets, Friends meeting-house; oldest in Philadelphia, built in 1804; since 1811 it has been used for the Philadelphia Yearly Meeting of Orthodox Friends, and is said to be largest in the world. (See Historic Burial Grounds.)

Southwest corner of Fourth and Arch Streets, site of residence built for William Smith, D.D., before 1762. First provost of the University of Pennsylvania.

Fourth Street, west side, below Arch, site of the Academy in 1749; beginning of the University, marked with tablet.

Southeast corner of Fifth and Arch Streets, Christ Church burial ground. (See Burial Grounds.)

Southwest corner of Fifth and Arch Streets, Free Quaker Building; tablet, inscription "By general subscription for the Free Quakers; erected in the year of our Lord 1783, and of the Empire 8." "Fighting Quakers," who fought in the Revolutionary War against peace principles of the sect. The Appren-

BENJAMIN FRANKLIN
From the collection in Independence Hall
Painted by B. T. Welch

THE COMMONWEALTH 35

tices' Library, organized 1820 in Carpenters' Hall, for many years only free library in Philadelphia, occupied the building after 1850. Later used by the Grand Lodge of Masons.

515 Cherry Street, residence of Bass Otis in 1819, who made the first American lithograph.

528 Arch Street, site, Pennsylvania College of Dental Surgery, first in Philadelphia, founded 1852; now absorbed by the University of Pennsylvania.

627 Arch Street, site, Woman's Medical College, first in America to graduate women physicians, founded 1850.

Southeast corner of Seventh and Arch Streets, residence of David Rittenhouse in 1770.

Northwest corner of Seventh and Arch Streets, Fort Rittenhouse; residence of David Rittenhouse, 1787; treasurer of Pennsylvania.

117 North Seventh Street, site, Mikveh Israel Synagogue, built in 1747. Removed to Broad and York Streets.

37-39 North Seventh Street, first United States Mint, 1792. David Rittenhouse, superintendent.

Southeast corner of Sixth and Market Streets, site of Robert Morris residence; next to it, on Market Street, 530-536, site of President Washington's mansion and John Adams, second President; originally built for Richard Penn.

700 Market Street, Penn National Bank. House where Thomas Jefferson wrote the Declaration of Independence.

801 Market Street, site, office of Thomas Jefferson, Secretary of State.

36   THE COMMONWEALTH

About 808 Market Street, site, residence of Thomas Jefferson, in 1791.

15 South Seventh Street, Franklin Institute, founded 1824; classic architecture, marble; John Haviland, architect.

COLONIAL WALK NO. 2

Southeast corner of Ninth and Chestnut Streets,

1. Continental Hotel. 2. Post Office. 3. Walnut Street Theatre. 4. Musical Fund Hall. 5. Potter House. 6. Jewish Cemetery. 7. Pennsylvania Hospital. 8. Morris House. 9. Holy Trinity R. C. Church. 10. Washington Square. 11. The Anthenaeum. 12. St. Mary's R. C. Church. 13. Old Pine Street Presbyterian Church. 14. St. Peter's P. E. Church. 15. Market. 16. Site Blue Anchor Inn. 17. Site Slate Roof House. 18. Stock Exchange. 19. St. Paul's P. E. Church. 20. Girard Bank. 21. St. Joseph's R. C. Church. 22. Contributionship Fire Insurance. 23. Dispensary.

site, Cook's Museum and Circus; first mummies brought to the United States are said to have been shown here.

Northwest corner of Ninth and Chestnut Streets, UNITED STATES POST OFFICE, built in 1884 on site of

THE COMMONWEALTH 37

the Mansion House, built for the official residence of President Washington, but never occupied; used for the University of Pennsylvania. Bronze statue of Benjamin Franklin, sculptor, John Boyle; Chestnut Street front, inscription by Washington: "Venerated for Benevolence, admired for Talent, esteemed for Patriotism, beloved for Philanthropy"; bronze bust, President McKinley in corridor; sculpture group on roof by D. C. French.

Northeast corner of Ninth and Sansom Streets, site, CHINESE MUSEUM; later, in 1835, Peale's Museum; exhibitions by the Franklin Institute were held here.

Northeast corner of Ninth and Walnut Streets, WALNUT STREET THEATRE, built in 1808; oldest theatre in the United States.

808 Locust Street, MUSICAL FUND HALL, built in 1824; oldest building in Philadelphia in continuous use as a hall; Dr. Charles H. Jarvis conducted classical soirées here before the Academy was built; has fine acoustic properties; it is on the site of the Fifth Presbyterian Church, which was moved to Tenth and Arch Streets.

260 South Ninth Street, POTTER HOUSE, built 1812; Joseph Bonaparte lived here two years; the cartoons, "Birth of Psyche," brought by him from Versailles, still form the mural decorations of the banquet hall.

Northeast corner of Spruce and Darien Streets, below Ninth, JEWISH CEMETERY, founded 1740; Rebecca Gratz, heroine in Scott's "Ivanhoe," is buried near the entrance.

225 South Eighth Street, MORRIS MANSION, built 1787; typical colonial model.

Eighth and Pine Streets, PENNSYLVANIA HOSPITAL, founded, 1751, by Dr. Thomas Bond and Benjamin Franklin; Georgian. Contains Benjamin West's famous painting "Christ Healing the Sick"; woman with white head shawl is said to be likeness of West's mother.

715 Spruce Street, residence of Nicholas Biddle in 1820; now used by the American Roman Catholic Society.

705 Locust Street, residence of E. L. Davenport, tragedian.

Southwest corner of Seventh and Locust Streets, site where Dr. Horace Howard Furness began his great variorum edition of Shakespeare.

618 Locust Street, residence of John W. Forney, journalist.

Southwest corner of Seventh and Walnut Streets, oldest Savings Bank in America; established 1816, by Mr. Condy Raguet with twelve directors; classic adaptation; Furness, Evans and Company, architects; among the oil portraits to be seen there are Lewis Waln and John C. Lowber, by Thomas Sully; G. Colesberry Purves, by William M. Chase, and Condy Raguet, artist unknown.

Southeast corner of Seventh and Chestnut Streets, site, residence of George Clymer, signer of the Declaration of Independence.

708 Chestnut Street, site, residence of Jared Ingersoll, signer of the United States Constitution; later, residence George M. Dallas, Vice-President of the United States. Opposite, on Chestnut Street below Eighth, eastern end of Green's Hotel, site,

THE COMMONWEALTH

residence of Thomas Fitzsimmons, signer of the United States Constitution.

632 Chestnut Street, site of Waln mansion.

615-17-19 Chestnut Street, site, THE ARCADE, built in 1826; the *Public Ledger* issued its first number here March 25, 1836.

605 Chestnut Street, bronze tablet front, inscription: "Site of First CHESTNUT STREET THEATRE, 1793-1855." "Hail! Columbia," composed by Joseph Hopkinson, first sung here, April 25, 1798, by Gilbert Fox. Fanny Elssler danced here in 1840; Jenny Lind sung, in 1850; Charlotte Cushman acted, in 1851; erected by The City Historical Society of Philadelphia."

Northwest corner of Sixth and Ranstead Streets, above Chestnut, site, The FALSTAFF HOTEL, from 1814-16; First City Troop met here.

130 South Sixth Street, site, residence Thomas G. Wharton; birthplace in 1824 of the Historical Society of Pennsylvania.

Southwest corner of Sixth and Walnut Streets, Curtis Publishing Company, on site of the Ludwig Building, a school erected by Christopher Ludwig, "Baker General" of the Revolution; see Architecture.

Southeast corner of Sixth and Walnut Streets, site, WALNUT STREET GAOL, 1775-1838; extended nearly to Fifth Street; in the rear, fronting Locust Street, then Prune Street, was the debtors' prison; Judge William Moore, also Provost William Smith, were confined here, in 1758, for publishing so-called seditious pamphlets on patriotism; the students went there to recite their lessons to him; Robert Morris, financier of the Revolution, was in prison here, in 1797, for debts incurred in a large private transaction; first successful balloon ascension in America was from the gaol yard, by J. P. Blanchard, French aëronaut, January, 1793.

Sixth to Seventh Streets, on Walnut, WASHINGTON SQUARE, patented by William Penn, 1704–05, as burial ground for strangers; hundreds of Revolutionary soldiers were buried here, also victims of the great yellow fever epidemic in 1793; in early times colored slaves gathered here to sing their native songs, and give wild African dances among the graves; named Washington Square by Councils, May, 1825, and improved for public use; monument to the Washington Grays, bronze, life-size figure of a private in original uniform.

215 South Sixth Street, site, residence of Hon. James Campbell, United States Postmaster General, appointed by President Pierce.

219 South Sixth Street, The ATHENAEUM OF PHILADELPHIA, founded, 1813, by students from the University, for a circulating library; first president, William Tilghman, Chief Justice of Pennsylvania; the Law Library was there many years, while Courts were Sixth and Chestnut Streets; was great chess center; architect, John Notman.

245 South Sixth Street, site, residence Commodore Barry, who succeeded John Paul Jones as head of the American Navy.

Locust Street below Sixth, south side, site, PRUNE STREET THEATRE; "Home Sweet Home" was sung here for the first time in America.

THE COMMONWEALTH 41

Northwest corner of Sixth and Spruce Streets, HOLY TRINITY ROMAN CATHOLIC CHURCH, built, 1739; circular building, alternate red and black bricks; body of Stephen Girard was buried here for many years; later removed to Girard College.

144-54 South Fifth Street, site, Free Quaker Cemetery.

127 South Fifth Street, site, PHILADELPHIA DISPENSARY, oldest in United States; founded by Dr. Benjamin Rush in 1786; now merged with Pennsylvania Hospital.

Northeast corner of Fourth and Walnut Streets, residence General Stephen Moylan, military secretary to Washington; Muster Master General of the Continental Army in 1775.

South side Walnut Street, above Fourth. John Marshall, Chief Justice of the United States, died here July 6, 1835.

Willing's Alley, south of Walnut Street, east of Fourth, ST. JOSEPH'S CHURCH; built in 1731; oldest Roman Catholic Church in Philadelphia; has painting, "Hagar and Ishmael," by Benjamin West; Washington is said to have been first referred to as "The Father of his Country" by the priest, in his sermon after Washington's death; Lancaster County makes the same claim.

309 Walnut Street, site, last residence of Bishop White.

212 South Fourth Street, PHILADELPHIA CONTRIBUTIONSHIP FOR THE INSURANCE OF HOUSES FROM LOSS BY FIRE, oldest fire-insurance company in America, founded 1752, by Benjamin Franklin;

known as "The Hand-in-Hand," from its seal; Classic architecture, built, 1835; portraits, Horace Binney by Thomas Sully; painted in 1837, and by George B. A. Healy in 1857; Dr. Charles Willing and Hon. John Welsh by Bernard Uhle; James Lewis Smith by Henry Inman; William Sellers and Ellis Yarnall by Percy Bigland, English; Alexander Biddle, Sydney P. Hutchinson and John T. Morris by Vonnoh; James S. Smith, 2d, by Van Morcken.

218–22 South Fourth Street, site, Edward Shippen mansion; President, Provisional Council, and First Mayor of Philadelphia; his daughter, Peggy Shippen, was married to Benedict Arnold.

Southwest corner of Fourth and Prune Streets, or Locust, residence of Dr. Caspar Wistar, in 1799; the garden extended to St. Mary's churchyard; is now headquarters of the Philadelphia Chapter No. 2 of Colonial Dames.

244–50 South Fourth Street, ST. MARY'S ROMAN CATHOLIC CHURCH, built, 1763, has a fine pieta by Boucher; in the graveyard are the tombs of Commodore Barry and of Thomas Fitzsimmons, members Continental Congress.

338 Spruce Street, residence, Joseph Hopkinson, born 1770, died 1842; author of "Hail! Columbia," 1798; it was called "The President's March," and always sung when Washington held state events; music by Henry Roth; he also wrote "The Battle of the Kegs."

Southwest corner of Fourth and Pine Streets, OLD PINE STREET PRESBYTERIAN CHURCH, brick, rough cast; classic; porch with Corinthian columns; built,

1857; graveyard is on both sides; east portion belongs to First Church, west to Old Pine.

Southwest corner of Leithgow Street, above Fourth and South Streets, SOUTH STREET THEATRE, 1766–1821; now used as a business building.

East side of Leithgow Street, west of Fourth, between South and Bainbridge Streets, site, APOLLO STREET THEATRE, 1811.

Spruce to Pine Streets, Third to Fourth, site, OLD ALMSHOUSE, 1731, and PHILADELPHIA HOSPITAL, 1732.

Northwest corner of Third and Lombard Streets, residence of CHARLES WILLSON PEALE, 1741–1827.

Southwest corner of Third and Pine Streets, SAINT PETER'S CHURCH, built, 1761; in the Churchyard are the tombs of Rev. Jacob Duché and Charles Willson Peale, artist, 1741–1827; it is often said, "To belong to old Philadelphia Society one must have an ancestor who entered Paradise through Saint Peter's graveyard"; (see Churches).

Northwest corner of Third and Pine Streets, site, residence of Colonel John Nixon, who read the Declaration of Independence.

Northeast corner of Third and Pine Streets, site, residence of Rev. Jacob Duché; later, British Military Hospital.

224 Pine Street, site, residence, Mayor John Stamper, 1760; Governor John Penn died here. "His funeral was very great, making quite a crowd."

237 DeLancey Street, above Pine, site, residence of Horace Binney, the great lawyer.

About 260 South Third Street, site, Bingham residence; later, in 1828, Joseph Head's MANSION HOUSE, known as the most sumptuous inn in America; John Quincy Adams stayed here in 1811; Pennsylvania Society of the Cincinnati gave a dinner in 1811, celebrating the unveiling of a monument to General Wayne; "Sons of Washington" held their annual dinner here on Washington's Birthday; French citizens gave a dinner in 1830, Peter Du Ponceau presiding, in popular demonstration after the French Revolution of the overthrow of Charles X.

256 South Third Street, site, "Washington Hall," built, 1814; erected by the Washington Benevolent Society; here General Andrew Jackson was fêted and dined, in February, 1819; Lafayette attended a dinner in 1824 given to Richard Rush, envoy to England from the United States, afterward member of Adams Cabinet; second Horticultural Exhibition was held in 1830.

244 South Third Street, residence of Samuel Powell, Mayor of Philadelphia, 1775-89; fine colonial architecture; many functions were held here during the Revolution; Washington celebrated his twentieth wedding anniversary here, January 6, 1779.

228 South Third Street, site, Thomas Willing residence, in 1746.

217-31 South Third Street, St. Paul's Protestant Episcopal Church, built, 1761; Headquarters of Philadelphia City Mission; Edwin Forrest, tragedian, is buried in the graveyard; (see Churches).

Southeast corner of Dock and Moravian Streets, below Walnut, publisher's office of *Burton's Gentleman's Magazine*, while Edgar Allan Poe was editor.

Southeast corner of Third and Walnut Streets, site,

THE COMMONWEALTH 45

residence of Alexander Hamilton, and site of Fort Wilson, residence of James Wilson, a signer of the Declaration of Independence.

301 Walnut Street, site, residence of Dr. Benjamin Rush, in 1791, a signer of the Declaration of Independence.

307 Walnut Street, site, residence of Judge Richard Peters.

Back part of Walnut Court, between 314-318 Walnut Street, site, Friends' Almshouse, 1713-1841.

Southeast corner of Third and Pear Streets (now Chancellor), Robert Bell's bookstore; Bell's imprints are sought by collectors.

116-120 South Third Street, GIRARD NATIONAL BANK, oldest banking building in America; Stephen Girard, financier of the War of 1812, bought it in 1812; it was his office until his death, December 26, 1831.

114 South Third Street, site, JAY COOKE'S BANKING HOUSE, financier of the Civil War.

Sansom Street, formerly Lodge Street, above Second; first successful locomotive, Old Ironsides, built in America was made by Matthias Baldwin in 1828.

Northwest corner of Second and Sansom Streets, site, residence of William Logan, 1750-60.

Southeast corner of Second and Sansom Streets, site, SLATE ROOF HOUSE, 1698-1867, built for William Penn; his son John was born here, January 29, 1700; sold to William Trent, founder of Trenton, in 1803, for eight hundred and fifty pounds; General Forbes, Governor of Pennsylvania, died here. "His funeral was of great splendor."

121 South Second Street, site, residence of Robert Fulton, artist and engineer.

123 South Second Street, site, residence of Captain Joseph Anthony; Assembly met here in 1828-30.

Back of 145-47 South Second Street, site of Indian reservation.

Second Street, southeast corner of Little Dock Street, site, Loxley House in 1720; Lydia Darrach is supposed to have lived here; Benjamin Franklin used the front door key in electricity experiment with a kite.

Water Street, between Walnut and Dock Streets, Hamilton's Wharf. FIRST ASSEMBLY BALLS were held here, in a large room, about 1740.

Second and Pine Streets, SECOND STREET MARKET, built, 1745.

200 Pine Street, site, residence of Charles Elias Boudinot.

South Street from South Street, corner of American, between Second and Third Streets, inscription on corner house: "In this street was birthplace of Edwin Forrest; Commodore Joseph Cresson; Alexander Wilson; and Joel B. Sutherland, first President of the Society of 1812."

Second Street below South, west side, SOUTHWARK BANK, built, 1825.

30 South Street, site, Plumsted House; MASON AND DIXON'S OBSERVATORY was near here.

Front and Pine Streets; probable site of the Penny Pot House.

Northwest corner of Front and Dock Streets, probable site of the BLUE ANCHOR INN, in 1682, where William Penn first landed in Philadelphia.

NOTABLE ARCHITECTURE

ARCHITECTURE should comprise beauty, fitness, and stability. It is classified by various styles from the past, necessarily developed by modern characterists. Eras of great national vigor invariably express themselves architecturally, by means of great scale. To illustrate, the Pyramids at Gizeh and the great temple at Karnak mark the zenith of Egyptian civilization; the Parthenon echoes the halycon days of Greece; Imperial Rome boasted the Baths of Caracalla and the Colosseum; the glorious Renaissance in Italy culminated in the grandeur of St. Peter's Church; and the consecration and craftsmanship of Gothic builders crashed to earth with the lofty vaulting of Beauvais. Also consider, in chronological order, the buildings of our own time, they present a mute record of the ever-increasing virility of the nation; in the lacelike tower of the Woolworth Building, piercing the blue heaven for a thousand feet, we read the tremendous advance and limitless possibilities of the country whose dreams become realities. Among the early COLONIAL or GEORGIAN buildings are, CARPENTERS' HALL, Chestnut Street below Fourth; CHRIST CHURCH, Second Street above Market; HAMILTON MANSION in Woodlands Cemetery, Thirty-ninth Street and Woodland Avenue; INDEPENDENCE HALL, group, Chestnut Street between Fifth and Sixth; OLD SWEDES' CHURCH (Gloria Dei), Swanson Street near Front and Christian Streets; PENNSYLVANIA HOSPITAL, Eighth and Pine Streets; ST. PETER'S CHURCH, Third and Pine Streets.

Egyptian. SYNAGOGUE ADATH-JESHURUM, Broad and Diamond Streets; Indiana limestone; architects, Thomas, Churchman, and Molitor.

Classic. ACADEMY OF MUSIC, Broad and Locust Streets. Interior classic; brick; built, 1850; architects, LeBrun & Runge; the audience room is very large, modeled after celebrated opera houses in Europe; plan of the balconies is now considered obsolete, but the general effect is undeniably fine, and has a flavor of the Second Empire. CATHEDRAL OF SS. PETER AND PAUL, Logan Square; brownstone, built about 1860; architects, Napoleon Le Brun for the building, John Notman for the façade; it is impressive and dignified. UNITED STATES CUSTOM HOUSE, Chestnut Street below Fifth; architect, John Haviland. GIRARD COLLEGE, Corinthian and Girard Avenues; architect, Thomas U. Walters; modeled after the Parthenon. GIRARD NATIONAL BANK, 116 South Third Street; portico of the Third Street front is Corinthian, studied from the Parthenon and Temple of Saturnus; it stands on a stylobate, elevated above the pavement by steps on three sides, which gives it emphasis and dignity, and marks it as the feature of approach to the building; this portico is flanked on either side by a pavilion of pilasters, of the same character as the columns of the portico, the space between the pilasters being pierced with windows which are adorned with architraves and cornices supported by carved brackets; the pilasters and columns are surmounted by a cornice pediment and balustrade of great elegance of detail and proportion, studied from the best class of Roman antique work; the tympanum of the pediment is enriched by

THE COMMONWEALTH 49

the date of the erection, 1795, and the American eagle in bas-relief carving, of excellent modeling; from the pavement to the apex of the portico is fifty-six feet; entire front is of Pennsylvania blue marble; the building was erected for the Bank of the United States in 1797, and followed closely the lines of the Dublin Exchange; architect, Samuel Blodgett; marble work was done by Claudius LeGrand in his yard at Tenth and Market Streets; this was the first building in Philadelphia to be erected with portico and pillars; in 1901, it was carefully renovated by James H. Windrim. GIRARD TRUST COMPANY, northwest corner of Broad and Chestnut Streets, built in 1908; architects, McKim, Mead & White, New York; Furness & Evans, Philadelphia; has steel frame and Gustavino dome faced with white marble; while the form of this building was probably suggested by the Pantheon at Rome, details of the order are rather Greek, and the colonetts, forming the mullions of the windows, suggest the Certosa di Pavia. RIDGWAY LIBRARY, South Broad and Christian Streets, Doric; built, 1880; granite; architect, Addison Hutton. OLD STOCK EXCHANGE, Second, Walnut and Dock Streets, white marble; has semicircular Corinthian colonnade, and lantern modeled after the Temple of Lysicrates; architect, William Strickland. ST. PATRICK'S CHURCH, Twenty-first and Locust Streets, Roman; classic; brick and granite; built, 1913; architects, LaFarge & Morris, New York; façade of this church is big in conception, full of dignity and repose, and forms a most successful termination to the vista when viewed from Rittenhouse Street. UNITED STATES MINT, Seventeenth and Spring Garden Streets, built, 1898; light gray granite; architect, James Knox Taylor.

Moorish. HORTICULTURAL HALL, Fairmount Park; built, 1876; architect, Herman J. Schwarzmann. RODEPH SHALOM SYNAGOGUE, Mt. Vernon and North Broad Streets.

Byzantine. FIRST BAPTIST CHURCH, Seventeenth Street above Chestnut, stone; Edgar V. Seeler, architect. JACOB REED'S SONS, store, 1424 Chestnut Street, brick, marble, and tile; built, 1904; Price & McLanahan, architects; façade is one of the most interesting in the city; the column caps are symbolic of the business conducted therein, as is also the tile work on the intrados of the arch, which depicts the shearing and manufacturing of wool and has the richness of an Oriental rug.

Gothic. ACADEMY OF THE FINE ARTS, Broad and Cherry Streets, Venetian polychrome Gothic, brick, limestone, and tile; architects, Furness & Hewitt; façade is interesting, as the most prominent example of the Venetian Gothic style, used in Philadelphia in the latter part of the nineteenth century. BROAD AND ARCH STREETS METHODIST EPISCOPAL CHURCH, white marble. ST. CLEMENT'S PROTESTANT EPISCOPAL CHURCH, Twentieth and Cherry Streets, Norman; built, 1857; brownstone; architect, John Notman; later improvements; new roof; apse; Lady chapel and parish buildings by Horace Wells Sellers. ST. JAMES' PROTESTANT EPISCOPAL CHURCH, Twenty-second and Walnut Streets, English decorated Gothic, with sculptured band around the tower; Ohio green sandstone and granite; architect, G. W. Hewitt. ST. LUKE'S

THE COMMONWEALTH 51

PROTESTANT EPISCOPAL CHURCH, Germantown Avenue and Coulter Street, granite and limestone; architect, Richard Upjohn of New York, who first used the principles of Gothic architecture in America; rectory, St. Margaret's Home, parish house, and the rood screen in the church are by Cope & Stewardson; organ screen is by Pierson. ST. MARK'S PROTESTANT EPISCOPAL CHURCH, Locust Street below Seventeenth, early decorated Gothic; brownstone; architect, John Notman; later improvements include the Lady chapel, architects, Cope & Stewardson. SECOND PRESBYTERIAN CHURCH, Twenty-first and Walnut Streets, French, with early English details; resembles the Parish Church in Norfolk, England; architect, Henry Sims. ST. STEPHEN'S PROTESTANT EPISCOPAL CHURCH, Tenth Street above Chestnut, early Gothic, with two octagonal towers; stone; interior decorated by Frank Furness; rich and unusual color. SOUTH MEMORIAL CHURCH OF THE ADVOCATE, Eighteenth and Diamond Streets, French; architect, C. M. Burns; built, 1897; interior profusely adorned with carving; windows by Clayton & Bell.

Romanesque. CHURCH OF ST. FRANCIS DE SALES, ROMAN CATHOLIC, Forty-seventh Street and Springfield Avenue, brick and terra cotta; Gustavino dome and mosaic, a very beautiful example of the style; built, 1912; architect, Henry D. Daggit. HOLY TRINITY PROTESTANT EPISCOPAL CHURCH, Nineteenth and Walnut Streets, Norman, brownstone; architect, John Notman. MASONIC TEMPLE, Broad and Filbert Streets, Norman with elaborately carved porch; gray granite; built about 1870; architect, James H. Windrim. CHURCH OF THE SAVIOUR, PROTESTANT EPISCOPAL, Thirty-eighth Street, north of Chestnut Street, Norman; architect, Charles M. Burns; the half dome and apse are decorated by Edwin H. Blashfield; said to be one of the finest examples of mosaic work in this country; alms boxes and reredos, designed by the late James Warner, are also of considerable interest.

Renaissance. ART CLUB, southwest corner of Broad and Chancellor Streets, Italian and French influences; brick and Indiana limestone; architect, Frank Miles Day. CITY HALL, open daily, 9.00 A. M. to 3.00 P. M., Broad and Market Streets, on site of Penn Square, formerly Centre Square, on which was a Friends' meeting-house in 1685; Rochambeau's Encampment, 1781; Wayne's Encampment, 1794; and the first city waterworks in 1801; this is the largest single building in America; covers four and a half acres, French, begun in 1871, white marble with granite base; built in the form of a hollow square, with passageways connecting both Market and Broad Streets; contains 662 rooms; the tower, on the north center, about 550 feet high, is surmounted by a colossal bronze statue of William Penn; center and corner pavilions have attic stories, and hanging stairs of polished granite; architect, John McArthur, Jr.; chief points of interest are the council chambers; mayor's reception room, with portraits of Philadelphia mayors; and state court rooms; from the roof is an excellent view of the city. To Alexander Milne Calder, Philadelphia is indebted for the applied sculpture, the artistic feature of the building, many scores of figures, symbolic of the history of this nation

CAPTAIN NICHOLAS BIDDLE
In the Tower Gallery of City Hall
Alexander Milne Calder, Sculptor

THE COMMONWEALTH 53

and the world, fine types of Indians, and other races; the negro heads being known among artists as the best of their kind; ornamentation symbolic of music, art, science, and commerce, is used as an integral part of this great public edifice, an inherent factor in true decoration, where it comes into its own, as well as in gardens, parks, boulevards, and plazas. Statues outside, on City Hall pavement, are, General John F. Reynolds, by Rogers; General McClellan; the Pilgrim by Saint Gaudens; the Quaker by Giuseppe Donato; Stephen Girard and John Wanamaker by J. Massey Rhind; Joseph Leidy, M.D.; President McKinley, and John C. Bullitt. COLLEGE OF PHYSICIANS, Twenty-second Street, above Chestnut, English; built, 1910; architects, Cope & Stewardson. DROPSIE COLLEGE, Broad Street below York, French; architects, Pitcher & Tachau. HAMILTON COURT, Thirty-ninth and Chestnut Streets, Italian; steel frame faced with brick and limestone; an apartment house built around an open court, recalling very strongly, both in color and detail, the earlier Venetian palaces. MEMORIAL HALL, Fairmount Park, German, granite; built, 1876; architect, Herman J. Schwarzmann; one of the best designed monumental buildings in the city. UNION LEAGUE addition, Fifteenth and Sansom Streets, Italian; steel frame, faced with limestone; built, 1912; architect, Horace Trumbauer: a very dignified and restrained elevation, suggestive of a Roman palace.

Spanish. THE FIRST CHURCH OF CHRIST SCIENTIST, Walnut Street above Fortieth; architects, Carrere & Hastings. PENNSYLVANIA INSTITUTE FOR THE

INSTRUCTION OF THE BLIND, Overbrook; Spanish mission; architects, Cope & Stewardson.

English. MELLOR, MEIGS AND HOWE OFFICE, 205 South Juniper Street, rough brick; architects, Mellor & Meigs.

THE ATHENAEUM of Philadelphia, 219 South Sixth Street; architect, John Notman; has best points of work done in 1850, showing traditions of the past, with developments and characteristics of its own; interior has a most beautiful reading room. THE UNIVERSITY BUILDINGS, from Thirty-fourth to Fortieth Streets, Walnut Street to Woodland Avenue, add much to the architectural attraction of West Philadelphia; entrances to the campus, near the dormitories, are fine Tudor gateways, wrought iron, with brick and stone piers. (See University of Pennsylvania.) Hon. James Arthur Balfour said in 1917, "The Americans build Brobdignagian cathedrals, and use them for office buildings." THE SKYSCRAPERS. ADELPHIA HOTEL, Thirteenth and Chestnut Streets, Italian Renaissance, brick and terra cotta; built, 1914; architect, Horace Trumbauer; the arabesque detail on lower stories of the façade, and pattern formed by projecting bricks, on the stories above, are worthy of notice; interiors are pleasing and architecturally correct. BELL TELEPHONE, a Parkway building, corner of Seventeenth and Arch Streets; height above ground 273 feet; stone; with interesting façade; architect, John T. Windrim. BELLEVUE-STRATFORD HOTEL, southwest corner Broad and Walnut Streets, French Renaissance; steel frame, faced with terra cotta; architects, Hewitt Bros. Most beautifully proportioned and artistic business building in Philadelphia. BOURSE, Fourth to Fifth Streets, below Market; adaptation of the François Premier; with fine feeling of dignity, in placing within the broad paving; architects, Hewitt Bros. BULLETIN BUILDING, Juniper and Filbert Streets, French; steel frame, faced with terra cotta; architect, Edgar V. Seeler. CURTIS PUBLISHING COMPANY, Sixth and Walnut Streets, modern adaptation of Georgian; steel frame, faced with white marble and brick; built, 1910; architect, Edgar V. Seeler; faces Independence Square, and although thoroughly modern, harmonizes perfectly, both in color and design, with the historic Georgian group, of which Independence Hall is the center, and adds to the quiet colonial atmosphere of the Square; interior is excellently designed; entrance, lobby, editorial offices, and the employes' dining room being of particular interest. Mechanical equipment is the finest of its kind in the world, producing an average of 5,558,600 complete paid for publications per issue of the *Ladies' Home Journal, Saturday Evening Post,* and *The Country Gentleman* for six months ending June 30, 1924. Twenty original paintings, and the mosaic "The Dream Garden," by Maxfield Parrish, a mural made of Tiffany favrile glass, the work proceeded through an entire year, in the Tiffany Studios, where each piece of glass was fired under the personal supervision of Mr. Tiffany and Mr. Briggs; time can never impair its freshness, color, or luminosity. Visitors will be shown the entire plant daily, except Saturdays and Sundays, between 9.00 A. M. and 5.00 P. M. FARM JOURNAL, Seventh Street and Washington

Square, Georgian; colonial brick and Indiana limestone; architects, Bunting & Shrigley. HARRISON BUILDING, Fifteenth and Market Streets, François Premier; built, 1895; architects, Cope & Stewardson; an unusual example of well-studied, though elaborate Renaissance detail; notice the graceful roof, recalling the charming chateaux along the Loire. LAND TITLE BUILDING, southwest corner of Broad and Chestnut Streets, modern adaptation of classic; steel frame, faced with gray granite and brick; architects, D. H. Burnham & Co., Chicago; contrast the scale of the order, in the newer portion of the building on Broad Street entrance, with the insignificant order in the old building. MANUFACTURERS' CLUB, Broad and Walnut Streets, Italian Renaissance; built, 1914; steel frame, faced with limestone; architects, Simon & Bassett; has a handsome façade, crowned by a daring Florentine cornice; interior unusually interesting in detail. RACQUET CLUB, Sixteenth Street below Walnut, Georgian; colonial brick, marble trimmings; architect, Horace Trumbauer. REAL ESTATE TRUST BUILDING, southeast corner of Broad and Chestnut Streets, Renaissance; architect, Edgar V. Seeler. RITZ-CARLTON HOTEL, Broad and Walnut Streets, modern adaptation, style of the Adam Brothers; built, 1912; steel frame, faced with colonial brick and Indiana limestone; architects, Warren & Wetmore, New York, Horace Trumbauer, Philadelphia, associate. The keynote of this structure is refinement and good taste; a recognition of the fact that commercialism and good architecture are by no means incompatible. STEPHEN GIRARD BUILDING,

THE COMMONWEALTH 57

Twelfth and Girard Streets, modern adaptation of Greek classic; built about 1894; steel frame, faced with brick and marble; architect, John T. Windrim; details of this building are interesting; note the bronze caryatid figures which support the heads of the second story windows; the wrought iron gates to the court on Girard Street rank with the best modern wrought ironwork in the city. WANAMAKER STORE, Chestnut, Market, Juniper, and Thirteenth Streets, modern adaptation of Italian Renaissance, built, 1910; steel frame, with light gray granite; architects, D. H. Burnham & Co., Chicago; exterior of this store is one of the finest in the city, it is simple, dignified, and impressive, without being monotonous; the great scale of the Doric order at the base, the severe wall treatment, and the splendid cornice, combine to express a purity and loftiness seldom equaled in commercial buildings; a guide may be had, upon application, who will conduct visitors through the entire building including the kitchens. WEST PHILADELPHIA HIGH SCHOOL, Forty-sixth and Walnut Streets, Tudor Gothic; rough brick and Indiana limestone; built, 1913, by the City Architect. WIDENER MEMORIAL HOME for crippled children, Broad Street and Olney Avenue, Georgian, built, 1906; Harvard brick and marble trimmings; architect, Horace Trumbauer; has a very beautifully designed wrought iron gateway.

To make a "City Beautiful" is to give it wide streets, lined with handsome buildings and houses, plenty of parks, boulevards, and to rid it of rows upon rows of semi-shanty premises, small, ill-kept, and unattractive. Each new building that is put up within the city limits should, in its arrangements and architecture, help toward making the locality in which it is erected more attractive than at the present time. This idea has been carried out in the CARNEGIE FREE LIBRARY buildings, scattered about within the limits of the municipality, as their varied exteriors are very distinguished, from an architectural point. The interiors are designed to avoid the multiplication of corridors; principal rooms used for reading, the art and reference rooms, are stately and fine.

An interesting GATEWAY is the entrance to the MANHEIM CRICKET CLUB, Germantown, Georgian; consisting of massive brick piers, surmounted by stone caps, connected at the top with a wrought iron supporting lantern, below which are the heavy wrought iron central gates; this, with smaller gateways, and a most attractive brick wall, forms the enclosure for the grounds; architects, McKim, Mead & White.

ART COLLECTIONS AND ART SCHOOLS

Philadelphia being the seat of government of colonial times, is extremely rich in historic portraits. They are in The Pennsylvania Academy of the Fine Arts; Independence Hall; Historical Society of Pennsylvania; Carpenters' Hall; American Philosophical Society; Pennsylvania Hospital; Academy of Natural Science; The Library Company of Philadelphia; Mercantile Library; College of Physicians; United States Mint; University of Pennsylvania; many banks and insurance companies.

PENNSYLVANIA ACADEMY OF THE FINE ARTS, Broad Street above Arch; open free daily, 9.00 A. M. to 5.00

A QUIET HOUR
Painted by John W. Alexander
Courtesy of the Pennsylvania Academy of the Fine Arts

P. M., Sundays, 1.00 P. M. to 5.00 P. M.; fee for special exhibitions; was the first art institute in America, founded, 1805; its history is in no small measure the history of American art itself, and dates back to 1791, when Charles Willson Peale attempted to organize in Philadelphia a school of art; from this grew, in 1794, the Columbianum, which held the first exhibition of paintings, in 1795, in Independence Hall. The permanent collection of paintings and sculpture now includes the Gallery of National Portraiture, with the largest number of portraits by Gilbert Stuart to be seen in any museum; and notable works by other early American painters—Benjamin West, Washington Allston, Matthew Pratt, the Peales, Sully, Neagle, Inman, Eichholz, Trumbull, and Bass Otis; the Gibson Collection, largely composed of the Continental schools; Temple collection of modern American paintings; important works by many of the world's greatest artists; and the Phillips collection of about forty thousand etchings and engravings. Annual exhibitions are, miniatures, water colors, illustration, and etchings in November and December; oil painting and sculpture in February and March, considered the salon of living American artists; also special exhibitions and lectures on art. The Academy coöperates with the system of International Catalogue Exchange.

Since the beginning of the Academy's existence, men and women whose names have become illustrious in the annals of American art have been enrolled as students. The schools are equipped in every way to teach the technique of painting and sculpture, the faculty is composed of representative artists of the day; collections, galleries, classrooms, models, and casts are admirably fitted to afford instruction fully equal to that obtainable in Europe. Many substantial prizes are awarded annually to students upon the merits of their work. The William Emlen Cresson Travelling Scholarships send, on an average, sixteen students abroad yearly for four months, and enable them to return to the Academy and continue their studies without payment of tuition fee. The Fellowship of the Pennsylvania Academy of the Fine Arts, organized 1897, sends out annually two exhibitions of original oil paintings by notable artists; one to other cities, the other to the Philadelphia public schools, where they remain one month in each school; while there, the paintings are explained by a member of the Fellowship to school children, thus teaching them true appreciation of art. A Picture Purchase Fund was established in 1912, with which pictures have been bought, from Fellowship Exhibitions, and placed in Philadelphia libraries and public schools.

JOHN GRAVER JOHNSON MUSEUM OF PAINTINGS, 510 South Broad Street, left by bequest April, 1917, to the City of Philadelphia, is open to the public; throughout Europe and America this vast collection of old and modern masters is famous for extent and merit. "No other American collection has so wide a range and so even a quality," says F. Mason Perkins; it contains scores of examples which could not be duplicated at any price. Noted for the completeness of different schools of painting.

PHILADELPHIA SCHOOL OF DESIGN FOR WOMEN, southwest corner of Broad and Master Streets; first industrial art school in this country; similar to the "Ecoles Professionelles des Femmes," in Paris; was founded in 1844 by Mrs. Sarah Peters, the American wife of the British Consul in Philadelphia, in her own house; later, the Franklin Institute assumed charge of the classes until 1853, when it was incorporated, and a Board of Directors elected. Its aim is to put art students in touch with business demands, as well as to cultivate, to the highest degree, their artistic ability. The Normal Art Course embodies all the special studies required by modern educators for teachers of art and design, and with courses in the fine arts, illustration, and costume illustration; has trained many women, now earning handsome emoluments and winning distinction. The residence on Broad Street, forming entrance to the school, which occupies large buildings in the rear, was the home of Edwin Forrest, a famous tragedian; the fine gallery which he erected to house his collection of paintings, now at the Forrest Home for Actors at Holmesburg, is used for annual exhibitions of the school's painting classes. Edwin Forrest died here in 1872 and John Sartain in 1897; John Sartain was celebrated as a mezzotint engraver, and lived here with his daughter, Miss Emily Sartain, then principal of the school, herself a skilled painter, and engraver in mezzotint; who with her well chosen faculty of eminent artists, carried to a prosperous fulfilment Mrs. Peters' initiative effort.

PENNSYLVANIA MUSEUM AND SCHOOL OF INDUSTRIAL ART was founded in 1876, as a concrete embodiment of the lessons taught by the Centennial Exhibition, and has developed forms of artistic craftsmanship that were practically unknown in America. The Museum is housed in Memorial Hall, Fairmount Park, memorial of the Centennial; Modern Renaissance; architect, Herman J. Schwarzmann. Open free, Mondays, 12.00 M., other days 9.30 A. M., closing 5.00 P. M., Sundays, 1.00 P. M. to 6.00 P. M. Established as a museum of art in all its branches and technical application, with a special view to the development of the art industries of the state. Among its important collections are the W. P. Wilstach paintings, about five hundred old masters, with their schools; and contemporary international paintings, belonging to the City of Philadelphia; with $700,000 endowment, interest to be used for their care and increase, by the Commissioners of Fairmount Park; among the many brilliant artists represented are, Whistler, Munkácsy, Sorolla, Zuloago, Velasquez, the Barbizon, Italian, and Dutch Schools of Landscape. The famous Bayeux tapestry is here; laces; vestments; porcelains; enamels; carved ivories; period furniture; some of the Edwin Atlee Barber collection of American pottery and porcelains; Lewis collection of Swiss stained glass, sixteenth and seventeenth centuries; Frishmuth collection of colonial antiquities. A Bureau of Identification is maintained where art objects may be classified.

The school is at the northwest corner of Broad and Pine Streets; porch of this building, facing Broad Street, is a fine example of Tuscan architecture, erected, 1828. The school has forty instructors. Free scholarships are given in each county of this state. This is the leading school in America in associating the study of art with practical training; through its equipment students not only design, but actually manufacture; it includes a complete textile plant with looms, dye house, and all related appliances which make possible the production of most artistic fabrics; other courses are cast and wrought metal; furniture; leather work; pottery; garden furniture in cement; mosaic; also the Normal Art Courses, illustration; architectural drawing; modeling; interior decoration; book binding. Classes are attended by men and women, who pursue exactly the same studies. Graduates are sought to fill lucrative positions as designers; artistic craftsmen; and art teachers.

DREXEL INSTITUTE, Thirty-second and Chestnut Streets. A day and evening technical school of Art, Science, and Industry for men and women; founded by Anthony J. Drexel, 1891; Renaissance, brick; architects, Wilson Brothers. The leading American and European current periodicals relating to art, science, and technology are in the library. Art Gallery contains collections owned by John D. Lankenau, works by modern German masters, and Anthony J. Drexel, works of International, contemporary, modern painters. The Museum, open free 10.00 A. M. to 5.00 P. M. daily, except Sundays, includes examples of Industrial Art and the Decorative Arts of India, Egypt, China, Japan, and Europe.

GRAPHIC SKETCH CLUB, 719 Catharine Street, founded by Samuel S. Fleisher in 1899, to provide, free, an art center which should give the culture craved by many intelligent young people, to whom it had been denied by circumstances. The Club House is open only at night, Saturday afternoons, and all day Sundays. This is an Art Club in effect, as well as name; rooms are artistically furnished in beautiful color harmonies, and embellished with choice bronzes bought at our Academy exhibitions, and fine porcelains. Students are educated in art, for the practical good it will do them, and cultural growth; all are day workers. The faculty is composed of well known artists; classes include portrait and still life painting; illustration and sculpture. From this school have gone some of the most original workers in the schools of the Academy of the Fine Arts. Landscape classes are in session during the summer. Lectures are given on art or musical topics. Membership in the Club is attained by attendance in the classes for three years.

PUBLIC ART SCHOOL, Park Avenue and Master Street, founded by Charles G. Leland, now under the direction of the Board of Public Education; open to pupils in grammar grades of public schools. A course of study was planned, including drawing, clay modeling, and wood carving, to train students to originate design, and do the manual work as well, so that the designer should be the artisan also.

ART CLUB, 220 South Broad Street. Annual exhibition of paintings and sculpture, gold medal awarded; and special shows by individual artists.

ART JURY, City Hall, Philadelphia, created by Act of Legislature, 1907, providing, "That in every city of first class, there shall be an Art Jury, composed of the Mayor and eight others, of whom shall be, one each, painter, sculptor, architect, and Park Commissioner, to pass upon design and location of all buildings; bridges; arches; fountains; or fixtures to be erected in the city."

CITY PARKS ASSOCIATION, City Hall.

DARBY SCHOOL OF PAINTING, Fort Washington, Montgomery County. Outdoor classes. Hugh H. Breckenridge, 10 South 18th Street, Philadelphia.

FAIRMOUNT PARK ART ASSOCIATION, organized, 1871. 320 S. Broad Street.

PENNSYLVANIA SOCIETY OF MINIATURE PAINTERS, organized, 1901. Annual fall exhibition, Pennsylvania Academy of the Fine Arts.

PHILADELPHIA CHAPTER, AMERICAN INSTITUTE OF ARCHITECTS, 1301 Stephen Girard Building; organized, 1869.

THE PHILADELPHIA SKETCH CLUB (men), 235 South Camac Street, organized, 1860. Annual fall exhibitions of members' work; also special exhibitions.

PHILADELPHIA WATER-COLOR CLUB. Pennsylvania Academy of the Fine Arts, annual international exhibitions; also Traveling exhibitions of members' work.

PLASTIC CLUB, women, 247 South Camac Street; organized, 1897. Annual and special exhibitions; lectures, and sketch classes.

T-SQUARE CLUB, 204 South Quince Street, founded, 1881. Annual architectural exhibition; drafting; decorative painting; modeling; and architecture in coöperation with Society of Beaux-Arts Architects, New York City.

The D'ASCENZO STUDIOS, for Stained Glass, 1604 Summer Street, founded twenty years ago, include designing; painting; firing; and glazing; work is begun and completed, in both modern and antique, with preference for the antique school, for architectural fitness and conventionality; also glass mosaic and mural decoration. D'Ascenzo's art may be seen in many important churches and buildings in this country; in the Chapel at Valley Forge, and in Philadelphia may be mentioned St. Mark's Protestant Episcopal Church, Frankford; St. James' Protestant Episcopal Church, Twenty-second and Walnut Streets; St. Patrick's Roman Catholic Church, Twentieth and Locust Streets; Synagogue Rodeph Shalom, Philadelphia.

WILLIAM WILLET AND ANNIE LEE WILLET STUDIOS, FOR STAINED GLASS, 226 South Eleventh Street, formerly of Pittsburgh. While all the world is deploring the loss of the magnificent old glass in the cathedrals of Europe, here the art of fused glass has been raised to such perfection that their great windows have all that the old work has, of depth, glow, and shadow, under modern conditions of stability; among their notable windows are, the Sanctuary Window, West Point Military Chapel, New York; Proctor Hall, the Graduate School, Princeton, New Jersey, great west window; many in the churches and public buildings of Pittsburgh, Chicago and elsewhere; in and near Philadelphia, in Summit Presbyterian Church, Carpenter and West View Streets, Germantown; St. Michael's Sanctuary window, High Street, Germantown; John Chambers Memorial Church; The Buchanan Memorial, St. Nathaniel's Church, Kensington; the Harrison Memorial; Holy Trinity Church, Nineteenth and Walnut; the Leta Sullivan in the Assumption, Strafford.

Notable private art collections in Philadelphia, that may sometimes be seen by writing for permit, which for variety and value, have few peers are:

THE TRAGIC MUSE
From the Edward Hornor Coates Memorial Collection
Painted by Violet Oakley
Courtesy of the Pennsylvania Academy of the Fine Arts

THE COMMONWEALTH

P. A. B. WIDENER'S, several hundred choice and rare paintings, mostly masterpieces of great artists of the Renaissance, and modern.

The W. L. ELKINS; many fine examples of medieval and modern portraiture, landscape and genre painting.

The JOHN MCFADDEN, best collection of solely eighteenth century English paintings in this country.

The EDWARD T. STOTESBURY, masterpieces of the English School and international contemporary art.

Should these collections accompany the WILSTACH, now in Memorial Hall, to the Municipal Art Museum in Fairmount Park, now under construction, it would begin its career with a wealth of paintings, more comprehensive and valuable than any that ever inaugurated a similar institution, not excepting the Louvre, Pitti, Dresden, National in London, and Metropolitan, New York, which grew from small beginnings, thus placing the highest products of art within equal and easy reach of all classes. This Museum will constitute the central feature of a comprehensive plan in progress, at the head of the Parkway, for a real art center, more imposing in scale and impressive in its entire effect than any similar art center in any American City. The PENNSYLVANIA ACADEMY OF THE FINE ARTS has been granted a site facing the Fairmount Plaza, also the PENNSYLVANIA MUSEUM AND SCHOOL OF INDUSTRIAL ART.

ARMY AND NAVY

THE FIRST CITY TROOP, Armory, Twenty-third Street, above Chestnut; founded in 1778. An exclusive social organization. Oldest military command in the United States in continuous active service; its traditions of active service are as loyally preserved as its rights as escort of the President, and other distinguished men. In the Spanish-American War in 1898, "The Troop" was the first body of cavalry landed at Porto Rico. The "Gentlemen of Philadelphia" met in Independence Hall, November 17, 1774, and formed a company of cavalry called, "The Light Horse of the City of Philadelphia"; they were dismissed by Washington after the Revolution in 1778, and reorganized immediately as the First City Troop; the Troop voted to give the certificate of dismissal, signed by Washington, to their captain, Samuel Morris; the paper is now in possession of the decendants of Elliston P. Morris, of Germantown. FRANKFORD ARSENAL, Bridge and Tacony Streets; local station, Bridesburg; open, free, daily, 7.45 A. M. to sunset. Established, 1814; President Madison was at the opening exercises. Lafayette stopped at the Arsenal in 1824. Here are complete small arms cartridge factory equipment; artillery cartridge factory equipment; and machine plant for the manufacture of inspecting instruments; sights for cannon; range finders; and other instruments for fire control at the fortifications, etc. PHILADELPHIA NAVY YARD, League Island, about 1000 acres; junction of Delaware and Schuylkill Rivers; deeded to the National Government by the City of Philadelphia in 1868. Open to the public daily between 9.00 A. M. and 4.00 P. M. Established about 1794 on the Delaware River front, at Prime Street. A large number of the old wooden ships of the Navy were built here, such as the ships of the line, *Franklin*, *Pennsylvania* and *North*

Carolina; frigates, *United States, Raritan,* and *Guerriere;* sloops of war, *Vandalia, Germantown,* and *Dale;* screw steamers, *Princeton, Wabash,* and *Lancaster;* side wheel steamers, *Mississippi* and *Susquehanna.* At present there are two dry docks; shops employ 2000 men; three large barrack buildings for the use of marines stationed at the Yard accommodate 1400 men. Admiral Benson, former Commandant, considers this the best Navy Yard in the Government's possession, being in the center of coal and iron industries, within short haul, both by rail and water, for all material required by a great navy yard; its nearness to great private shipyards on the Delaware provides skilled mechanics in the art of ship-building, and the fresh water feature, being unique, is of great importance; barnacles accumulated in salt water drop off in fresh water, simply by docking here for short periods. There is also a large Reserve Basin called the Back Channel, where ships out of commission can be laid up until wanted. The berthing facilities may be indefinitely extended by constructing additional sea wall and piers. FORT MIFFLIN, below mouth of the Schuylkill, has casement dungeons, and earthen banks of early warfare, and was prominent in the Revolutionary War; designed and built by Major Louis de Tousard in 1798. Now, in the magazines, ammunition from government battleships is stored, before they enter the Navy Yard; the magazines are surrounded by poles, on each pole is a lightning rod. UNITED STATES NAVAL ASYLUM, Gray's Ferry Avenue below Bainbridge Street, classic, marble; has Museum of Uniforms.

HISTORIC BURIAL GROUNDS

The earliest were connected with churches; some date almost from the beginning of the city.

Baptist. BLOCKLEY CEMETERY, Meeting-House Lane, between Lancaster Avenue and Haverford Street; ground given, 1804. Church is at Fifty-third Street and Wyalusing Avenue. DUNKER, Germantown, on Germantown Avenue above Sharpnack Street; oldest meeting-house of the German Baptists, or Dunkers, in America; erected, 1770. Burial ground opened, 1793; in it lie Alexander Mack, founder of the sect, and Harriet Livermore, the "Pilgrim Stranger" of Whittier's "Snow Bound." MENNONITE, Germantown Avenue above Herman Street; church was built, 1770; many early Germantown settlers are buried in the yard. PENNYPACK, or LOWER DUBLIN, Krewston Road near Pennypack Creek, one mile from Bustleton; here is oldest Baptist church edifice in Pennsylvania, built about 1707; in the old time graveyard are many curious moss covered tombstones.

Friends. When the graves are marked the stones are always small and inconspicuous. FAIRHILL MEETING, Germantown Avenue and Cambria Street; ground granted by William Penn; a large and beautiful old cemetery and near "Fairhill," the great Norris estate. THE MEETING HOUSE, Fourth and Arch Streets, was built in 1804, but the ground was used for burials many years before; it is one of the oldest cemeteries in Philadelphia. Some of the most prominent citizens of very early days lie here with nothing to mark their resting-place; it is computed that twenty thousand persons are interred here.

Jewish. MIKVEH ISRAEL, on Spruce Street, near Ninth; ground was granted to Nathan Levy by John Penn in 1738; here lies the beautiful Rebecca Gratz, original of Rebecca in Scott's "Ivanhoe." In August, 1913, the little burial ground was opened for the interment of her grandniece, the first burial for thirty years. MOUNT SINAI, Frankford Avenue, near Bridge Street, has imposing entrance, erected, 1854.

Lutheran. ST. MICHAEL'S, Germantown Avenue and Phil-Ellena Street, joins the church built about 1730; a notable grave, with flat marble stone resting on four columns, is that of Christopher Ludwig, "baker general" to the American army during the Revolution.

Methodist. ST. PAUL'S, Catharine Street near Sixth. Church is now used as an Italian mission; has a small graveyard.

Presbyterian. OF FIRST AND THIRD CHURCHES, Southwest corner of Fourth and Pine Streets, First Church, Seventh and Locust Streets, has the eastern section. When the First Church abandoned its old Market Street site for the present locality, the bodies were moved whenever possible, and many of the old headstones were inserted in the south wall of the new graveyard. The Third Church, called "Old Pine," divides the grounds, using the west section; both are most interesting, with many people of note interred, including David Rittenhouse; William Hurry, who is said to have rung the Liberty Bell when proclaiming independence; Dr. William Shippen, Director General of Hospitals during the war for Independence; many Revolutionary soldiers; and Captain Charles Ross of the First City Troop.

Protestant Episcopal. ALL SAINTS, Bristol Turnpike, Torresdale. Established 1772–73, when the first church edifice was built. CHRIST CHURCH has two burial-grounds, one attached to the church on Second Street, North of Market, dating from the earliest days of the church, the other southeast corner of Fifth and Arch Streets, where first interment was made in 1730; graves of Benjamin Franklin and Deborah, his wife, are in the northwest corner; may be seen from Arch Street through an iron railing set in the brick wall; in these graveyards are buried may distinguished Americans; among them Peyton Randolph, first President of the Continental Congress; Commodores Truxton, Biddle, Bainbridge, and Dale; Robert Morris; several signers of the Declaration of Independence; Dr. Benjamin Rush, Dr. Philip Syng Physick, Bishop White, and Dr. William Augustus Muhlenberg. GLORIA DEI (Old Swedes'), Front and Swanson Streets, south of Christian; church built, 1700, being the oldest church building in Philadelphia; a most interesting graveyard surrounds it; the celebrated ornithologist, Alexander Wilson, is buried here. ST. JAMES, KINGSESSING, Sixty-eighth Street and Paschall Avenue; church erected, 1762; General Josiah Harmer, of the Revolution, is buried in the graveyard. ST. JAMES THE LESS, Hunting Park Avenue and Clearfield Street; this beautiful little Gothic church, brownstone, built 1847, has a number of fine monuments in the burial ground; John Wanamaker is buried here. ST. LUKE'S, Germantown Avenue and Coulter Street, church dates from 1818; the famous Philadelphia annalist, John Fanning Watson, is interred in the churchyard. ST.

PETER'S, southwest corner of Third and Pine Streets; in the graveyard lies the body of Commodore Stephen Decatur, the grave surmounted by an Ionic column supporting an American eagle; other notable names here are Chew, Cadwalader, Mifflin, Binney, Biddle, Peale, Waln, Meade, McCall, Duché, Norris, Kuhn, Montgomery. TRINITY, Oxford, near Fox Chase, east of old Second Street Pike; present church dates from 1711; began as a log meeting house, 1698; tombstones date as early as 1708; the inscriptions on some are quaint and original.

Roman Catholic. HOLY TRINITY, northwest corner of Sixth and Spruce Streets, dates from 1789; on the old tombstones may be deciphered names of many of the early German and French inhabitants of Philadelphia. Stephen Girard was buried here until 1851, later his body was removed to Girard College. MOST HOLY REDEEMER, Richmond Street, opposite Hedley Street, Bridesburg; many of the Redemptorist Fathers are buried here.

OTHER NOTABLE BURIAL GROUNDS

NORTH CEDAR HILL, Frankford Avenue corner of Foust Street, incorporated, 1857; a soldiers' monument to the Civil War soldiers from Frankford is in the older part. CRISPIN, Holmesburg; contains grave of Thomas Holme, who laid out the city of Philadelphia; plot is under care of the Crispin Association, formed of descendants of Holme. GLENWOOD, Ridge Avenue and Twenty-seventh Street, opened, 1850, has notable monument of the Scott Legion Association, formed among the surviving soldiers of the Mexican War.

GREENWOOD, Asylum Pike and Arrott Street, Frankford; established, 1869, by the benevolent order of the Knights of Pythias, as a burial place for members and their families; occupies the "Mount Airy" estate, once residence of Commodore Stephen Decatur. HOOD, or "THE LOWER BURIAL GROUND," on Germantown Avenue at Logan Street, opened in 1693, having been presented to the borough of Germantown by Jan Streepers. Many early settlers of Germantown lie here; among them Frederic William Post, the Moravian missionary to the Indians, and Condy Raguet, founder of the Saving Fund in Philadelphia; in 1847, William Hood built the front entrance, of Pennsylvania marble, the wall and railing. IVY HILL, East Mount Airy Avenue, above Stenton Avenue, chartered, 1867; about 80 acres; the Second Baptist Church has removed to Ivy Hill about 300 bodies from its old burial place on New Market Street; an imposing monument is here in memory of David Lyle, Chief Engineer of the Volunteer Fire Department from 1859–67. NORTH LAUREL HILL, East bank of Schuylkill River and Ridge Avenue, organized, 1835; formerly "Laurel," country seat of Joseph Sims. "Fairy Hill," seat of Pepper family, now CENTRAL LAUREL HILL, and "Harleigh," William Rawle's place, now SOUTH LAUREL HILL; historic dead and artistic monuments fill these cemeteries; Commodores Murray and Hull, General George Gordon Meade, and Mrs. Cornelius Stevenson, "Peggy Shippen" of the *Ledger*, are among those who lie here; the Lea Memorial, sculptor A. Sterling Calder, is very beautiful, the chapel is early English. Just across the Schuylkill River, on Belmont Avenue, at Pencoyd

THE COMMONWEALTH 75

Station, is WEST LAUREL HILL, opened in 1869. General Herman Haupt is among those buried here. MONUMENT, Broad Street and Montgomery Avenue, was laid out by Dr. John A. Elkinton in 1836; an obelisk monument, on a pedestal, erected, 1859, in honor of Washington and Lafayette, was designed by John Sartain, artist, who is buried near base of shaft. MOUNT MORIAH, Sixty-second Street and Kingsessing Avenue, opened, 1855; has grave of Betsy Ross, over which a flag floats perpetually. MOUNT PEACE, Lehigh Avenue and Thirty-first Street, was originally country seat of the Ralston family, known as Mount Peace estate. MOUNT VERNON, Ridge and Lehigh Avenues, opposite Laurel Hill, chartered, 1856; the Gardel monument was long considered handsomest in the country. NATIONAL CEMETERY, Haines Street and Limekiln Pike, land acquired by the United States Government in 1885, it is well wooded, and the grounds are laid out with flowering plants; about 2700 Union soldiers are buried here; their graves marked by long rows of small granite slabs, bearing their names and the States from which they came. Soldiers of three wars lie here; a granite monument, erected by the United States, marks the burial place of 184 Confederate soldiers and sailors. PALMER, at Palmer, Belgrade, and Memphis Streets, owes its origin to Anthony Palmer; in 1730, he purchased a large tract of land in "The Northern Liberties," on which he laid out a town and named it Kensington; his daughter carried out his wishes, and bequeathed ground for a burial place for those living in Kensington. RONALDSON'S, Tenth and Fitzwater Streets, now neglected, was founded by James Ronaldson in 1826 as a burial place in which persons of moderate means could find a grave without any of the restrictions which attended interments in the churchyards; he gave the ground, almost a city square, decorated it with trees and shrubbery; so beautifully was it kept that it was considered "The model burial place of the City," until the opening of Laurel Hill. UPPER BURIAL GROUND, or AX'S, Germantown Avenue near Washington Lane. John Frederick Ax was caretaker from 1724-56; many early settlers are buried here, the oldest known grave being that of Cornelius Tyson, who died in 1716; there are also graves of some American soldiers and officers, killed in the Battle of Germantown; over them, John Fanning Watson placed a marble headstone. WOODLANDS, Thirty-ninth Street and Woodland Avenue, was in early times the country seat of William Hamilton, known as "The Woodlands"; acquired by Woodlands Cemetery Company in 1840. Many distinguished men and women are buried here, among them Commodore Thomas Stewart, who commanded the *Constitution* in 1812; General John Stewart, Major Generals D. B. Birney and Abercrombie of the Civil War; Rembrandt Peale; William K. Hewitt and P. F. Rothermel, Artists; John Davenport, Actor; Colonel Thomas A. Scott and J. Edgar Thomson; Frank and Louise Stockton; Dr. S. Weir Mitchell and Anthony J. Drexel.

HISTORIC CHURCHES IN PHILADELPHIA

Among the eight hundred and five churches in Philadelphia, are:

The Philadelphia BAPTIST, whose Association celebrated its two hundredth and tenth anniversary in 1917. FIRST CHURCH, Seventeenth Street below Chestnut, open daily, is a consistent example of Byzantine architecture with American modifications; stone; architect, Edgar V. Seeler. Windows made by Heinecke & Bowen are copies of the Byzantine leaded glass; lights and shadows in drapery are all done with leaded strips of glass, not painted. TEMPLE, Broad and Berks Streets, famous on account of its pastor, Rev. Russell H. Conwell, was dedicated, 1901; at that time it was the largest church edifice in the United States, excepting the Mormon Temple at Salt Lake City; auditorium seats 3135 people: Romanesque, with two low towers on the front, surmounted by large copper domes, which give an Oriental touch; architect, Thomas Lonsdale. Fine rose window in front, said to have been made by John LaFarge; other windows are by J. & R. Lamb and R. S. Groves: the Hope-Jones organ, built by the Rudolph Wurlitzer Company, is one of the largest in this country; it has all the orchestral accompaniments. TABERNACLE, Chestnut and Fortieth Streets, Gothic, stone, has a window by William Willet. There are about one hundred Baptist churches in Philadelphia.

Christian Science. FIRST CHURCH OF CHRIST SCIENTIST, Walnut Street near Fortieth; Spanish architecture.

Congregational. CENTRAL, Eighteenth and Green Streets, Gothic, stone, built in 1872; architect, D. Supplee; organized in 1864; first services were held in old Concert Hall, 1217 Chestnut Street, afterwards used as first Free Library Building; sermon "Recognition," was preached by Rev. Henry Ward Beecher; other sermons of early days, by Richard S. Storrs, D.D. About nine or ten churches of this denomination are in Philadelphia.

Friends' or Quaker Meeting-Houses.

"What dignity breathes from the lofty space
  And amplitude of hospitality
  In these old-fashioned Quaker shrines!
  Most friendly seems the long, high, sturdy roof,
  Most friendly the all-welcoming old walls
  Seen through the sheltering trees.
  O mighty oaks and noble sycamores,
  With trunks moss-silvered and with lichened limb,
  Breathe soft to me the storied memories
  And treasured records of the long rich years
  That blessed the meeting-houses."

(From "Old Meeting-Houses,"
by John Russell Hayes.)

For more than one hundred years there has been no change in the general style of architecture; before that time, the earliest meeting-house in Philadelphia, at Second and Market Streets, was built with a central lantern or cupola; probably copied from a meeting-house of similar form in Burlington, New Jersey, built, 1682; where the yearly meeting for New Jersey and Pennsylvania was first held: later it met alternately at Philadelphia and Burlington, but since 1750 in Philadelphia, Fourth and Arch Streets. One of the most interesting old meeting-houses, built in 1696, is at MERION, near Narberth Station, Pennsylvania Railroad, in which William Penn preached; another, that he attended, is the old HAVERFORD, built in the early eighteenth century, near Cobb's Creek, opposite St.

THE COMMONWEALTH 79

Dennis Roman Catholic Church. RADNOR and PLYMOUTH are also interesting old houses; all these last named are now owned by the HICKSITE BRANCH of Quakers, who also own over seventy other meeting-houses throughout the state. Among those owned by the ORTHODOX BRANCH within Philadelphia are the Fourth and Arch Streets, not only the most important, but of great charm architecturally; it is very large and stands on ground originally given by William Penn to George Fox, and by the latter to Friends in America; and may be taken as typical of the later and best Quaker architecture; built in 1804, following the style of the pre-Revolutionary days of the houses just named, but adapted in material and size to the increased numbers worshiping within; it is of brick, set in ample grounds, with abundant shade; the ground about it, and much also covered now by the building and by Arch Street, is a very old burial ground, filled over several times. James Logan is buried under the pavement of Arch Street. TWELFTH STREET MEETING-HOUSE, brick, built in 1812, is second in importance, and one of the most beautiful bits in old Philadelphia. The oak timbers in its roof are said to have come from the "Great Meeting-House," which succeeded that with the cupola at Second and Market Streets; oak timbers are also exposed with good effect in the upper room of the Arch Street house; the two houses are of the same general type and severely plain, but form, together with that at Sixth and Noble Streets, a most dignified trio of places for worship; remarkable for true proportion and dignity of outline, they are typical of the wealth and solidity of the Friends at their most flourishing period. THE MEETING HOUSE, Sixth and Noble Streets, known as "North Meeting," once accommodating a large congregation, has been reduced in members by removals; the Yearly Meeting has therefore taken over its use as an adjunct to the settlement work, carried on by Friends at "Noble House."

Jewish. Rosh Hashana, or the Jewish New Year's Day, is the oldest festival celebrated in the civilized world, 1917 will usher in the year 5678; it commences the great series of fall holidays: ten days later is "Yom Kippur," the Day of Atonement, most sacred of the year, when the Jews fast from sunset to sunset and attend the synagogues, and a week later "Succoth," corresponding to our Thanksgiving Day, which lasts a week. The principal synagogues are ADATH-JESHURUN, Broad Street above Diamond, Egyptian; limestone and brick; architects, Churchman, Thomas & Molitar, has leaded glass windows by Nicolo D'Ascenzo. KENESETH ISRAEL, Broad Street above Columbia Avenue, Italian Renaissance, brick with limestone trimmings; architect, Hickman. MIKVEH ISRAEL, Broad and York Streets, organized, 1747; moved from Seventh Street near Arch; French Renaissance, limestone; architects, Pitcher & Tachau. RODEPH SHALOM, southeast corner of Broad and Mt. Vernon Streets, Moorish, sandstone; built, 1869; architects, Furness & Evans; has leaded glass windows by Nicolo D'Ascenzo.

Lutheran. The THEOLOGICAL SEMINARY of Philadelphia, 7301 Germantown Avenue, was founded in 1864; removed to present location, 1889; site, residence of Chief Justice Allen; afterwards a military school of some distinction, "Mount Airy College." The administration building was erected by James Gowen for a residence in 1848, and adapted to the wants of the Seminary; on the grounds are twelve buildings, including Krauth Memorial Library, perpendicular Gothic, stone, built, 1908; contains portraits; the Refectory, once residence of the Miller family, built, 1792, colonial; and the Ashmead-Schaeffer Memorial Chapel, Gothic, stone. ST. MICHAEL'S, Germantown Avenue and Phil-Ellena Street, first church, built, 1730; British soldiers took refuge in the church and demolished the organ during the Battle of Germantown; corner-stone of present church laid, 1896. OLD ST. JOHNS, Race Street between Fifth and Sixth, first English Lutheran Church in America, colonial, brick; congregation organized in 1806, largely through efforts of General Peter Muhlenberg; contains a fine oil portrait by John Neagle, painted in 1853, of Dr. Philip F. Mayer, first pastor 1806–58; and woodcarvings in front of the gallery by William Rush. ZION (German), Franklin Street above Race, Romanesque, brownstone, built, 1870, moved from southeast corner of Fourth and Cherry, founded 1766; a memorial service was held here for Washington in 1799, by General Charles Lee. THE MARY J. DREXEL HOME AND PHILADELPHIA MOTHERHOUSE OF DEACONESSES, Twenty-first Street and South College Avenue, modified Gothic with numerous towers, brick trimmed with sandstone, built, 1888; provides a training school for Deaconesses of the Lutheran Church; home for the aged and a children's hospital; a Gothic chapel on the second floor, has altar cloths from Neuendettelsau, Bavaria; and stained glass by Meyer, Munich; portraits of the

Lankenau and Drexel families are here, and an Italian marble bust of Mr. Lankenau by Moses Ezekiel of Rome.

Methodist. SAINT GEORGE'S, 229 North Fourth Street, oldest Methodist church in the world, used continuously for worship; dedicated, 1769; Bishop Francis Asbury preached his first sermon in America here; three memorial tablets mark the front: to John Dickens, founder of the Methodist Book Concern, buried rear of the church, in 1798; to Ezekiel Cooper, his successor, buried in front, and one commemorating the first Methodist Conference in America, held in this church July 14, 1773. CALVARY, Forty-eighth Street and Baltimore Avenue, Gothic, stone, has mural painting, "Sermon on the Mount," by H. Hanley Parker, and two Tiffany windows. Other Methodist Episcopal churches with good architecture are, ARCH STREET, Broad and Arch Streets, Gothic, white marble, and GRACE, Broad and Master Streets, Renaissance.

Presbyterian. FIRST CHURCH, Seventh and Locust Streets, facing Washington Square; oldest Presbyterian Church in Philadelphia, founded, 1699; present building erected, 1820, classic, brick, rough cast; with Ionic porch; architect, Theophilus P. Chandler: contains Paxton memorial window by Frederick Wilson, interesting old tablets, and a copy of Calvin's "Institutes." SECOND CHURCH, Twenty-first and Walnut Streets, French Gothic, with early English detail; erected, 1872; architect, Henry Sims; Richmond granite is used in the base, the walls are of Trenton stone, Cleveland sandstone for tracery of windows and moulding of doors, with red sandstone, blue sandstone,

THE COMMONWEALTH 83

and green serpentine for special parts, in contrasts of color and decorative effects: interior is faced with buff-colored brick imported from Raubon, Wales: the richly ornamented pulpit is of Caen stone. Windows, a double one, by John LaFarge; seven representing old Testament subjects, by Tiffany; and five apse windows from England. SCOTTS, Broad Street below Morris, founded, 1766: third oldest organization in the Philadelphia Presbytery; is still under its original charter; original church was at Fourth and Bainbridge Streets, later on at Spruce Street above Third; Louis Philippe lived in the parsonage during his residence in Philadelphia in 1796; John Purdon, father of Purdon's Digest, was its first elder; President John Adams attended the church. OLD PINE STREET CHURCH, Fourth and Pine Streets, classic, brick, rough-cast, with Corinthian porch; erected, 1857, one of the walls being that of the original church built in 1768; the first pastor, George Duffield, was chaplain of all the Pennsylvania militia, and also served as chaplain of the First Continental Congress after Jacob Duché; he was with Washington during the retreat through New Jersey; was in the battles of Princeton and Trenton, and the British offered a price of 50 pounds sterling for his head; he is buried under the central aisle of the lecture room, and his portrait is in Independence Hall: John Adams, when President, was a communicant here; when the British occupied the city, they used this church as a hospital; pews and other woodwork were burned as fuel, and later the church was used by the dragoons to stable their horses. HOLLAND MEMORIAL, Broad and Federal Streets, Romanesque; buff

Massillon stone, with red sandstone trimmings, from the Ballaclunyle quarries of Scotland; architect, David S. Grendell; windows by Tiffany, in the south arcade, are from originals by Frederick Wilson; other windows are by Alfred Godwin and Maitland & Armstrong; there are four large rose windows, in one, the patriarch Joshua stands in the center, clad in full armor; color scheme is based upon the rose window of Saint Chapelle, Paris; makers, William and Annie Lee Willet: under each window is a group of five arcade windows, some of them copies from originals of Sir Edwin Burne-Jones, for windows in Brighton and Salisbury Cathedrals. TABERNACLE, Thirty-seventh and Chestnut Streets, is one of the finest Gothic church edifices in Philadelphia, in decorative English style, with tower 130 feet high, erected, 1886; granite, with Indiana limestone for tracery of windows and doors; no wood being used in its construction, it thus resembles the cathedrals of the old world; chapel is connected with the manse by a cloistered porch. WEST ARCH STREET, Eighteenth and Arch Streets, Roman classic, with dome 170 feet above the ground, stone, plastered; has fine Corinthian porch. MARKET SQUARE, Germantown, founded, 1738: President Washington worshiped here, while living opposite in the old Morris house, during the yellow fever epidemic in Philadelphia in 1793; during the battle of Germantown, a battalion of Virginians, prisoners of the English, were lodged in this church; the old bell, cast, 1725, which was in the shingle roof steeple of the old church, is still intact, and preserved as a relic; also the "Trumpet angels in their gold array," part of the original organ from Holland:

THE COMMONWEALTH 85

present building, French Gothic, stone, was erected in 1886.

The WITHERSPOON BUILDING, Walnut Street below Broad, has sculpture by A. Stirling Calder and Samuel Murray.

Protestant Episcopal. ST. ALBAN'S, Olney, consecrated, 1915; decorated French Gothic; buttresses run up to above the cornice line, ending in gables with crockets and finials; there is a belfry tower and porch; interior lines are very beautiful; the high arches and lofty piers give an impression of great dignity and simplicity, well adapted for rendering the services, with all the accompaniment of advanced churchmanship; architect, George T. Pearson. CHRIST CHURCH, Second Street north of Market; first Protestant Episcopal Church in the province; hours of service, September to July, Sundays 10.00 A. M., 11.00 A. M., 3.30 P. M., open daily 9.00 A. M. to 3.00 P. M.; founded in 1695, under a provision in the original charter of King Charles II to William Penn. John Penn, last male member of this line, is buried near the steps of the pulpit. Present building, Georgian, erected 1747; Dr. John Kearsley, Building Director; the old roof, its wooden balustrade with carved spindles, and the steeple are ever of interest to architects and antiquarians.

Here the colonial governors had their state pew, marked by coat of arms, bearing the monogram of William and Mary; the parish was subsidized by King William III, William of Orange; Communion silver presented in 1709 by Queen Anne; baptismal font dates from 1695, and was used for the baptism of Bishop White in infancy. The chime of bells pealed forth the

Declaration of Independence, in response to the Liberty Bell, July 8, 1776; they were made in England, and came over in the same ship with the Liberty Bell, were taken to Allentown with the Liberty Bell, and subsequently rehung; are referred to by Longfellow in "Evangeline." George and Martha Washington regularly occupied pew 58 from 1790–97; it was also the official pew of John Adams while President, and was used by Lafayette in 1824; Franklin had pew 70, still used by his descendants; Robert Morris' pew was 52; Francis Hopkinson's, 65. General Charles Lee, of the Continental Army, is interred beside the southwest door, and near by is General Hugh Mercer; Rt. Rev. William White, D.D., first Bishop of Pennsylvania and long Presiding Bishop of the United States, is interred before the chancel rail, and his Episcopal chair is beside the altar. The church was organized; its constitution framed; and the amended Prayer Book adopted in this church, in 1785; Bishop White and Provost William Smith, D.D., were the Committee for revising and altering the liturgy of the English Prayer Book, for use in America. Rev. Jacob Duché was rector for many years. Windows illustrate the history of the Christian Church; made by Heaton, Butler and Bains. ST. CLEMENT'S, Twentieth and Cherry Streets, Norman Gothic, brownstone, built, 1857; architect, John Notman; new roof of nave, apse, and high altar; choir and lady chapel; architect, Horace Wells Sellers; the sanctuary is beautifully designed, with effect heightened by a magnificent reredos; artist, Frederick Wilson of Briarcliff, New York, leaded glass of apse, and lady chapel, by Alfred God-

BISHOP WILLIAM WHITE
Painted by Gilbert Stuart
Courtesy of the Pennsylvania Academy of the Fine Arts

win, Philadelphia. ST. ELIZABETH'S, corner of Sixteenth and Mifflin Streets, early Italian, with high Campanile; medieval exterior and interior give an exact idea of old Italian churches; brick; architects, Bailey and Bassett; the choir is raised eight steps from the nave, giving view of the crypt, and dignified elevation of the high altar; over the altar is a copy of Correggio's "Marriage of St. Catharine"; fine jeweled door of the Pyx on the altar; Lady chapel has an altar of richly carved and gilded wood, finished with a high reredos, copy of an original in Santo Spirito, Florence; paintings set in are copies of works by Fra Filipo Lippi. CHURCH OF THE EVANGELIST, now part of Graphic Sketch Club, Catharine Street above Seventh, brick, is a gem of medievalism; Italian Basilican style; red brick, relieved by stone trimmings; pillars of portico rest on backs of lions; architects, Furness & Evans; frescoes by Nicolo d'Ascenzo and by Robert Henri; original compositions and adaptations of great paintings in Italy; font, late English Gothic, with a richly carved stone; above it is the Strasbourg window, containing a figure of the prophet, Jonas; this piece of glass, before the Franco-Prussian War, was in the Cathedral of Strasbourg, and was taken from one of the windows after the Germans had directed their fire on the church and smashed the glass: paving of the Chapel of the Holy Sepulchre is of Mercer tiles; Rood screen of polished marble, is modeled after that at St. Marco, Venice; Altar rail modeled after that in a chapel at Monreale, Sicily; the reredos, of the high altar, is a copy of a famous altar-piece by Carlo Crivelli; original now in the National Gallery, London. GLORIA

DEI (Old Swedes'), on land given by Swan Swanson, corner of Front and Swanson Streets, near Christian Street; formerly Wecacoa (Indian name for pleasant place); was dedicated in 1700. Georgian architecture, with steep pitched roof; brick work of walls, Flemish bond, headers coated with vitreous, blue black glaze, doubtless the arch bricks in the kiln; great square windows. Erected by the Swedish Lutherans; after the Revolution, care of the Swedish churches was committed to the American Church, and became part of the Diocese of Pennsylvania. This congregation first worshiped in a block house, used also as a fortress from 1677; the font used then is still in the present church. HOLY TRINITY, Nineteenth and Walnut Streets; Norman Romanesque; architect, John Notman; has fine memorial windows. ST. JAMES, Twenty-second and Walnut Streets, founded, 1807; present building, English decorated Gothic with sculptured band around the tower, from which rises the graceful memorial spire; Ohio green sandstone and granite, built, 1870; architect, G. W. Hewitt: pulpit; altar; reredos of fine perpendicular work in Caen stone, rich in ornamentation and sculpture, which also extends around the chancel, with two marble pilasters having delicately carved capitals; all designed by Cram, Goodhue and Ferguson; mosaics of the twelve apostles, in the walls of the nave, suggest those of the Popes in the Church of St. Paul, outside the walls, in Rome; leaded glass by Nicolo d'Ascenzo; font has a bas-relief in white marble, angel scattering flowers, made in Florence, Italy. ST. JAMES THE LESS, near main entrance to Laurel Hill Cemetery; thirteenth century

Gothic; brownstone; once said to be the choicest specimen of church architecture in the United States. ST. JOHN CHRYSOSTOM, corner Twenty-eighth Street and Susquehanna Avenue, almost an exact copy of St. Stephen's Church, London, designed by Sir Christopher Wren; Renaissance, granite; architects, Bailey & Bassett; adapted to a square lot, the interior shows form of Greek cross, with inner octagon; rosettes and decorations of the dome are graceful and beautiful; columns, placed on rather high pedestals, are Vermont marble, with very beautiful veining, surmounted by Corinthian capitals: the church is almost entirely white, with no stained glass, and gives an impression of complete harmony. ST. MARK'S, Locust Street above Sixteenth, built, 1849; fine specimen of fourteenth century, decorated Gothic, brownstone; plans furnished by the Ecclesiological Society of Cambridge, England; modified by John Notman; altar and reredos are richly carved stone; also the pulpit and choir screen; notable features are the rood beam, with cross and figures; carved sanctuary door; choir and clergy stalls; the altar at head of north aisle is alabaster. Lady chapel, erected, 1900, contains a silver altar of elaborate magnificence, probably finest in the world, of the same style as the one at Florence, Italy, by Pallajnoli, but richer, containing twelve scenes from the life of the Virgin, and studded with precious stones, some four hundred emeralds, sapphires, and opals, a monumental work, which will remain a very splendid presentation of twentieth century English ecclesiastical art; altar rail is silver and bronze; stained glass windows in the church are notable; the sacred vessels and vestments surpass any in the Angelican Communion, in their extraordinary richness; silver processional cross is supposed to be that of the Palermo Cathedral, in 1520; among old vestments are the coronation robes of Louis XV from Rheims Cathedral, of light blue velvet, heavily embroidered with twenty-two karat gold bullion. The first curate was the Rev. Morgan Dix, ordained priest in this church, who became the famous rector of Trinity Church, New York. ST. MARY'S, 3916 Locust Street, on ground given by William Hamilton, of Woodlands; first Protestant Episcopal Church in West Philadelphia, organized, 1820; frame church erected, 1824; Bishop White laid the corner-stone; present building, Gothic, consecrated, 1890. Memorial Gothic altar, retable, and reredos are from famous studios in Rome, Italy, said to be the finest example of ecclesiastical mosaic work in this country: windows are from London, Paris, Munich, and Philadelphia. Rev. Thomas C. Yarnall celebrated his fiftieth anniversary as rector of St. Mary's in 1894. ST. PAUL'S, east side of Third Street, below Walnut; classic; erected, 1761; third Protestant Episcopal Church in Philadelphia and largest in the province; now headquarters of the City Mission. The General Convention met here in 1814, when Bishop Moore of Virginia was consecrated; Bishop Hobart preached the sermon. St. Paul's Club, 411 Spruce Street, makes a specialty of giving aid to the down and out drunkard, sobering him up, fitting him for a job, and getting him one; in the five years of its existence to 1917, it has registered 45,000 transient visitors and temporary guests on its books. ST. PETER'S, corner of Third and

Pine Streets, second church erected in Philadelphia, fine example of Georgian architecture, in beauty of line; brick; built, 1761; tower and spire, 218 feet high, were added, 1842; stone finials of gateposts were cut in England; present wall erected in 1784, after the old wooden fence had been taken for fuel by the British. Interior still retains the high-backed box pews, President Washington's among them, pew 41; the pulpit, surmounting the clerk's desk, soars upward at the far end, opposite the altar; Provost William Smith preached the consecration sermon; very beautiful stained glass by Myeres, London; remarkable for richness of color and design; many interesting relics in the church's history are in the sacristy. CHURCH OF THE SAVIOUR, Thirty-eighth Street above Chestnut, architect, C. M. Burns, has a splendidly impressive chancel; decoration by Edwin Howland Blashfield and furnishings are memorial to Anthony J. Drexel. Memorial window by William and Annie Lee Willet, "Christ and Nicodemus," has strong decorative quality and richness of color. SOUTH MEMORIAL, CHURCH OF THE ADVOCATE, Eighteenth and Diamond Streets, French Gothic, suggested by Amiens Cathedral; built, 1897; stone; architect, Charles M. Burns; interior profusely adorned with carving, and sixty-five stained glass windows by Clayton and Bell, London. ST. STEPHEN'S, Tenth Street above Chestnut; founded, 1823; early Gothic, with two octagonal towers; stone; designed by William Strickland; contains notable sculpture; the Burd Memorial, "Angel of the Resurrection," finest Italian marble, by Carl Steinhauser, native of Bremen, who studied in Rome under Thorwaldsen; and recumbent effigy of Colonel Burd; also font by Steinhauser, represents three cherubs supporting on their wings a large marble bowl, with sculpture in relief; the church, decorated by Frank Furness, with color, rich and unusual, sets off admirably the beauty of the memorial marbles; the stately reredos, with its brilliant Venetian mosaic picture, "The Last Supper," was made in 1889, by Salviati, Venice, from cartoons by Henry Holiday, London, and under his own supervision; large double window in transept also by Holiday; a Tiffany window is, "Christ Among the Lilies," the only flower He mentions in the Evangels, and accepted as symbol of the resurrection; the window, showing the angel sitting on the edge of the tomb with partly unfolded wings, is copy of a picture by Axel Ender, over the altar of a church in Molde, Northern Norway; near the reredos is "The Angel of Purity," sculptor Augustus Saint Gaudens, which suggests his "Amor, Caritas," owned by the French Government, now in the Luxembourg; here is also a basrelief by Charles Grafley of Dr. David D. Wood, organist of St. Stephen's for forty-six years; the great organ was built by C. T. Haskell, Philadelphia, in consultation with Dr. Wood; pipes were voiced in the church, resulting in a sweetness and just proportion of tone; its echo organ, located about two hundred feet away, is in the loft over the chancel. Parish house is on site of the old graveyard, tombstones are in pavement of cloister; architect, George C. Mason, Jr. TRINITY, Oxford, Oxford Road and Second Street Pike; colonial; founded, 1698. Present brick church erected 1711–12; the transepts and tower later; was the first house of worship in Pennsylvania, owned and occupied by the Quakers, and presented by them to the Church of England, for Episcopal use and worship. Chalice and paten sent by Queen Anne, engraved "Anne Regina," 1713; she died in 1714, it is probably the last one she sent to America, and has been used in every Holy Communion for over two centuries. Tiffany altar window, "The Baptism of Christ." The altar, of walnut and oak, is beautifully carved. This is the mother of many flourishing missions, St. Luke's, Germantown; Our Saviour, Jenkintown; St. Mark's, Frankford; Emmanuel, Holmesburg; Holy Trinity, Rockledge; and Trinity Chapel, Crescentville; today it stands, vigorous and full of life, in its old age, greatly enlarged and carefully restored; the utmost care has been taken to disturb none of the old walls, and to keep the historic features intact; the glass, in the body of the church, is an opaque yellow, harmonizing with the colonial buff of the walls and barrel ceiling. The churchyard is of great interest, one stone, dated, 1686, is said to mark the grave of an Indian.

The Reformed Church in the United States, which brought its beautiful and significant emblem, "The lily among thorns," from the fatherland, is derived from the Reformed Churches of Switzerland and Germany; these churches are largely to be found in the counties east of the Susquehanna River. William Penn's mother, Margaret Jasper, was reared in this faith; noted members who came here were Michael Schlatter, in 1746, from St. Gall, Switzerland; sent to establish an ecclesiastical organization; he was practically the first superintendent of public instruction in

Pennsylvania; died, 1790, and was buried in the Reformed graveyard in Philadelphia, now Franklin Square; Colonel Henry Bouquet, from Switzerland, proved the saviour of the early settlers in Pontiac's war and obtained the restoration of all captives to their homes; three hundred and seventy were brought back; and Baron von Steuben, who had served on the staff of Frederick the Great at the siege of Prague, drilled our men into efficiency to cope with the British regulars; later he commanded at the Siege of Yorktown, which he pressed so vigorously that Cornwallis was obliged to surrender. Zion Reformed Church at Allentown sheltered our Liberty Bell and the Christ Church bells during the Revolution; among their thirty churches in Philadelphia and vicinity, of Gothic architecture, stone, are the FIRST CHURCH, Fiftieth and Locust Streets; oldest of this denomination in Philadelphia; moved from Tenth and Wallace Streets; PALATINATE, Fifty-sixth Street and Girard Avenue; ST. JOHN'S, Fortieth and Spring Garden Streets; and TRINITY, northeast corner of Broad and Venango Streets. There are also five churches of the Dutch Reformed.

Roman Catholic. The churches of this denomination are all notable for good architecture, interior sumptuous, ecclesiastical decoration. CATHEDRAL OF SS. PETER AND PAUL, finely situated on Logan Square and the Parkway; Classic Renaissance, brownstone; built 1846–64; architect, Napoleon LeBrun; "The Crucifixion," back of the high altar, genuine fresco painting, is by Constantine Brumidi, who, about the same time, executed important decorations, in the same medium, in the dome of the Capitol at Washington; on entering the church, in chapels on both sides of the door, are mural decorations by Henry J. Thouron, said, by high authority, to be the best mural paintings in the United States; the first was placed in 1911 as a fitting background for a statue of the Virgin and Child by Louis Madrazzi, which Mr. Thouron brought from Paris as a gift to the Cathedral; in the north transept is a painting, "The Dead Christ," attributed to Titian; a work of art of exceptional merit is a large ivory crucifix, the master work of Carlo Pazenti, an Augustinian lay brother, about 1840; acquired for the church, with much difficulty, by the venerable John N. Neumann, fourth Bishop of Philadelphia; when, during the Civil War, the Sanitary Fair was being held in Logan Square, Archbishop Wood, then Bishop Wood, exhibited this beautiful work daily, for the benefit of the great cause; it was returned each evening to its place in the Cathedral. ST. JOHN THE EVANGELIST, Thirteenth Street above Chestnut, for a short time the cathedral; early English, Gothic; interior, perpendicular Gothic; corner-stone laid by Bishop Kenrick, third Bishop of Philadelphia; church opened April 8, 1832: a flagellation of Christ, much darkened, by Garacci, was presented to the church by Joseph Bonaparte soon after its completion: Mozart's "Requiem Mass" was rendered, for the first time in America, at St. John's Church, and the music there today, is said to be the best church music in Philadelphia. ST. PATRICK'S, Twentieth Street below Locust, originated in a frame church in 1839, on east side of Nineteenth Street near Spruce; the seventy-fifth anniversary was celebrated in 1916, was attended by many notable dignitaries of the church. Windows by d'Ascenzo. ST. FRANCIS DE SALES, Forty-seventh Street and Springfield Avenue, Romanesque, with Byzantine details; built, 1907–10; architect, Henry D. Dagit, Philadelphia; the leaded glass is particularly beautiful; windows are of the antique school and extremely rich in color, including four rose windows, designed and made by Nicolo d'Ascenzo, Philadelphia. Four old historic churches rather near together, ST. JOSEPH'S, on Willing's Alley, south of Walnut, below Fourth Street; built on site of first Roman Catholic Church in Pennsylvania, established by a member of the "Society of Jesus" from Maryland, in 1731; ST. MARY'S, Fourth Street, above Spruce; ST. AUGUSTINE'S, Fourth Street, above Race; and HOLY TRINITY, northwest corner of Sixth and Spruce Streets, had their origin in the eighteenth century, the first two long before the Revolution. St. Augustine's is on site of a building erected in 1801, by the hermits of the Order of St. Augustine; it had William Rush's wooden sculpture "The Crucifixion," but this was burned in 1847. Holy Trinity, German, is of somewhat earlier date; the wayfarer who now looks in on any of them may readily picture them as they were over one hundred years ago. In St. Mary's Church is a very fine pieta by Boucher, a modern French sculptor.

Swedenborgian, or The New Church, grew out of the teachings of Emmanuel Swedenborg, scholar, traveler, scientist, and religious writer, born in Stockholm, Sweden, in 1688. A school of the New Church was started in Philadelphia in 1854. FIRST "NEW

THE COMMONWEALTH

JERUSALEM" CHURCH, Twenty-second and Chestnut Streets, Gothic, brownstone, was built in 1884; architect, Theophilus P. Chandler. Connected with it is a free library and reading room.

Unitarian. FIRST CHURCH, Chestnut Street near Twenty-second, built, 1885; was organized, 1796, in a room of the University of Pennsylvania; in 1797 Dr. Joseph Priestly delivered an address to this Society, and enrolled himself among the members. William Henry Furness was ordained pastor in 1825, in the church at the corner of Tenth and Locust Streets; present church contains some interesting memorials, Dr. Furness, bust by M. Launt Thompson, New York; circular window to Dr. Priestly by John LaFarge; other windows are English; and some are by Tiffany, New York. GIRARD AVENUE UNITARIAN, Girard Avenue above Fifteenth Street, organized by the Rev. Charles G. Ames, in the late seventies; Gothic, granite. GERMANTOWN UNITARIAN, corner of Chelten Avenue and Greene Street, built, 1866; Gothic; architect, Frank Furness; has good stained glass windows, made by Heaton, Butler and Bayne, London. Rev. Samuel Longfellow, brother of the poet, was pastor for some years; also the Rev. Charles G. Ames.

FAIRMOUNT PARK

On east and west banks of the Schuylkill River, and Wissahickon Creek; second largest municipal park in the world, 3597 acres; its only superior in acreage being Blue Hills Park, Boston, with 4906 acres. The ravines, "unkempt and wild," all have springs of clear, cold water. Main entrance at Green Street is also approach to the proposed PHILADELPHIA MUSEUM OF ART, on a raised terrace, like a Greek Temple, facing the Parkway; Horace Trumbauer, C. C. Zantzinger, and Charles L. Borie, Jr., architects; part of the plan for development of Philadelphia within a radius of thirty miles: here also is the "Washington Monument," sculptor, Professor Siemering of Berlin, erected by the "Society of the Cincinnati." Continue drive, to the Schuylkill River, proposed Ericsson Memorial, Paul B. Cret, architect, was commissioned to prepare a design for development of the entire basin, from boat houses to Spring Garden Street, including the AQUARIUM, formed, 1911, using the classic marble buildings of the old waterworks; it is said to be the best equipped in the world; walls of exhibition tanks are covered with calcareous tufa, rock shell formation from the Ohio River Valley, full of holes, in which deep water vegetation is planted to suggest sea bottom; Arctic and tropical life have their own temperatures; also hatching rooms. This tract and Rocky Hill, of the old waterworks, five acres, between Green and Callowhill Streets, was named by William Penn, FAIR MOUNT; it was used as the terminal pillar of the British redoubts, stretching across the city from the Schuylkill to the Delaware, in 1777–78. Acquired by the city in 1812 as site for the city waterworks, moved from Centre Square, for park purposes. This was the beginning of Fairmount Park; to beautify the grounds, walks were laid out up to the reservoir, and the rock decorated with sculpture, chiefly woodcarving, by William Rush, including the groups, "The Schuylkill in an Improved State," and "The Schuylkill in Chains," which are still over the entrances

THE COMMONWEALTH 99

to the wheel houses; "Justice" and "Wisdom," full-length statues, carved for decoration of the triumphal arch in front of the State House at Lafayette's reception in 1824, are now in the hatching room; and "Leda and the Swan," modeled in 1812 from Miss Vanuxen, a Philadelphia belle, a bronze reproduction is here now. Boat houses are of decorative construction. THE SCHUYLKILL NAVY, said to be the most complete association devoted to rowing in the world, is the center for test trials of skill and endurance, of national interest; it is known as the American Henley; the course above Columbia Avenue bridge is ideal for oarsmen, and the banks rise like seats of an auditorium. On the main drive from the Aquarium are the LINCOLN MONUMENT, bronze, sculptor, Randolph Rogers, made in Rome, cast in Munich; Iron Spring, and a bronze group, "Lioness Carrying to Her Young a Wild Boar," sculptor, August Cain; near Brown Street entrance is bronze group, "Silenus and the Infant Bacchus"; original in the Louvre, credited to Praxiteles; and the bronze group, "The Wrestlers," from original antique in the Royal Gallery, Florence; both reproduced by Barbedienne, Paris.

LEMON HILL MANSION, built by Henry Pratt about 1800, near site of favorite home of Robert Morris. "The Hills," planned by Major L'Enfant, built, 1773; the property was bought by the city in 1844, and dedicated, in 1855, as a Public Park. Northwest on main drive is GRANT'S CABIN, headquarters of General U. S. Grant in siege of Richmond, 1864-65, brought to the Park from City Point, Virginia, at close of Civil War; opposite is SEDGELEY GUARD HOUSE, formerly the porter's lodge of the Sedgeley Park Estate, site of a Gothic mansion, built, 1800, by William Crammond; acquired for the Park by public-spirited citizens; on same drive, near east end of Girard Avenue bridge, is the replica bronze equestrian statue of "JEANNE D'ARC," sculptor, Fremiet, Paris; among the best examples of modern French equestrian sculpture. The original is in "La Place des Pyramids," Paris.

RIVER DRIVE near boat houses, "Tam O'Shanter," four figures, red sandstone, sculptor, Thom; from the last boat house, or the Beacon Light, to Girard Avenue bridge will be the ELLEN PHILLIPS SAMUEL MEMORIAL, for which she left $500,000 in 1913; Fairmount Park Art Association, legatee; "On top of stone bulkhead I will have erected, 100 feet apart, on high granite pedestals, uniform in size and style, the History of America, symbolized in a system of statuary"; model made by Edgar V. Seeler. Near are the heroic bronze bust of James A. Garfield, with allegorical figure, sculptor, Augustus Saint Gaudens; the colossal bronze equestrian group, "Lion Fighter," on natural jutting rock, sculptor, Professor Albert Wolff, cast, 1893; and scattered along, five bronzed iron fountains, replicas of those at Rond Point, Champs Elysees, cast in Paris at foundry of Val D'Osne.

North of tunnel, above Girard Avenue bridge, on River Drive, bronze equestrian statue, "Cowboy," sculptor, Frederick Remington; a band of cowboys and Indians participated in the unveiling; River and Fountain Green Drive, heroic bronze equestrian statue, "General U. S. Grant"; sculptors, Daniel Chester French for Grant, Edward C. Potter for horse, modeled

THE COMMONWEALTH 101

from the nineteen-year-old gelding, "General Grant," sired by an Arabian stallion (Leopold), presented to the General in 1878 by the Sultan of Turkey; cast by Bureau Bros., Philadelphia, mounted on Jonesboro granite pedestal, designed by Frank Miles Day and Brother. Columbia Avenue entrance, fountain of "Orestes and Pylades," bronze group, on Richmond granite pedestal, with bronze masks; sculptor, Carl Steinhaeuser, Calsruhe, Germany; cast in Philadelphia; near is the Children's Playground building, erected by Richard and Sarah Smith in 1898; and a park mansion, MT. PLEASANT, land bought from Phineas Bond by John MacPherson, who built the house in 1761, after style of a house in Scotland owned by the chief of his clan, the MacPhersons of Clunie; in 1779, purchased by Benedict Arnold; on his conviction for treason, it was confiscated by the state; in 1781-82 Baron von Steuben occupied it, and here wrote the army regulations which created the American Army; in 1868 it became property of the city, and was added to Fairmount Park.

ROCKLAND comes next, on west side of Dairy Ball Field, occupied 1750-65 by John Lawrence, a notable mayor of Philadelphia; near Rockland is ORMISTON, colonial, owned by Edward Burd, prothonotary, Supreme Court of Pennsylvania, named for Scotch home of Mrs. Burd, daughter of Lord Haliburton of Ormiston, who founded the Burd Orphan Asylum; near Dauphin Street entrance, Grand Fountain, bronze and iron, and park trolley station.

Northwest is WOODFORD mansion; ground deeded by Penn to Dennis Rockford in 1693; house built, 1742, by William Coleman, an original member of the Junto Club; friend of Franklin and Judge of the Supreme Court of Pennsylvania, colonial, brick; original oak floor is still in fine state of preservation; boards doweled together; laths are hand-cut, and handwork on cornices and wainscoting most beautiful; fireplace and mantel in main room are worthy of attention, although now marred by paint; later it became the home of the Franks family; EDGELEY ball field, site of residence built by Philip Syng Physick, 1828–36, Professor of Surgery at University of Pennsylvania and first American to be elected member of the Royal Academy of France; the RANDOLPH MANSION is west of Edgeley; interesting colonial house with beautiful handwork in cornices.

STRAWBERRY MANSION, near Dauphin Street entrance; residence of William Lewis; then called Summerville, now used as a restaurant; name was given when added to the park; fine colonial architecture; main hall shows still how beautiful it must have been, with exquisite handwork on cornices, wainscoting, and niches in the hall ornamented with hand tracery.

Along the river drive we pass other country seats known as Harleigh, Fairy Hill, and the Laurels, now South, Central, and North Laurel Hill. Near the Falls on east side of Ridge Road, stood the home of Governor Thomas Mifflin, the fighting Quaker; from the Falls bridge a fine view is obtained of the Schuylkill Navy's race course.

Farther up is the WISSAHICKON Creek, Wisamickan (Catfish Creek), or Wisaucksickan (yellow colored stream); we enter the deep recesses of this ravine, where the waters empty into the Schuylkill River; tradition says that on the northwest bank stood a flour mill; in Revolutionary times the owner ground glass or plaster, with the wheat, for the patriot army, for this crime some of Washington's soldiers hanged him on a tree in front of his mill; here General Armstrong's corps attacked the Hessian and British soldiers, October 4, 1777, while the Battle of Germantown was in progress: up the Wissahickon drive is Maple Spring Hotel, decorated by grotesque figures of animals and birds, carved out of native laurel; beyond this, across the stream, are abrupt bluffs, from one, the most prominent, called Lover's Leap, tradition says, a young Indian and the girl whom he loved, being forbidden to marry, plunged into the waters below and were drowned; a steep grade leads to the six-mile stone; here Paper Mill Run empties into the Wissahickon, and here Nicholas Rittenhouse had his grist mill; just beyond, close beside an old bridge, is a quaint old house, inside is a stone tablet marked "C. W. R. 1707," here DAVID RITTENHOUSE, the famous astronomer, was born; on Paper Mill Run, the first paper mill in this country was erected, about 1690, by William Rittenhouse: a portion of this land near Tulpehocken Street, within park limits, once belonged to the Queen of Spain; farther is the Blue Stone Bridge, and just beyond is Lotus Inn.

Northward, the east shore becomes more steep, to Mom Rinker's Rock, she is said to have been a witch; upon the height stands a statue of WILLIAM PENN, with the single word "Toleration" cut on the pedestal; the statue and land were given to the city, for park purposes, by Hon. John Welsh, ex-minister to England.

One quarter mile farther is Kitchen Lane, and the HERMIT'S WELL, dug by Johannes Kelpius, scholar and mystic, who came from Germany with his followers, forty men, the number of perfection, in 1694, "to the new world, to see the dawn of the millennium; the pathway to the Light Illumitable, in the glory of religious liberty in Pennsylvania"; they were followers of the Essenes who lived in the solitudes of the Dead Sea, of which St. John the Baptist is said to have been a member; the Ridge and Valley of the Wissahickon gave them a temple of sacred grandeur; places there are now known as Hermit's Land, and Hermit's Glen; the piety and humility of Kelpius made him renowned; John Rogers of Connecticut and leaders of other colonies came long distances to consult this great Magister, he lived wholly to the service of God and his fellow men; the Baptistry, a place in the creek, is shown where the monks immersed their converts; after Kelpius' death, about 1710, his followers built the monastery, replaced in 1752 by a stone house, built by Joseph Gorgas, also called the monastery; ruins still there: the bones of these faithful men are interred under the floor, in the chancel of St. Michael's Protestant Episcopal Church, High Street, Germantown; also some of their original headstones are there: their books were given, in 1728, to Christ Church, Philadelphia, where they may still be seen: the cult is now found about Ephrata, among the Seventh Day Baptists.

Beyond the monastery, near Livezey's Lane, are caves, said to have been the abode of hermits. Half a mile farther is Livezey's mansion, built, 1698, said to have been neutral ground where British and American officers met during 1777–78; now headquarters of the Valley Green Canoe Club; above is Cresheim Creek, a small tributary flowing into the Wissahickon Creek, among great masses of huge rocks, under tall pines, making a dark pool, called the Devil's Pool; said to be bottomless; scene of an engagement during the Battle of Germantown. Just beyond is Valley Green, a quaint old wayside inn; here is a stone bridge with strong buttresses and single arch; the reflection makes a clear oval; farther is the first drinking fountain erected in Philadelphia, "Pro Bono Publico," placed in 1854; white marble; half a mile beyond, at east end of Rex Avenue Bridge, is Indian Rock, summit crowned by heroic statue of Tedyuscung, last of Indian chiefs to leave the shores of the Delaware. Northwest the ravine is deep and the hills steep, winding toward Chestnut Hill. It is proposed by the city to extend Fairmount Park, on both sides of the Wissahickon, to Fort Washington, and include Militia Hill at Whitemarsh, famous in the Revolution, making the Park one thousand acres larger.

WEST PARK, west end of Girard Avenue Bridge, ZOÖLOGICAL GARDENS, open daily, including Sundays; in front, bronze group, "The Dying Lioness"; sculptor, Professor Wilhelm Wolff, Berlin, cast in Munich. The inclosure embraces SOLITUDE, a mansion built in 1785 by John Penn, the poet, grandson of the founder and cousin of John Penn of Lansdowne; was last property owned in America by the Penn family; notable decorations are in the ground floor room; ceiling, fine example of French stucco, Louis XV period. The Zoölogical Gardens were incorporated in 1859; oldest incorporated body of its kind in America; on an area of forty-one acres arranged by H. Schwarzmann in 1873. opened, 1874, with large and attractive buildings, in which representative species of living animals are shown; it is a private organization; the Pathological Laboratory has for its objects, assistance in the hygienic control of the Garden; collection of statistics upon diseases of wild animals; and research: many species of water, and other birds, are on the large lake, and inclosures scattered through the Garden.

Opposite, on Girard Avenue, is WILLIAM PENN'S HOUSE, originally in Letitia Street, near Second and Market; first brick house in Philadelphia, built, 1683, removed in 1883; LANSDOWNE ENTRANCE to the Park, under two spacious elliptical arches of the Pennsylvania Railroad viaduct, carrying the railroad across Girard Avenue, is a dignified and handsome structure. Near is bronze group, "Hudson Bay Wolves," sculptor, Edward Kemeys, cast in Philadelphia.

In 1732, "The State in Schuylkill," a fishing club, first social club in Philadelphia, leased an acre of land near here, and built a hut; annual rental, three sun perch, presented on a pewter plate; they were here for ninety years; now in New Jersey; the members espoused the Revolutionary cause, and in 1774 formed a Company, called "The Light Horse," afterwards, in 1778, became the First City Troop.

On Lansdowne Drive is SWEET BRIER MANSION, built by Samuel Breck about 1810; colonial, in the hall is an interesting wrought iron grill; in front is bronze Indian group, THE STONE AGE, sculptor, John J. Boyle; cast in France. THE SMITH MEMORIAL

GATE, to Pennsylvania men distinguished in the Civil War, is at entrance to the Esplanade; architects, James and John T. Windrim, erected, with statuary, 1897-1912; sculpture all colossal; equestrian, Major General Hancock, sculptor, J. Q. A. Ward; and Major General McClellan, sculptor, Edward C. Potter; statues, Major General Meade, sculptor, Daniel Chester French; Major General Reynolds, sculptor, Charles Grafly; Richard Smith, sculptor, Herbert Adams; busts, Admiral Porter, sculptor, Charles Grafly; Major General Hartranft, sculptor, A. Stirling Calder; Admiral Dahlgren, sculptor, George E. Bissel; James H. Windrim, sculptor, Samuel Murray; Major General S. W. Crawford, sculptor, Bessie O. Potter Vonnoh; Governor Curtin, sculptor, Moses Ezekiel; General James A. Beaver, sculptor, Katharine M. Cohen; John B. Gest, sculptor, Charles Grafly; two eagles and globes, sculptor, J. Massey Rhind.

The JOHN WELSH MEMORIAL, President of the CENTENNIAL EXPOSITION, formal Garden, with fountain, on site of Centennial main building, Parkside Avenue approach to Memorial Hall; "Florentine Lions," cast by Harrison, Winans and Eastwick at Alexandroffsky, Russia, in 1849, from pair at entrance of Imperial Mechanical Works, originals at entrance to Loggia di Lanzi, Florence; MEMORIAL HALL, front terrace, bronze, Spanish cannon, Miltiades, date, 1743; bronze, Spanish cannon, Semiramis, date, 1737; bronze, Spanish mortar, date, 1731, from fortifications in Cuba; carved decorations with Spanish royal arms of Philip and Elizabeth Farnese; two bronze groups: "Winged Horses," led by muses of epic and lyric poetry, Calliope and Clio; sculptor, Pilz, made for Vienna Opera House, Austria; Memorial Hall, German Renaissance; architect, Hermann J. Schwarzmann; contains complete model of the arrangement of the Centennial buildings, made to scale by John Baird; first International Exposition held in America; when our national art was invigorated by competition with masterpieces of other lands, and now challenges comparison with the best: also Pompeian collection of paintings, illustrative of Pompeian life; and bronze face and hands of Abraham Lincoln; casts taken from first replicas, of original casts from life, in 1860; sculptor, Leonard W. Volk, Chicago; for collections, see Art. North of Memorial Hall is heroic bronze equestrian statue, MAJOR GENERAL GEORGE GORDON MEADE, sculptor, Alexander Milne Calder.

HORTICULTURAL HALL, erected 1876, on site of LANSDOWNE MANSION, built by Governor John Penn in 1773; stone; Italian; in 1816, leased by Joseph Bonaparte for two years, accidentally destroyed by fire in 1854. In 1866, the land was acquired from Barney family for the park; Moorish style, architect, Hermann J. Schwarzmann, also responsible for plan of adjacent sunken garden: no other building for similar purposes in this country can approach it, in dignity of design: contains marble statue "Il Penseroso," sculptor, Mosier, acquired, 1874. Notable plants housed in this building are a gigantic specimen of *Attalea Cohiene*, bay oil palm, from Central America, possibly most superb palm to be seen under glass anywhere; *Phœnix Canariensis* from the Canary Islands; *Seaforthias* from Australia; *Howeas* from Lord Howe's Island; Cocoa palms; *Ceroxylon*, wax palms, towering sixty or seventy feet; giant Rubber trees; *Araucarias* from Australia; Bamboos from the Orient; and lofty Tree Ferns from New Zealand unite to produce a wonderfully impressive scene, not unlike a glorified tropical forest, emphasized by training creepers up the lofty stems, growing ferns and orchids in crotches of the limbs, and by the strange aerial roots which reach down from these clinging plants to seek nourishment in the soil below, as in the tropical jungle. The Cactus house is arranged to give something the effect of arid regions, by planting in sterile soil; the Fern houses, with superb collections of Tree Ferns, and smaller growing *Adiantums*, *Nephrolepis*, *Acrostichums*, recall the effect of mountain ravines. A special house is given to the Cycads or Sago palms, survivals of vegetation of fossil beds, of which this collection is unique in this country. Another tropical house contains the *Bromeliad* or pineapple family, collection unique in many respects.

In the gardens, most striking features are the rare trees, golden larch, Pseudo-Larix; the Gordonias, *Franklinias;* oaks. East front has bronze busts of SCHUBERT, granite pedestal with bronze bas-relief; "Music," sculptor, Henry Baerer, New York; HAYDEN, a trophy won by United Singers of Philadelphia at the National Saengerfest; VERDI, on artistic sandstone pedestal, with carved figure; "Religious Liberty," marble, sculptor, Moses Ezekiel; presented by the Hebrew Society B'nai B'rith. A short walk east, near Columbia Avenue bridge, is said to be Tom Moore's cottage; the poet was a frequent guest both at Belmont and Ormiston, with communication by boat.

THE SUNKEN GARDEN, west, rearranged to conform to Moorish ideals of garden approaches, is now a pool, about eight hundred feet long, similar to that before the Taj Mahal, flanked on both sides by spreading Oriental planes; beyond this central feature are flower gardens, following the Oriental in color arrangement, making an effect of noble proportions. A bronze SUNDIAL shows the variations for each month of the year, and the time at twelve o'clock in twelve principal cities of the world; on Tennessee marble pedestal, with four supporting female figures, emblematic of the four seasons; sculptor, A. Sterling Calder. Bronze statues of Schiller, made in 1886, granite pedestal with bronze panels in bas-relief representing poetry, history, drama; and of his friend Goethe, made in 1890, granite pedestal decorated with bronze laurel wreaths.

Roman Catholic CENTENNIAL FOUNTAIN, erected by the Total Abstinence Societies, sculptor, Herman Kern. JAPANESE TEMPLE GATE and lotus pond, near Belmont Avenue, part of Japanese exhibit in St. Louis, in 1904, showing best Japanese work of three hundred years ago; also on way to George's Hill are, the Ohio, English, and Rhode Island Centennial buildings. GEORGE'S HILL, eighty-three acres, acquired by bequest to the City of Philadelphia, in 1868, through the Fairmount Park Commission, for the health and enjoyment of the people forever.

BELMONT MANSION, built, 1743, by William Peters, stone, on estate of two hundred acres, approached by avenue of tall hemlocks, ninety feet high. Washington and Lafayette both planted trees here; view down the Schuylkill is like the Rhine; City Hall Tower focuses the eyes in the distance; Richard Peters, his son, wit and scholar, born here, was made Judge of the United States District Court of Pennsylvania by Washington; who was entertained here; also Hancock, the Adamses, Jefferson, Steuben, Talleyrand, and Louis Philippe.

North of Belmont is RIDGELAND, once private residence; continue northeast near Park Trolley Station, CHAMOUNIX mansion, formerly known as Mount Prospect for its fine situation; built, 1802, by George Plumstead, a Philadelphia merchant.

OTHER SQUARES AND PARKS

William Penn, in his city plan, laid out five squares. PENN SQUARE, Broad and Market Streets, site of early waterworks; now occupied by City Hall; WASHINGTON, Sixth and Walnut Streets; first Potter's Field; RITTENHOUSE, Eighteenth and Walnut Streets, remodeled like a French park; playground for children of city's social center; LION AND SERPENT, bronze; sculptor, Barye; replica of one in the Garden of the Tuilleries, Paris; THE DUCK GIRL, bronze; sculptor, Paul Manship; BILLY, sculptor, Albert Laessle. LOGAN, on the Parkway; SWAN MEMORIAL FOUNTAIN to be in center, sculptor, A. Sterling Calder. This was the second Potter's Field, and place of public executions; site of Sanitary Fair, in 1864, for the Civil War, visited by President and Mrs. Lincoln, pronounced most brilliant affair ever held in America. FRANKLIN, Sixth and Race Streets, formerly a burial ground.

Broad Street, running north and south, is 113 feet wide and 12 miles long from League Island to City Line. BURHOLME, near Fox Chase, museum and library given and maintained by provision in will of Robert W. Ryerss; over forty-eight acres; opened to public in 1910. CLARK'S, Forty-third Street and Chester Avenue, has artistic bronze group, DICKENS AND LITTLE NELL, made in 1890; sculptor, Frank Edwin Elwell; awarded gold medals, Philadelphia, 1891; Chicago, 1893. COBB'S CREEK, 338 acres, formed, 1904; follows Cobb's Creek on east bank; chiefly steep, tree-covered slopes for 107 acres; crossing at Mount Moriah Cemetery; widens, north of Market Street, into rolling landscape; has public golf links. FERNHILL, ten acres, bounded by Wissahickon Avenue, Roberts Avenue, Schuyler Street, and Abbottsford Avenue, Germantown; memorial to Mr. and Mrs. Thomas McKean, part of their old homestead, given by their children to Park Commissioners with endowment. FISHER, twenty acres; near North Penn branch, Reading Railway; acquired by gift, 1909. HUNTING PARK, with lake, eighty-seven acres; crossing Northeast Boulevard at Nicetown Lane. LEAGUE ISLAND and United States Navy Yard; part of Southern Boulevard. MORRIS, twenty acres; extension of Cobb's Creek Park; beautiful forest, watered by Indian Run Creek, acquired by gift, 1912. PENNYPACK, near mouth of Pennypack Creek to Rhawn Street, 532 acres, acquired in 1905; beautiful fertile valley with stream, widened in places, with half ruined mill dams and their waterfalls; quaint masonry bridges, either in single arch or series of spans. REYNOLDS, Snyder Avenue and Seventeenth Street, contains memorial to General John F. Reynolds, a hero of Gettysburg; granite shaft, six feet high, with bronze medallion of General Reynolds; sculptor, H. K. Bush-

THE DUCK GIRL
From the Fountain in Rittenhouse Square
Paul Manship, Sculptor

Brown; unveiled, 1915. WISTER'S WOODS, contains fine trees and profusion of dogwood; forty-four acres; East Germantown; bird sanctuary.

Total amount of space devoted to park, square, and boulevard purposes within city limits is 8,037.32 acres.

THE FAIRMOUNT PARK ART ASSOCIATION organized 1871, to express high civic ideals, in forms of beauty and dignity, synonymous with art, have had large mounted photographs of the sculpture in Fairmount Park placed in Philadelphia public schools.

HISTORIC INSTITUTIONS OF PHILADELPHIA

ACADEMY OF NATURAL SCIENCES, on the Parkway at Logan Circle, was founded, 1812, in the house of Thomas Say, Esq., northwest corner of Second and Market Streets. The Museum, for its historic value and extent of its collection, is one of the most important in existence; arranged in two series, an exhibition for the public, and reference for specialists. Library contains about 60,000 volumes, nearly all on natural sciences; several important publications are issued by the Academy, and numerous lectures on natural history are given annually. Contains portraits of founders, Thomas Say, Gerard Troost, William Maclure, Charles Lesueur, Sir Joseph Banks, Samuel L. Mitchell. All painted by Charles Willson Peale, and hung in Peale's Museum; others by noted artists are Robert Bridges, Isaac Lea, Joseph Leidy, by Bernard Uhle; Jacob Gilliams by P. F. Rothermel; William Hempbell and George Ord by John Neagle; Samuel G. Morton by Paul Weber; W. S. W. Ruschenberger by William K. Hewitt; Isaac Wistar by Robert Vonnoh; also a fine study model of Alexander Wilson, the ornithologist, by Charles Grafly, and statuette of same by Alexander Calder.

AMERICAN PHILOSOPHICAL SOCIETY, 103 South Fifth Street, on lot in State House yard, given the Society by the state in 1785; colonial, brick; built, 1789: originated in "The Junto" formed by Benjamin Franklin, 1727, with the object of mutual improvement; received its name 1769, "The American Philosophical Society in Philadelphia, for Promoting Useful Knowledge." Benjamin Franklin, then in Europe, sole American plenipotentiary to France from the thirteen provinces, was elected first president, and continued until his death in 1790. David Rittenhouse, second president, served until his death in 1796; he, with other members, successfully observed the Transit of Venus, June 3, 1769, giving the first approximately accurate results to the world, in the measurements of the spheres; he also constructed an orrery for measuring heavenly bodies. Thomas Jefferson, third president, served eighteen years, while he was also Vice-President and President of the United States, and established its library and cabinet. Present President, Dr. W. W. Keen. Its membership is world wide. At the meetings, held regularly, the most advanced thought in scientific investigation is presented. The Society now owns most of the Franklin papers in existence, recently calendared in five volumes by Dr. I. Minis Hays; field notes of Lewis and Clark expedition; original copy of Penn's Charter of Privileges, dated 1701; manuscript volume, Laws of Pennsylvania prior to 1700, and original broadside, Declaration of Independence. Oil por-

THE COMMONWEALTH 115

traits of all its Presidents are here and of many leading members; notably, George Washington, by Gilbert Stuart; President Jefferson, Benjamin Rush, John Vaughn, Caspar Wistar, P. S. DuPonceau, all by Thomas Sully; David Rittenhouse and Samuel Vaughn by C. W. Peale; Joseph Priestly and Chief Justice William Tilghman by Rembrandt Peale; Daniel G. Brinton by Thomas Aikens; Professor Alexander Dallas Bache by Huntington; General Isaac Wistar and Joseph Henry by Bernard Uhle; several notable busts of Jefferson, Turgot, and Condorcet by Houdon; Benjamin Franklin by Caffieri; and of Lafayette, Alexander Hamilton, and Nicholas Biddle.

THE FRANKLIN INSTITUTE, Seventh Street above Chestnut; organized, 1824; open free daily; classic, marble, built, 1825; John Haviland, architect. First organization in the United States to combine science with practice; the lecture course presents, free to the public, latest advances in useful arts and sciences, by distinguished technologists; also popular illustrated addresses on topics of the day; school of Mechanic Arts includes instruction in mechanical and architectural drawing, said to be one of the most thorough and practical in the United States. Library is second to none, in extent and completeness, as reference for scientific literature; *The Franklin Journal*, published since 1825, monthly, is the only record extant of a number of early United States patents. They held first exhibition in America of American manufactures, 1824, in Carpenters' Hall, and first electrical exhibition in America. Portraits include Dr. Benjamin Franklin and Matthias W. Baldwin by Sully, Daguerre by Abraham Whiteside, and bust of Henry Clay by William Rush, carved wood. Among relics are typesetting and electrical machines, used by Benjamin Franklin, and early models of machinery. Will be moved to Parkway, Race Street, east of Nineteenth Street.

☛ THE HISTORICAL SOCIETY of Pennsylvania, 1300 Locust Street, in mansion of General Robert Patterson, enlarged and made fireproof; founded, 1824. Open 10.00 A. M. to 6.00 P. M.; July and August, closes at 4.00 P. M.; publishes the *Pennsylvania Magazine of History and Biography*; contains probably the largest collection of sources of American history assembled in any one place; includes over 100,000 bound books, 250,000 pamphlets, 7000 volumes of manuscripts and some 3500 volumes of newspapers, which are invaluable to the student of colonial and Revolutionary history; an INDEX TO THE MARRIAGES AND DEATHS, in Dunlap, Claypoole and Poulson's AMERICAN DAILY ADVERTISER, creates a constant demand for the files of that newspaper for genealogical purposes; Tom Paine's AMERICAN CRISIS, 1776, and many other rare imprints of Americans. The Society has a large and exceedingly rich collection of oil paintings; practically all the governors of the state are represented in portraiture on its walls, some of the mayors of Philadelphia, and portraits of many Revolutionary officers; a portrait of Johannes Kelpius, the "Hermit of the Wissahickon," by Christopher Wick, in 1704, is believed to be the earliest portrait in oil painted in America; portraits of Gustavus Hesselius, his wife, and of Robert Morris, Sr., father of the financier, painted by Gustavus Hesselius, are of historic interest; a fine collection of original

GEORGE WASHINGTON
From the collection in Independence Hall
Painted by Rembrandt Peale

portraits, drawings, studies, and manuscripts by Benjamin West, includes the full length portrait of William Hamilton of the Woodlands, and his niece, Mrs. Ann Hamilton Lyle, probably the most beautiful of West's portraits in this city; other artists represented are Charles Willson Peale, Jacob Eicholtz, Thomas Sully, Rembrandt Peale, John Neagle, Charles Gilbert Stuart, Robert Edge Pine, John Singleton Copley, Walter G. Gould, Henry Inman, Paul Weber, and William E. Winner. Among the miniatures are those by John Trumbull, James Peale, and Robert Fulton. Marble busts are of Washington, Franklin, Milton, Henry Clay, Major General Robert Patterson, T. Buchanan Read, and Dr. Joseph Parrish. Relics of great historic interest include the Ephrata Printing Press, the Charter of the City of Philadelphia, and the "Great Belt of Wampum," representing the famous Shackamaxon Treaty between William Penn and the Indians, " never signed and never broken."

MASONIC TEMPLE, Broad and Filbert Streets; Norman architecture; built, 1870; John T. Windrim, architect. Rooms with notable decorations are the Egyptian; Oriental, Moorish style from sketches made in the Alhambra by John Sartain; and Corinthian, copied from well-known standards of architecture, ornament and familiar figure composition. Museum said to be the greatest existing Masonic museum, contains aprons of Past Grand Masters of the three oldest Lodges in the world; and George Washington's apron, made by Madame Lafayette and presented to him by the Marquis, worn by Washington at laying of the corner-stone of the Capitol at Washington; an ancient

Templar Cross, original Crusader's Cross, found in a grave at Tyre, Syria, A.D. 1250; notable jewelers' art of England, Denmark, Germany, France, and Great Britain, in badges, including one owned by Napoleon I; tablet from Temple of Herod; Sephar Torah, ancient scroll of the law found in Germany, over eighteen feet long, and from three hundred to five hundred years old. Library, Byzantine decorations, with coats of arms, of various Guilds and Grand Lodges, in the ceiling. The Great Hall, or front entrance, contains portraits and paintings, among them "The Puritans" by F. J. Waugh and "A Marine Scene" by Richards; Seals of the States of the Union, and paintings portraying the Pan Athenia, Greek festival. On the second floor are the Grand Lodge Room, representing a Corinthian temple, constructed to appear roofless; the columns, reproductions of the Lysicrates, Athens; mural paintings represent the mythology of the Greeks, "Weighing of the Soul," "Ulysses Passing the Island of the Sirens," "Birth of Athena," "Judgment of Paris," "The Golden Fleece." Renaissance Hall, the Tabernacle, contains the Veils of the Temple. Two paintings at either end represent a High Priest, and a Scribe. Ionic Hall and Norman Hall have characteristic ornamentation; Egyptian Hall, decorations are copied from Temples of Karnak, Elephanta, Philae, Rameses, the Cataracts and Tombs; Ceiling from Temple of Denderah; also the scene "Weighing the Soul," showing Egyptian mythology allied with Greek.

MINT OF UNITED STATES AT PHILADELPHIA, Sixteenth and Spring Garden Streets, open daily, except Sundays and holidays, 9.00 A. M., to 3.00 P. M. Classic Ionic, granite, built, 1901, by the Supervising Architect of Washington, D. C. Main lobby finished in Italian marble with mosaic ceiling; panels illustrate ancient methods and processes of coinage; artist, W. B. Van Ingen. Largest and most completely equipped Mint in the world. Numismatic room, accessible to the public, contains large collection of coins and medals; among them the widow's mite, found in ruins of Temple in Jerusalem.

PENNSYLVANIA BIBLE SOCIETY, 701 Walnut Street, organized in Philadelphia, 1808. First Bible Society on American continent; present building erected, 1853. First President, Right Rev. William White, D.D.; first meeting, called by Robert Ralston in his own home; object, to further our country's welfare through the Bible, the Book teaching love, unity, and forbearance; therefore qualified to band the people together and advance national betterment. The establishment of such an organization in our land was recognized by gift of £200 by the British and Foreign Bible Society, London. All denominations have been represented in the line of Presidents; during Bishop Whitaker's incumbency the Pennsylvania Bible Society was connected with the American Bible Society in New York, now the national organization. General Lafayette in 1824 was presented by this Society with a specially prepared copy of the Scriptures. At the centennial of this Society, in 1908, celebrated in the Academy of Music, Bishop Ozi W. Whitaker, D.D., presided; Right Hon. James Bryce, British Ambassador, made an address and presented to Bishop Whitaker a beautifully embossed Bible, sent by the British and

Foreign Bible Society, emblems on the cover were from early Christian examples, similar to those on the Coronation Bible given to King Edward VII; Ambassador Bryce was in turn presented with a richly made copy of the Scriptures, by the Pennsylvania Society; greetings were received from President Theodore Roosevelt and Governor Edwin S. Stuart of Pennsylvania, and from other Bible societies. At the Tercentenary celebration of King James version of the Englisg Bible, in the Academy of Music, 1911, James A. MacDonald, LL.D., of Toronto, spoke of "The Influence of the Bible Upon the Commonwealth." Letters were read from King George V of England, and President William H. Taft. This Society now circulates between two and three hundred thousand Bibles per annum, printed in over fifty languages and dialects, for Pennsylvania, New Jersey, and Delaware, over which this house has especial jurisdiction. Any separate book of the Bible may be obtained for two cents.

PHILADELPHIA COMMERCIAL MUSEUM, Thirty-fourth Street below Spruce, organized, 1894, is the only Commercial Museum in the United States; it received immense collections from the Chicago "Columbian Exposition," over forty governments being represented; many subsequent collections from other international expositions; and special exhibits, illustrating the people and products of the world. A free reference library is here, of Foreign and American Commerce and Travel, which could not be duplicated, and courses of free lectures are given which cover subjects of geographic, commercial, and industrial importance, illustrated by colored lantern slides and motion pictures; colored slides, with lantern screen and typewritten lectures, covering same field of geography, commerce, and industry, are loaned, free of cost, to public-school teachers, in all parts of Pennsylvania; they reach tens of thousands; also collections of specimens, to aid teachers, are sent free of cost, as a gift to Pennsylvania public schools; they are arranged, showing important raw material, and process of manufacture. Manufacturers are furnished with information on all matters pertaining to foreign trade; the Foreign Trade Bureau is the acknowledged leader of such organizations in the world.

THE PENNSYLVANIA HORTICULTURAL SOCIETY, 1600 Walnut Street; first in America, organized at meeting in Franklin Institute, 1827, to promote horticulture and create love for flowers, fruits, and vegetables by their cultivation. Minutes of the Society and list of membership is complete from formation to present time. Lectures by an expert in the various branches of horticulture are given at each monthly meeting, from November until May. Annual exhibitions are, Spring Flower Show before Easter, three days; Peony, outdoor grown Rose and Sweet Pea Show in Philadelphia suburbs, from May to July, according to season; Dahlia Exhibition, in September; Chrysanthemum, early November. The Society has a library of several thousand books on agriculture and horticulture, some very rare and of great value, and all recommended works, of recent publication, in Europe and America. "Great gardens educate people in gentility as well as in horticulture."

WAGNER INSTITUTE, southwest corner of Seventeenth

Street and Montgomery Avenue; founded by Professor William Wagner, 1847. Circulating and reference library open daily except Sunday, 9.00 A. M. to 9.00 P. M. Museum collections, chiefly in reference to geology and mineralogy, open Wednesday and Saturday afternoons. Courses of lectures conducted through the collegiate year.

LIBRARIES

THE LIBRARY COMPANY OF PHILADELPHIA, Locust Street, east of Broad; first circulating library in the United States; founded by subscription in 1731, by Benjamin Franklin and his friends of the Junto Club; charter granted by John, Thomas, and Richard Penn in 1781; original building, Fifth and Library Streets, designed by Dr. Thornton, now the Drexel Building; present building, architect, Frank Furness in 1889; is a haven for scholars interested in historical research; also has important collections of books on costume, foreign literature, and complete set of Punch, begun in 1840; among historic relics are original sketches made for Watson's Annals of Philadelphia; William Penn's desk from Pennsburg; John Dickinson's reading desk, and Heraldic Hatchment, used at his funeral; and the André collection. THE RIDGEWAY BRANCH, Broad and Christian Streets, founded by bequest of Dr. James Rush; architect, Addison Hutton; built, 1878, Doric, granite; contains terra cotta bust of Minerva, heroic size, probably French work; formerly behind the Speaker's chair in the Continental Congress, Sixth and Chestnut Streets, given to the Philadelphia Library, 1783, also some articles of Boule, and illuminated manuscripts.

MERCANTILE LIBRARY, Tenth Street above Chestnut; was established 1821, at 100 Chestnut Street, present building, originally a market house, with room seventy-four by two hundred feet, and high-arched ceiling, makes ideal condition for library work on one floor; this is a circulating library of general literature for stockholders and members, who only are admitted into the reading room, where they have unrestricted use of books.

PHILADELPHIA CITY INSTITUTE, 218 South Nineteenth Street, was founded, 1852, by public-spirited citizens, for the purpose of benefiting young men, by establishing a free library and night school; library free to the public.

THE FREE LIBRARY OF PHILADELPHIA, northeast corner of Thirteenth and Locust Streets, chartered, 1891, from endowment fund, left in will by William Pepper, M.D., LL.D., for a free library in the city of Philadelphia: opened temporarily in City Hall; removed to old Concert Hall, 1217–21 Chestnut Street, now in old building of College of Physicians; contains bust of Dr. Pepper, by Carl Bitter, and portraits; a large new library building is in process of construction on the Parkway, Nineteenth and Vine Streets. Growth and usefulness, from its inception, are due to the management of the late Dr. John Thomson, Librarian; now includes a main building, 26 branches, as well as deposit stations and traveling libraries; total circulation for home use in 1916, 2,767,310. Hearty coöperation exists between the public schools and the Free Library; school extension lectures are given to the children of the grammar grades; and "story hours" are weekly events for younger children in the branch libraries. Reference and periodical departments contain works on art, architecture, and archæology, extremely valuable to the practical student and designer; here are facsimiles of many most noted, of early printed books and manuscripts, Bible codices, etc.; the "open shelf" system is used in all departments. Fine buildings of the branch libraries have been developed in their architectural proportions and decoration, on the traditions of French and English Renaissance, or local expression of the Georgian; always with top lighting, considered extremely important: in the basement of the branch at Seventeenth and Spring Garden Streets is a large and valuable collection of government documents; the Josephine Widener Memorial Branch, Broad Street and Girard Avenue, has reference books of priceless nature and rare prints, issued before A.D. 1500.

HISTORIC MEDICAL COLLEGES, HOSPITALS, AND DISPENSARIES

CHRIST CHURCH HOSPITAL, Wynnefield Station, Park Trolley and P. R. R.; Gothic stone building; organized, 1772, by Dr. John Kearsley; endowed by Jacob Dobson in 1804; is a home for gentlewomen, communicants of the Protestant Episcopal Church, in the Diocese of Pennsylvania; 150 acres; the Board of Managers include three of the vestry, each, of Christ Church and St. Peter's Church.

COLLEGE OF PHYSICIANS OF PHILADELPHIA, Twenty-second Street, above Chestnut; founded about 1787, and modeled on lines of The Royal College of Physicians in London. A scientific paper was read by Dr. Benjamin Rush at the first meeting. English Renaissance, brick, laid Flemish bond, with basement, cornices, pilasters, and other trimmings of Indiana limestone; finest building of a medical society in the world, with the largest medical library, save one, in the United States, and a fine collection of portraits of presidents of the Society, painted by most notable artists. This is not a teaching institution, but a Medical Society, composed of men of professional distinction.

HAHNEMANN MEDICAL COLLEGE AND HOSPITAL, 226 North Broad Street. Oldest homeopathic college in the world; founded in 1848; first located at 229 Arch Street. Consolidated with the Homeopathic Medical College in 1869; moved to present site in 1901. Its collections include the world-famous dissection of entire cerebro-spinal nervous system by Dr. Rufus B. Weaver; Dr. Hering's complete writings of Paracelsus; Dr. A. R. Thomas's library of old and rare anatomical books; Hahnemann's works in the original; it has the most complete library of homeopathic literature in existence. Portrait of Dr. W. B. VanLennep; artist, Henry Rittenberg.

HOME OF THE MERCIFUL SAVIOUR, 4400 Baltimore Avenue, on grounds adjoining the Clarence Clark Park; incorporated, 1882; eight houses and chapel, all memorials, with a summer home at Avon-by-the-Sea. A home for crippled, homeless, and helpless children. First of its kind in America where vocational training is taught.

HOSPITAL OF THE PROTESTANT EPISCOPAL CHURCH, Front Street and Lehigh Avenue. Main group of buildings, pure Norman. Founded by the Right Rev. Alonzo Potter, Bishop of Pennsylvania, and Dr. Caspar Morris, in the ancestral home of two parishioners on the present site. Jenny Lind made the first cash contribution.

JEFFERSON MEDICAL COLLEGE, Tenth and Sansom Streets; founded through the efforts of Dr. George B. McClellan; opened, 1825. Present building erected, 1904.

JEFFERSON HOSPITAL, Tenth and Sansom Streets; last word in hospital construction and equipment; originated in the Infirmary established in Jefferson College, 1825; present site was bought, 1875, and the building opened for use in 1877. Amphitheatre is one of the largest in the world. Museum contains casts and wax models of interesting cases. Notable portraits in the building are Dr. Forbes, by Aikens; Dr. DaCosta, by Vonnoh; Dr. Keen, by Chase; Mr. William Potter, by Breckenridge; Dr. William Pancoast, by Uhle; also bronze bust of Dr. Marion Sims, by C. Duboi, Paris, 1876; marble bust of Dr. George McClellan; bronze busts of Daniel Webster and Thomas Jefferson.

JEWISH HOSPITAL, Logan Station; Old York Road and Olney Avenue, entrance is marked with six granite columns from the old United States Mint, formerly on Chestnut Street. Includes twenty buildings, on twenty-two acres of ground, with modern scientific equipment for treatment of sick, care of aged and incurable. A number of art works said to be of considerable value are here.

MUNICIPAL HOSPITAL, Luzerne, near Front Street,

4000 north; on extensive grounds bisected by a well-wooded ravine. Established in 1774, on State Island, for the isolation and treatment of contagious diseases; probably most complete of its kind in the world.

PENNSYLVANIA HOSPITAL, between Spruce and Pine Streets, Eighth and Ninth Streets; colonial; brick; with great trees and beautiful open spaces in the grounds. First hospital in the United States, founded, 1751, by Dr. Thomas Bond and Benjamin Franklin. Corner-stone on present site, laid, 1755, can still be seen; part of this land belonged to William Penn, which he donated. In 1756, here was the first clinical amphitheatre in America. Noah Webster delivered a lecture for the benefit of the hospital in 1786; other benefits received about this time were, a charity sermon preached by Rev. George Whitefield in St. Paul's Protestant Episcopal Church; and a painting by Benjamin West, "Christ Healing the Sick," made while he was in London; the English refused to allow the original to come to America; they used it to start the National Gallery; so a replica was painted; it now hangs in the hall; for years the hospital made money by charging a fee to see it. At the Pine Street front is a leaden statue of William Penn, presented by his grandson, John Penn, from Wycombe Park, Bucks, England, estate of Lord le Dispenser. Benjamin Franklin was the first Secretary and the second President; his minute books are still to be seen there, with clear fine handwriting; and interesting letters and documents of colonial and Revolutionary times.

PHILADELPHIA ALMSHOUSE AND GENERAL HOSPITAL, Thirty-fourth and Pine Streets, Blockley; first almshouse was opened in 1713 by the Quakers; not municipal, open only to their sect; located on Walnut, between Third and Fourth Streets. First city almshouse was established in 1732; second in 1767; in 1772 it was the most extensive hospital on the continent. During the Revolutionary War, wounded were cared for here. In Longfellow's poem, Evangeline becomes a Sister of Mercy and ministers here to the yellow fever sufferers in Philadelphia. Present institution built, 1834; architecture of administration building, Corinthian, marble. The Medical Department antedates the Pennsylvania Hospital.

PHILADELPHIA COLLEGE OF PHARMACY, 145 North Tenth Street; established, 1821, at meeting in Carpenters' Hall: consists of five large buildings connected by a central building, Romanesque, Pompeian brick and Seneca red stone; largest and first institution in the United States devoted to pharmaceutical and chemical instruction. Laboratories and equipment are without a peer, for most advanced training of men and women as pharmacists and chemists. Museum has a large number of paintings of famous scientists, also the Martindale Herbarium of over 200,000 plant specimens. Library has about 14,000 volumes; around the gallery hang portraits of men who have given largely of their time and substance to the development and advancement of the College, and to the progress and betterment of the city; artists represented, Charles Willson Peale, Hugh H. Breckenridge, Henry R. Rittenberg. Collection of photographs of pharmaceutical subjects, many rare and very valuable.

PRESTON RETREAT, Twentieth and Hamilton Streets,

on site of William Penn's residence; classic, marble: founded by Dr. James Preston in 1837, for married women of good character and indigent circumstances, about to be confined. One of the best equipped in the world.

ST. JOSEPH'S HOSPITAL, Girard Avenue and Sixteenth Street; colonial, brick. Established first in the parish of St. Joseph's Church, near Fourth and Walnut Streets, for Irish famine refugees who became ill on overcrowded and unventilated ships. Incorporated, 1849. Was third general hospital in Philadelphia.

WILLS' HOSPITAL, Eighteenth and Race Streets, facing Logan Circle; classic, marble; founded, 1832, by James Wills, Jr., for the indigent blind and lame. Now one of the best in the world as an institution for the study and practice of ophthalmy.

WOMEN'S HOSPITAL OF PHILADELPHIA, North College Avenue. Oldest and largest hospital in the world for women and children: organized, 1861. Its motto is, "Woman's work for woman by women."

WOMAN'S MEDICAL COLLEGE OF PHILADELPHIA, Twenty-first Street and North College Avenue; first college in the world organized for the education of women for the medical profession. Incorporated, 1850. Dr. Ann Preston, of first class to be graduated, was the founder of the Women's Hospital. Contains bas-relief tablet, "The Woman Physician"; sculptor, Miss Clara Hill.

HISTORIC MUSICAL INTERESTS OF PHILADELPHIA

ACADEMY OF MUSIC, Broad and Locust Streets. Seats 3000; established, 1857, for representation of operas in English, and distinguished entertainments; opened with a magnificent ball, such as was never before witnessed in Philadelphia; now home of the Philadelphia Orchestra, which has had three conductors since its organization in 1900, Fritz Scheel, Carl Pohlig, and Leopold Stokowski; all of whom have brought the splendid body of players to a high standard of musical excellence. Dr. Stokowski has said of the Academy: "The architect must have had great knowledge of the laws governing sound, as the volumes are marvelously arranged."

The Mahler Symphony was given here in 1916, first time in America, Stokowski, director, with chorus of 1000 voices. A memorial to Siegfried Behrens will be in wall of lobby, portrait figure in relief, with Muse of Music holding laurel wreath, Cararra marble, seven feet high, on base of dark marble; sculptor, Guiseppe Donato.

THE MAENNERCHOR SOCIETY, 1643 North Broad Street. A men's chorus of active and associate members, founded, 1835, by Philip Mathias Wolsieffer, director for eighteen years. The Maennerchor was the first men's chorus in America; they have sung for twenty-eight years at opening of the German-American Charity Ball, in the Academy of Music. They sang with the Vocal Union, choral parts of Beethoven's Ninth Symphony in 1874, first time given in America, William W. Wolsieffer conducting. Won three prizes at National Saengerfest in Brooklyn, Baltimore, and Newark.

MUSICAL FUND HALL, Locust Street, west of Eighth Street, built, 1824. Acoustic properties unsurpassed.

THE COMMONWEALTH 131

Jenny Lind sang here. Now used by a Labor Organization.

Philadelphia has over two hundred singing societies, and a long list of very prominent musical organizations.

THE PRESSER FOUNDATION OF PHILADELPHIA, organized 1916, is the first institution of its kind to be established in America. All of its resources have been given by Mr. Theodore Presser. It includes a Home for Retired Music Teachers, suggested by the Founder's visit to the Verdi "Casa di Riposo per Musicisti," in Milan in 1899. Scholarships to institutions of learning, the students to be selected by the President, and Directors of the Musical Departments, and emergency aid relief to musicians.

THE UNIVERSITY OF PENNSYLVANIA AND OTHER HISTORIC SCHOOLS

THE UNIVERSITY OF PENNSYLVANIA, Thirty-fourth Street and Woodland Avenue, with a campus of one hundred and seventeen acres along the west bank of the Schuylkill River and equipment of seventy buildings; originated in the Charity School, organized, 1740, at Fourth and Arch Streets; made an academy through the interest of Benjamin Franklin, in 1749; chartered, "The College of Philadelphia," with power to confer honorary and collegiate degrees, being the third oldest college in the United States; in 1799 was organized and chartered as "The University of the State of Pennsylvania," making it the first institution in the United States designated a university; also the first to establish professional schools distinct from the college. The School of Medicine was added in 1765, and has always maintained the most advanced requirements and highest standards of scholarship for graduation; it was founded by Dr. John Morgan, who held the first medical professorship in America; he was physician in chief of the Continental Army, 1775–77. The first American University Professorship in Law was established here, 1790; James Wilson held the position; President Washington attended his lectures. In 1799, the University conferred on Washington the degree of LL.D., and later, in 1826, set apart his birthday as University Day, on which honorary degrees are conferred, with appropriate exercises. Nine sons of this University signed the Declaration of Independence; seven, the Constitution of the United States; twenty-one were members of the Continental Congress; nine, in the United States Senate; eight were Attorney-Generals of states or of the United States; six were Justices of the Supreme Court; seven, Governors of states; and many others were Officers in the Army and men in public life, who had received their education in the old building, Fourth and Arch Streets, before 1800.

In 1802 the University was moved to Ninth and Chestnut Streets, and occupied the presidential mansion, now site of the Post Office; in 1872, moved to the present site in West Philadelphia. In 1912, under the administration of Provost Edgar Fahs Smith, The University Extension Courses were formed, and the college made into three departments with a dean for each. The COLLEGE, founded 1740, includes School of Arts; Summer School; College Courses for Teachers; Courses in Biology and Music. THE

TOWNE SCIENTIFIC SCHOOL, founded, 1875, includes, Architecture, Chemistry, Science, Technology, Mechancal, Electrical and Civil Engineering. WHARTON SCHOOL OF FINANCE AND COMMERCE, founded 1881, includes, School of Accounts and Finance in Philadelphia; and the Extension Schools of Finance and Accounts in Scranton and Wilkes-Barre.

DEPARTMENT OF MUSIC, through the unceasing and wise direction of Dr. Hugh A. Clarke, has graduated hundreds of students in music, after a four years' course in Harmony, Counterpoint, Composition, and Orchestration. The degree of Bachelor of Music has been conferred on many who qualified to meet the requirements. THE GRADUATE SCHOOL was founded, 1882; courses lead to degrees of master of arts, and doctor of philosophy.

Other Departments are, the LAW SCHOOL, Thirty-fourth and Chestnut Streets; building dedicated University Day, 1900, architects, Cope & Stewardson, style similar to the English Renaissance as de-developed by Sir Christopher Wren; Indiana limestone and dull red brick; contains the Biddle Law Library, 55,000 volumes; The Black Memorial Collection of English Legal Engravings, most complete in America; several original documents by Benjamin Franklin, George Washington and other colonial men; many objects of historical interest to members of the bar; a fine collection of portraits include those of Algernon Sydney Biddle, by Cecilia Beaux; Charles Chauncey, by Henry Inman; Thomas McKean, LL.D., by Robert W. Vonnoh; Richard Coxe McMurtrie, LL.D., by William M. Chase; James Wilson,

LL.D., by Albert Rosenthal, from a miniature; marble busts of Daniel Webster and Jeremiah Sullivan; tablets and memorials.

LABORATORY OF CHEMISTRY, Thirty-fourth and Spruce Streets; dedicated, 1894; shows the broad projecting eaves of brick architecture in the Italian Renaissance; architects, Cope & Stewardson; it is one of the best equipped chemical laboratories in America. The ENGINEERING building, Thirty-third and Locust Streets; dedicated, 1906; Georgian, dark brick with limestone trimmings, architects, Cope & Stewardson; houses the civil, electrical, and mechanical engineering departments; best equipped of its kind. In its collection of portraits is that of John Henry Towne, by William M. Hunt.

LABORATORY OF HYGIENE, includes the Psychological Clinic; Department of physical education; and Franklin Field, Thirty-third and Spruce Streets, dedicated, 1895, seating capacity of the stadium about 62,000, was for many years scene of annual football between the United States Military and Naval Academies; gymnasium, facing Thirty-third Street, erected, 1903, English Collegiate, Gothic, dark red brick, with black headers laid in Flemish bond, terra cotta and Indiana limestone trimmings, floors and columns concrete; comprises Weightman Hall, exercising rooms, and a large swimming pool; architects, Frank Miles Day & Brother; in front on the terrace is statue of Benjamin Franklin at seventeen, as he first entered Philadelphia in 1732; sculptor, Dr. R. Tait McKenzie, pedestal designed by Professor Paul P. Cret. In the entrance is bronze tablet in relief, full figure portrait of

Charles S. Bayne in baseball uniform, "1895 College," sculptor, R. Tait McKenzie; also other memorials.

DEPARTMENT OF ARCHÆOLOGY, founded, 1889, by the late Provost William Pepper, M.D., LL.D., museum, Spruce Street, near Thirty-fourth Street, open free daily, 10.00 A. M. to 5.00 P. M.; Sunday 2.00 to 6.00 P. M. The treatment of this building and the courtyard, begun 1897, is among the most successful works of architecture in this country; it was inspired by the round, arched, brick architecture of Northern Italy, about twelfth century; details especially suggesting the old Church of San Stefano in Bologna; roof of Spanish tiles gives added charm; architects in coöperation, Wilson Eyre, Jr., Cope & Stewardson, Frank Miles Day & Brother. Has valuable collections illustrating the history of mankind; Egyptian, Cretan, Etruscan, and Babylonian antiquities, famous tablets from Nippur, and the Dillwyn-Parish collection of Græco-Roman papyri, among which are the oldest known fragments of the Gospel of St. Matthew. During 1916, the museum maintained four expeditions in the field: in Egypt, China, Siberia, and one on the Amazon, which will return with collections they have gathered. Among the portraits in the museum are, Mrs. William D. Frismuth, donor of collection of musical instruments, and Franklin Hamilton Cushing, ethnologist, both by Thomas Eakins; bronze statue of Dr. William Pepper, by Carl Bitter, is in the Italian garden; free public illustrated lectures are given Saturdays, 3.30 P. M., from November to March.

LIBRARY, founded, 1749, with volumes bearing accession dates of 1749, given by Benjamin Franklin; First Provost, William Smith; Louis XVI of France; and others, now contains about 450,000 volumes, and many special collections; present building dedicated, 1891, Thirty-fourth and Locust Streets, red brick, sandstone, and terra cotta, Furness, Evans & Company, architects; among the portraits here are Benjamin Franklin, LL.D., replica, by Thomas Gainsborough, R.A., of his original; William Wordsworth, poet, from life, by Henry Inman in 1844; Joseph G. Rosengarten, LL.D., by B. A. Osnis, and the entire class of 1811 minus one, in silhouette, cut at Peale's Museum; here also is the famous orrery and large clock made by David Rittenhouse for this university.

HOUSTON HALL, memorial to Henry Howard Houston, Jr., class of '78, Spruce Street above Thirty-fourth. North Conshohocken and Indiana limestone; architect's design of two students of the School of Architecture, developed by Frank Miles Day; was planned by Provost C. C. Harrison, to weld the cosmopolitan body of students into one democratic brotherhood, which has now become a world-wide movement in college life; contains trophy rooms, pool tables, and publication office of "Old Penn," until 1918 the official weekly; courses of Free Public Lectures are given by members of the Faculty, and men from other American and foreign Universities; services by eminent ministers are conducted each Sunday morning. Among the many portraits in Houston Hall are, Henry Howard Houston, Jr., by Cecilia Beaux; David Rittenhouse, by Charles Willson Peale; Henry Reed, and Henry Vethake, both by Sully.

THE UNIVERSITY HOSPITAL, Thirty-fourth and Spruce Streets; founded by the late Provost Dr. William Pepper, 1874, covers two city blocks; medical staff consists of more than one hundred and fifty physicians and one hundred nurses; the Surgical Building erected, 1914; Jacobean style, brick and limestone, architects, Brockie & Hastings, contains marble bust on pedestal of Dr. William Pepper, Provost, 1881-94; bronze mural tablet with portrait of late Dr. John H. Musser, sculptor, Dr. R. Tait McKenzie; and many bronze memorials. The MEDICAL LABORATORY, dedicated, 1904, on Hamilton Walk, English Collegiate, of Middle seventeenth century, hard burnt brick and buff Indiana limestone; architects, Cope & Stewardson; interior finished in white Italian marble; is one of the largest and best equipped in America. Contains nearly complete collection of oil portraits of staff of physicians from 1765, including painting of David Hayes Agnew, M.D., LL.D., at the close of a clinic in Medical Hall, all the subordinate figures in the group are likenesses, among them, Dr. J. William White, Dr. Joseph Leidy, Jr., and the artist, Thomas Eakins; Professor John Morgan, founder of the Medical School, after the original by Angelica Kauffman; Professor William Osler, LL.D., and De Forest Willard, by W. M. Chase; Professor Philip Syng Physick, first American to be elected member of Royal Academy, France, by Henry Inman, from life in 1836; Professor Benjamin Rush, by John Neagle; Dr. J. William White, by John S. Sargent; and bronze bust on pedestal of Dr. Joseph Leidy.

THE WISTAR INSTITUTE OF ANATOMY AND BIOLOGY,

Thirty-sixth Street and Woodland Avenue, founded, 1892, for extension of Wistar and Homer Museums; first university institute exclusively for research in anatomy and biology, buff brick and light terra cotta, fireproof, built, 1808, architects, George W. and W. D. Hewitt; in 1905 this institute became the clearing house for anatomy in America, and in 1906 was appointed Central United States Institute for Brain Investigation; the five principal independent anatomical journals of the United States are published here. Open to the public daily, except Sundays and holidays, 9.00 A. M. to 4.00 P. M., Saturdays, 9.00 A. M. to 12.00 M. Contains bronze bust, sculptor, Samuel Murray, 1890, of General Isaac J. Wistar, Sc.D., who gave the building and endowment; in bronze vase are his ashes; also in three bronze vases are the ashes of Joseph Leidy, M.D., LL.D., John Adams Ryder, Ph.D., and Professor Edward Drinker Cope. Opposite is THE ARCHITECTURAL SCHOOL, Thirty-sixth Street and Woodland Avenue, second only in importance and numbers to the *Ecole des Beaux Arts,* Paris: the *esprit de corps* of faculty and students is most pronounced; students and graduates, of late years, have won more competitive prizes, and scholarships, than those of all other American schools combined. The four years' course leads to degree; special two years' course, and summer six weeks' course.

THE BOTANIC GARDENS, established, 1894, face Hamilton Walk, open to visitors from sunrise to sunset; greenhouses filled with rare plants from all the world; lily and lotus ponds are attractive feature of the campus. Open-air plays are given here. The Vivarium, established 1898, has fresh and salt water aquaria, first vivarium ever connected with any educational institution. ZOÖLOGICAL LABORATORY, on Hamilton Walk and Thirty-ninth Street, built, 1910; architects, Cope & Stewardson, hard burnt brick and Indiana limestone, English Collegiate, of middle seventeenth century; considered best working laboratory for its purpose in this country, contains many famous collections.

VETERINARY BUILDING AND HOSPITAL, Thirty-ninth Street and Woodland Avenue, constructed about a square courtyard; one of best equipped of its kind. Architects, Cope & Stewardson, English Collegiate, seventeenth century, hard burnt yellow brick and limestone trimmings, roof green slate, built, 1906–07.

SCHOOL OF DENTISTRY, "Thomas W. Evans Museum and Dental Institute," Fortieth and Spruce Streets, Collegiate Gothic, time of Henry VIII, hard burnt red and black brick and Indiana limestone, built, 1914, architect, John T. Windrim; the grotesques ornamenting the band courses, while in the spirit of the Middle Ages, are modern in subject and caricature; most complete edifice in the world, devoted to the science of dentistry. Museum contains the priceless Evans collection, gifts from the nobility of Europe, portraits and busts of Dr. Evans.

HENRY PHIPPS INSTITUTE for the study, prevention, and treatment of tuberculosis, founded, 1903, northeast corner of Seventh and Lombard Streets; facing Starr Garden Park, a civic center of the Playgrounds Commission; is colonial style, designed by Grosvenor Atterbury, New York, brick trimmed with white marble.

FLOWER ASTRONOMICAL OBSERVATORY at Llanerch on West Chester Pike, architect, Edgar V. Seeler, 1895. Open to visitors every Thursday evening during collegiate year, 7.00 P. M. to 10.00 P. M.; is equipped with an 18 inch equatorial telescope, and other instruments of latest and most approved design.

DORMITORY HOUSES, Jacobean, thirty in number, begun in 1895, suggest the Oxford and Cambridge colleges; carved grotesque bosses on main cornices are reminiscent of the Gothic period; they are amusing, and display an unusual amount of imagination; material, hard burnt yellow brick and Indiana limestone; architects, Cope & Stewardson; entrance through two gateways known as Memorial Tower, gift of the Alumni, dedicated in 1901, in memory of University of Pennsylvania men who served in the Spanish-American War, corner-stone was laid by General Miles, in 1900; and the Provosts' Tower, named as memorial to the Provosts of the University of Pennsylvania, whose twelve names are carved on medallions, from William Smith to Charles Custis Harrison.

WILLIAM PENN CHARTER SCHOOL, 8 to 10 South Twelfth Street, was planned in 1684 at a meeting of the Provincial Council, Governor Penn presiding. In 1689, William Penn, writing from England to Thomas Lloyd, President of Council, instructed him to set up a "Public Grammar School in Philadelphia," the school was incorporated in 1698, and George Keith engaged as head master, 1699. In 1701, William Penn, while on a visit to America, granted the school a charter from his own hand; on the same day he chartered the city itself. This school is the oldest existing chartered school in America; a second and more liberal charter was granted, 1708, and a third charter, under which the school is still conducted, 1711; the originals of all three of these charters are in the school's possession. The school will be moved to Pinehurst, the Waln estate, twenty-two acres on School Lane near Wissahickon Avenue, Germantown, acquired by gift; field now used for their athletic sports, surface having been adapted for the purpose by the Newhall Engineering Company, Philadelphia, who made there a football oval; an eighteen foot quarter-mile track; and an eighteen foot 220 yard straightway; drainage of these tracks and oval is such, that in eight years, not one scheduled contest has been postponed on account of condition of the ground.

CENTRAL HIGH SCHOOL, Broad and Green Streets; established, 1836. In view of the increasing income and diminishing debt of the nation, the United States Congress in 1836 passed a law, authorizing the distribution of surplus revenue among the states, to be disposed of as their legislatures might enact; Pennsylvania devoted her share, over $70,000, to public education, and the controllers erected a high school in Philadelphia, which was completed, 1838, east side of Juniper Street, below Market Street. In 1853, the original building was sold; present structure occupied in 1900. Conferring of academic degrees dates from 1849. Memorial window to Edward T. Steel in assembly room.

GIRARD COLLEGE, College and Corinthian Avenues, for the care and training of orphan boys; founded by Stephen Girard, a native of France, who at his death, in 1831, left his estate for this purpose. Main building, architect, Thomas Ustick Walter, architect of the Capitol at Washington, probably the finest architectural specimen in Philadelphia, modeled after a Greek temple, white marble, covers an area of 34,344 feet, exclusive of eleven marble steps by which it is approached on every side; a colonnade of 34 Corinthian columns aid in supporting the marble roof, each column 6 feet in diameter and 55 feet high, the diameter of corner columns being increased $1\frac{1}{2}$ inches to overcome apparent reduction of size from their insulated position; bases 9 feet 3 inches in diameter, 3 feet 2 inches high, capitals 8 feet 6 inches high and 9 feet 4 inches wide; each shaft, as well as the bases, consists of a single piece, without vertical joints; at each end of the three story building is a vestibule, the ceilings of which are supported by eight columns, whose shafts are composed of a single stone; corner-stone was laid July 4, 1834, and the completed building transferred to the Board of Directors, 1847. In the first vestibule is white marble sarcophagus, with body of Stephen Girard, and his statue by Gevelot; the memorial room contains portrait of Girard, by J. R. Lambdin, copy from posthumous portrait by Bass Otis in Masonic Temple; interesting collection of furniture; pictures; china; silverware, and fine marble bust of Napoleon I, by Canova, presented to Girard by Joseph Bonaparte.

Present capacity, 1520 boys, admitted from six to ten years of age and graduated fourteen to sixteen years of age, preference of admission is given to those born within the old Philadelphia city limits, next in consideration those born in Pennsylvania, and third

THE COMMONWEALTH 143

group, boys born in the cities of New York and New Orleans. There are several hundred on waiting list.

Equipment comprises ten white marble buildings for school and house purposes, chapel seating 1600, and other buildings, also plant for heat, light, and power, inclosed on forty acres with a ten-foot high stone wall. Endowment now about $29,000,000. Soldiers' and sailors' monument on campus, in memory of the graduates who served in the Civil War; sculptor, J. Massey Rhind. Clergymen are excluded by Girard's will, "that the boys might be kept free from denominational controversies." Bible has always had a foremost place in the teaching of the college; Chapel speakers are laymen of prominence in the professional and business world.

OTHER PLACES OF HISTORIC INTEREST

RESIDENCE OF JOHN FITCH in 1791, 462 North Second Street; in 1790 John Fitch's steamboats made regular trips; Petty's Island was used as a port for the *Perseverance*, one of the five steamboats that Fitch constructed for use on the Delaware, before Robert Fulton placed his *Clermont* on the Hudson; it was blown up at moorings on this island. RESIDENCE OF EDGAR ALLAN POE from 1843–44 west side of Seventh Street, above Spring Garden (old number 234). BUSH HILL MANSION, on west side of Seventeenth Street below Spring Garden, erected by Andrew Hamilton in 1740; front lawn sloping to Vine Street, was scene of a Fourth of July celebration held in 1788, after the last of the nine states that made the Constitution effective came in; the procession dispersed here at "Union Green,"

James Wilson, a signer of the Constitution, delivered an oration, and there were other ceremonies. SPRINGETTSBURY, built 1736–39, called after the name of William Penn's first wife, manor-house of the Penns; burnt in 1808; part of site is now occupied by the Preston Retreat, Eighteenth Street below Spring Garden. Northeast corner of Broad and Walnut Streets, site of VAUXHALL GARDEN; a ball was given here in honor of General Andrew Jackson after his victory at New Orleans, January 8, 1814. PENN TREATY PARK, Beach Street and East Columbia Avenue. KNIGHT'S WHARF at edge of Green Street, in Northern Liberties; near here Poole's bridge crossed Pegg's Run at Front Street, it was named after one Poole, a Friend, whose mansion was here, recalls the Mischianza invitation: "The favor of your meeting the subscribers to the Mischianza at Knight's Wharf, near Poole's Bridge, tomorrow at half past three, is desired. (Signed) Henry Calder. Sunday, 17th May, 1778. For river parade to the Garden." Preparations for this magnificent entertainment, the erection of numerous and vast pavilions around the Wharton mansion, and their decorations by André, Delancey, and other gallant officers, was the talk of the town for weeks. The Wharton mansion, Walnut Grove, used by the family in summer, was where Fifth Street, near Washington Avenue, is now; the British had possession there in the spring of 1778; Miss Peggy Shippen's portrait was sketched by Major André in Mischianza costume. Philadelphia then excelled all other colonial cities in size, culture, and importance. SOUTHWARK SHOT TOWER, built, 1809, Carpenter Street between Front and Second, first plant in the United States which made bullets. SITE OF HILL'S SHIPYARD, Queen Street wharf below Cathrine Street. Original Swedish houses on both sides of Queen Street below Front. Site of United States first navy yard, 1201 South Front Street.

Obelisk northeast corner Twenty-third and Market Streets gives a history of the old Market Street bridge, built 1801–05; inscriptions to be recut.

HISTORIC GERMANTOWN

Colonial and Revolutionary suburb, six miles from Philadelphia; founded in 1683 by Francis Daniel Pastorius from Sommerhausen, Germany, one of the best educated men in the Colonies; he had received the degree of Doctor of Laws at Nuremberg; was a member of the Assembly from 1687–91. Earliest settlers were Friends and German Religionists, highly cultivated, and skilled in weaving, paper-making, printing, and other trades. First railroad in America to use steam was the Philadelphia and Reading to Germantown in 1832. First successful locomotive made in America was Matthias Baldwin's "Old Ironsides," used on this road, only taken out in fair weather. GERMANTOWN AVENUE follows an old Indian trail, made a turnpike in 1800, on which are still many historic houses of quaint colonial architecture; rough native stone with overhanging hipped roofs and a projecting pent, over doorstep. STENTON, built in 1728, brick, colonial, near Wayne Junction, residence of James Logan, Secretary to William Penn, 1727–34;

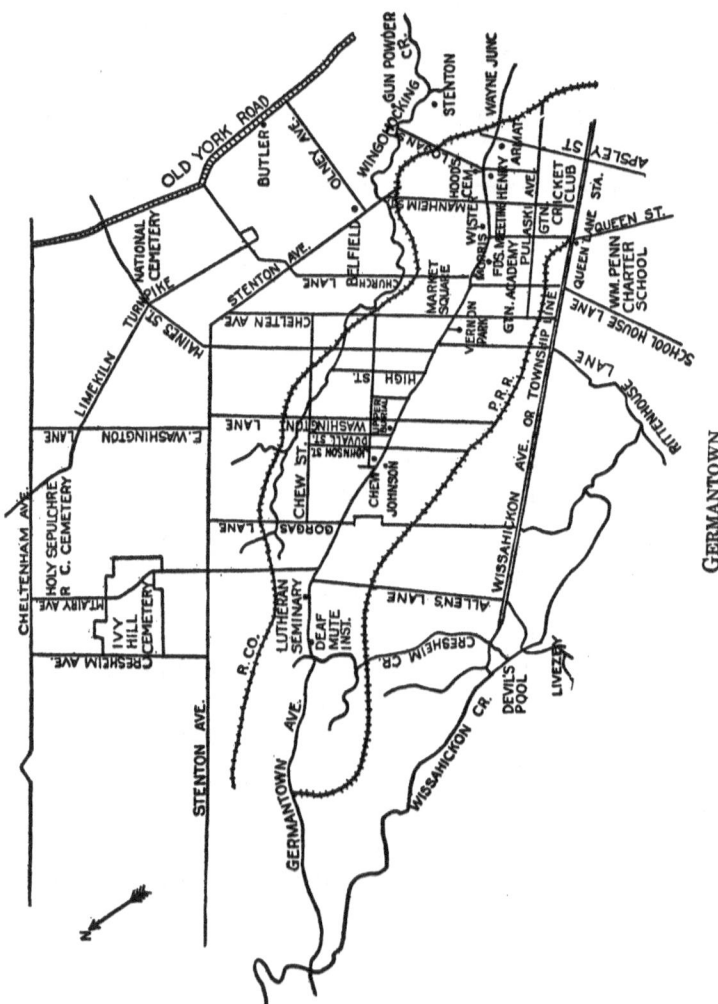

President of Council, Chief Justice of the Supreme Court of Pennsylvania; his guests were Franklin, Jefferson, Madison, Monroe, Lafayette, John Randolph; occupied by General Washington, August, 1777, on way to the Battle of Brandywine; by General Howe during Battle of Germantown; Washington dined here with Dr. Logan, July, 1787, while the Constitutional Convention was in session. There is a curious underground passage from cellar to stable; the stream on the place was named "Wingohocking" for an Indian chief, who himself took the name of Logan; now in charge of the Pennsylvania Society of Colonial Dames, who have refurnished it with original pieces and relics of the Logan family; open daily 1.00 P. M. to 6.00 P. M., excepting Sunday and Thursday. Admission fee, fifteen cents. Northwest corner of Apsley Street and Germantown Avenue, LOUDOUN, built in 1801, residence of Thomas Armat, now occupied by Armat and Logan descendants; many wounded Americans died and were buried here in Battle of Germantown. 4825 Germantown Avenue, house built by Christopher Ottinger in 1781; walls two feet thick; rafters unhewn trees; his son, born here in 1804, was Captain Douglas Ottinger in the United States Revenue Marine; he invented the Ottinger life car which, in 1849, equipped eight life-saving stations on the New Jersey coast. 4810 Germantown Avenue, site of Wagner house, built, 1747; used as hospital after the Battle of Germantown, stable doors were taken for operating tables; many died and were buried in a trench in the rear. 4908 Germantown Avenue, built in 1760, was bought, 1828, by John S. Henry, whose son, Alexander Henry, was three times Mayor of Philadelphia and a member of Congress.

Northeast corner of East Logan and Germantown Avenue, Lower or HOOD'S BURIAL GROUND, presented to borough in 1693 by Jan Streepers; John F. Watson placed stones over graves of General Agnew and Colonel Bird, British officers killed in Battle of Germantown; see Burial Grounds. 5109 Germantown Avenue, site of Thones Kunder's home, part of original north wall is still standing; first meetings of the Society of Friends in Germantown were held here; and a public protest against slavery was made in 1688; the paper, written and signed by Pastorius and three others, was forwarded to the Yearly Meeting in Burlington; Thones Kunder, by trade a dyer, was the ancestor of the Conard and Conrad families, also of Sir Samuel Cunard, founder of the Cunard Steamship Line; he died in 1729.

South side of Manheim Street, west of Germantown Avenue, residence of Jacques Marie Roset, who came to America in 1792, first to introduce the tomato plant into Germantown; his granddaughter was the wife of Anthony J. Drexel, Esq.; opposite, 153 Manheim Street was Taggert's field; British Infantry encamped here. Manheim Street, corner of Morris Street, GERMANTOWN CRICKET CLUB, organized in 1854; William Rotch Wister, was the first American to study the science and points of the play, and teach it; he was known as "The father of American cricket"; first American field, "Belfield Cricket Club," Stenton and Olney Avenues, was the Wister pasture and orchard; second club, "Young America," field, rear

THE COMMONWEALTH 149

of residence of Thomas A. Newhall, Esq., Manheim and Hansberry Streets; they consolidated in 1889. Queen Lane, west of Pulaski Avenue, site of Potter's Field in 1765, a burial place for "all strangers, negroes and mulattoes as die in any part of Germantown."

5106 Germantown Avenue, residence of Commodore James Barron, Commandant Philadelphia Navy Yard in 1842; Captain of the *Chesapeake*, when captured by the British ship *Leopard*; in 1807 he killed Commodore Stephen Decatur in a duel at Bladensburg, Maryland. 5157 Germantown Avenue, residence and printing office, now altered, of Philip R. Freas; publisher of *The Village Telegraph*, in 1830; later *The Germantown Telegraph*. ST. STEPHEN'S METHODIST CHURCH, opened in 1856; site of Frederick Fraley's carpenter shop; gun carriages were made here for the American Army; Washington was a frequent visitor. 5140 Germantown Avenue, residence of GILBERT STUART, 1794–95; the barn was used as his studio; portrait of Washington, now in the Athenaeum of Boston, was painted here; also a full length portrait of "Cornplanter," the Indian chief. 5253–55 Germantown Avenue, formerly one dwelling, OWEN WISTER, novelist, was born here July 14, 1860, son of Dr. Owen J. and Sarah Butler Wister; his mother was a daughter of Pierce and Fanny Kemble Butler. 5219 Germantown Avenue, residence of John Bringhurst, carriage maker, 1775–95; a founder of the Germantown Academy; in 1780 he made a "chariot" for General Washington, whose arms and crest were properly displayed; cost £210 in gold; Martha Washington rode to Mount Vernon in it. Colonel Bird, British officer, died here. 5249 Germantown Avenue, built by Dr. Owen Wister, was his residence from 1860–70, he then moved to Butler Place on York Road; 5253 Germantown Avenue site of CHRISTOPHER SAUR'S residence and printing office, who arrived in Germantown, 1724; secured a printing outfit from Germany in 1738; published the first German newspaper in America, 1739; printed the first Bible in European language in America, 1743; Christopher Saur, Jr., was Bishop of the Dunkard Church, 1753. 5242–44 Germantown Avenue, site of Indian Queen Tavern, which gave the name to Queen Street. 5261 Germantown Avenue, erected by John Wister in 1744, stones were quarried from a hill in the rear; joists from oaks in Wister's woods; family removed to Penllyn during occupancy by British, where SALLY WISTER, a daughter, wrote her charming "Diary." The British General, James Agnew, lived here at the time of Battle of Germantown; was brought back wounded, and died here; now owned and occupied by Wister descendants. 5300 Germantown Avenue, corner of Queen Street, parsonage of TRINITY LUTHERAN CHURCH; was one of the Saur properties; first type cast in America, in 1772, was made in the cellar of this house; church built, 1837; many well-known Germantowners lie in the graveyard. 5275–77 Germantown Avenue, Germantown National Bank, 1825–68; John Fanning Watson was cashier, he lived at 5277; building was occupied by Thomas Jefferson, Secretary of State, and Edmund Randolph, Attorney General of the United States, in 1793, during the yellow fever in Philadelphia.

Northeast corner of Germantown Avenue and Coulter Street, ST. LUKE'S PROTESTANT EPISCOPAL CHURCH, first Episcopal Church in Germantown, built, 1811; land given by Thomas Armat, Esq.; John Fanning Watson, the annalist, is buried in the churchyard. Northwest corner of Germantown Avenue, and Coulter Street, FRIENDS' MEETING, land given by Jacob Shoemaker, fifty acres, in 1693; in the library is a photograph of the first protest against slavery. 5425 Germantown Avenue, Masonic Lodge room; site, residence of A. Bronson Alcott, where LOUISA MAY ALCOTT, authoress, was born. 5430 Germantown Avenue, residence of Captain ALBERT ASHMEAD, of the Philadelphia County Troop who commanded a troop of cavalry, and escorted General Lafayette from Bristol to Philadelphia in 1824; French Embassy during 1793. 5434 Germantown Avenue, residence of John Ashmead, father of Captain Albert Ashmead; who designed and made the first carriages known as Germantown wagons, in 1824, in the shop at rear of house; also first plows with wrought iron mold board; Lafayette purchased four, for his La Grange farm in France.

MARKET SQUARE, Battle of Germantown fought here, September 25, 1777; here was the market house, prison, stocks, and public scales; in February, 1764, several hundred Paxtang boys, from banks of the Conestoga and Susquehanna Rivers, encamped here; they came east to murder the peaceful Moravian Indians, sheltered in Philadelphia, and were met by Benjamin Franklin, Thomas Willing, Benjamin Chew, and others, who persuaded them to return. Monument erected in 1883, to Civil War soldiers and sailors, pedestal with tablets, containing names of Germantown soldiers and sailors, at base are two coast defense mortars from the Civil War, two bronze cannon on wheels from the United States Arsenal; the enclosure is of musket barrels and bayonets, used during Civil War, and broken cannon from British frigate *Augusta*, sunk by American batteries during Revolutionary War. MARKET SQUARE PRESBYTERIAN CHURCH, originally German Reformed, built in 1733; Count Zinzendorf preached his first sermon in America here, December, 1741, and last on leaving, June, 1742; Washington worshiped here while living in the Morris house opposite; a battalion of Ninth Virginia, captured by the British, was confined here.

5442 Germantown Avenue, MORRIS HOUSE, Washington's summer residence, in 1793-94, built by David Deshler, 1772-73; Sir William Howe occupied it after the battle in 1777; in 1804, it was bought by Mr. Perot for a country residence, and became the property of his son-in-law, Mr. Morris; the yard is kept in the simple elegance of colonial times. 5450 Germantown Avenue, in 1790 residence of Thomas Armat, who lived later at "Loudoun." 5452 Germantown Avenue, erected in 1711 by John Ashmead, great grandfather of Captain Albert Ashmead; front rebuilt 1790. 5454 Germantown Avenue, occupied in 1742 by Count Zinzendorf; commencement of Moravian Seminary, now in Bethlehem, Pennsylvania. Saving Fund Building, site, residence of Jacob Tellner, first stone house built in Germantown; William Penn present at the roof raising; he once preached here.

THE COMMONWEALTH 153

School House Lane and Greene Street, GERMANTOWN ACADEMY, built, 1759; colonial, native stone; founded by Christopher Saur, and others of German birth, to furnish education in "English, High Dutch, and the German language." It has always held high rank as a school; the bell was brought to Philadelphia in 1774, in the tea ship Polly, the cargo was not allowed to land, it was taken back to England, and returned here when the war was ended; telescope used by Washington during battle, when the building was used as a hospital, is here; several British soldiers were buried in the yard; cricket was first played in America here, by British officers; Bank of Pennsylvania was brought here, escorted by McPherson's Blues in 1798, during the second yellow fever epidemic in Philadelphia; gymnasium on Green Street, modern. On School House Lane, farther west, is Cricket Field of the William Penn Charter School.

Northeast corner of School House Lane and Germantown Avenue, Mutual Fire Insurance Company, in the office is "Shag Rag," an old hand engine, imported from England, 1764; site, De la Plaine house, Whitefield preached from balcony to about 500 people in the Square. Northwest corner of Germantown Avenue and School House Lane, Germantown Bank, chartered, 1813; site of Germantown Library in 1806; used by United States Bank in 1798, escorted from Philadelphia by body of Light Horse. 5516-18-20 Germantown Avenue, site, KING OF PRUSSIA TAVERN in 1757, the sign was painted by Gilbert Stuart; a stage coach, with awning, ran from King of Prussia to the "George Inn," Second and Arch Streets, three times a week. Germantown Avenue north of Chelten Avenue, Vernon Park, residence of John Wister, member of Congress until 1883; now belongs to the city; mansion, built in 1803, is used as museum by the Site Relic Society; marble statue of John Wister, near the door, made in Italy, given by his son, Jones Wister, who posed for the figure. Free library building in Park. South side of Haines Street, east of Chew, still stands a farmhouse; residence of Christopher Ludwig in 1777; appointed "Baker General" to American Army; said to be the original of Harvey Birch in Cooper's novel, "The Spy."

Southeast corner Germantown Avenue and High Street, site of the Morris-Littell house, was residence of DR. CHRISTOPHER WITT, physician, botanist, musician, artist, astronomer, poet; originally one of the hermits of the Wissahickon; friend of John Bartram and Francis Daniel Pastorius; an oil portrait of Johannes Kelpius, painted by Dr. Witt in 1705, is said to be the first oil portrait painted in America, now at Pennsylvania Historical Society; he started the first botanical garden in America, twenty years earlier than Bartram's. Now yard of high school building. South side of High Street, two squares east from Germantown Avenue, ST. MICHAEL'S PROTESTANT EPISCOPAL CHURCH; window of St. Michael after Guido Reni by William and Annie Lee Willet; grave of Dr. Christopher Witt is here; died in 1765, aged 90; site of old Warner burial ground; British and American soldiers were buried here.

METHODIST CHURCH, 6019 Germantown Avenue, site, Green Tree Tavern in 1748, kept by Francis Daniel

Pastorius until 1754; General Anthony Wayne came this far, time of battle; Pastorius was the hero in Whittier's "Pennsylvania Pilgrim." Died in 1719; was buried, probably, in the Friends' burial ground, Germantown Avenue above Coulter Street. Southwest corner of Walnut Lane and Germantown Avenue, "WYCK," built in 1690; thought to be the oldest house now in Germantown; was used as hospital and operating room after battle; Lafayette was entertained here July, 1825. 6043 Germantown Avenue, southeast corner of Walnut Lane, was bought in 1775 by Dr. William Shippen as a summer home; center of fierce skirmish during battle; Pennsylvania manual training school was here under Dr. George Junkin, who was afterwards President of Washington and Lee University; his daughter was married to General Stonewall Jackson; in 1832, Dr. Junkin was President of Lafayette College, Easton; in 1851 this property was bought by Charlotte Cushman, actress.

Germantown Avenue above Herman Street, MENNONITE MEETING HOUSE, founded, 1708; present building erected, 1770; William Rittenhouse, first pastor; Brigadier General Agnew was mortally wounded near here. 6205 Germantown Avenue, site of house built in 1738 by Dirck Keyser, a silk merchant, who came from Amsterdam in 1688. 6239 Germantown Avenue, was known as Washington Tavern in 1793. 6306 Germantown Avenue, Johnson House, in thickest of fight; time of battle the British swarmed through, and cleared everything edible; family fled to the cellar. Germantown Avenue, north of Washington Lane, built, 1775, Concord School House; now

Charter Oak Library. North of library is the Upper Burial Ground; has probably the oldest existing stone to a German in Pennsylvania, Cornelius Tyson, buried in 1716; graves of the Lippard family are here, ancestors of George Lippard, author; American soldiers' memorial stone was erected by John Fanning Watson. Southeast corner of Germantown Avenue and Duval Street, site, "Pomona," residence Colonel Thomas Forrest, artillery officer; later member of the Sixteenth and Seventeenth Congress. 6338 Germantown Avenue, site, the Ship House, built, 1760; had representation of a ship on south gable; rear, site of first public hall in Germantown.

Northeast corner of Germantown Avenue and Johnson Street, CHEW HOUSE, "Cliveden," known as the "Germantown Battle Field," built in 1760 by Benjamin Chew, Attorney General of the Province, member of Council, later Chief Justice; colonial, solid and heavy masonry; forming admirable fortification; was the scene of most important battle in Germantown, October 4, 1777; family were away; house partly furnished was left in charge of servants, the building was battered with bullets, holes still shown in the doors. Northwest corner of Germantown Avenue and Johnson Streets, UPSALA, one of the finest examples of colonial architecture; built in 1798 by John Johnson; is still occupied by his descendants; during the battle, Americans put their cannon in the yard to fire on the Chew House, opposite. Northeast corner of Germantown Avenue and Upsal Street, Billmyer house, built in 1727; Washington stood on the horse block, telescope in hand, to penetrate the smoke of battle, and discover force of the

THE COMMONWEALTH 157

enemy at Chew House. Woodwork bears marks of bullets and attempts by soldiers to set it on fire; bought by Michael Billmyer in 1788, a celebrated German painter, whose business plant was here; tablet placed by Site and Relic Society.

6611 Germantown Avenue, parsonage of DUNKARD MEETING HOUSE, said to be over two hundred years old; near it, in the battle, General Nash was mortally wounded and Major Witherspoon, son of Rev. John Witherspoon, President of Princeton College, killed by the same cannon ball; they were buried in St. Michael's Lutheran Churchyard. 6613 Germantown Avenue, mother church of the Brethren, or DUNKARDS, in America; who came here in 1719; Church was organized by Peter Becker, first pastor, in 1723, present building, erected, 1770, has tablet to Christopher Saur in the meeting house, he published the first American quarto edition of the Bible, 1743; in the graveyard is buried Alexander Mack, founder of the Dunkard sect in Germany, who came to America, 1729.

Southeast corner of Germantown Avenue and Phil-Ellena Street, ST. MICHAEL'S LUTHERAN CHURCH, founded 1737; in 1742, Rev. Henry Melchoir Muhlenberg had charge here, and of St. John's in Philadelphia; pews were placed in 1750; during the battle, the organ was destroyed by British soldiers, who ran along the streets blowing the pipes; in the graveyard is buried Christopher Ludwig, and other patriots. 6749 Germantown Avenue, residence George Hesser; Elizabeth Drinker's journal, written while staying here in 1793, during yellow fever epidemic in Philadelphia, gives interesting local details of life in Germantown.

7301 Germantown Avenue, opposite Allen's Lane, LUTHERAN THEOLOGICAL SEMINARY, site, "Mount Airy," summer residence of Chief Justice William Allen; Lafayette was entertained here; later a school was conducted by Benjamin C. Constant, "The American Classical and Military Institute." General Meade and his brother, also General Beauregard, were educated here. Southeast corner of Germantown and Gowen Avenues, now part of Lutheran Theological Seminary; residence, in 1792, of Joseph Miller, whose daughter was married to James Gowen; their son, Franklin B. Gowen, was born and lived here many years, also his brother, James E. Gowen.

7406 Germantown Avenue, Mount Airy, PENNSYLVANIA INSTITUTION FOR DEAF, semi-deaf and blind-deaf; founded in 1820 by David G. Seixas, who gathered deaf street roamers in his home, taught, fed, and clothed them; a school was planned, Bishop White presiding; constitution adopted, and directors chosen; now a splendidly equipped trade teaching department for boys and girls; articulation, and lip reading taught; architecture, Norman.

INTERESTING PLACES WEST, NOT ON GERMANTOWN AVENUE

Queen Lane, two blocks west on Wissahickon Avenue, CARLTON, residence of Henry Hall; Washington's headquarters, August, 1777, and two days in September, before and immediately after the Battle of Brandywine; when the British occupied Germantown, the Hessian detachment encamped from here to the Schuylkill River: General Kuyphansen's headquarters: be-

THE COMMONWEALTH 159

yond the house, toward Queen Lane reservoir, is a granite monument erected by Sons of the Revolution in 1895 to commemorate the earlier encampment of the American army at this point. Corner of Rittenhouse Street and Lincoln Drive, birthplace of David Rittenhouse, Pennsylvania's first and greatest astronomer, born April 8, 1732; house erected in 1707; his grandfather, William Rittenhouse, came to America in 1690; first paper maker in America; mill located near the house.

PLACES OF INTEREST EAST

East Logan Street, across Wissahickon Avenue, the picturesque WAKEFIELD MILLS and residence of Thomas and Sarah Fisher, née Logan, in 1795, granddaughter of James Logan, of Stenton; passing Wakefield, Old York Road is soon reached. JEWISH HOSPITAL on the right. Old York Road, on left, residence of Pierce Butler, bought in 1812; he was a member of the Constitutional Convention, and Senator from South Carolina; his son, Pierce Butler, Jr., married Fanny Kemble; present residence of Owen Wister, their grandson; the British outpost was stationed near here. Church Lane and Wingohocking Creek, site of Roberts Mill, built in 1683; first in the country; built by Richard Townsend, a passenger on the *Welcome* with William Penn; back of mill, British had a small redoubt, guarding their encampment in Germantown. Northeast corner of Church Lane and Dunton Street, Spencer farmhouse; Thomas Godfrey, inventor of the quadrant, was born here; he died in 1749. Northwest corner of Haines Street and Limekiln Turnpike, PHILA-

DELPHIA NATIONAL CEMETERY, thirteen acres, founded in 1885; soldiers of the War of the Rebellion are buried here. Farther along Limekiln Turnpike left wing of Washington's army moved down this road, and a sharp encounter occurred with an outpost of British.

II
BUCKS COUNTY

AUTOMOBILE ride of historic interest through Washington's itinerary to New Hope. Return to Philadephia via Bristol and Frankford.

One of the first three counties established by William Penn, 1682, named for Buckinghamshire (Bucks), England, Penn's ancestral home. From HATBORO, Montgomery County, take the Old York Road to WARMINSTER, site where John Fitch, in 1785, made a model of the first successful steamboat, marked by monument; he ran a boat, with side wheels, by steam, on a pond in 1786, and on the Delaware River, during session of Federal Constitution at State House in Philadelphia, 1787; twenty years before Robert Fulton's trial trip on the Hudson; before Fitch, first model of steamboat in United States was made by William Henry, of Lancaster, 1763. Approaching Hartsville, is site of Log College, origin of Princeton University, founded by Rev. William Tennent, 1740, near Christ's Home, where everything is obtained through prayer. Neshaminy Church in a grove of very old oak trees, where William Tennent preached, is one of the oldest Presbyterian churches in Pennsylvania. HARTSVILLE, Cobe Scout's shop, on Little Neshaminy; bulk of American army was at Neshaminy Camp, with General Stephen and Lord Sterling, when Lafayette joined it, and was handed his commission by General Washington in Moreland house, near the bridge; marked, inscrip-

BUCKS COUNTY

BUCKS COUNTY 163

tion, "Washington's headquarters, August, 1777, Bucks County Historical Society." First Pike west of Hartsville, wooden covered bridge over Little Neshaminy; inscription, "Bucks County Bridge, 1821, 20 mi. to P." Continue York Road beyond Jamison's Corner, seven arch stone bridge over Big Neshaminy at Bridge Valley, built, 1800; beyond bridge, first left road, over Crawford's Hill, fine view of Neshaminy Valley.

Via Pebble Hill to DOYLESTOWN, county seat, settled, 1778, population 3857; court house, native gray stone; concrete fountain in front, Renaissance, with benches and lamp posts, designed by William R. Mercer, Jr., erected by borough, 1912, in commemoration of one hundredth anniversary of the county seat. Bucks County Historical Society, Library and Museum, built, 1915, of reinforced concrete, interior groined arch construction, designed, built, and presented to the Society by Dr. Henry C. Mercer; the court, surrounded by four galleries, contains collections illustrating history of the United States by means of utensils of American pioneers; unique of its kind in America; includes Indian relics, decorated stove plates, illustrated in a booklet "The Bible in Iron"; arms and relics of the Rebellion. Former library building, now the Auditorium, brick, built, 1904; colonial, designed from "Homewood," Baltimore residence of Charles Carroll of Carrollton; was presented to the Society by William L. Elkins, Esq.

Fountain House, Main Street, opposite National Bank, oldest hostelry in continuous use in upper Bucks County, built, 1745, rebuilt, 1758, low, two story, with porches, was the old stagehouse to Easton; contains large collection of colonial furnishings and old prints. "Aldie," residence of William R. Mercer, Jr., has notable pheasantry, rare fowls from eastern Asia; concrete garden ornaments made by Mr. Mercer; and antique sculpture from pre-Christian era; Font Hill, outside borough limits, residence, Dr. Henry C. Mercer; beamed and vaulted ceilings; roof terraces and many windows, entirely of reinforced concrete; walls and ceilings adorned with mosaics and tiles made by Dr. Mercer at the neighboring "Moravian Pottery and Tile Works." Living room decoration, Bible pictures in tiles, adapted from Pennsylvania German stove plates; Columbus room, ceiling and pavement tiles, discovery and exploration of America; Bow room, ceiling tiles, Cortez' maps of ancient Mexico, pavement, Aztec picture writings; Yellow room tiles, story of Bluebeard; also collection of classical and Renaissance mosaics, and ancient tiles, from historic buildings; may be seen by writing to the owner for admission.

Near Doylestown, National Farm School, four hundred acres, pioneer Jewish institution of its kind in America, founded, 1898. From Doylestown southwest, two miles, CASTLE VALLEY, Prospect or Spruce Hill, fine view, and grave, according to county tradition, of Lenape Chief, Tammany, whose name is used in Tammany Hall, New York; continuing the automobile route, Buckingham turnpike near Doylestown, small stone bridge, said to be 179 years old; facing masonry, more modern; date stone, 1814. BUCKINGHAM, Tavern, General Green's headquarters, lunch room restored in ancient style; Friends Meeting House, with lost graves of Continental soldiers along roadside;

BUCKS COUNTY 165

Buckingham Mountain and Wolf Rocks, center of runaway slave settlement, old negro church on summit; left of Old York Road, ancient limestone quarries and kilns; HOLICONG or "Conkey Hole" deep funnel-shaped depression with water hole in neighboring field; residence of Colonel H. D. Paxson, contains unique collection of light and fire making apparatus, and of North American Indian objects including the Lenape Stone; LAHASKA, Dr. Staveley's residence, "Bleak House." AQUETONG, Logan's or Ingham Spring, one of the largest limestone springs in East United States, residence of Samuel Ingham, General Jackson's Secretary of State; north of York Road, SOLEBURY, Friends Meeting House.

CENTER BRIDGE, on the Delaware, house in which William G. Whittier, the poet, lived. Residence of Edward W. Redfield, landscape painter, many of his paintings are made from scenes in this vicinity. NEW HOPE, summer art colony, residence W. L. Lathrop, and other artists; Parry House, "Cintra," stone, with walls of great thickness, said to have been built by William Maris in 1816, is so strikingly like the famous Octagon House in Washington, D. C., that both were probably from the same model, a wing of the old castle "Cintra" near Lisbon, Portugal; the heavy paneled cherry doors, with silver-plated knobs, on first floor, are said to have been originally part of Robert Morris' house, "The Hills," in Fairmount Park; Mr. Maris is credited with several buildings in New Hope, also, near New Hope, "Spring Dale," with octagonal entrance hall, once the home of Dr. Charles Huffnagle, who was United States Consul to Calcutta and later United States Consul

General to British India; who brought a notable collection of curios from the Orient which for many years were on exhibition at Spring Dale.

In December, 1776, four brigades under Generals Sterling, Mercer, Stephen, and De Fermoy, were posted from Yardley's to Coryell's Ferry, now New Hope, to guard fords above Trenton. Farmhouse of William Keith above Brownsburg, built, 1763; marked, inscription, "Washington's headquarters previous to Battle of Trenton, December 14–25, 1776." Old Eagle Tavern to right, fine view of river, hills, and valley southward; picturesque valley of Knowles Creek along Jericho Hill, site of American Army camp. North, line of William Penn's first Bucks County purchase from the Indians, near site of Indian town Playwicky; below, "Lurgan," near river, named in honor of James Logan's birthplace in County Armagh, Ireland. On December 25, Washington and army crossed the river at McConkey's Ferry, now TAYLORSVILLE, before midnight; nine hundred-foot bridge there now; twenty-four hundred troops were transported by 3.00 A. M. December 26; marched to Trenton, in two divisions, under Generals Greene and Sullivan, conquered the Hessians, and recrossed the river same evening, with nearly one thousand prisoners, arms, and several cannon.

At NEWTOWN, then county seat, Washington wrote of his victory to the President of Congress, December 27, 1776, in residence of John Harris; his headquarters until December 29. Old Brick Hotel, built, 1684, enlarged, 1764, called, "The Red Lion," Hessian prisoners were brought here; in 1829, residence of Major

Joseph O. V. S. Archambault, born at Fontainebleau, France, aide to Napoleon in Battle of Waterloo, member of his household at St. Helena; was visited here by Prince Murat and Joseph Bonaparte. Old Friends Meeting House; old Court House; and Bank, robbed by the Doans after the Revolution. North of Newtown, one mile, WRIGHTSTOWN, Lenape monument, on site of chestnut tree, land given by Miss Martha Chapman, inscription, "To the memory of the Lenni-Lenape Indians, ancient owners of the region, these stones are placed on this spot; the starting point of the 'Indian Walk,' September 19, 1735, Bucks County Historical Society, 1890." Friends Meeting House; nearby, in fields, site of cave house of John Chapman, first settler: very beautiful views beyond Buckmansville toward Wrightstown, Solebury Mountain in plain view. On Richboro Pike, at RICHBORO and CHURCHVILLE are Dutch Reformed churches, about 200 years old; near is Southampton Baptist Church, built, 1764. From WRIGHTSTOWN, through YARDLEYVILLE to MORRISVILLE, population 3639; opposite Trenton; Island off lower part was first Pennsylvania land occupied by Europeans, 1624; first ferry, 1640. "Summer Seat," built by Thomas Barkley, 1773, conveyed to Robert Morris, 1791, still standing; was Washington's headquarters December 8 to 14, 1776; Lincoln Highway enters Pennsylvania here. FALLSINGTON, Friends Meeting House and quaint old buildings.

Return to Philadelphia on Bristol and Frankford Turnpike; "The King's Highway," laid out by Provincial Council, first road cut through Bucks County; early milestones still standing; pass Wheat Sheaf to

Pennsbury, site of William Penn's country house, frames and other work brought from England; he lived here one year. EDGELY, greenhouses where "Queen of Edgely Rose" originated; Landreth's seed farms above BRISTOL, population, 10,273, named for Bristol, England, home of William Penn's wife, Hannah Callowhill; the Keene house, built by Major Lenox, 1816, American minister to England, his niece, Sarah Lukens Keene, inherited and died here, bequeathing it to the Protestant Episcopal Church of Philadelphia, in trust, as home for aged gentlewomen; St. James' Protestant Episcopal Church, built, 1712, has silver communion service presented by Queen Anne, church was used for stable by cavalry during the Revolution; interesting burial ground, tomb of Captain John Green of American Navy, said to have been first to carry the American flag in voyage around the world. Farmers' Bank of Bucks County, Radcliffe Street, Grecian, Ionic, built by James Craig, nephew of Nicholas Biddle, for residence, bought for bank, 1830.

LANGHORNE, residence of Joseph Richardson, Esq., built, 1738, Edge Hill stone, with white oak joists and rafters, sawed by hand with pit saw, now occupied by his descendants; headquarters of Lafayette and Dr. Peter Yarnall. "Night after battle of Trenton, part of Washington's army came to Attleboro," now Langhorne: old Galloway House, Trevose, residence of Jeremiah Langhorne, part owner of Durham Furnace. One mile east, on Lincoln Highway, is stone mansion, one of the oldest in Pennsylvania, exterior is in original state, residence of the late A. Haller Gross, Esq., notable for its art, architecture, and landscape gardening; an addition, in French chateau style, built, 1911, has rooms and floors enriched by very beautiful tiles, designed and made by Dr. Henry C. Mercer; his work is further shown on the terraces and gardens; in a fountain of green enameled tiles; the concrete balustrade, and pavilion dragons and other devices are in the sunken Moorish garden; and in the Italian garden, with its pergola, sun dial and fountain. BYBERRY, birthplace Dr. Benjamin Rush in 1745, house still standing; and Friends Meeting House, with large library. EDDINGTON, St. Francis Roman Catholic Industrial School, built and endowed by the Drexel family; CORNWELLS, "Castle of State in Schuylkill"; ANDALUSIA, named by John Craig, Philadelphia merchant, in memory of successful ventures in Spain; here is Church of the Redeemer and King Free Library. Old Red Lion Inn, on the Pike, near three-arched stone bridge, over Poquessing Creek, Washington's army encamped around it in 1781, on march to Yorktown; seven years earlier, Massachusetts delegates to the First Continental Congress stopped here.

TORRESDALE, Philadelphia County, place of fine residences; Eden Hall now Convent of St. Elizabeth. BUSTLETON, old Baptist Church, with interesting burial ground. Over Pennypack Creek, two arched stone bridge, date, 1800, style has been reproduced in the Fairmount Park trolley bridges. HOLMESBURG, Edwin Forrest Home, "Spring Brook," and one hundred and eleven acres, bequeathed by him, for retired actors, men and women; bought in 1865 for his country seat; House of Correction, accommodates 1000; well-kept grounds. Over Pennypack Creek, stone bridge built 1697–8, in good repair, oldest in Pennsylvania; about a mile distant, near Rowland Station, is old Crispin Cemetery, contains monument, inscription, "In memory of Thomas Holmes, died, 1695, age 71, Surveyor General for William Penn, he drafted the plan and laid out the City of Philadelphia." BRIDESBURG, United States Arsenal. FRANKFORD, site of a Delaware Indian Camp, on banks of Frankford Creek; many arrowheads have been found in this locality; Indian names are retained at Tacony, Tackawanna, Wissinoming; an interesting Roman Catholic Church, Gothic, is at Tacony, also Louis A. Burk's Japanese garden and orchid farm. Swedes settled here in 1667, and were followed by the English. Philadelphia delegates to the First Continental Congress came to Frankford in 1774 to meet the Massachusetts delegates on their way to the city, and held a conference here relative to the Independence of the colonies, which decided the destiny of the nation. In 1781 General Washington and his army marched through Frankford from New York to Yorktown; a stop was made at the "Jolly Post Hotel," built, 1680, on Frankford Avenue north of Orthodox Street.

In 1824 Lafayette passed through Frankford from Bristol to Philadelphia, riding in an open carriage drawn by six cream-colored horses, with postilions; he was escorted by a detachment of the City Troop under command of Captain Albert Ashmead, Captain of the Philadelphia County Troop; the Washington Grays, and several other companies of mounted volunteers. Rooms of the Frankford Historical Society, Frankford Avenue north of Sellers Street, contain many objects of interest, illustrating this locality in old times. Residence of Commodore Stephen Decatur is on Powder Mill Lane. The old Friends' Meeting House, corner of Unity and Waln Streets, was organized in 1682; first log church built, 1698; present building, 1775.

Rehoboth Methodist Church, formed in 1830; used the old Academy; the Supreme Court met here in 1800; now on Paul Street below Unity Street; present building Spanish architecture, dark brick, erected, 1879. St. Mark's Protestant Episcopal Church was a Mission of Trinity, Oxford; started in 1709; present church, Frankford Avenue below Sellers Street, erected in 1908; English, Fourteenth century Gothic; Port Deposit granite with Indiana limestone trimmings; architects, Watson and Huckle; windows by D'Ascenzo and Tiffany. Frankford Presbyterian Church, corner of Frankford Avenue and Church Street, was originally German Reformed; corner-stone laid, 1770; for many years the church was supplied with a preacher from the Market Square Church, Germantown; present building erected, 1859; architect, McArthur. St. Joachim's Roman Catholic Church, corner of Church and Franklin Streets, built, 1874; Gothic, brownstone and sandstone; has a very beautiful tower, resembling that of Magdalen College, Oxford; architect, Edwin Durang; contains three carved marble altars; also a large mosaic, and memorial windows from Munich.

Automobile, north from Centre Bridge, River Road, to DURHAM, commands some of the most beautiful views in eastern Pennsylvania; through LUMBERVILLE, Devil's Half Acre; right, at Like Kiln, site of important Indian fishing village, many relics have been found here. POINT PLEASANT, mouth of Tohickon Creek,

Indians quarried argillite rock for blade material; RIDGES ISLAND, Indian village site; grave of Edward Marshall of the "Indian Walk," in his family graveyard. Tinicum Creek, picturesque gorges, ringing rocks, cliffs of the narrows, with fine view from Table Rock, very rare "ice plant" grows here. Hill Presbyterian Church, built, 1761, on Durham Road near OTTSVILLE.

KINTERSVILLE, ruins of Durham Furnace, built, 1727, stone, thirty-five feet square at base, thirty feet high; large leather bellows used to give the blast, were operated by a water wheel; charcoal fuel was made in pits close at hand; in 1758, Durham was regarded as best iron works in the country; in 1773, one thousand acres were reserved for the furnace; fire backs and stove plates were made here until 1794, when it blew out; eight genuine, Durham fire backs are at "Stenton," Germantown, home of James Logan, who was one-fourth owner of the furnace, three bear the date, 1728; cannon balls for the Revolutionary war were made here in quantities, specimens may be seen in the Bucks County Historical Society; in 1773 Joseph Galloway became first individual owner, it then comprised over eight thousand acres, and was leased to George Taylor, at one time a filler at the furnace; he later was a signer of the Declaration of Independence; scanty remains of the once celebrated Durham Cave, destroyed for its limestone as flux for iron ore. The road passes site of Indian village of Pechequeolin, jasper quarries worked by Indians for arrowheads on neighboring Rattlesnake Hill. Fine old stone arch bridges over Tohickon and Durham

Creeks. RIEGELSVILLE, old Reformed and Lutheran Churches.

Places of interest in Bucks County, north and west of Doylestown, via Easton and Dublin Turnpikes, PLUMSTEADVILLE, beautiful views of Haycock Mounttain, and upper county, Moses Doan's grave, marked with inscription; west, DUBLIN to HILLTOWN, two Mennonite and Amish meeting houses, stone arch bridge over Deep Run. PERKASIE, Trinity Lutheran Church, mural painting in chancel, "Angel with Trinity Symbol," the late H. Hanley Parker, artist.

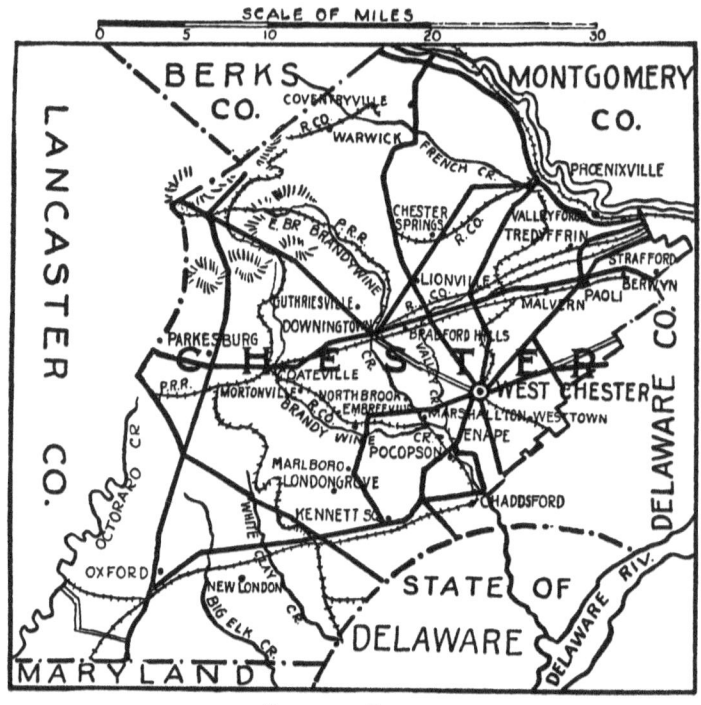

CHESTER COUNTY

III
CHESTER COUNTY

THIRD county formed by William Penn; named for Chester, England. This is rich agricultural district; its broad well-kept farms, great gray barns, and comfortable homesteads of stone or brick, many still occupied by descendants of the original Quaker settlers; together with the gently rolling surface of the country and its many beautiful streams, all combine to give the county a character of its own, of quiet pastoral charm. Both the family names and place names indicate in a general way the character of the original settlement of the county, Birmingham, Bradford, Marlborough, and Kennett indicating the settlements of the English Quakers in the central and southern portion of the county: Tredyffrin and Berwyn, those of the Welsh in the east; while the Germans came later into parts of the north; and the Scotch-Irish Presbyterians into the southwest.

The Lincoln Highway, Lancaster Pike, enters the county at STRAFFORD; St. Peter's Protestant Episcopal Church, built, 1823; Eagle schoolhouse, 1772, on site of Lutheran log church, 1767, one of the cradles of the nation in education; now contains historical library and relics of the neighborhood; site, of "Spread Eagle Inn," built, 1732, post and relay station.

PAOLI, 535 feet above sea, Tredyffrin township. "The General Paoli Inn," built by General Joshua Evans, who was elected to State Legislature, 1820;

recruiting went on briskly here for War of 1812. Road southwest to West Chester, nine miles. One mile south of Paoli, colonial homestead, "Waynesborough," birthplace of General Anthony Wayne, built, 1724, in original condition, now residence of Captain William Wayne; contains many relics of the General; Lafayette was guest here one night; marked with bronze tablet; near Paoli is Great Valley Baptist Church, second oldest in state, built by Rev. Hugh Davis, from Wales, 1722; present church, 1805; interesting burial ground. DUFFRYNMAWR Post Office, "The Green Tree," George King, builder and host, died 1792, native blue limestone, stopping place for Mennonites and Amish.

MALVERN, terminus of the West Chester Railroad in 1833, cars were then drawn by horses; "The Warren Inn," stopping place for Lancaster County Germans, sold to John Penn, 1776; British army quartered here before Paoli Massacre; in 1786, sold to Casper Fahnestock, member of German Mystic Community at Ephrata; three fugitive French princes were here in 1789, Louis Phillipe, Duke de Montpensier, and Count de Beaujolais.

One mile southwest of Malvern, site of Paoli Massacre, 1777; two monuments, marble, 1817, granite, 1877, same inscriptions, erected by Republican Artillerists of Chester County and citizens; here General Wayne's company, fifteen hundred men, were surprised by a greatly superior force of British under General Grey, and charged with bayonet before they could arm for defense; Wayne saved his artillery.

DOWNINGTOWN, birthplace of Jacob Eicholtz, artist.

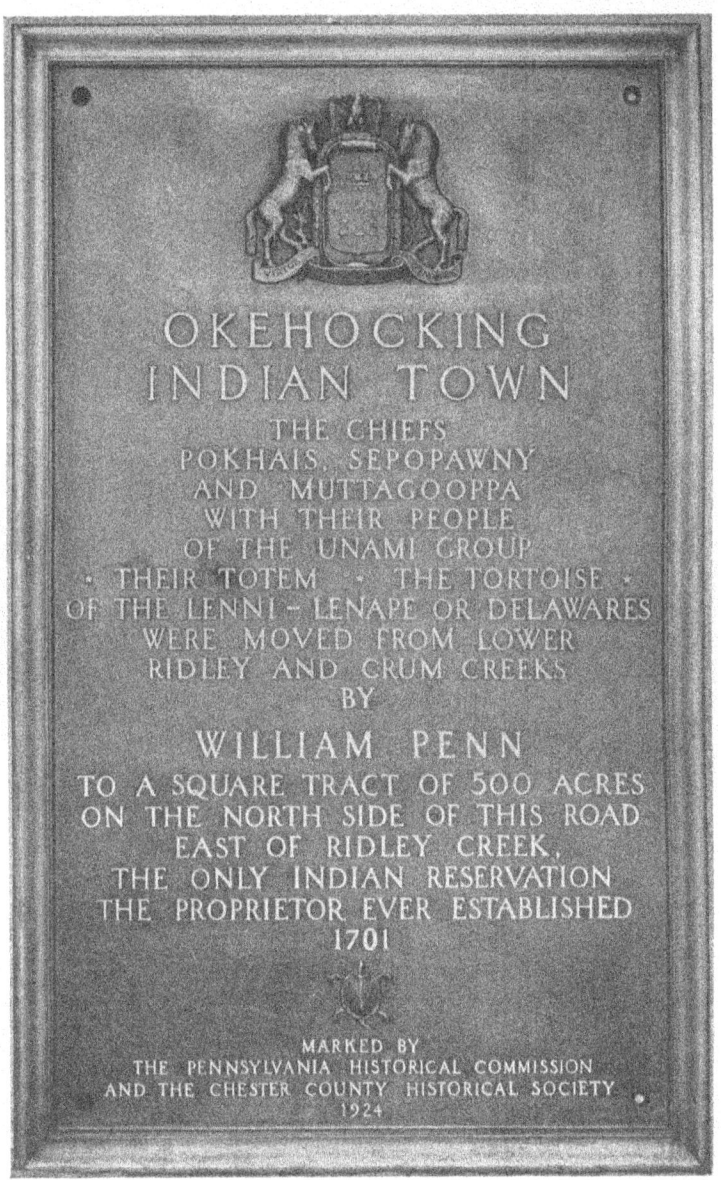

BRONZE TABLET IN BOULDER
This is located on the farm of Dr. Thomas G. Ashton, near Willistown

Designed by Paul P. Cret

CHESTER COUNTY 177

"General George Washington Inn" known as Downings, now a dwelling. Interesting colonial mansion of the Thomas family, well preserved, now, Public Library. "The Ship Tavern" one mile west, old sign perforated with bullet holes by Continental soldiers, now a residence. Old gray stone bridge across the East Brandywine, built, 1741.

Two miles north, near Guthrieville, birthplace of Thomas Buchanan Read in 1822, poet and artist; marked, bronze tablet.

On the limestone road, following Indian trail, leading from Parkesburg to Oxford and south, are Faggs Manor, six miles northeast of Oxford, classical school, established, 1739; marked, bronze tablet. St. John's Presbyterian Church, early burial ground; Whitefield stood under the old oak trees.

An interesting early highway known as the "Street Road," laid out in part by William Penn, has almost the directness and width of a Roman road; entering the county near Westtown, and crossing Brandywine Creek at Pocopson, to London Grove, original name, Marlborough; Street, stately old Quaker Meeting House at London Grove; wonderful oak trees.

WEST CHESTER, county seat, formed, 1786, population 11,717. In one block, High Street between Gay and Market Streets, are good specimens of the three great orders of Grecian architecture, designed by Thomas U. Walter, architect of Capitol at Washington; National Bank of Chester County, built, 1836, Doric, white marble; First National Bank, Ionic, white marble; the Court House, Corinthian, built, 1847, Pictou stone; on Court House lawn is Soldiers'

Monument to Civil War patriots, bronze figure, granite base, erected, 1915; sculptor, Harry Lewis Raul. Public Library, North Church Street, memorial to Bayard Taylor, contains interesting collection of his manuscripts; "The Story of Kennett," his books, sketches, and other relics; also marble bust of General Anthony Wayne; sculptor, W. Marshall Swayne. The new Library of the State Normal School contains portrait of Washington by Peale, painted at Valley Forge; historic autograph letters; Indian stone relics; large herbarium; and small permanent collection of original paintings, among them works by Hugh Breckenridge and Mary Butler; annual exhibitions of modern paintings and sculpture are held; Della Robbia reproductions in auditorium; Chester County Historical Society rooms are here, containing many interesting local historical collections; addresses on subjects of local historic interest are frequently given, and published in their bulletins.

Churches noteworthy for architecture, Holy Trinity, Protestant Episcopal, South High Street, native serpentine stone, Gothic; and Westminster Presbyterian, South Church Street, tower suggests famous one of Magdalen College, Oxford. At north end of High Street, stone drinking fountain, surmounted by bronze figure of boy, sculptor, Martha J. Cornwell; placed by New Century Club. Marshall Square, a public park, contains rare collection of trees. West Chester, noted for men of repute in scientific world, was the residence of the late Dr. Joseph Trimble Rothrock; in 1893 he drew up a bill creating a Forestry Commission, to investigate and report upon the forestry conditions of

CHESTER COUNTY

Pennsylvania, this bill was passed, and in 1895 he was appointed Commissioner of Forestry.

Favorite drives, with succession of beautiful vistas, are along the East Brandywine from Downingtown south, and West Brandywine, from Mortonville south. At MORTONVILLE, three miles southeast of Coatesville, is fine, old, gray stone bridge, with four arches, graduated in width, and rounded buttresses; built, 1826.

Following the stream, and crossing several picturesque wooden covered bridges, through EMBREEVILLE, a half mile east of which is Point Lookout, where sentries were posted to guard supplies for American Encampment at Valley Forge; marked by Chester County Chapter of the Daughters of the American Revolution; opposite is "Star Gazers' Stone," set by Mason and Dixon, 1764, in running a base line for boundary between Pennsylvania and Maryland; here they made various astronomical observations; calculated the force of gravity; and measured a degree of latitude on the earth's surface southward; this stone was walled and marked, with bronze tablet. Several places in the vicinity, connected with the Lenni-Lenape Indians, are also marked; in County Home, grounds, grave of Indian Hannah, last of her race in this county; site of her cabin half mile south of NORTHBROOK; Indian cemetery half mile west of Northbrook; and Indian Rock, just west of Northbrook; from the latter point the Indian chief, Checochinican, claimed that land had been reconveyed to the tribe up to source of stream, a mile on either side; these negotiations, in the picturesque language used by the chief, are among the records of the provincial assembly; Okehocking, Indian Town, has been marked by tablet.

Just east of Northbrook, birthplace of Humphry Marshall, botanist; two miles north, at MARSHALLTON, adjoining his old home, is interesting arboretum, still containing many trees planted by him; marked with bronze tablet.

Continue drive to LENAPE, amusement park, where East Branch of the Brandywine, from Downingtown, unites with western; down main stream, skirting, just above Pocopson, a beautiful spot, Dungeon Bottom; and passing several antique, covered, wooden bridges, to CHADDS FORD; here the ranks of British, Hessians, and Continentals charged to and fro at Battle of Brandywine, September 11, 1777; two miles northeast, old BIRMINGHAM meeting house, used as hospital by troops, and center of some of the fiercest fighting; many points connected with the battle were marked with tablets by Chester County Historical Society, in connection with State Historical Commission, in 1915.

On State Highway, six miles west of Chadds Ford, Kennett Square, birthplace of Bayard Taylor, poet and traveler, and his later home "Cedar-Croft," built by him, one mile south, both marked with bronze tablets; he was buried at Longwood Meeting House, about two miles east; artistic monument, a cylindrical stone; at this meeting house, of "Progressive Friends," many prominent leaders of anti-slavery spoke before the Civil War. This region was center of anti-slavery sentiment, many of the old Quaker homesteads were stations of the so-called "underground railroad," by which fugitive slaves were protected and carried north-

BAYARD TAYLOR MONUMENT, LONGWOOD

CHESTER COUNTY

ward. Half mile north of Longwood Meeting House is "Pierce's Park," now owned by Pierre du Pont, Esq., contains wonderful trees, planted over a century ago by Samuel and Joshua Pierce, who rode on horseback to the Dismal Swamp for cypresses and brought them home in saddlebags. Mr. du Pont has recently added an unusually beautiful flower garden and conservatory; visitors admitted free on week days.

KENNETT SQUARE, Bayard Taylor Memorial Library, contains first editions of his books, his paintings, and his drawings; also busts of Bayard Taylor and John Welsh; sculptor, W. Marshall Swayne. In Advent Protestant Episcopal Church, memorial window to Bayard Taylor. Ten miles southwest, NEW LONDON Academy, founded, 1743, marked by bronze tablet; here were educated three signers of the Declaration of Independence, Thomas McKean, George Reed, and James Smith, and other men of prominence.

Other places of interest, in north of county, are VALLEY FORGE, chiefly in Montgomery County. PHŒNIXVILLE, population 10,484; farthest inland point reached by British, September 21-22-23, 1777; marked by low granite monument opposite Fountain Inn. St. Peter's Protestant Episcopal Church, stone; stained glass windows by Meyer Bros., Munich, Germany; Parish House interior designed by the late George Wattress, pure English, dark oak, with tiled floors; early Iron Industry, Phœnix Iron Company, marked, bronze tablet.

Ten miles northwest of Phœnixville is COVENTRYVILLE, old Coventry Forge, 1717, earliest in county, second in Pennsylvania; Mordecai Lincoln, ancestor of Abraham Lincoln, worked here and was part owner in 1725. WARWICK, Warwick Furnace, Potts and Rutter, proprietors, 1737; here was cast the first Franklin stove, and others with quaint designs and Biblical verses; cannon and cannon balls were made here for the Revolutionary Army; marked. Seven miles west of Phœnixville, at CHESTER SPRINGS, is summer art school of the Pennsylvania Academy of the Fine Arts, forty acres, with buildings for studios, and lodging houses for the students; one of these buildings was used as a Revolutionary Hospital, marked; former name, "Yellow Springs," a watering resort in colonial days.

Marking on all places has been by the Chester County Historical Society unless otherwise stated.

IV
LANCASTER COUNTY

FORMED May 10, 1729, by request of the proprietaries, on site of an Indian village; it was named for Lancashire, England, derived from Lan-Castra, the Camp at Lan, permanent camp of Roman occupation of Britain two thousand years ago. Earliest settlers, Swiss Mennonites, who, in 1710, had warrants for ten thousand acres of land on Pequea Creek; leader, Bishop Hans Herr; his stone house, built by himself on this tract, is still standing, with initials and date cut over front door, "C. H. H. 1719." A fine Mennonite meeting house, lately built, is here; on the grounds is huge boulder, marked by the Lancaster County Historical Society. This is the richest agricultural county in the United States, of unexampled fertility; the tourist is impressed with the mammoth barns of this region; luxuriant crops of tobacco are of special note. The Conestoga River, with its affluents, drains an area of 315 square miles, it is crossed by many bridges. On the border of the city limits is a nine arch stone bridge, built by Abraham Witmer in 1800, which leads the Lincoln Highway over the Conestoga. At Pequea is St. John's Protestant Episcopal Church, according to a quaint old Vestry Book "Built of wood in 1729, to perform Divine Adoration . . . after ye manner of ye Episcopal Church of England," the itinerant missionaries of the Society for the Propagation of the Gospel of England holding service; corner-

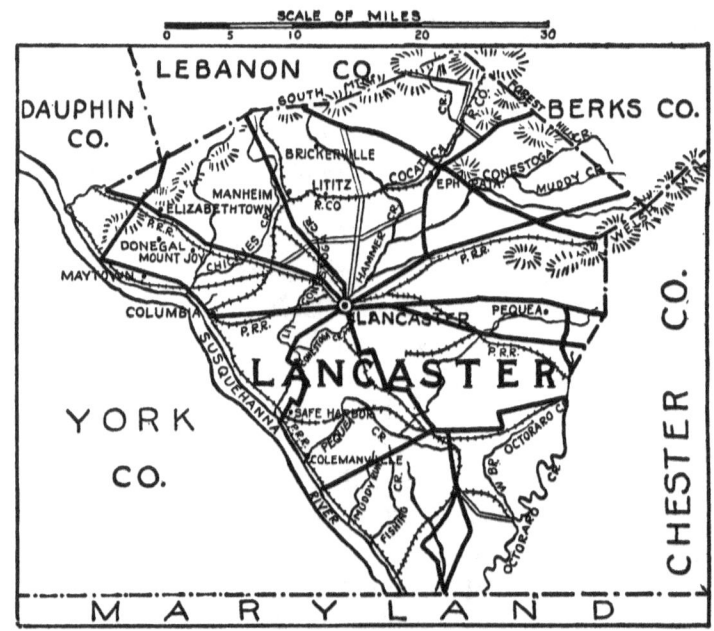

Lancaster County

stone of present church building was laid by Bishop Onderdonk, the rector at that time being Rev. Edward Young Buchanan, brother of President James Buchanan; the parish possesses two vestry books of great historic value.

Most famous group of historic buildings are those erected by the Seventh Day Baptists, founded by Conrad Beisel in 1722, at EPHRATA, on the Cocalico; monastery still in original condition, with cells and rooms; and the adjoining chapel little changed; the brothers and sisters lived, each in their narrow cell, like monks of the Middle Ages; a printing press was set up in 1743, on which were printed the largest books in America prior to 1860; first Sunday schools in America were said to have been started here in 1740; and Henry William Steigel introduced glass making. Joining the Cloister Settlement is Clare Point Stock Farm, now occupied by the Redemptorist Fathers, a Roman Catholic order, founded in 1732 by St. Alphonsus Maria Leguori, in Italy; of strict discipline and singleness of purpose, designed to work among neglected country people; this is their only mission in Pennsylvania.

County seat, LANCASTER, 418 feet above sea, population 53,150; laid out by Governor Gordon in 1730; near by is the Conestoga River, named by Conestoga Indians, a tribe of the Delawares; the Dutch who lived here invented the wagon, with big covered tops, drawn by six horses, and named it for the river. It is said that here was first given to Washington the title "Des Landes Vater." This is a square city, lines run north and south, east and west, with outlying districts;

one, Rossmere, was named in honor of George Ross, a signer of the Declaration of Independence.

The Continental Congress arrived here from Philadelphia the very day Sir William Howe entered that city; the next day they moved to York. This was the Capital of the State from 1799–1812, and birthplace of Simon Snyder, Governor of Pennsylvania 1808–1817. In center of Penn Square is a monument to soldiers and sailors of the Civil War. One block away is the court house, on East King Street, built about 1850; architect, Samuel Sloan; Corinthian; contains portraits of Hon. Isaac E. Hiester by Isaac Williams, and Hon. W. U. Hensel by Lazare Raditz, Philadelphia. Jail, East King Street, Norman castellated, red sandstone, built, 1850, architect, John Haviland. Fountain, East King Street, on reservoir grounds, made, 1905, memorial to John Williamson Nevin; bronze lion, sculptor, Blanche Nevin.

Michael Schlatter and Henry Melchior Muhlenberg, leaders of the Reformed and Lutheran Germans, were in favor of higher education, and established Franklin College in 1787, forming the beginning of Franklin and Marshall College; built on an eminence west of city; main building Elizabethan, brick, built, 1854–55, with beautiful entrance door, contains portraits. In the Watts de Peyster Library are bronze busts of the father and mother of General de Peyster. St. Stephen's Chapel has memorial window to Rev. John W. Nevin, D.D., LL.D., made by Armstrong, New York. On the campus is bronze heroic statue of Abraham de Peyster, made in New York, 1895, replica of one facing New York Custom House. The

MAIN BUILDING FRANKLIN AND MARSHALL COLLEGE, LANCASTER

LANCASTER COUNTY 187

scientific building contains oil paintings, among them one by J. D. Wiltkamp, "The Three Women of Grève-Coeur." Buchanan Park, opened, 1905, joins the college campus and grounds of the Reformed Theological Seminary. "Wheatland," residence of President James Buchanan, is near, on Marietta Pike, colonial, brick, built prior to 1812. St. Joseph's Hospital and Roman Catholic Church are near college; hospital contains portrait of Henry E. Muhlenberg, M.D., by Caroline Peart Brinton; the church windows are from Munich and Innspruck.

Among Lancaster's numerous churches are, the Moravian, West Orange Street, rear part stone, built, 1750, oldest in the city, brick front added, 1820. First Reformed, East Orange Street, brick; Romanesque; built, 1852–54; two steeples, contains lectern and other pieces of woodcarving by A. Lang of Oberammergau, nephew of Anton Lang, made, 1905; decorations by J. F. Lamb, New York; windows from Tiffany and D'Ascenzo studios; bronze memorial tablet by Martha Hovenden. St. James Protestant Episcopal, corner of East Orange and North Duke Streets, Norman, brick; main walls built, 1820, added to 1870 and 1910; chancel windows from England, others by Lamb and the Tiffany Studios, New York; oil painting, "The Crucifixion," artist, Jacob Eicholtz; pictorial tile base at altar, by Dr. Henry Mercer; in parish house is fifteenth century oil painting, Urbanean School. St. Anthony's Roman Catholic, East Orange Street, bronze altar and statues from Oux et Cie, Paris; frescoes by Ludwig Reingruber are adaptations of old masters. Trinity Lutheran, South Duke Street, brick; fine old Georgian style, compares with Christ Church, Philadelphia; built, 1761; tower and spire added, 1794; wood sculpture, four evangelists, at base of tower; original pipe organ built, 1771, was utilized in new organ; memorial windows by the Tiffany Company, and by Joseph Lauber, New York City.

Fulton Opera House, Prince Street between Orange and West King Streets, on site of massacre of Conestoga Indians by Paxtang boys in 1763, over entrance, life-size statue, carved wood, of Robert Fulton, made, 1852, sculptor, Hugh Cannon: the Lancaster County Historical Society placed a tablet on the wall of Robert Fulton's birthplace, built, 1765; southern part of Lancaster County, Fulton Township, A. Herr Smith, Memorial Free Library, North Duke Street; Italian villa style; contains portraits of notable men identified with Lancaster County. Post Office and Revenue Building, North Duke Street, Italian Renaissance; Indiana limestone; built by United States Government. Guaranty Trust Company, North Duke Street, Ionic, marble, built, 1912. The Henry G. Long Asylum, corner of Marietta and West End Avenues, contains two portraits by Jacob Eicholtz. The Iris Club, founded by Miss Alice Nevin, has annual exhibition of paintings.

In Woodward Hill Cemetery, southern part of city, on the Conestoga, is tomb of President James Buchanan. Greenwood Cemetery, end of South Queen Street, has stone entrance, made, 1895, by Rothenberger. Tomb of Thaddeus Stevens, white and black marble and granite, is in Shreiner burial ground. West Chestnut Street, corner of Shippen and Ross Streets, is inclosure and small brick monument topped by stone sphere, site of George Ross's mansion. Bountiful markets held on the curbs, as well as in the market houses, are a distinctive and picturesque feature of the town; the presence of the Mennonite, Amish, and other sects lends a peculiar aspect to the scene.

Near Rockford, south, is brick colonial mansion, built before 1775, residence of the Revolutionary general, Edward Hand, marked with tablet by local Historical Society. The birthplace of Dr. David Ramsey, historian, built, 1749, is still standing. Williamson Park, end of South Drake Street, on Conestoga River, acquired by gift in 1902, has wild scenic beauty. Long's Park on Harrisburg Pike, two miles from city, acquired by gift, scenic, opened, 1903. Between Mount Joy and Maytown is Donegal Presbyterian Church, built prior to the Revolution, a quaint building with gambrel roof; interesting burial ground with the witness tree; Cameron family bury here.

HERSHEY, the chocolate town, a model village, out of which daily roll fifteen cars loaded with candies and chocolate; in 1915 Dunkards came from all over the United States to the annual conference of the "Church of the Brethren," held in convention hall which seats six thousand, built for them by M. S. Hershey, largest meeting in the history of their church.

LITITZ, settled by Moravians, 1748, has Moravian boarding school for girls, "Linden Hall," founded, 1749; in the town park are the famous Lititz Springs;

Lititz is also famous for pretzels, first made by William Rauch in 1710.

MANHEIM, laid out by Henry William Steigel, 1762, was named for his German home town; here he built a large glass factory, first in the United States; skilled workmen from Europe were employed; a few rare specimens of this glass, owned by collectors, show fineness of quality, richness of color, and a peculiar bell-like ring, some specimens are in the Danner Museum, open Tuesdays, free, to visitors, which outrivals some, more noted, in the rarity and variety of its collections: in 1772 Steigel gave to the Lutherans at Manheim a piece of ground on which to build a church; payment to be five shillings and an annual rental of one red rose; on the second Sunday in June, crowds attend the Baron Steigel Memorial Church, and at these services a descendant of the Steigels receives the red rose; the chancel is often filled with red roses dropped there individually as a tribute; in 1752 Steigel had married a daughter of John Jacob Huber, who owned a small iron furnace near Brickerville, he purchased land and became interested in several furnaces, one he named for his wife, "Elizabeth"; the Elizabeth furnace, in 1776, came into possession of Robert Coleman of Lebanon, in 1777 it was overtaxed with large orders of shot and shell for the Continental Army, and the government sent about two hundred Hessian prisoners, taken at Trenton, to work there; many remained and became good citizens. Mr. Coleman's residence was at Elizabeth furnace, here he entertained Washington as his guest, who, at his request, sat for a portrait to

LANCASTER COUNTY

Gilbert Stuart, which is now owned by B. Dawson Coleman, Esq.

Lancaster County furnaces in the Conestoga Valley, Caernarvon Township, were owned by David Jones in 1736; old mines are still there that bear his name; in 1743 David Branson built the Windsor forges, in the same township; among his partners was Lynford Lardner, who married his daughter Rebecca. On the banks of Furnace Run, near Colemanville, may be seen an old cinder heap, which is all that remains of the Martic Furnace, built 1751-52 on 3400 acres of land, with the usual houses and shops; during the Revolution, round iron was drawn under the hammer at the forge, and bored out for musket barrels; negro slaves were always employed here; among the past owners of this furnace, from 1777-93, was a Philadelphia merchant, Michael Hillegas, who became first Continental treasurer in 1775; in 1777 he was appointed first treasurer of the United States and continued in that office until 1789.

Near, just below Safe Harbor, in the Susquehanna River, is Indian Rock, with a number of inscriptions on it, the writing may be seen when water is low; same writing is found in Beaver County. The bridge over the Susquehanna River from Columbia to Wrightsville has been replaced several times, one was burned to stem the tide of the Confederates. At Elizabethtown are the Masonic Homes of Pennsylvania, on 982 acres, with Grand Lodge Hall, 437 feet long by 160 feet wide, seventeen dwelling houses, and other buildings. Georgian architecture, designed by Zantzinger, Borie and Medary.

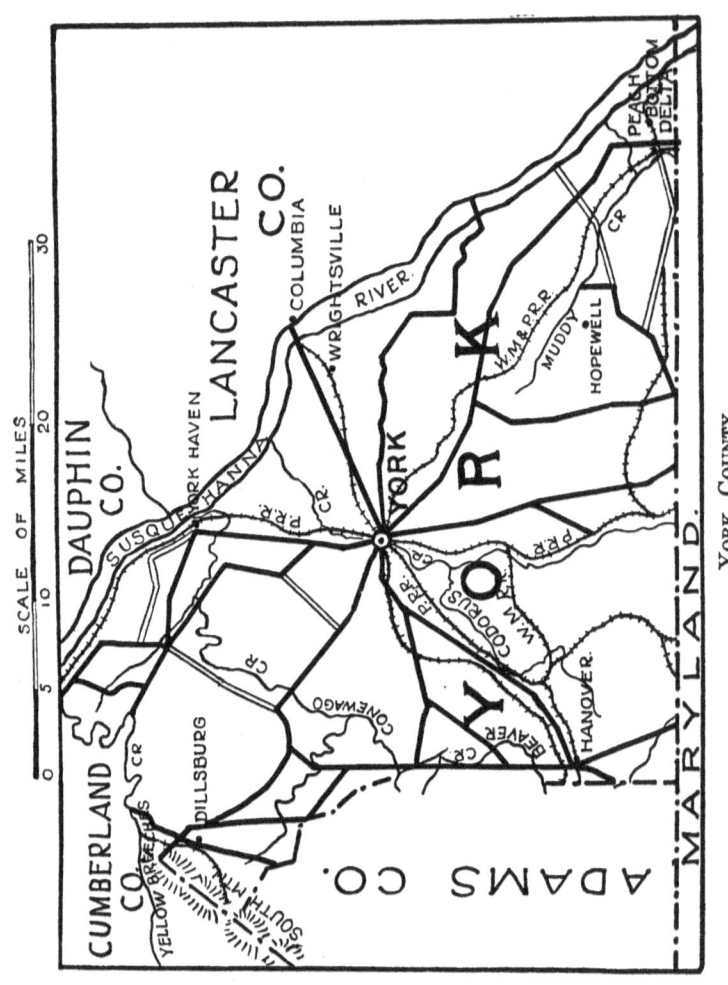

V
YORK COUNTY

FORMED August 9, 1749; named for the House of York, England. An agricultural region of great fertility. First authorized settlements were made in 1733. Before the white settlers came, the territory west of the Susquehanna River was hunting ground for the Conestoga Indians, a branch of the Mohawks, who migrated to New York State about 1750; also for the Susquehannocks and Conewagos, who had their village at present site of York Haven. When a treaty with the Indians at Albany, in 1736, gave Penn's heirs right to the territory from west of the Susquehanna to the South Mountain, immigrants from Europe flocked into York County, in vast numbers, and proved a strong and influential part of the population. During the colonial period four companies of soldiers from this county assisted in driving the French and Indians from the western part of the province before 1758.

At beginning of the Revolutionary War it is said that the first military company from Pennsylvania that arrived at Washington's headquarters, siege of Boston, in 1775, shortly after Battle of Bunker Hill, were from York County; this company, and one commanded by Captain Morgan of Virginia, were first American troops to use rifles; they became the terror of the British regulars, who still used the old-time flint musket. When the British attacked New York City and the Battle of Long Island followed, Pennsylvania troops camped at Perth Amboy; here two regiments from York County were formed out of the militia; and became a part of the Flying Camp, a body of ten thousand men from Pennsylvania, Virginia, and Maryland, which joined Washington before the Battle of White Plains; they were also in the battles of Princeton and Trenton. Colonel Thomas Hartley, a member of York County bar, commanded a brigade under Washington at battles of Brandywine and Germantown; and after the Revolution he represented York County in Congress for twelve years; he was first member of the Pennsylvania bar to be admitted to the Supreme Court of the United States. President Washington was entertained in his house in 1791, site marked by tablet.

Shortly before the Battle of Brandywine, September 27, 1777, the Continental Congress adjourned from Independence Hall to meet in Lancaster; they were there one day, then crossed the Susquehanna and made YORKTOWN the seat of government until June 27, 1778, when they returned to Philadelphia. Twenty-five Congressmen came on horseback over the old Monocacy Road, and took up quarters in the town and vicinity. The personnel of Congress was constantly changing; no less than sixty-four different members were present from first to last. The mansion, corner of Center Square, where the Colonial Hotel now stands, had been rented to General Roberdeau; quarters were found there for the leading Congressmen, Adams, Lee, Harrison, Laurens, and others. John Adams, in letters to his wife Abigail, complained of his straitened quarters, and the Dutch cooking.

YORK COUNTY 195

James Smith, a signer of the Declaration of Independence, gave his law office in Center Square to be used by the Committee of Foreign Affairs; and the Board of War.

The noted chest of papers, belonging to Congress, which John Adams declared "was worth more than Congress itself," was kept by Thomas Paine at the Cooke's House, a house of entertainment, still standing, in the bend of Codorus Creek, then away from town; here he wrote parts five and six of "The Crisis." On September 30, 1777, with John Hancock as President of Congress, the first session was held in the brick court house, built, 1756; site marked by Yorktown Chapter, Daughters of the American Revolution; soon after Congress assembled here, news was brought of the surrender of Burgoyne to General Gates, with six thousand British and Hessian troops, at Saratoga. A motion, made by Richard Henry Lee of Virginia, to set apart a day for Thanksgiving was unanimously adopted; Thursday, December 18, 1777, was appointed, and a few days later this historic document was written, and sent by post riders to the governors of each of the thirteen original states; this was the first national Thanksgiving proclamation in America, in the sense of its observation, on the same date, by the thirteen states.

Soon after, General Lafayette arrived in Yorktown and was received in open session by Congress; the victory of General Gates had made him the hero of the hour; Washington had been defeated at Brandywine and Germantown, and gone into winter quarters at Valley Forge; knowing that a large number of the delegates in Congress at Yorktown favored a plan to displace him from the head of the army, and promote General Gates to that position, Washington never visited Congress here; he wrote a private letter to Robert Morris, saying, "If Congress adjourns, *sine die*, I wish it understood, I will oppose British invasion, in the mountains of Pennsylvania and Virginia, rather than give up our cause for Independence, promulgated July 4, 1776"; this historic letter was read at an open meeting in Zion Reformed Church.

Congress called General Gates to York, and made him President of the Board of War; he gave a banquet at his headquarters; among the guests was Lafayette, twenty-one years of age; speeches were made favoring the promotion of Gates to position of general in chief of the army, when Lafayette arose and offered the following toast: "To General George Washington, head of the American Army; may he continue to hold that position until a Treaty of Peace is signed with England, acknowledging the freedom of this country, in whose cause I am listed for its defense." It was this incident that caused the collapse of the Conway Cabal, instigated by General Conway, opponent of Washington and friend of Gates.

Lafayette visited York in 1825, then sixty-eight years old, and last surviving Major General of the Revolution; he stopped overnight at McGrath's Hotel, on site of the Rupp Building, where a reception and banquet were given him; among the toasts was, "Lafayette, we love him as a man, hail him as a deliverer, revere him as a champion of freedom, and welcome him as a guest"; to which he responded,

YORK COUNTY 197

"The Town of York, the seat of our American Union in our most gloomy time; may her citizens enjoy a proportionate share of American prosperity."

At request of Washington, Baron Steuben came to Yorktown early in 1778, and was immediately appointed to the rank of major-general; from here he went to Valley Forge and began to drill and discipline the Army, in the military tactics used by Frederick the Great. In May, 1778, a nephew of General Putnam, who crossed the Atlantic in the Mercury, a fast flying vessel of Congress, which landed at Portsmouth, New Hampshire, brought a letter to Henry Laurens of South Carolina, President of Congress, from Benjamin Franklin, saying, "The King of France has resolved to send $600,000 in silver, an army and a fleet, to aid the Americans in their struggle for Liberty." The Articles of Confederation were formed here, and adopted in Philadelphia the following June. Much Continental money was ordered by Congress, which was printed in a house, at the corner of Market and Beaver Streets, marked by tablet.

Penn Park has a soldiers' monument, to men of York County in Civil War; this has been the scene of many military gatherings; several insubordinates of the Pennsylvania line were shot here, by order of General Wayne, before the forces under him marched to Virginia; and large hospitals were built here during the Civil War, when York County was the high-water mark of the Southern Confederacy. On June 28, 1863, General Jubal Early of Virginia, with 10,000 Confederate troops, took possession of York. John B. Gordon, leading a brigade of Georgia troops, was first to enter town; he marched on to Wrightsville with twenty-eight hundred men, where a skirmish took place, and when the bridge across the Susquehanna was burned by the Union forces on the Lancaster County side; Early remained in York two days, with four brigades, and received word to fall back immediately to Gettysburg. The first engagement took place in the streets of HANOVER, between Confederate cavalry under Stuart, who were defeated by Union cavalry under Kilpatrick; they were prevented from reaching Gettysburg until evening of second day of battle, which probably turned the tide in favor of the Union; this event is commemorated in the Center Square by a statue, that ranks with the best Art in Pennsylvania, a cavalryman, bronze; sculptor, Cyrus E. Dallim, Boston.

YORK, county seat; population 47,512; is oldest town in Pennsylvania west of the Susquehanna; the general plan embraced streets forming perfect squares, with widened space in center of town, junction of Market and George Streets, for market purposes; these privileges are still used. Court house in east Market Street, classic; porch with granite Ionic columns; built, 1903; architect, J. A. Dempwolf; contains portraits of York County judges; Museum of York County Historical Society, open every afternoon except Sunday; has large collection of Indian implements, of war and peace; and etchings by Rosenthal. An annual art exhibition is held in York. Post Office, classic, Ionic. Among the many places of worship, several now standing were erected more than one hundred years ago, including St. John's Episcopal, in which is tablet to Colonel Thomas Hartley. In burial ground of First Presbyterian Church is tomb of James Smith, the signer, who died, 1806; another

CAVALRY STATUE, ERECTED IN 1904, CENTER SQUARE, HANOVER

Cyrus E. Dellam, Sculptor

signer, Philip Livingston, of New York, who died while Congress was in session here, is buried in Prospect Hill Cemetery, where also are the tombs of General William B. Franklin of the Civil War; his brother Rear Admiral Samuel R. Franklin; Judge Jeremiah S. Black; and several hundred Civil War soldiers.

In mentioning the notable men of York, we must include Colonel Hance Hamilton, first sheriff of York County in 1750; Colonel Richard McAllister, founder of Hanover, first President Justice of the County Courts under the Constitution of 1776, and later President of the Supreme Executive Council of Pennsylvania; James Ross, born, 1762, served two terms in the United States Senate, making there an eloquent speech favoring the Louisiana Purchase, which led to its result; and Senator Matthew S. Quay, born in Dillsburg, 1833, whose father was pastor of the Presbyterian Church. Other places marked by tablet are, site of building of the Franklin Press, where valuable papers were published during the Revolution, and building of General Anthony Wayne's headquarters.

In 1761, the Mary Ann Furnace was built on Furnace Creek; at the same time a road was cut from there, to connect with the road to the Conewago settlement leading to Baltimore; the furnace was started by George Ross of Lancaster, the signer, his brother-in-law, George Stevenson, a lawyer of York County, and William Thompson, later a general in the Revolution; and continued for fifty years, under other owners; besides making pig iron, stoves, and household iron ware, cannon balls and grapeshot were cast here. The Spring Creek Forge was erected by George Ross, previous to 1772, and was active many years.

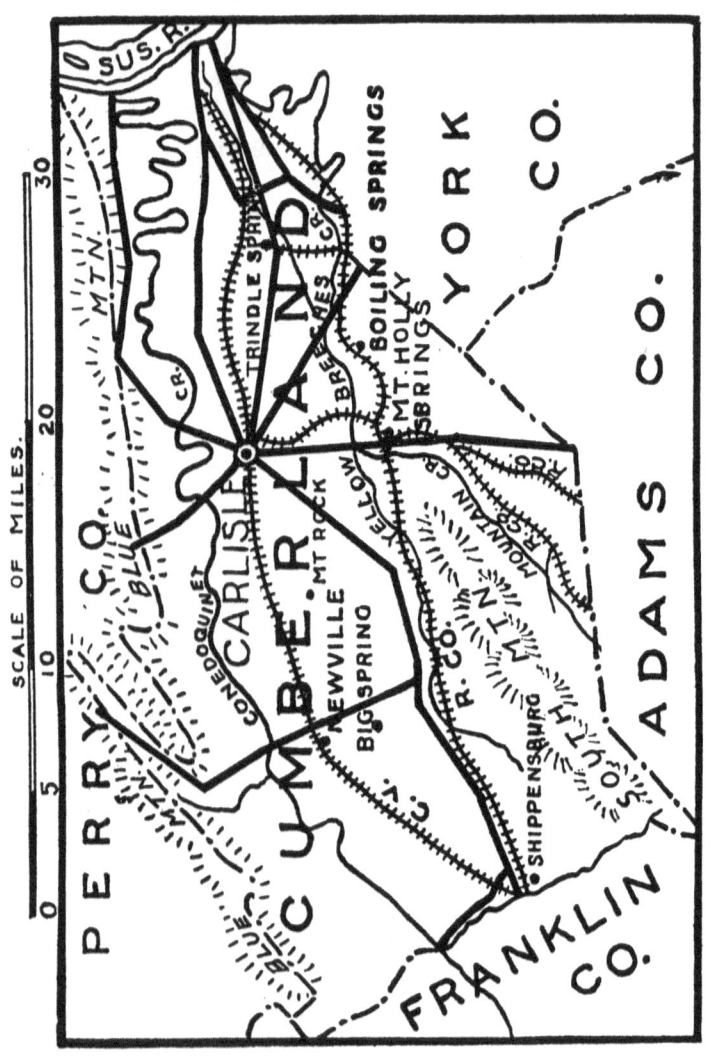
Cumberland County

VI
CUMBERLAND COUNTY

FORMED January 27, 1750; named for county of Cumberland, England. One of the two or three rich agricultural valleys in the United States. Early industries were iron furnaces and forges. First settlers, Scotch-Irish, men of stout heart and wonderful nerve; almost contemporaneous with their building forts and providing means of protection for themselves and families, they established Presbyterian churches, the fine springs of the valley being selected as sites, namely, Silver Springs Church, nine miles west of the Susquehanna; Trindle Spring, now a Lutheran Church; Meeting House Spring, now First Presbyterian Church of Carlisle; curious old carvings are in Meeting House Springs burial ground; Big Spring Church, at Newville; and Middle Spring Church, above Shippensburg, a monument to Revolutionary soldiers is here; all continue in active existence. The early pioneer countenanced the institution of slavery, at one period as many as 307 negroes were held as slaves in this county, the last of them in 1840; on November 1, 1780, an act was passed, directing that all slaves and those held as such in Pennsylvania should be registered; but thereafter all should be free men and women.

SHIPPENSBURG, population 4372, first permanent settlement in the county, founded in 1730, was the only town on the line of the "Great Road" when it was laid out from John Harris' Ferry, on the Susquehanna, to the Potomac, from 1735–44; this road was the first effort to connect the wilderness west of the Susquehanna with the civilization in the earler settlements. First bridge erected in the county was over Letort Spring, on east Main Street, Carlisle, about 1780, replaced in 1795 by a stone bridge; several stone arch bridges are over the Yellow Breeches Creek; at the eastern end is Miller's Mill bridge, over one hundred years old, three arch stone, in good condition; Alexander's bridge is one mile north of Carlisle on the Conodoguinet Creek, colonial with wooden cover, one span, is very old.

County seat, CARLISLE, named for shiretown of Cumberland County, England; population 10,916; the town is laid off at right angles, with a large public square in center; Bellair Park on the banks of Conodoguinet Creek is one mile from center of town; Lindner Park faces Franklin and Louther Streets, five squares from center; Mount Holly and Boiling Springs Parks are outlying, reached by trolley. The courthouse faces Center Square, Corinthian, Bryant & Witt, architects, built, 1846, one of the portico columns shows marks, in broken flutings, of the shelling of Carlisle, captured by General Lee, during the Civil War; contains portraits of judges of the local court. First Presbyterian Church also faces Center Square, main auditorium built in 1757, Greco-Roman, blue limestone with white marble linings, showing early bonding in stone masonry; tower added and parish house built, 1873. The Young Men's Christian Association half square from Center, on High Street, French Renaissance, built, 1908; architect, M. I. Kast, Harrisburg.

CUMBERLAND COUNTY 203

County jail, one square from Center, corner High and Bedford Streets, Tudor, built, 1854, brownstone, is a small copy of the Castle of Carlisle, England, note the limestone arch in east wall of the yard; architects, Myers & Gutshall. Post office, two squares from Center, corner of Pitt and Louther Streets, classic Renaissance, built, 1909, J. Knox Taylor, architect, Washington, D. C. Historical Society, corner of Pitt Street and Dickinson Avenue, brick, built 1878–80, architect, George Rice, contains historical library, papers, and museum.

DICKINSON COLLEGE on campus of seven acres, with law school one square south, Conway Hall one square west, and the Herman Bosler Biddle Memorial Athletic Field, with colonial gateway, made in 1909, architect, H. E. Yessler, three squares west; Main Building, "Old West," built, 1803; blue limestone mellowed by time, with façade of fine proportions; arched doorways and windows; architect, Colonel Latrobe, first government engineer and architect, brought from England; auditorium contains portraits of John Dickinson, Dr. Nisbet, and others; the James W. Bosler Memorial Hall; Romanesque; built in 1885; George Rice, architect; contains portraits of notable alumni, including President James Buchanan and Dr. Benjamin Rush, also marble bust of James Bosler, and fine copy of Salvator Rosa's "The Conspiracy of Cataline," original in the Pitti Palace, Florence; the J. Herman Bosler Memorial Library, architects, Baldwin & Pennington, Baltimore; classic; built, 1899; white marble entrance vestibule, lighted by memorial window, Burne-Jones design, made by

Maitland Armstrong & Company; Denny Memorial Recitation Hall, Collegiate Gothic, built, 1905, M. I. Kast, architect.

St. John's Protestant Episcopal Church faces Center Square, has memorial altar, white marble, with Caen stone reredos, and windows made by Maitland Armstrong & Company; First Lutheran Church, one square east of Center, corner of High and Bedford Streets; Italian Renaissance; yellow brick, black and white trimmings; built, 1900; J. A. Dempwolf, architect, York, Pennsylvania. The second Presbyterian Church, corner of Hanover and Pomfret Streets; Gothic; built, 1869, has memorial window over door, Moorish design; and fine fretwork choir rail. St. Patrick's Catholic Church; east Pomfret Street, has rose window of Tiffany glass; and other windows from Munich; also memorial marble altar.

Ashland Cemetery, York Street, nearly a mile east from Center, contains bronze statue, "Angel and Child," made by Lamb & Co., in James W. Bosler's lot. The "Old Grave Yard," three squares from Center, on east South Street, contains Mollie Pitcher's grave and monument; bronze portrait figure standing, on granite pedestal, with bronze reliefs of battle scenes extended on both sides; sculptor, J. R. Schweizer, Philadelphia; a Civil War cannon is in front; old English and German carvings from the year 1700 are in this cemetery. At Mount Rock, five miles west of Carlisle, is the Ionic Monument, in memory of Governor Ritner from 1835–39; erected by the state in 1902; architect, J. W. Ely, Mechanicsburg, Pennsylvania.

DICKINSON COLLEGE, "OLD WEST," CARLISLE

CUMBERLAND COUNTY 205

THE INDIAN SCHOOL, one mile northeast from Center, was formerly a military post, buildings were destroyed by Fitz Hugh Lee in 1863, excepting the old guard house, built by the Hessian prisoners during the Revolution, in 1777; this was the original "West Point" for the training of officers and artisans, and for the manufacture of arms and munitions. In 1776, and throughout the War, anthracite coal was taken down the Susquehanna River from the Wyoming mines to the armory at Carlisle, said to have been the first shipment of anthracite coal in this country; there are now about twenty-five or thirty buildings, brick, of varied architecture, on twenty-five acres of ground; gateway, Georgian, M. I. Kast, architect, built, 1910; native Indian art is on exhibition in the Leupp studio. George Washington joined the army of 15,000 men, as Commander in Chief, at Carlisle, for suppression of the Whiskey Insurrection in 1794; he was the guest of Ephraim Blaine; the army was located on the opposite side of the town from the military post.

The Civic Club of Carlisle is placing classic art prints in the public-school buildings. Interesting colonial houses: residence of Ephraim Blaine, built, 1795, now law office and dwelling of Edward Stiles, built, 1815; of Stephen Duncan, built, 1815, used by the Fraternity of Owls; and that of Isaac B. Parker, built, 1820, the home of the Elks.

In 1762, Richard Peters of Philadelphia obtained a patent for 388 acres of land at Boiling Springs, and executed a deed to John S. Rigby & Co., for twenty-nine acres on which they had already commenced the erection of a blast furnace, they bought two ore banks at the foot of South Mountain, and soon after added 1614 acres of land, and called the property "Carlisle Iron Works"; it passed through several ownerships, until, in 1792, Michael Ege became sole owner; the furnace produced twelve to fifteen tons of metal a week, mostly pig iron, but they also cast stoves, fire backs, and hollow ware. William Denning, in 1776, made two wrought iron cannon in Mount Holly Gap, about six miles south of Carlisle, the first ever made; one in use at the Battle of Brandywine was captured by the British and deposited finally in the Tower of London; the British Government offered a large sum of money and an annuity to William Denning, to instruct them how to make wrought iron cannon, but he refused; he died in 1830, age ninety-three, at his home near Newville, his monument there, given by the state, shows a square marble base surmounted by a cannon. Pine Grove Furnace was built on Mountain Creek, halfway between Carlisle and Gettysburg, the recorded ownership dates from a proprietary grant in 1762 for 450 acres on Mountain Creek to Thomas Pope; it is now part of the State Forestry reservation.

VII
NORTHAMPTON COUNTY

FORMED March 11, 1752; named by Thomas Penn; prior to the Revolution comprised all the northeast section of Pennsylvania; chief industries, Bethlehem Iron and Steel Works, where 15,000 men are employed day and night; silk mills, graphite works, and other manufactories. Here were Washington's storehouses along the Delaware River, with supplies for all branches of the army; a point of attack by the British battling between West Point and Trenton, buildings are still in evidence. The famous backwoods rifles used by two thousand Pennsylvanians against the British at Boston were made here.

County seat, EASTON, founded by Thomas Penn, 1751; at "The Forks of the Delaware, where the water is deep and smooth," population 33,813. In center of the public square is the monument to soldiers of this county in the Civil War, on site of the old Northampton court house that stood for a hundred years; on its threshold was promulgated the Declaration of Independence, the same day as in Philadelphia; the old court house bell, that rang out then, is still doing public service. The first flag, combining stars and stripes, as an emblem of a new nation, was made here, showing thirteen eight pointed stars and thirteen stripes in the field, this flag is said to be the one now in the Easton Public Library, deposited in 1821, after being used in the War of 1812; in a special room of the

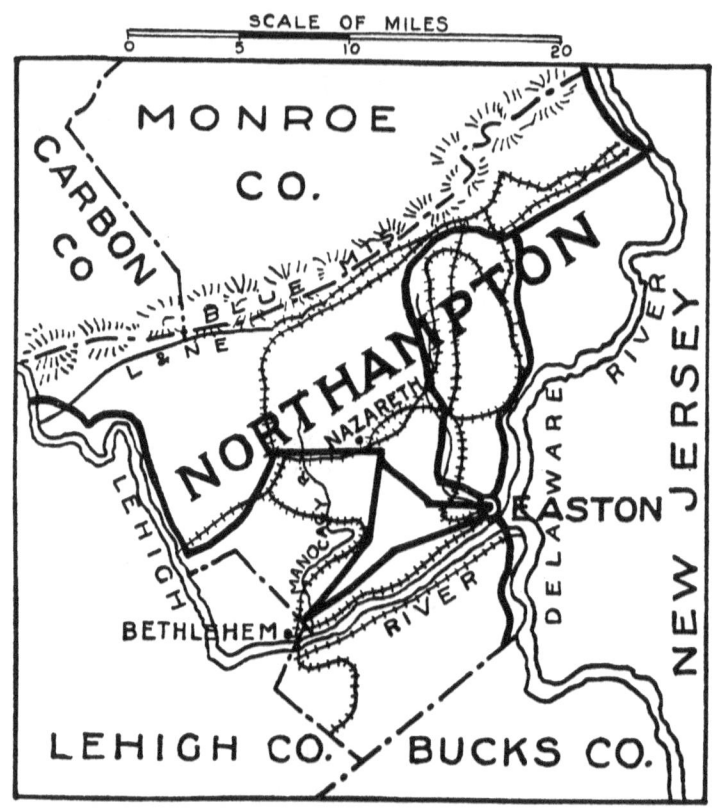

Northampton County

NORTHAMPTON COUNTY 209

library is the private collection of Samuel Sitgreaves, with rare volumes of American history. Next to Sitgreaves' office was the home and shop of Henry Derringer, a gunmaker of the Revolution, whose son invented the Derringer pistol. On the public square, Light Horse Harry Lee, from Virginia, recruited his troop of Pennsylvania Germans, and horses. Valuable papers and moneys belonging to the state and national government were placed in the custody of Robert Levers, during British occupancy of Philadelphia.

The old Union Church, now the Reformed, on North Third Street, stone, colonial, built, 1775–76, was used as a hospital in the Revolution; this is the principal residential street, and entrance to LAFAYETTE COLLEGE, founded, 1832, by James Madison Porter, Secretary of War; has interesting collection of portraits of Lafayette, in oil and black and white, also valuable old engravings; on the campus is statue of Lafayette, by Daniel Chester French, given by Morris L. Clothier, Esq. In the New Century Art Club, New and Porter Streets, lectures on art and exhibitions are given. A bridge leads across the Delaware to Phillipsburg, New Jersey, first wooden bridge built, 1797; north of the bridge is Riverside Park, leading to North Delaware Road and the Delaware Water Gap; the Wind Gap has precipitous sides; very beautiful scenery is on the River Road.

In July, 1782, Washington came from Bethlehem to Easton. BETHLEHEM, in Lehigh County, is the seat of government of the Moravian economy, from Moravia in Bohemia, in the western hemisphere, dating back to 1740; these pioneers belonged to the Church of the Brethren, organized in 1457 by followers of John Huss about forty years after he had been burned at the stake for conscience' sake; the little church was revived in Saxony in 1722; to this church Count Nicholas L. Zinzendorf granted an asylum on his own estate; the count visited the Brethren here in 1741. On July 25, 1782, Washington, with Colonel Trumbull and Major Welker, stayed overnight at the Sun Inn; Brother Ettwein and others of the Fraternity called to pay their respects; the Sun Inn was built in 1761, Peter Warbas the first host; the suite occupied by General Washington and his wife is still shown to visitors. During the Revolution the Moravian settlement experienced many horrors and discomforts of war; the tramp of armed men through its quiet streets began in July, 1775; in December most of the houses were taken for hospitals, being on the main route of travel from the eastern states; many distinguished soldiers were here, Greene, Knox, Gates, Stirling, Sullivan, Schuyler, von Steuben, De Kalb, Pulaski, de Chastelleux, also Samuel and John Adams, Hancock, Laurens, Livingston, Boudinot, Reed, Rittenhouse, Gerard; in autumn of 1777, Lafayette, under careful nursing of a Moravian sister, Liesel Beckel, rapidly recovered from a wound received in the Battle of Brandywine. General hospital of the Continental Army was here, 1776–78.

The Moravian Church, plain and dignified architecture, after a German model, is full of sunlight within, contains Moravian archives and Schussele's large oil painting, "Power of the Gospel," showing Zeisberger preaching to the Indians; the organ and vocal music is exceptionally fine. The Moravian College and Semi-

NORTHAMPTON COUNTY 211

nary for young women includes instruction in housekeeping; moral training is a particular feature. The Widows' house, built, 1768, endowed by John Jordan, Jr., Philadelphia, for widows and daughters of Moravian ministers and other women who have served the church. The Sisters' house, formerly first Brethren's house, was used for home of unmarried women of advanced age; now a boarding house. Second Brothers' house, where unmarried men could live and still gain independent support, is now "Colonial Hall," a part of the Seminary. Corpse house still stands with its weeping willow tree; because of the small rooms of the houses, the body was taken from the home to the corpse house for three days; the trombone choir announced a death from the church steeple by a particular choral that designated whether it was for man, woman, or child; at the burial the trombone choir met the procession at the cemetery gate and took part in the service at the grave; in the Moravian burial ground are graves of many Indians, among them that of Uncas, in Cooper's "Last of the Mohicans," inscription, "In memory of Tschoop, a Mohican Indian, who, in holy baptism, April 16th, 1742, received the name of John, one of the first fruits of the mission at Wycomico, whereby he became a distinguished teacher among his nation. He departed this life in full assurance of faith at Bethlehem, August 27, 1746." The graves are in rows, sisters and brothers separate, with small stone markers. Bethlehem had the second waterworks system in the United States, 1760.

A covered wooden bridge over one hundred years old, to be replaced by modern structure, crosses the

Lehigh River to SOUTH BETHLEHEM, Northampton County, seat of Lehigh University, built, 1866; in 1865, Asa Packer gave $500,000 for founding a free technical college for boys in South Bethlehem, largest single benefaction any American college had received up to this time; this was the beginning of Lehigh University, opened the following year; later a classical department was opened at Mr. Packer's direction, who gave the University $1,500,000 during his life, and left it by will another $1,500,000, to ease the struggle upwards of boys with whose ambitions he sympathized; this University is particularly noted for its course in engineering, with the Fritz Engineering Laboratory, endowed with over $1,000,000; there are also a gymnasium with swimming pool, and a stadium.

The BACH FESTIVAL, announced by the trombone players from the tower of Lehigh University Chapel, has been held annually since 1911, first performance was in 1888. In 1780, the settlement had an orchestra, said to be the first in America, flutes, horns, viols, and trombones were permanent factors in their church music, which undoubtedly led up to the present development; frequently referred to as the American Bayreuth; a quartet of trombones summoning the people, as do the trumpets in Germany; in 1901, the Christmas Oratorio was given in its entirety, first in America; they have also given the Passion, and the Mass in B Minor; J. Frederick Wolle, pupil of Rheinberger, organist of the Lutheran Church, has charge of the music; choir consists of 200 voices, natives of Bethlehem, excepting leading soloists; the orchestra and instrumental soloists vary, the Philadelphia Orchestra has played here. Location of Bethlehem is scenically quite as beautiful as Eisenach in the Thuringian forest, where the famous Wartburg, with memories of Tannhaeuser, Bach, and Luther attract thousands of tourists and pilgrims. In NAZARETH are old stockaded forts of the Indian wars, where were maintained 365 settlers from beyond the mountains, now used by the Moravian Historical Society for their collection of relics, curios, and portraits of noted Indians. Whitfield house, built, 1755, old English, contains Moravian Historical Collection; Nazareth Hall, built, 1748, was school for young men. At Boulton, near Nazareth, is Benjamin West's first tragic painting, "Death of Socrates."

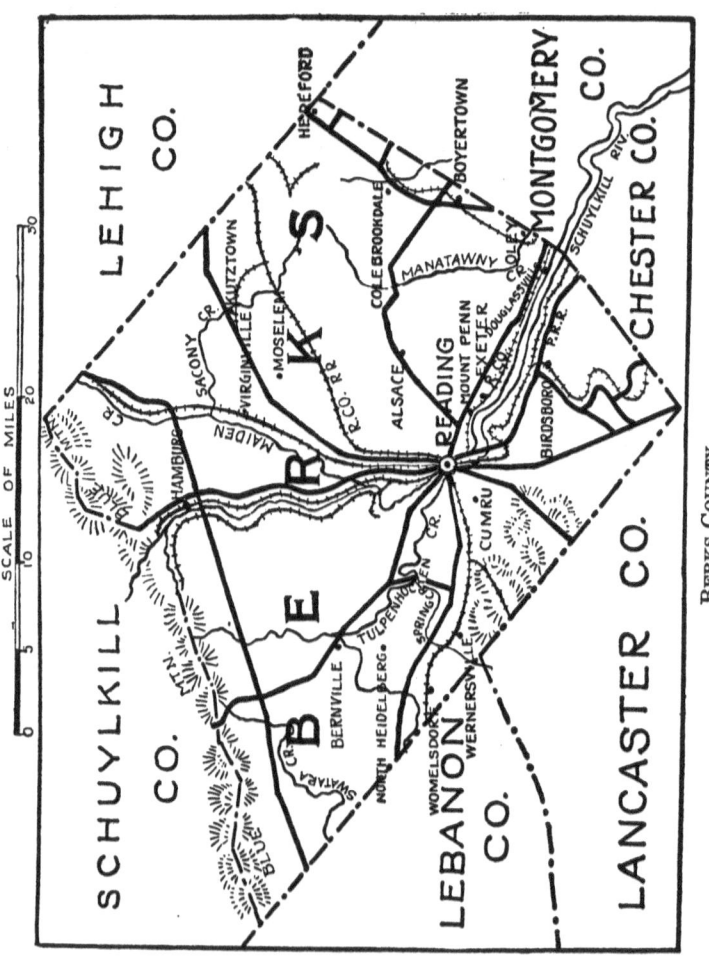

BERKS COUNTY

VIII
BERKS COUNTY

FORMED March 11, 1752; reduced to present limits, 1811; named for Berkshire, England, where Penn family had large estates; has broad, fertile plains and valleys, intermingled with rough hills and mountains containing mineral wealth in iron. First settlers were Germans, and Friends from England, 1704-12, among whom was George Boone, ancestor of Daniel Boone of Kentucky, who was born here, in Exeter Township, 1735. Mordecai Lincoln, great-great-grandfather of Abraham Lincoln, also lived in Exeter Township; he owned one thousand acres of land, had interest in iron forges; and built a small stone house in 1733, that now forms one end of the present homestead, which remained in the Lincoln family until 1912; the Lincoln men of Berks County were all men of note, several holding public positions; one, Abraham, married Anna Boone; he died, 1806.

In 1729, Conrad Weiser came over with Germans from the Palatinate and settled near Womelsdorf, where he is buried in the family burial ground; marked by boulder; his granddaughter was married to the "Patriarch" Henry Melchoir Muhlenberg; farm and burial ground of Conrad Weiser, purchased by the Burks County Historical Society, is to be maintained as a Memorial Park. The Dutch came in 1730; their descendants still reside on their ancestral estates; they named the river, flowing through the county,

Schuylkill (hidden creek); Indian name was Manai-unk. When war was declared between England and France, the French found the Indians eager to join them against the British, and after Braddock's defeat at Fort Duquesne in 1755, they devastated these peaceful settlers, by fire and slaughter, until 1778, when they were driven beyond the Alleghenies. This region has become famous for wine making; vines are grown on Mount Penn, Neversink, and the Alsace Mountain slopes; over fifty years ago, George L. Reiniger left the fertile vineyards of Wurtemberg and settled here, where the soil, scenery, and environment seemed so much like the fatherland; these vineyards are now used for the cultivation of dahlias.

READING, county seat; population 107,784; was laid out in 1748 by agents of Richard and Thomas Penn; named for Reading, in Berkshire, England. Courthouse on Penn Common, Fifth and Penn Streets, built, 1762; present building in 1840, on north Sixth Street; colonial with Ionic porch; cupola eighty-four feet above the roof. In the park are equestrian statue of General David McMurtrie Gregg, by H. Augustus Lukeman, New York; the Firemen's Monument; "The First Defenders"; and Frederick Lauer, all designed and made by P. F. Eisenbrown, Sons & Company, Reading; the bronze statue of President McKinley, reliefs and eagles, was designed by Edward L. A. Pausch, Buffalo, New York. Prison, Penn Street and Perkiomen Avenue, red sandstone, castellated Gothic, built, 1846; architect, John Haviland. A two story building, northeast corner of Fifth Street and Penn Square, was built in 1764 for a tavern; Washington stayed here in

THE JAIL AT READING

John C. Haviland, Architect

BERKS COUNTY 217

1794, en route to join troops against the Whiskey Rebellion; now Farmers' Bank; it is marked as the oldest building in town. The Hessian camp ground, southwest of Reading, is also marked.

Trinity Church, most important Lutheran Church in this country, is a fine example of Georgian architecture, northwest corner of Sixth and Washington Streets; was built, 1791. Christ Protestant Episcopal Cathedral, Gothic, brownstone; built in 1864; architect, Potter, New York; has good windows. The Reading Museum and Art Gallery, Eighth and Washington Streets, has a good collection of paintings, representing foreign and American artists, including sixty paintings given by Mrs. William Littleton Savage, as memorial to her parents, Mr. and Mrs. George DeBenneville Keim, and other works of art and natural history; it is open free to the public. The Historical Society of Berks County, 38 North Fourth Street, has a good historical collection. Among the notable artists who have lived in Reading are Christopher H. Shearer, represented in permanent collection at Pennsylvania Academy of the Fine Arts, Philadelphia; Benjamin F. Austrian, noted still-life painter, born here, 1870; James A. Benade, landscape; F. D. Devlan, animal painter and cartoonist; during the Civil War he furnished many cartoons for Frank Leslie's illustrated newspaper; George Seiling, mural decorator, born in Bavaria, 1818, his paintings are in St. James' Church," The Transfiguration," and Calvary Church, "Christ Bearing the Cross." Calvary Reformed Church has stone mosaic decoration in chancel by H. Hanley Parker.

Charles Evans Cemetery, acquired by gift in 1864, has Gothic gateway, dark sandstone; made in 1847; architects, Calver & Hall, Philadelphia; the chapel is brownstone, Gothic, built, 1854; architect, John M. Gries, who was a major in the Union Army, killed in battle of "Fair Oaks"; here is the Soldiers and Sailors Monument, with bronze tablets; erected, 1889.

Reading was the resort of many fugitives families from Philadelphia while British were there in the winter of 1776–77, and became the scene of much gayety. General Mifflin, afterwards governor, had his country seat at Cumru, three miles southeast of Reading, now used as the County Almshouse and Hospital buildings. In the different wars of this country Berks County men were among the first to offer their services; the Ringgold Light Artillery, Captain James McKnight, is said to have been the first company that reported at Harrisburg in response to President Lincoln's Proclamation in 1861, and was one of five Pennsylvania companies to arrive first at Washington in defense of the Capital.

At KUTZTOWN, settled by Germans in 1733, is the Keystone State Normal School, originally MAXATAWNY Seminary, but since 1866, the Normal School, enlarged after most improved models of school architecture. Four miles distant is VIRGINSVILLE; here is a natural curiosity, the "Crystal Cave," of vast dimensions, with crystal formations in every shape and color; it is lighted by electricity. BOYERTOWN, with two large academies, and BIRDSBORO, with fine churches and residences, are noted for their iron furnaces. HAMBURG is the home of the Berks County State Sana-

BERKS COUNTY

torium No. 3 for tuberculosis; Spanish architecture. Berks County has several picturesque old bridges, the oldest, with one arch, stone, built in 1822, spans the Wyomissing Creek at its mouth, opposite Reading. Thirteen other stone arch bridges, the longest, over Maiden Creek, four arches, built in 1854; and twenty-five wooden covered bridges, are decided artistic assets.

Historic iron furnaces in Berks County are at BIRDSBORO, Hay Creek Forges, built, 1740, by William Bird on land obtained by warrant and survey; he also erected Hopewell Furnace in 1759, and the Berkshire Furnace in Heidelberg about 1760; his son, Mark Bird, inherited the property, and built Spring Forge and Gibraltar Forge; in 1796, John Louis Barde became the owner; his daughter was married to Matthew Brooke, who subsequently purchased the property, which has become an extensive iron works. COLEBROOKDALE, famous as the seat of the first blast furnace in Pennsylvania, was on Iron Stone Creek, named for the Colebrookdale furnace, in Shropshire, England; it was founded by Thomas Rutter and Thomas Potts in 1720: in 1724, the output was forty-eight tons of pig iron per annum, each ton valued at £5; this was the first furnace to cast pots, kettles, and other hollow ware by the use of sand moulds; it had a long and prosperous career. HOPEWELL, a cold blast, one stack furnace, employed one hundred and seventy men and boys, the iron ore was obtained from the Hopewell mine, about two miles away, water from Hopewell Creek formed the motive power; a dam was constructed a quarter of a mile above the furnace and conveyed by a race to the big water wheel; the property covered 5163 acres, chiefly woodland; stoves were cast here with much detailed design, marked with the name of Bird; also cannon for the Revolutionary Army; Hopewell furnace, although idle for many years, is not dismantled, and the village street of ironworkers' homes is much the same as it must have been in early times.

OLEY FORGE, south of the little hamlet called Oley Churches, and about ten miles from the confluence of the Manatawny and Schuylkill rivers, was organized by John Ross in 1744, and was in active operation for one hundred and twenty years. In 1760, a valuable deposit of iron ore was found in Oley Township, and in 1765 Dietrich Welcker erected OLEY FURNACE, near the mountain; it was owned by General Daniel Udree during the Revolution. PINE FORGE was among the earliest of those erected in the Manatawny district, on land conveyed by William Penn to Thomas Rutter; the original patent is in possession of the Rutter family. There is every evidence that the group of early forges and furnaces had a general interchange in their business affairs, as the owners of the plants were almost identical; William Bird, in 1733, was cutting wood for the use of Pine Forge, at two shillings ninepence a day. Ten years later we find him renting one-eighth of Pine Forge at £40 per annum.

The management of the old forges was patriarchal in its character; grist mill, sawmill, and the village store were all under control of the company, and the records of the old forges and furnaces are filled with human interests of an earlier day. WINDSOR FURNACE,

TRINITY CHURCH, READING, BUILT IN 1791

on Furnace Creek, under shadow of the Blue Mountains, besides making pig iron and the usual hollow ware cast in colonial times, was noted for remarkable artistic work under the management of Jones, Keim & Co.; one casting, being a copy of Leonardo da Vinci's "Last Supper," is now in possession of the Philadelphia Exchange.

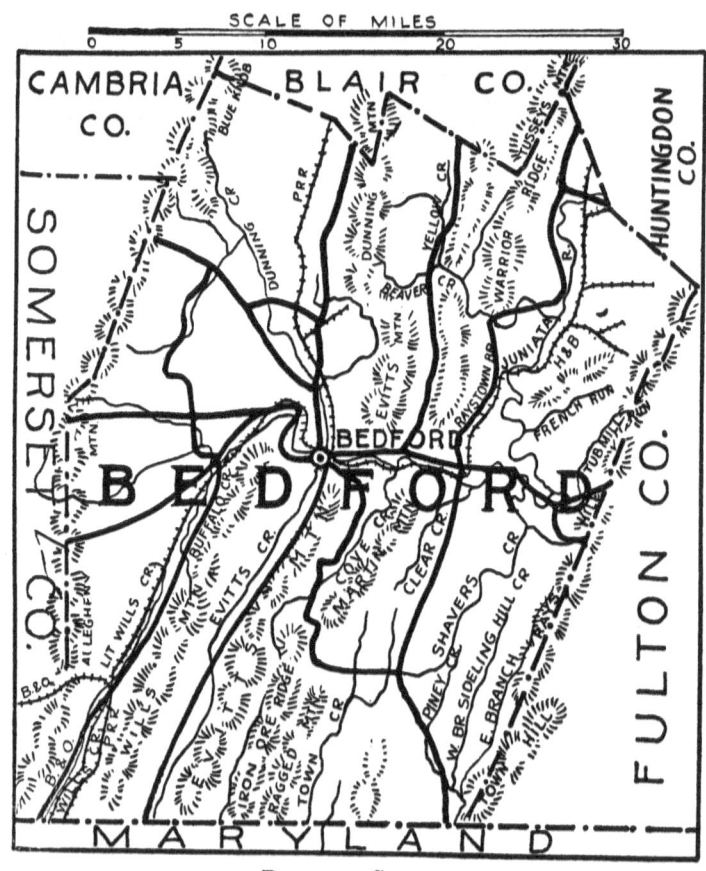

BEDFORD COUNTY

IX
BEDFORD COUNTY

FORMED March 9, 1771; named by Governor John Penn, in 1776, from fort of this name in the county. Is widely known for its mineral springs. When first established it embraced entire southwest part of the province. Mean altitude 1100-1200 feet above sea level; in northwest at Blue Knob, near Blair and Cambria County line, is highest elevation in Pennsylvania, 3136 feet above sea level. Surface is broken by parallel ranges of mountains, with narrow, beautiful valleys, in a high state of cultivation. Chief industries are farming, stock raising, and apple growing. It is said that the most important fields of bituminous coal in Pennsylvania are largely in the northeast of this County known as "The Broad Top Coal Fields." Population Scotch-Irish, German, and English.

First permanent settlement was made in 1750, by a Scotchman named Ray (McRay), an Indian trader, near present site of Bedford, then Raystown. In 1755, Colonel James Burd was appointed by the province to construct the first wagon road, from Fort Louden, Franklin County, to join Braddock's road near Turkey Foot, Somerset County, passing through Raystown (Bedford), practically identical with the Chambersburg and Bedford Turnpike, now Lincoln Highway. On western border where this road crosses main range of the Alleghenies, at a point two-thirds of the ascent, is a view unsurpassed in the picturesque charm of the landscape, stretching far and wide. The highway follows the main course of the Raystown Branch of the Juniata, crossing this stream at least four times; bridges are iron or old wooden ones.

The fort at Raystown was constructed in 1758 by the vanguard of General Forbes' army; it embraced about seven thousand square yards, occupying the bluff now bounded on the east by Richard Street; south, Pitt Street (Lincoln Highway); west, Juliana Street; north, the Raystone River; it was the most prominent military stronghold in the central part of the province, and the principal rendezvous of troops forming the right wing of General John Forbes' army in his expedition against Fort Duquesne, 5850 men, besides wagoners; largest single contingent was 2700 Pennsylvania provincials under Colonel Bouquet, who had chief charge of entire force, until General Forbes arrived; the 1600 Virginians were under command of Colonel George Washington and Colonel William Byrd. In 1759, Geneal John Stanwix, then in command of the garrison, had the name changed to Fort Bedford, in honor of the Duke of Bedford; now no trace of the fortification remains.

In 1794, Bedford became the headquarters of General Henry Lee, Governor of Virginia, who was commander in chief of the army of 13,000 troops raised to quell the Whiskey Insurrection; President Washington, after reviewing the troops at Carlisle and Cumberland, came to Bedford and made his headquarters in a stone house on Pitt Street, house still standing.

BEDFORD, county seat, population 2330; laid out, 1766, by Surveyor General John Lukens, with a com-

BEDFORD COUNTY

modious square, in the most convenient place. Courthouse erected, 1828, colonial with clock tower, architect and contractor, Solomon Filler, faces the square. Opposite is the United States Post Office, built, 1915, Indiana limestone, classic, Doric columns, architect, Oscar Wenderoth; also facing the square are the Presbyterian Church, colonial, built, 1828, on site of an earlier one built in 1810; and the Lutheran Church, fine two-story building and parsonage. The Soldiers' Monument in honor of Bedford County volunteers in Civil War occupies center of square. Handsome memorial colonial gateway forms entrance to Bedford Cemetery, stone, with bronze tablets.

The therapeutic qualities of the Mineral Springs are believed to be second to none anywhere in the world, and justly entitle Bedford to the name of the Carlsbad of America; one and one-half miles south of the borough, within an area of a few square rods, several varieties of water are to be found; most famous is the Magnesia Spring, efficacious in disturbances of the digestive organs; others are known as the Black Sulphur, Limestone, Chalybeate, and Sweet Water Spring. Colonial Hotel has a colonnade of Doric columns, twenty feet high, made of native solid trees; the links for the Scottish game of golf are on a place earlier named Caledonia. The Bedford Chalybeate Springs, about one mile northeast of the town, contain waters showing analysis of carbonate of calcium, magnesium, iron and sodium, and sulphite of calcium. Ten miles southwest of Bedford are the White Sulphur Springs in Milliken's Cave, second largest health resort in the country; waters are unexcelled in health-restoring properties.

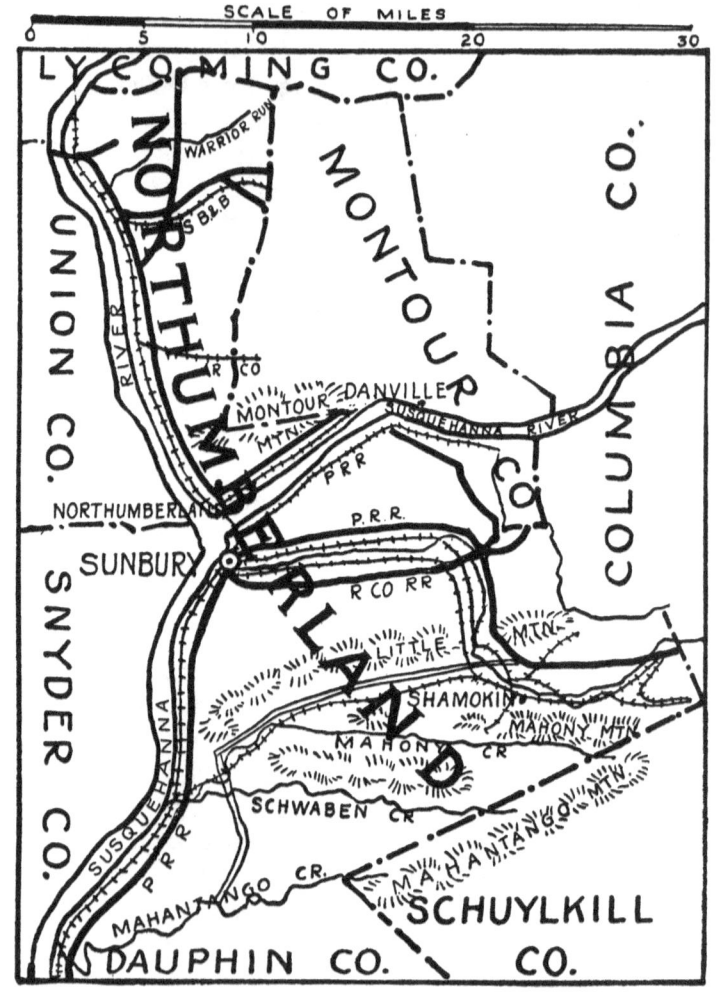

NORTHUMBERLAND COUNTY

X
NORTHUMBERLAND COUNTY

FORMED March 21, 1772; named for the Duke of Northumberland. Mountainous, with great amount of fertile land, watered by the Susquehanna River and tributaries. Chief industry is coal mining.

County seat, SUNBURY, population 15,721, on site of a populous Indian village named Shamokin, occupied variously by different tribes; in 1745, the town contained about fifty houses and three hundred inhabitants; the Six Nations used it as a tarrying place for their war parties against the Catawbas of the South.

It was the residence of Shikellimy, an Oneida chief sent by the Iroquois, who claimed the land by conquest in 1728, he was the Indian diplomat, and land agent of the three great tribes of Pennsylvania, New York and Delaware, with supervision of the Delaware, Shawnee, and other tribes. He also had to look after all matters relating to the settlement and purchase of Indian lands by the whites. In 1742, Count Zinzendorf, with Conrad Weiser and others, came to Shamokin; Shikellimy gave them a hearty welcome, and promised to forward their design of having a Moravian Mission there; it was established in 1747 by Martin Mack and his wife; Bishop Cammerhoff and Zeisberger visited the town the next year. In 1748 Shikellimy died; "the Chief who never swerved in his friendship to the Province"; he had been baptized in the Christian faith in Bethlehem, and was buried just outside of what was later Fort Augusta; James Logan, his second son, was perhaps the best known of his children; made so by the murder of his family, near the mouth of Yellow Creek, on the Ohio, in 1774, and the famous "Logan's Lament." A large boulder, with memorial tablet, marks Shikellimy's grave; it was placed, in 1915, by the Fort Augusta Chapter, Daughters of the American Revolution, and the Pennsylvania Historical Commission; the boulder is of very close grained rock, of the kind used by the Indians for their hardest and strongest implements; it was quarried near Wapwallopen, about forty miles above Sunbury; this rock boulder, from our local mountains, will resist the forces of nature for centuries to come, as it has done for ages past.

Shamokin (Sunbury) was also the residence of Allummapees, or Sassounan, the head chief of the Delawares, so that this place was, in every sense of the term, the Indian capital of Pennsylvania from 1728–48, and was deserted in 1749 on account of a severe famine along the Susquehanna. At the north of Sunbury, along the river drive, is site of Fort Augusta, built in 1756 by Colonel Miles and Captain Trump of the Second Pennsylvania Battalion; it was the frontier, after Forts Muncy, Brady, and Freeland were destroyed in 1779 by British and Indians; the powder magazine, and well, built of brick, are still intact and in good preservation. This was said to have been the most strategic point in the whole section; a monument on either side of the roadway marks the place. On the site of the fortifications is a brick mansion; within are many relics taken from the fort, and draft of original plan.

NORTHUMBERLAND COUNTY 229

Visitors are welcome. Site of Fort Freeland on north side of Warrior's Run, four miles east of Watsontown; it was a large stockaded log house, built in 1773, enclosing about half an acre.

SUNBURY was laid out 1772, by William Maclay and John Lukens, by order of Governor Richard Penn, who named it. William Maclay, first United States Senator from Pennsylvania, built his stone residence, still standing, on the river bank in northwest part of town; the city plan is like that of Philadelphia, and many of the streets have the Philadelphia names; Market Street faces a public square between Second and Third Streets, known as Cameron Park, in which is the Civil War Soldiers' Monument, granite shaft surmounted by a life-size, granite statue of Colonel James Cameron, who organized a regiment from this county. Courthouse, Second Street, facing west side of Cameron Park, originally built in 1866; Georgian; brick with Hummelstown brownstone trimmings; was remodeled in the same style in 1915 and enlarged, in the rear, with a cross wing, giving two fine courtrooms, last architect, William H. Lee, Shamokin. The prison, one block away, at the corner of Second and Arch Streets, medieval castle style, built, 1878, dark gray stone, with stone wall twenty feet high, surrounding the whole structure, has wing used as a penitentiary, where prisoners serve out their sentences; they weave carpets and make coarse hosiery.

NORTHUMBERLAND, settled, 1772, population 4061. Dr. Joseph Priestly, chemist and philosopher, was its most noted inhabitant; he emigrated here in 1794, to be with his son, and died, 1804; in 1874, Scientists of America celebrated here the centennial of Dr. Priestly's discovery of oxygen; his house, built, 1796, is still standing, in excellent preservation; a portrait of Dr. Priestly, by Gilbert Stuart, is owned by Miss Priestly. The Academy was erected in 1803, mainly through the efforts of Dr. Priestly; Rev. Isaac Greer, first principal.

XI
WESTMORELAND COUNTY

FORMED February 26, 1773, named for the County of Westmoreland, England. Chief industries, coal, coke, gas, and manufactories. Ruins of old furnaces abound in this section, relics of the iron industry about 1800. The Lincoln Highway crosses this county, formerly the Philadelphia and Pittsburgh Turnpike, entering near LAUGHLINSTOWN, at the base of Laurel Ridge, elevation, 2700 feet; here is a museum of relics, shown in an old tavern of stage coach days, built about 1800, where Daniel Webster is said to have stopped, and Zachary Taylor, in 1848, held a reception. Three miles west is LIGONIER, on site of a fort built by Captain Burd under the direction of Colonel Bouquet, a Swiss; named for Sir John Ligonier, a famous English general; all traces of the fort have been obliterated; a descriptive tablet, erected by the Daughters of the American Revolution, is in the town square. In the High School Library is an engraving, from a painting by Sir Joshua Reynolds, of Sir John Ligonier. Near by is Idlewild Park.

At Bushy Run the Indians made a furious attack on Bouquet and his company but were utterly routed and they retreated beyond the Ohio; Bouquet then marched to Fort Pitt and recovered it in 1763; next year he led an expedition beyond the Ohio River, the Indians sued for peace, and he compelled them to

WESTMORELAND COUNTY

WESTMORELAND COUNTY

bring all their captives to Fort Pitt. One and a half miles west of Ligonier is residence of General Arthur St. Clair, from 1767-72, "The Hermitage," rebuilt, excepting one room, which is well cared for; there is a well-grounded tradition that Washington sent from Mount Vernon two expert carpenters, whose quaintly designed woodwork, mantelpiece and wainscoting doubtless saved this room from destruction; the house was marked in 1913, by the Phœbe Bayard Chapter, Daughters of the American Revolution, of Greensburg.

Four miles west of Latrobe is St. Vincent's Monastery and Church, dedicated in 1905, brick and stone buildings, with highly decorated interiors, containing the main altar, onyx, set with jewels, and fine wood carvings from Italy. North, on William Penn Highway, is NEW ALEXANDRIA; here, owned by Elizabeth Craig, is a Rattlesnake Flag, in use before the Revolution, made of crimson silk; in the upper left-hand corner is the English coat of arms; on the field is a rattlesnake with thirteen rattles, indicating the thirteen colonies; underneath are the words "Don't tread on me," J. P. F. B. W. C. P.—for John Proctor's First Battalion Westmoreland County, Pennsylvania; by whom it was adopted.

GREENSBURG, population 15,033, formerly called Newtown, settled in 1782; made county seat in 1786, and name changed in honor of General Nathaniel Greene, who had died at Savannah, Georgia, that same year; many of the Westmoreland County soldiers served under him in the Revolution. It now has its fourth courthouse, a dignified building, French Renaissance, white granite, the façade surmounted by a well-proportioned dome, dedicated, 1908; architect, William Kauffman; contains portraits of judges and lawyers. Among the churches of good architecture are the United Brethren, classic, Doric, architects, Winkler & Macdonald; and the First Presbyterian on South Main Street, Gothic, stone, architects, Cram & Ferguson. Other notable buildings are the Post Office, classic, Ionic; the Y. M. C. A., an adaptation of Colonial, and St. Joseph's Academy, with beautiful grounds, overlooking the whole town.

In St. Clair Cemetery is a monument to General Arthur St. Clair, who is buried here. About five miles distant is Oakford Park. Fells Church in Rostravor Township southwest is said to be the second Methodist Church west of the Alleghenies, built of logs in 1792; present stone building in 1834; in the burial ground are many pioneers of western Pennsylvania.

XII
WASHINGTON COUNTY

FORMED March 28, 1781; named for President Washington; originally part of Augusta County, Virginia. First court held here was two miles west on the Gabby farm, marked by granite block; inscription, "On this spot, was held in 1776, the County Court, for the District of West Augusta, Virginia; the first Court held by English-speaking people, west of the Monongahela River. Erected by Washington County Historical Society 1905." Chief industries, between 1860–80 raising fine stock and wool growing; in 1884, oil was discovered and for ten or fifteen years this county became an oil center, with some of the largest wells; now coal is being shipped all over the country from seemingly boundless veins.

WASHINGTON, county seat, laid out in 1782, population 21,480. Courthouse, built in 1900, on Main Street, Italian Renaissance, Columbia sandstone and granite; architect, F. J. Osterling; contains portraits, also collections made by the Washington County Historical Society; ground given by David Hoge of Virginia, who owned large tracts of land where the town now is. Town Hall, corner-stone laid by General U. S. Grant, in 1869; contains Public Library, gift of Dr. Francis J. Le Moyne. Washington and Jefferson College, combined in 1870, from Washington College founded 1787, and Jefferson College founded in Canonsburg, 1802; both flourished until the Civil

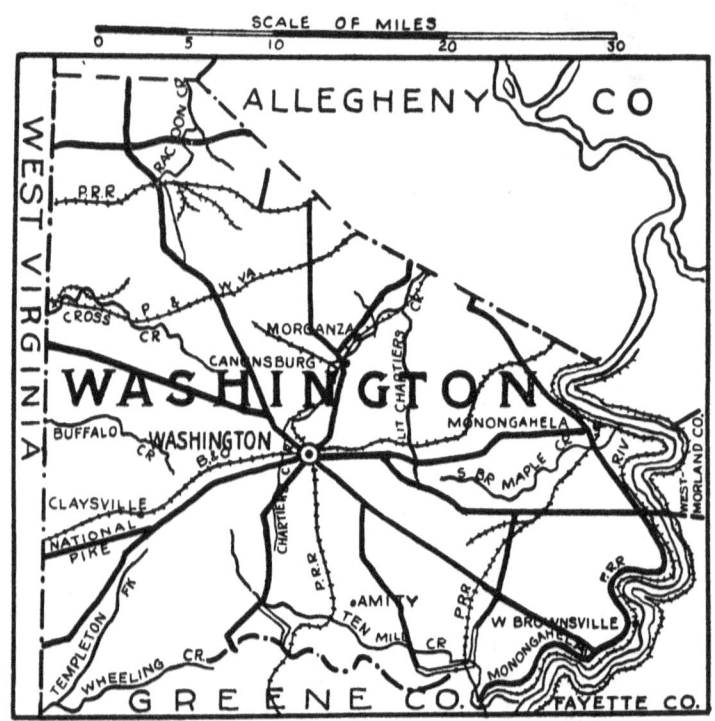

WASHINGTON COUNTY

WASHINGTON COUNTY 237

War, when many students enlisted and financial depression followed; located one square east of the courthouse; oldest part, two story, stone, erected, 1793; main building, brick, 1836, enlarged, 1875, houses the Y. M. C. A., the museum, classrooms, and laboratories; several other fine buildings of brick and stone are on the campus; chapel contains portraits.

Washington Seminary, recognized as one of the oldest and best institutions for women students, one square south of college, was built, 1836. Bradford House, first stone house in this locality, was built, 1794, by Colonel William Bradford, a leader in the Whiskey Insurrection. Residence, Dr. Francis Julius Le Moyne, native of this town, built in 1812, East Maiden Street near Main, is one of the landmarks; he was a brilliant scholar, abolitionist, and promoter of the underground railroad; he built the first crematory in America, located south of Washington, first cremation, Baron de Palen, in 1876. Dr. Le Moyne was cremated, 1879. The Presbyterian Church leads, with the other principal denominations represented, also Jewish Synagogue. West from Washington, the Campbell family founded the Disciples, or Christian Church, on Buffalo Creek.

The Cumberland Road, built, 1811, brought an almost unbroken stream of home seekers through this town, en route to the west; bridges and culverts built about the same time still stand, models of solid masonry and good engineering, one is between Washington and Claysville, town named for Henry Clay, who had an interest in the road and frequently came here.

CANONSBURG, laid out, 1787, by Colonel John Canon,

population 10,632, a portion of his first grist mill is on original location near Chartier's Creek. Jefferson College chartered, 1802; oldest building erected in 1830; on North Central Avenue, highest ground in town; was outgrowth of Dr. John McMillan's Log Cabin Latin School from 1782; first classical school west of the Allegheny Mountains, his cabin stands on the campus, marked by a bronze tablet, placed by the Phi Gamma Delta Fraternity, custodians; having been removed from its original site, two miles south of town; Franklin Hall, converted into a Memorial Hall in 1900, contains portraits of college presidents and professors between 1802–69, also collections of old books from several early libraries and literary societies; may be seen by applying to any of the Memorial Hall Committee. Stone edifice, opposite campus, built by John Roberts, Esq, who conducted a school and kept post office here in 1801, parts of walls are said to be part of stone Academy Building, erected by Colonel Canon, for which he donated the ground in 1790; it was merged with the Log Cabin School to form Jefferson College.

Two-story building at northeast corner of Central Avenue and Pike Street, now grocery and hardware store, was site of the Joshua Emery's Hotel; here President James Monroe was entertained in 1817. On east side of North Central Avenue, between Pike and College Streets, vacant lot, site of Black Horse Tavern, notable as the resort of men who rifled the mail sacks, when letters supposed to contain evidence against violaters of the excise laws were stolen, *en route* to Philadelphia from Pittsburgh, 1794. Residence 62–68

East Pike Street, built by Dr. Jonathan Letherman, before 1830, here Dr. John McMillan died in 1833; the flower garden, with brick wall, was laid out by a landscape gardener brought from Philadelphia by Dr. Letherman, original designs still retained. The Hutchinson house, north side, West College Street, corner of Hutchinson Avenue and adjacent lots, once the Hutchinson farm, was where the "Whiskey boys" encamped in 1794, here also "musters" were held before the Civil War. Chartiers Presbyterian (Hill) Church and burial ground, one mile south of Canonsburg, is where Dr. John McMillan began his pastorate in 1775, and was buried; here, Woodrow Wilson's father was also a former pastor; this site became a rendezvous for the Whiskey Insurrectionists in 1794.

A natural park of seventy acres, within east side of the borough, acquired by gift, is a beautiful breathing spot for the whole community. About one mile northeast of Canonsburg, at Morganza, is the Western Pennsylvania Industrial School; the Morgan Lands, eleven hundred acres, was the home of General George Morgan, Indian agent in Pittsburgh 1775–79; a portion of his residence is still standing, about midway between Morganza and Pollock; here he was visited by Aaron Burr in 1806. General Morgan and his two sons were summoned to Richmond, as witnesses, when Burr was tried for treason.

MONONGAHELA, an important town, first called Parkinson's Ferry, then Williamsport; the men here took an active part in the Whiskey Insurrection, 1794. It furnished its quota of soldiers, known as the Williamsport Rangers, for the War of 1812. Monument to

Colonel Hawkins, and to the Philippine veterans. James Gillespie Blaine was born at West Brownsville in 1830. AMITY, southern part of Washington, near county line, was the residence of Solomon Spalding, born in Connecticut, minister of the Congregational Church; here he wrote the "Manuscript Found," or Book of Mormon; he was not a robust man, and spent many hours writing this romance, with no idea of founding a religious sect; he would read his book in the evenings to the men gathered in the general store; died, 1816, age fifty-five, grave marked by large granite block.

XIII
FAYETTE COUNTY

ORGANIZED September 26, 1783; named in honor of the Marquis de Lafayette; occupied prominent place in Indian, Revolutionary, and later wars. On Jacobs Creek, a mile and a half above the point where it empties into the Youghiogheny River, stands the ruins of the first furnace for the production of pig iron, west of the Allegheny Mountains; the furnace was put in blast November, 1790, and was known as the Alliance Iron Works, operated by William Turnbull and Peter Marmie of Philadelphia; it continued in blast until 1802 using the native ores from the neighboring hillsides, and charcoal burned from the surrounding forests; in 1792 the company cast four hundred six-pound shot for the Fort Pitt Arsenal at Pittsburgh. Coal mining and coke are now the chief industries. Connellsville coke is known throughout the industrial world.

Aboriginal inhabitants were the Shawnee Indians, who made various earthworks and burial mounds, along the Monongahela and Youghiogheny Rivers before their migration southward; it was part of the "Hunting Grounds" of the Iroquois Confederation; the "Indian Title" was extinguished by treaty at Fort Stanwix, 1768.

In 1749 Nemacolin, a Delaware Indian, guided Colonel Thomas Cresap from Wills Creek, Cumberland, Maryland, to the mouth of Dunlap's Creek, where

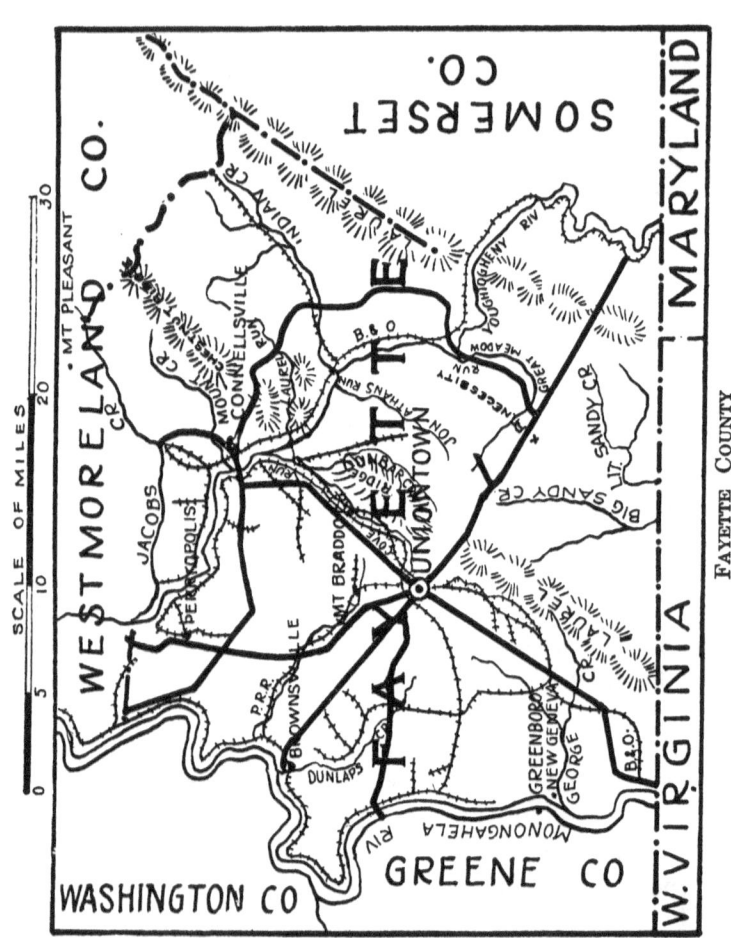

FAYETTE COUNTY

FAYETTE COUNTY 243

Fort Burd was erected in 1759, on site of "Redstone Old Fort," an Indian earthwork, now Brownsville; this was called Nemacolin's trail, and was the best course for the Ohio Company to reach the Ohio River. It was followed by Washington, with Christopher Gist, to the French forts in 1753, the first actual step here, in conflict with France. During the "French and Indian War" Fayette County was the scene of some of the most thrilling events in American history. In 1745 Washington's expedition to gain possession of the Ohio Valley followed this trail to drive the French from "The Forks" (Pittsburgh); he advanced to Gist's Plantation at Mount Braddock, then retreated to The Great Meadows, Fort Necessity, marked by tablet at Mount Washington, where he was defeated by the French under M. Coulon de Villers; previous to this, Washington had met a detachment of French soldiers under M. Coulon de Jumonville, in which Jumonville was killed, grave marked by tablet; first blood shed in French and Indian War.

In 1755 Major General Edward Braddock's expedition against Fort Duquesne followed Nemacolin's trail to Mount Braddock, thence over Catawba trail, which enters Fayette County at mouth of Dunkards Creek; northward through Uniontown, crossing the Youghiogheny (Stewarts Crossing) at Connellsville, on through Mount Pleasant to Westmoreland County, Hunkers, Circleville, to McKeesport; crossing the Monongahela, then recrossing below at mouth of Turtle Creek. General Braddock, mortally wounded in the battle of the Monongahela, was carried back over the road he had opened to a point on the Cumberland Road, National Pike, where he died and was buried; Washington read the Episcopal burial service over him; grave marked by monument, erected by officers of his old regiment, the "Coldstream Guards of England." Braddock's Road became the main highway for settlers of Southwest Pennsylvania and Kentucky; the entire course is full of historic interest; sites of encampments, blockhouses and Indian forts; some are marked.

UNIONTOWN, county seat, formed, 1776; population 15,692. Courthouse, Italian Renaissance; stone; architects, E. M. Butz and William Kauffman, Pittsburgh. Presbyterian Church has fine Tiffany windows. Mr. James Hadden, the historian of Fayette County, has a life-size bust of Washington, cut by himself from the wood of a wild cherry tree, which grew within the lines of Fort Necessity, in 1784. Washington owned the land on which the tree stood. Two miles south is Fort Gaddis, only frontier or settlers' fort now standing in Fayette County, marked by tablet in 1908; there were sixteen such forts in this county, built of heavy logs, making durable houses for the frontiersmen, and safe retreat for neighboring settlers.

CONNELLSVILLE; population 13,804. On grounds of the Carnegie Free Library is a bronze statue of Colonel William Crawford, pioneer and patriot, who, in 1765, built the first cabin home within limits of Connellsville; killed by Indians in 1782; sculptor, Charles S. Kilpatrick; tablet on base placed by Pennsylvania Historical Commission. Trinity Lutheran Church, Italian Renaissance; native white sandstone, trimmed with Indiana limestone; built, 1911; contains

FAYETTE COUNTY

copy of Bougereau's "Resurrection." In the tower is chime of twelve bells. Architect, J. C. Fulton, Uniontown.

Lafayette was entertained, in 1825, at "Friendship Hill" near New Geneva, the home of Albert Gallatin, member of Congress, Minister Plenipotentiary from the United States to two courts of Europe, signer of the Treaty of Ghent, Secretary of the Treasury in Jefferson's and Madison's administrations; the house was built, 1789, enlarged, 1882, and with the estate of seven hundred acres, is still of great beauty; Albert Gallatin's library remains just as he left it, on a high eminence, overlooking the Monongahela River, on the edge of a precipice three hundred feet above the river, the view is said to be similar to that from Heidelberg Castle; the main entrance is near the old Morgantown Road, an historic highway,

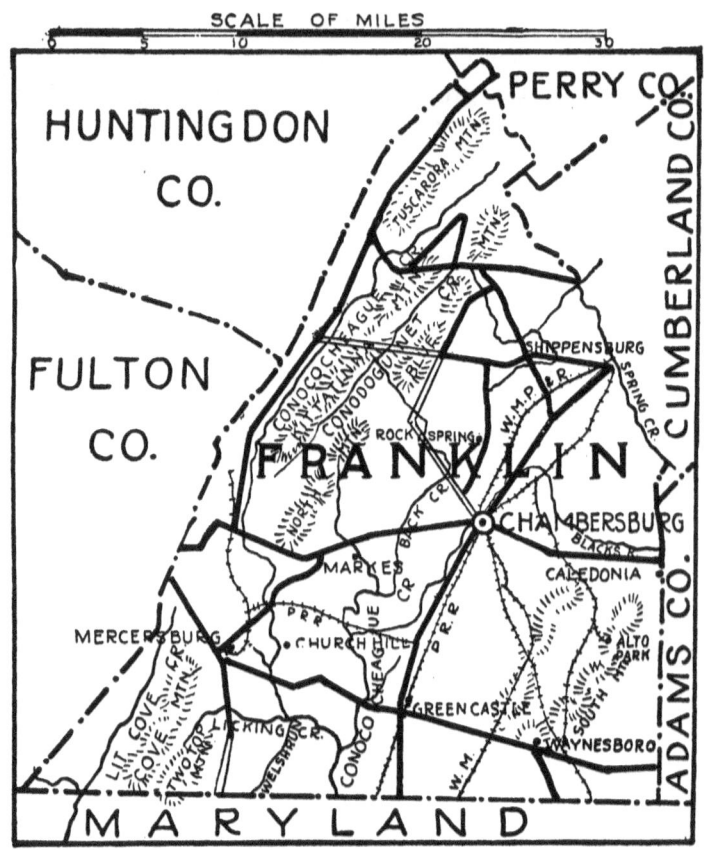

FRANKLIN COUNTY

XIV
FRANKLIN COUNTY

FORMED September 9, 1784; named for Benjamin Franklin, whose fame was then world-wide. Earliest settlers Scotch-Irish, later Germans. Chief industry agriculture, the land east is limestone and very fertile; west, slate lands prevail, abounding in pure streams and rich meadows; the Conococheague and Conodoquinet Creeks drain the central part of the county, they are crossed by many stone arch bridges of graceful architecture, the most notable is at Hiester's Mill, three arches. The principal road, now part of the Lincoln Highway, enters the county near the historic Thaddeus Stevens Iron Works, built, 1837, at Caledonia, which comprised about 20,000 acres, now in State Forestry Reservation, and with the Mont Alto tract, makes a total of about 40,000 acres; the mill and machinery were entirely destroyed, in 1863, by order of General Early, on account of Stevens' well-known activity as an abolitionist; this road was route of greater part of Lee's Army to and from the battle-field of Gettysburg to Chambersburg; site of encampment before the battle, a little beyond the hospital, east from Chambersburg. Other roads leading west, of historic interest, are the Two Mountain, and the Path Valley, formerly Indian trails.

County seat, CHAMBERSBURG, settled, 1764, population 13,171. In Centre Square is a boulder with tablet commemorating the burning of Chambersburg by Confederate Cavalry, July 1, 1864. Facing the square are the brick courthouse, Southern colonial with fluted columns, cupola and clock, contains portraits of judges; and the Central Presbyterian Church, with Tiffany windows. Near are, Miller's drug store on site of Jack Tavern, where the first court was held in 1784, large mortar in front was made from one of the pillars of the burned courthouse. United States Post Office, Main and King Streets, built, 1912, semi-classic, light colonial brick with gray stone facing. Masonic temple, built, 1823, saved by Confederate Masons when the town was burned. Zion Reformed Church, built, 1812, exterior unchanged, particularly good lines in steeple, has Tiffany windows. On King Street stands the house John Brown occupied, second from Union Baptist Church; Nicklas store, on Main Street near Queen, is site of old tavern where President Washington and Alexander Hamilton spent the night, *en route* to quell the Whiskey Insurrection in 1794; Market House, Second and Queen Streets, built, 1830, brick, colonial, with clock tower.

WILSON COLLEGE comprises seven buildings, including Thompson Memorial Hall, built, 1904, modified Gothic, with auditorium and fine organ, architect, George C. Baum, Philadelphia. Falling Spring Presbyterian Church and Chapel, organized, 1736, services first held in Benjamin Chamber's sawmill, present church built, 1803, chapel, 1873, native stone, has Tiffany memorial windows to Judge and Mrs. Alexander Thomson, parents of Frank Thomson, Esq. Rocky Spring Presbyterian Church, four miles northwest from Chambersburg, built, 1794 by the Scotch-

FRANKLIN COUNTY 249

Irish, colonial, with high, straight-backed pews, and original old high pulpit, with sounding board, pewter Communion service from England and ten-plate stoves. Dr. McIntosh preached here; has an interesting old graveyard, keys kept at adjoining farmhouse.

The "MONT ALTO PARK," formerly a famous picnic ground, now in charge of State Forestry Commission, in the South Mountain, in old maps named "The Valley of a Thousand Springs," contains an old Protestant Episcopal Church, near which is a native boulder, with granite tablet, marking the place where Captain John E. Cook, of John Brown's Army of Liberation, was captured and disarmed, October 25, 1859, erected by the Kittochtinny Historical Society, 1909. The STATE FOREST ACADEMY is here, where the state educates its foresters, free of all cost; in 1900, the Bureau of Forestry had grown to the point where it should be raised to the rank of a department, of which the chief should be a member of the Governor's cabinet; there was strenuous oppositon, but owing to the flood of letters received by members of the Legislature, from the women of the State Federated Clubs, the change was made, and Pennsylvania takes a commanding place in the Forestry and Conservation movement. The WHITE PINE, STATE SANATORIUM, No. 1, free for consumptives, is also here, one of the largest in the world. South is WAYNESBORO; good roads and notably fine scenery in this section.

GREENCASTLE, birthplace of Robert McClelland in 1807, see Honor Roll; directly north, on State Road, is monument, to mark where Corporal William H. Rhil fell, first soldier killed on Northern soil in Civil War.

MERCERSBURG, settled between 1730–35, population 1663; named for General Hugh Mercer, who was killed in the Battle of Princeton. Mercersburg Academy, Main Hall, built, 1833, used as hospital for wounded soldiers, on retreat from Gettysburg, is a notable example of Southern colonial architecture, with fine pillars and surmounted by a cupola; the '88 Dormitory, given largely by class of 1888 of Princeton University, is Tudor Gothic, brick and white stone; Kiel Hall, the refectory, interior, baronial Gothic with frescoes and hangings by Tiffany; over mantel, in wood, carved by John J. Maene, is "The Boar Hunt" from design by A. Stirling Calder; notable collection of University shields in glass and wood; mosaic armorial design in hearth; Laucks Hall, Tudor Gothic, has mural painting in trophy room, "The Victor," representing a Mercersburg boy being crowned victor in athletic skill, artist, Edward Howland Blashfield, also collection of portraits of distinguished men, including President James Buchanan, Thomas A. Scott, and W. M. Irvine, by William Merritt Chase; Dr. E. E. Highbee, by Carroll Beckwith; and Dr. Thomas Apple by John W. Alexander; the new gymnasium, architect, Frank Miles Day, has stained glass by Tiffany.

Historic houses on Main Street, one in which Harriet Lane Johnston was born, built, 1788, by Colonel Robert Parker, friend of Lafayette, has interesting interior woodwork; and residence of Dr. William Magaw, who dressed Lafayette's wounds after the battle of Brandywine, grounds now in campus of Academy. Near Mercersburg, Irwinton Mills, a picturesque spot on the west branch of the Conoco-

THE VICTOR
In trophy room of the Mercersburg Academy
Painted by Edwin H. Blashfield

FRANKLIN COUNTY 251

cheague, birthplace of Jane and Elizabeth Irwin, who were married to the Harrison brothers; Jane was mistress of the White House in 1841, Elizabeth became the mother of President Benjamin Harrison. East of town, birthplace of William Findlay, see Honor Roll. President James Buchanan was born at Cove Gap, three miles from Mercersburg, birthplace marked by monument erected by will of his niece, Harriet Lane Johnston; the house was later removed to Lafayette Street, Mercersburg.

The famous Packer's Path, used by pack horses, leads from Stony Batter across the mountains to Pittsburgh. Site of Fort McCord, near Yankee Gap, at North Mountain is where twenty-seven pioneer settlers were massacred or carried into captivity by Indians in 1756, and thirty-two provincial soldiers killed or wounded in their effort at rescue; marked by native stone monument 1914, erected by the Enoch Brown Association, and Pennsylvania Historical Commission. Northeast is the Enoch Brown Park, with monument sacred to the memory of Enoch Brown and eleven scholars massacred by Indians here in 1764, during the Pontiac War. Large collection of Indian curios found near here are owned by Benjamin Snively, Jr. South, is site of Fort Loudoun, marked.

Natives of Franklin County, in the World's Honor Roll are, Samuel Adams, Senator from Mississippi; George Washington Buchanan, United States District Attorney for Dakota; James Buchanan, 1791–1868, schoolboy in Mercersburg, lawyer, member of the legislature and of congress, Minister to Russia, member of United States Senate, Secretary of State, Minister to

Great Britain, fifteenth president of the United States; Edmund R. Calhoun, Rear Admiral, United States Navy; Hugh S. Campbell, United States District Attorney for Dakota; George Chambers, 1786–1866, Judge of the Supreme Court of Pennsylvania; Matthew St. Clair Clark, Clerk of the United States House of Representatives; Colonel Thomas Hartley Crawford, Judge of the United States Court, District of Columbia, and Commissioner for Indian Affairs; George Eyster, Assistant United States Treasurer at Philadelphia; William Findlay, 1768–1846, State Treasurer, United States Senator, Governor, Assistant United States Treasurer at Philadelphia; Henry Harbaugh, 1817–67, theologian, poet, hymn-writer; Robert Johnston, Collector of Excise, appointed by President Washington; John Maclay, member of the convention at Carpenters' Hall; Samuel Maclay, United States Senator; William Maclay, first United States Senator from Pennsylvania, died, 1825; Robert McClelland, United States Secretary of the Interior, Governor of Michigan; James McLane, Member of the Supreme Executive Council and of the Pennsylvania Council of Censors, member of the convention at Carpenters' Hall; John Williamson Nevin, 1803–86, President of Franklin and Marshall College, theologian, author, preacher; William M. Nevin, 1806–92, poet, teacher; James Potter, Major General of the Continental Army; John Rowe, Surveyor-General of Pennsylvania; Thomas A. Scott, Assistant Secretary of War, President Pennsylvania Railroad; Frank Thomson, President Pennsylvania Railroad; Joseph Williams, Chief Justice of the Supreme Court of Iowa.

XV
MONTGOMERY COUNTY

FORMED September 10, 1784; named in honor of General Richard Montgomery; ranks third in state as to amount of money at interest paying state tax; notable for fine suburban residences and for Washington's itinerary and Camp at Valley Forge, with 11,098 men. The Valley Forge Park Commission acquired, in 1893, 472 acres, partly in Chester County, to maintain and preserve forever the Revolutionary camp ground; American army here from December 19, 1777, to June 19, 1778; soldiers built their huts 16 x 14 feet by 6½ feet high, each to accommodate twelve men, and bore their sufferings from cold, starvation, and sickness like heroes; facts of interest are:

Baron von Steuben came from Germany with his secretary, Peter S. Du Ponceau, after having served as aide-de-camp to Frederick the Great; he was appointed inspector general of the American army, and gave them military training and discipline; Mrs. Washington came to Valley Forge February 27, 1778; on May 18, a detachment under Marquis de Lafayette moved to Barren Hill, but the British came in force against them, and they retreated over Matson's ford, Conshohocken, on a bridge of rafts; on June 18, British evacuated Philadelphia, June 19, Washington and army left Valley Forge in pursuit.

A marker is placed where General Sullivan and soldiers built a bridge across the Schuylkill in 1778;

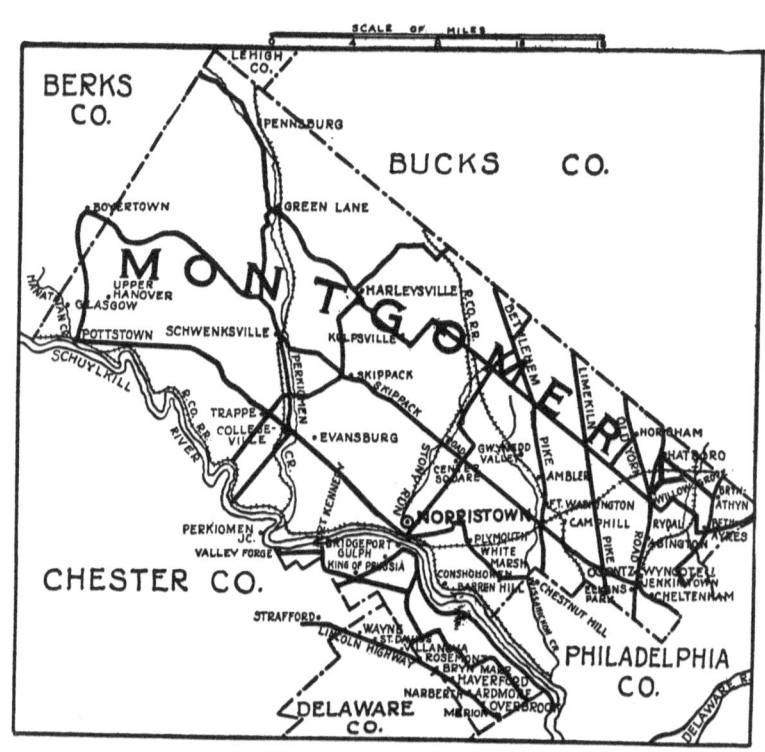

MONTGOMERY COUNTY

redoubts and intrenchments have been restored; every point of interest has been marked with granite tablets by various historical societies, and by the states whose sons suffered here; bronze equestrian statue of General Anthony Wayne, sculptor, H. K. Bush-Brown, made, 1908, marks site of cantonment of his troops; near this is replica of a brigade hospital, a soldier's hut; and the bronze statue of General Friederich Wilhelm von Steuben, granite pedestal with bronze relief; sculptor, J. Otto Schweizer, erected, 1915, by National German-American Alliance. National Memorial Arch, one of the most beautiful structures of its kind, granite, designed by Paul P. Cret, was erected by the United States Government in 1914, as a tribute to General Washington and his regiments.

Washington's headquarters (home of Isaac Potts), open daily, 8 A. M. to 6 P. M., is arranged as when he occupied it; Washington Inn was used as army bakery during encampment, ovens in basement, originally home of Colonel William Dewees, sheriff of Philadelphia, and owner, with John Potts, of the forge; the Star Redoubt; the Defenders' Gate; Cemetery; and View from observatory on Mount Joy are interesting; Museum of American History contains rare relics of Washington and the war.

Washington Memorial Protestant Episcopal chapel, and the Cloister of the Colonies, in which each of the thirteen colonies will be represented by a bay, in the center of each is the colonial seal in brass; ceiling, hand carved oak, in the central boss of each, the state coat of arms; the Cloister incloses the Garth in which is a bronze statue, "Sacrifice and Devotion," by Bela Pratt, in honor of the mothers of the nation; the porch gates were wrought by Samuel Yellin, hammered in the iron are the symbols of the four Evangelists, the lock has a miniature Liberty Bell as a keeper, and the sliding bolt passes through the knapsack of a Continental soldier, guarding the lock; windows in the chapel from D'Ascenzo Studios. Waterman Monument marks the grave of only identified soldier buried here.

Across the Schuylkill is Fat Land built by James Vaux; Washington slept here September 21, 1777; the next day, Sir William Howe came here and almost caught him. At Port Kennedy, one and one-half miles east of Valley Forge, prehistoric bones of sabretooth tigers and extinct animals are found. West of Valley Forge, Mill Grove, built, 1762, still standing, residence of John James Audubon; here he studied, painted, and wrote about "Birds of America" that have made him world-famous. Near, at the mouth of Perkiomen Creek, Washington's army encamped at Richardson's Ford, September 21, after marching all night, wet breast-high, and hungry, one thousand men without shoes. Howe moved on west of Schuylkill toward Reading, the depot of American supplies, having burned buildings at Valley Forge on his way, and reached Phœnixville, Fountain Inn. Washington marched his troops to Upper Hanover, within four miles of Pottstown; his headquarters was residence of John Potts, built 1753; and sent General Wayne with fifteen hundred men to harass the rear of British army under General Gray, but they were outnumbered by the British, and massacred at Paoli; marked by two monuments.

PERKIOMEN BRIDGE, BUILT 1798, COLLEGEVILLE
Photograph by Fred P. Powers

MONTGOMERY COUNTY 257

POTTSTOWN, founded by John Potts, population 17,431; noted for its iron industries since 1716; Mill Park Hotel, built, 1752, for residence of founder, who was visited here by Washington. Friends Meeting House, built, 1752, ground given by John Potts; he also gave ground for Zion Lutheran Church, Georgian, 1753. Residences of founder's three sons, Dr. Jonathan Potts, Director General of Hospitals, Northern Department, in the Revolutionary War, "Stowe," west of Pottstown; Samuel Potts, east of Pottstown, now "Hill School"; John Potts, Jr., a Tory judge, corner of High and Hanover Streets, center of town, later, residence of General Arthur St. Clair; Daughters of the American Revolution tablet on side. Emmanuel Lutheran Church, architects, Lechman & Murphy, windows from D'Ascenzo Studios; Christ Protestant Episcopal Church, Gothic; brownstone; good memorial windows; was received in Convention in 1827; Pottstown Hospital is controlled by Board of Women Managers, also the Library, in which art exhibitions are shown.

Not until William Penn came was any effort made to manufacture iron in Pennsylvania. Having iron furnaces of his own at Hawkhurst, England, he was interested to encourage the industry here. Thomas Rutter, Bailiff of Germantown from 1705-06, after Pastorius, moved up the Schuylkill on patent of land from William Penn, deed still in the family, and established in 1717, the "Pool Forge," on Manatawny Creek, three miles above Pottstown; he was first in Pennsylvania to manufacture iron; ore is still being mined from the same beds. Among the great names in our early iron industry, Rutter and Potts stand preeminent; the list of forges and furnaces on the Manatawny and its branches, owned by their intermarried families, before the Revolution, include Mount Pleasant furnace and forge; Spring forge; Colebrookdale furnace and forge; Amity forge; Rutter's forge; Pool forges; Pine forge and Little Pine forge.

Near Boyertown is Ringing Rocks, a natural curiosity; they make a complete octave. Michael Schlatter preached at Manatawny in 1748, also in the Reformed Church, built in 1743. McCalls, or Glasgow Forge, on Manatawny Creek, still in operation, was erected in 1725, on land conveyed by William Penn to his son, John, in 1701; 14,600 acres; sold to George McCall of Glasgow, Scotland, in 1735; who also had interest in Colebrookdale furnace managed by Thomas Potts, Jr., which supplied McCall's forge with pig iron. Green Lane Forge, on Perkiomen Creek, notable for its excellent blooms, was built in 1733 by Thomas Mayberry; earliest settler in Marlborough township, who bought 1210 acres, supplied with pig iron from Durham Furnace, Bucks County; equipment, water wheel, huge bellows, tuyere pipe, open hearth forge, melting pots, and conelike charcoal kilns.

MONTGOMERY COUNTY AUTOMOBILE TRIP TO VALLEY FORGE

(Return by Schuylkill River Drive to Philadelphia)

From Thirty-second and Market Streets, Philadelphia, out Lancaster Avenue, first turnpike in United States, completed in 1794, pattern for all subsequent roadbeds; main highway to Pittsburgh, once

MONTGOMERY COUNTY 259

thronged with teams, coaches, and Conestoga wagons with six horses, making twenty miles a day; trip from Philadelphia to Pittsburgh and return, 333 miles, in six weeks; wayside inns were located a mile apart. Originally part of Indian trail; later King's Highway; Lancaster Pike; Main Line; now Lincoln Highway, made free of tolls July 15, 1917. OVERBROOK, Roman Catholic Theological Seminary, St. Charles Borromeo, contains painting, "Crucifixion," by the late Thomas Eakens. The Pennsylvania Institution for the Instruction of the Blind, designed by E. A. Allen, Spanish Renaissance, 1898, architects, Cope & Stewardson, considered finest residential school for blind in the world, particularly well-equipped for the purpose. Montgomery County, near NARBERTH station, old Merion meeting house, built, 1695, stone, sharp roof, curious pointed gables over doors, peg is still shown where William Penn hung his hat when he rose to preach; beyond is site of Penn cottage, built, 1695. MERION, Dr. Barnes' Art Museum, built of imported French limestone; modern art. ARDMORE, St. Paul's Lutheran Church and burial ground, log church, built, 1769, present church, 1873. Red Lion Inn, still standing.

HAVERFORD, Haverford College for boys, founded in 1833 by Society of Orthodox Friends, life is focused inward, neither sight nor sound of the outer world reaches the campus of 225 acres, on which are farm and woodland, cricket and football fields, tennis courts, a running track and skating pond; the arrangement of buildings, chiefly modern colonial, from 1833–1912, shows the result that comes only by slow growth and care; architects, W. S. Vaux; Cope

& Stewardson; W. F. Price; Baily & Bassett. Library contains over four hundred Babylonian clay tablets, from 2500 B. C.; Harris collection of Oriental manuscripts; seven hundred reproductions in fictile ivory, of ancient and medieval carved ivories in British Museum, from second to eighteenth centuries; Roberts autographs, more than 11,000 items, covering period from late fifteenth century to present day; some portraits of Haverford alumni. Old Haverford meeting house, near Cobb's Creek, stone, built, 1696, has horse block used by William Penn in dismounting; chimney had curious openings in outside wall, through which fire wood was introduced to the hearth, their position is still traceable. The Buck. Tavern, built, 1732, now Haverford House.

BRYN MAWR, 415 feet above sea level (Welsh, great hill). Bryn Mawr College, founded by Dr. Joseph W. Taylor, of Burlington, New Jersey, in 1880, to establish "An institute for advanced learning, for women to have equal advantages with men." The college has continued a high standard of academic work, and maintains graduate school for women doing research work in all branches. Buildings, chiefly varieties of Gothic architecture, stone, date from 1882–1913, architects, Addison Hutton, Cope & Stewardson, C. Francis Osborne, Lockwood de Forest, and Winsor Soule; the Library, Jacobean Gothic, period, 1630, incloses cloister garden with center fountain, bosses of cloister arches are carved by hand, sculptor, Alec Miller from England. Memorial brasses, set in wall, were designed by Lockwood de Forest. Reading room contains portraits of President M. Carey Thomas, by John S.

Sargent, and ex-President James E. Rhoads, by William M. Chase.

ROSEMONT, residence, Alba Johnson, Esq., late Tudor, is typical of Main Line residences, many of them Norman or English; grounds in woodland and best traditions of English landscape gardening; marble statue of Eve, made 1855, by Bartholomew, Rome; lead statuary, Neptune and horses fountain, from Bronze Grove Guild, Worcester, England, Walter Gilbert, sculptor; the grounds may sometimes be seen by writing to owner for permission. VILLA NOVA, Roman Catholic College and monastery. Bernard Corr Memorial Hall, old English Gothic, built, 1912–14; architects, Durang & Son.

RADNOR, Delaware County, Friends meeting house, built, 1718, used as hospital for Morgan's riflemen and Potter's brigade in 1778; St. David's Church, built, 1715, by the congregation, named for patron Saint of Wales; native stone, used as hospital in Revolutionary War, leaden sash, melted for bullets; Swedish missionary at Wicaco held first services here; General Anthony Wayne, vestryman, is buried in church grounds; his monument was erected by Pennsylvania Society of the Cincinnati in 1809; Judge William Moore and wife, buried under the door-step; their daughter was the wife of the first Provost, William Smith, U. of P. Communion service given by Queen Anne. WAYNE, General Wayne Inn, hotel since 1707, Wayne's encampment near in 1792, before his western campaign against Indians. Chester County, Lincoln Highway to Strafford, Township Line Road to VALLEY FORGE, see page 253.

Return, Montgomery County, Valley Forge road to "King of Prussia" Inn, built, 1749; continue on Gulph Road to Gulph Mills, stone, built, 1747, Boulder Monument, inscription, "Gulph mills, the main Continental Army commanded by General George Washington, encamped in this vicinity December 13 to December 19, 1777, on way to Valley Forge, erected by the Pennsylvania Society, Sons of the Revolution, 1892." Over Gulph Creek near Gulph station, Philadelphia & Western Railroad, is stone bridge, inscription "Montgomery County, Upper Merian (Merion) Township, 1787; In the second year of the Foederal (Federal) Union." WEST CONSHOHOCKEN. Matson's Ford, over which Lafayette retreated from the British in 1778, continue along Schuylkill River drive to Belmont Avenue, through Fairmount Park to Philadelphia.

MONTGOMERY COUNTY AUTOMOBILE TRIP ON OLD YORK ROAD, TO DOYLESTOWN, BUCKS COUNTY, LEADING TO CENTER BRIDGE

Old York Road, original stage route to New York, laid out in 1711, from city line to Center Bridge. ELKINS PARK station. Residence of the late P. A. B. Widener, "Lynnewood Hall," notable for one of the finest art collections in the United States; near by, residence of William L. Elkins has notable art gallery, both galleries may sometimes be seen by writing to owners for cards of admission. South of Chelten Avenue, stone bridge, two arches, date, 1793; opposite is only milestone of old series south of the Neshaminy,

MONTGOMERY COUNTY 263

it is the seventh milestone mentioned in Washington's orders for the attack on Germantown. West, is residence of the late Lucretia Mott, Oak Farm, near La Mott, now Latham Park. OGONTZ, residence of the late Jay Cooke, financier of the Civil War; named for an Indian chief whom he had met. Over Tacony Creek is stone bridge, inscription, "Cheltenham bridge, 1798, 7½ miles to Phila." Church Road, near Myers Mill, Cheltenham, site, country residence of William Penn; on part of this land is country residence of the late John Wanamaker. At Washington Lane, southeast boundary of Jenkintown, is large oak tree where Washington rested his white horse.

A quarter of a mile east of Jenkintown is Abington Friends meeting house, organized, 1682, built, 1697 by William Jenkins from Wales; stone; long piazza; old shutters with strap hinges and iron hooks, door latch and knobs; all in keeping with its period of construction, fine old trees in grounds are well cared for. One mile north, RYDAL station, Ogontz School for Girls, lately in Jay Cooke mansion, organized about 1850, by Misses Bonney & Dillaye: Collegiate Gothic, built, 1917; architects, Cope & Stewardson, has Art Department. Through Meadowbrook, one mile east to BETHAYRES, residence, Henry McCarter, artist.

One mile north, BRYN ATHYN, name means "Hill of Cohesiveness," a Swedenborgian educational community. Library contains the most valuable collection of Swedenborg's writings in the world. Here is being erected a cathedral; architect, Ralph Adams Cram, gift of John Pitcairn; like the cathedrals of old, all work is prepared on the grounds; wood-carving and stonecutting by hand; glass manufactured, models made; the workmen in consultation with the donor and the architect to obtain the best results. Return to York Road. ABINGTON, library, originally Jenkintown Lyceum, built, 1830, lately remodeled, modern colonial, contains valuable collection of books bequeathed by John Lambert, artist, who also left $50,000 in trust for purchasing paintings by young artists at annual exhibitions in Pennsylvania Academy of the Fine Arts. Presbyterian Church built, 1714, is said to be third in this country; in 1740 George Whitefield preached here to three thousand persons in one day.

WILLOW GROVE PARK; pleasure resort; fine concerts given throughout the summer season, by *Sousa* and others. North on Doylestown Pike, HORSHAM, Graeme Park, colonial, stone house, hipped roof, residence, Sir William Keith, from Scotland, Baronet of Ludquhairn, Aberdeenshire, Lieutenant Governor of Pennsylvania, 1717-26; he laid foundation of the military system, encouraged putting out paper currency, and inaugurated a military display at Penn's death; property later owned by Dr. Thomas Graeme, his son-in-law; Governor Keith's coat of arms is on a large iron plate in the fireplace; in the yard is an antique slave bell and stone strength tester. Quaker meeting house, built, 1803. Approaching HATBORO, stone bridge leads York Road over Pennypack Creek, inscription "Hatborough, 1780, 16 M. to P." It is said this bridge was built in 1824, stone taken from an older bridge. Battle of "Crooked Billet," name of near-by tavern, fought in 1778, a small company of Americans

MONTGOMERY COUNTY

under Colonel John Lacy were attacked by British under Lieutenant Colonel Abercrombie, and nearly all killed; white marble monument was erected here in 1861. Continued in Bucks County.

MONTGOMERY COUNTY AUTOMOBILE TRIP FROM CHESTNUT HILL TO CAMP HILL AND FORT WASHINGTON

(Return by Norristown to Philadelphia)

At Chestnut Hill, on Bethlehem Pike, we enter Whitemarsh Valley (Umbilicamince), named from mists of Wissahickon Creek; near by is ERDENHEIM, Carson College, on one hundred acres of ground, richly endowed by Robert N. Carson, for orphan girls, that they may have the same benefits which Girard College has accorded to orphan boys; the architect, Albert Kelsey, has planned his design to be an allegorical vision of woman's life, combining beauty, utility, and sympathy; he eliminates the usual large central buildings, the administration and classrooms being in the nature of a college settlement which make up in beauty what they lack in size, and may be expanded as occasion demands. Passing the Wheel Pump and Black Horse, famous early hotels. Colonial houses; Presbyterian and Lutheran churches with their burial grounds; to junction with Skippack Road.

St. Thomas Protestant Episcopal Church, contains Communion service given by Queen Anne, first log chapel built by Edward Farmer, 1690; stone church built, 1710, on first site; during the Revolutionary War, church was occupied by various military forces, used as fort by British with guns in windows; the gravestones, long, flat pieces of slate on four columns, used as cooking stoves, with fires lighted underneath, upright stones were marks for target practice, bullet holes may still be seen in them. American forces camped here November 22, 1777; being warned by Lydia Darragh of a British attack, when the enemy made their appearance, General Wayne opened fire from Fort Washington, the British retreating with a loss of one hundred men. Whitemarsh church is repeatedly mentioned in Washington's diary as a center of operations; present church, near first site, consecrated, 1881. Gothic, native stone, interesting interior, with high pointed roof and narrow lancet memorial windows, all made abroad but one, "Angel of the Resurrection," by Tiffany; high on west wall is a rose window; three small lights in the George and Anna Catherine Sheaff window are said to have been painted by Albrecht Durer; reredos, "Christ Breaking the Bread," painted in Italy; altar, Indiana limestone with carved angels kneeling; the rood screen with loft, English quartered oak, is exquisitely craved. Encircling a window is mural decoration by Marianna Sloan. In the burial ground is an Iona Cross, marking last resting place of Henry Howard Houston, for whose memorial Houston Hall was given to the University of Pennsylvania.

View from north door of church shows, east, Camp Hill; in valley below, Washington's headquarters, stone house two and a half stories, one-half mile east from Camp Hill station, Pennsylvania Railroad, left wing of army, posted rear of house; here Washing-

MONTGOMERY COUNTY 267

ton decided to establish fortified encampment at Valley Forge; December 12, whole army ordered to march to Valley Forge, via Swedes Ford, Norristown, where they crossed the Schuylkill on a bridge of wagons, with rails laid over them; "Swedes Ford," hotel built, 1723, still standing, at Bridgeport.

North of St. Thomas Church we locate Fort Washington by its flagstaff, in center of earthwork thrown up by General Anthony Wayne's men. West, from Church, Militia Hill, where some of the stones, used as anchors for tents, are still in position; at foot of hill is Wissahickon Creek, over which leads the high railroad bridge belonging to the Trenton cut-off of the Pennsylvania Railroad. Passing Fortside Inn, north, on Bethlehem Pike, is stone marker, inscription "About 700 feet south of this stone is an American Redoubt and site of Howe's threatened attack, December 6, 1777; from here Washington's army marched to Valley Forge. Erected, 1891, by the Pennsylvania Society, Sons of the Revolution."

Farther on Bethlehem Pike, over Sandy Run, is the village of FORT WASHINGTON, now home of the Darby School of Painting, a summer art school conducted by Hugh H. Breckenridge, member of the faculty of the Pennsylvania Academy of the Fine Arts, there science of color is taught in its fullest significance. On Engertown Road is old Friends meeting house. Farther, on Limekiln Pike, is Pennsylvania School of Horticulture for Women, post office, Ambler, founded in 1910, thorough training, through all seasons, eliminates waste of costly inexperience, and fits a woman for a life that is healthful, attractive, and remunerative. Near Sumneytown and Butler Pike is "Three Tuns Inn."

Gwynedd, meeting house, built, 1700, Welsh Quakers worshiped here.

Down Butler Pike to AMBLER, residence of Dr. R. V. Mattison, built, 1890, Scotch baronial style, wrought iron gates designed in Munich; opposite is Trinity Memorial Church, Romanesque, noted for its beautiful windows, designed by F. S. Lamb, original, and adapted from paintings by world famous artists, of scenes in Christ's life, made by J. and R. Lamb; interior paneled in oak, similar to House of Parliament, London; font, Italian marble, good design. Through Morris Road, over bridge crossed by Washington's army, between Morris and Skippack roads, one mile west of Ambler, is stone residence, built by Abraham Dawes in 1736, was Washington's headquarters, October 21, 1777.

Out Skippack Road, on road from Center Square to HEEBNERVILLE, Washington's headquarters, October 16; residence of Peter Wentz, still standing, two story, stone, built, 1758. Out Township line to KULPSVILLE, on Sumneytown Road, Baptist or Mennonite meeting house, here are buried General Francis Nash of North Carolina, and other officers who died of wounds received in the Battle of Germantown. Northwest, one mile, HARLEYSVILLE, residence of Henry Funk, Bishop of Mennonite Church, who with the Dunkards of Ephrata, made translation, in 1748, from the German, of Tielman Jan van Braght's great historical book of the Mennonites, termed the noblest specimen of American colonial bibliography; Henry Funk's mill, still standing, known as Musselman's Mill, contains a parchment deed, date, 1733, with great seal of the province and signature of Thomas Penn.

Return to Skippack Road, to Pennypacker's Mills, SCHWENKSVILLE, residence of the late Governor Samuel Pennypacker, two story, stone house, Washington's headquarters before and after Battle of Germantown; army marched down Skippack Road, 7.00 P. M., October 3, to attack the enemy; here October 7, Washington received a committee of Friends, appointed by the Yearly Meeting, against war; Schwenksville was settled by Schwenkfelders from Silesia in 1734; Casper Schwenkfeld preached, in 1523, doctrines accepted by George Fox in 1648, were forerunners of Quakers. Perkiomen Seminary, at Pennsburg, originated in a school founded by Schwenkfelders, 1764. Down Perkiomen Creek road, over finest old stone bridge in state, five arches, built, 1799, architect, George Lewis, carries Ridge Road over Perkiomen Creek at COLLEGEVILLE, Ursinus College; Co-ed Lutheran, portraits by Albert Rosenthal. And old Providence meeting house.

One mile west, at TRAPPE, Augustus Church, oldest Lutheran church in United States; built, 1743; unaltered; used as hospital for American soldiers during Revolutionary war; Henry Melchior Muhlenberg was sent from Halle, Germany, in 1742, to organize this church in Pennsylvania; first regularly ordained preacher, reports he sent to Halle supply much early, original information. His sons, born here, were General Peter Muhlenberg, pastor of church in Shenandoah Valley, who called on his congregation to enlist in the Revolutionary War, and Frederich Augustus, speaker, First National Congress, 1789. EVANSBURG, St. James Protestant Episcopal Church and schoolhouse, built about 1700, contains Bible, prayer book, and old walnut Communion table, sent over by the English Society in 1723, to its foreign mission. Revolutionary soldiers are buried in the church yard. Here is an eight arch stone bridge, date 1792.

NORRISTOWN, county seat, settled, 1784, population 32,319. Courthouse built, 1791, native white marble; on grounds is Rittenhouse monument, granite shaft, dedicated 1876, marks the meridian. Jail, built, 1851, red sandstone, castellated Norman, architect for courthouse and jail, N. Le Brun. Historical Society of Montgomery County has local historical collections. St. John's Protestant Episcopal Church, Gothic, dedicated, 1815, Revolutionary soldiers are buried in its grounds. Montgomery Trust Company, Greek, Ionic, Westerly granite and Indiana limestone, facing public square, on site of first hotel in Norristown. In Montgomery Cemetery are buried Charles Heber Clark (Max Adler), and General Winfield Scott Hancock.

PLYMOUTH MEETING, old Friends meeting house, built, 1715, stone, used as hospital during Revolutionary War, Thomas Hovenden, artist, buried in grounds; residence of Mrs. Thomas Hovenden (Helen Corson), was a noted underground railway station for refugee slaves. Stone bridge over Plymouth Creek, date, 1796; stone bridge carrying Germantown and Reading Railroad over Plymouth Creek, date, 1802. BARREN HILL, Lafayette and detachment of army attacked here by British, May 18, 1778. ROXBOROUGH, Philadelphia, St. Timothy's Protestant Episcopal Church has frieze, procession of angels. Through Ridge Avenue to Wissahickon Drive, Fairmount Park, to Philadelphia.

XVI
DAUPHIN COUNTY

SEAT of state capital; formed March 4, 1785; named for title of the Dauphin of France, then Louis XVI, in recognition of aid rendered to the colonies in Revolutionary War. Chief industries iron and steel; in the north, anthracite coal. High mountain ranges, with valleys of rich rolling farm lands, intersected with many streams, show much scenic beauty.

HARRISBURG, county seat; laid out in 1785; population 75,917. The state capitol's best approach is from Third and South Streets, the massive pile looms up in exquisite proportion, one is impressed with the inherent dignity of the façade, controlled by a well-proportioned dome; dedicated in 1906; architect, Joseph W. Huston; Roman and Italian Renaissance, with influence of Greek Corinthian; dome suggests St. Peter's in Rome; bronze doors, designed by J. W. Huston, were modeled by Otto Jansen; superb groups of statuary on either side of the main entrance typify, "The Joy, and Burden of Life," sculptor, George Gray Barnard; within the rotunda is the splendid collection of battle flags, 378, owned by the state; one of the most interesting of the kind.

Mural decorations, the Rotunda; Economic "Triumphs of the State," artist, Sir Edwin A. Abbey; from large lunettes show the "Spirits of Commerce, Oil (Light), Coal, Steel"; four pendentives contain single

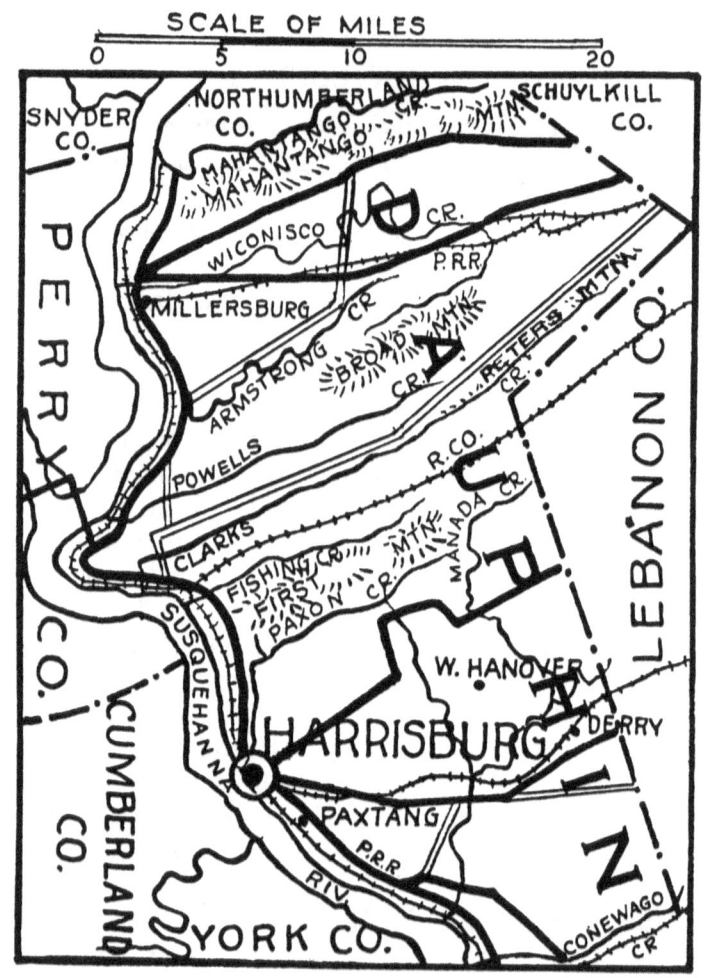

DAUPHIN COUNTY

DAUPHIN COUNTY 273

allegorical figures, Religion, Art, Literature, Science; governor's reception room; frieze, artist, Violet Oakley, "Foundations of the State of Liberty Spiritual." Lunettes, artists, John W. Alexander and W. B. Van Ingen, "Growth and Expansion of the State of Liberty Spiritual," by the establishment of various religious bodies that came to the new colony. House of Representatives; wainscoting of marble from the French Pyrenees; above the large windows are stained glass by W. B. Van Ingen; paintings by Abbey, "The Apotheosis of Pennsylvania," with figures that stand as portraits, "Penn's Treaty with the Indians," and "The Reading of the Declaration of Independence," planned by Abbey and finished in his studio after his death; the dome contains his exquisitely painted decoration, symbolical of the "Passage of the Hours"; only one of Abbey's paintings for the senate room was finished, his "Valley Forge," it has been placed with his others in the House of Representatives; Miss Oakley's paintings were unveiled there in February, 1917; she will also decorate the Supreme Court Room.

The Moravian tiled pavement was designed and manufactured by Dr. Henry C. Mercer; these artists were all born in Pennsylvania; the consecutive line of historical and idealistic thought in the decorations was a conception of the architect. In Capitol Park, sixteen acres, notable for shrubbery and flowers, is a bronze equestrian statue, General and Governor John Frederick Hartranft; sculptor, Frederick W. Ruckstuhl; also Mexican monument, white marble, erected by the state in 1868, in memory of citizens lost in war with Mexico, 1846-48. An elementary course of art is taught in nearly every public school in Pennsylvania, prepared by the Department of Public Instruction at Harrisburg, the basis of all art instruction in normal schools; nearly every summer school in the state offers a course in freehand drawing, and special courses for both grade teachers and supervisors.

Harrisburg is famous for her park system, the 972 acres extend along the river front, and to the center of the city for over a mile. Harris Park, four acres, from Paxton Street to Mulberry Street; contains monument to John Harris, first settler, and John Harris, Jr., founder of the city; facing the park, below Mulberry Street, is the Harris residence, stone, built in 1766; little changed from the original form; Lincoln Park, two and one-fourth acres, from Mulberry Street to Market Street, contains memorial, "In memory of J. Conrad Weiser, 1696–1764, Provincial Interpreter, and his friend Shikellimy, 1683–1748, an Oneida Chief." Erected about 1911. Facing this park is the building of the Historical Society of Dauphin County, with interesting museum. Promenade Park, three and one-half acres, Market to State Streets; and the D. W. Gross Park, two acres, Water to Herr Streets, with bronze memorial statue, a charging soldier, in memory of Sylvester P. Sullivan. Reservoir Park, eighty-eight acres, contains the city reservoir, giving a lake setting, with elaborate planting of flowers and shrubs; best scenic view is from this elevation. Wildwood Park, 666 acres, has a large lake for boating. The Boulevard or Parkway, 146 acres, is along streams, through ravines, and meadows; landscape architect, Warren H. Manning.

THE JOY AND BURDEN OF LIFE
Harrisburg State Capitol

George Gray Barnard, Sculptor
Photographed by Boyd P. Rothrock, Curator

DAUPHIN COUNTY

St. Patrick's Procathedral; architect, George I. Lovatt; Renaissance; main altar, marble, is reproduction of Bernini's altar in St. Peter's, Rome. In Grace Protestant Episcopal Church is a painting by E. Irving Couse, "Adoration by the Shepherds." Soldiers' Monument, State and Second Streets, "To the Soldiers of Dauphin County, in 1861-65; erected by their fellow citizens in 1869." Bronze tablet in west wall of the Camp Curtin School House, corner of Sixth and Woodbine Streets; commemorating site of old Camp Curtin, 1861-65; placed in 1911, by Keystone Chapter, United States Daughters of 1812. Memorial Market Street entrance to the City of Harrisburg; eastern approach to new bridge, formerly the old "Camel Back," includes two columns from the old burned state capitol, and commemorative bronze tablets, designed by A. Sterling Calder; architect, Albert Kelsey; presented by the Henry McCormick Estate under auspices of the Harrisburg Civic Club; erected and dedicated in 1906.

The Susquehanna River, one mile wide here, is spanned by three other bridges; Mulberry Street viaduct is said to be largest reinforced concrete bridge in the world, designed and erected by James H. Fuertes; stone arch bridge of the Pennsylvania Railroad at Rockville, said to be the largest four-track stone bridge in the world. Historic buildings; residence of William Maclay, first United States Senator from Pennsylvania, built in 1791; original building intact, with large wing added; on upper river front above South Street, used later by the Harrisburg Academy. Old Derry Church, Derry Township, a Presbyterian settlement since 1724, first log church built in 1732; present stone building on first site, built, 1883; has burial ground of much historic interest; Old Hanover Church, Presbyterian, eleven miles from Harrisburg, first log church built on Bow Creek in 1735; present building closed; the ancient burial ground is chief point of interest. Old Paxtang Church, Presbyterian, three miles east of Harrisburg, first log church said to have been built in 1716, with burial ground; present stone building built, 1740. Bronze gate and tablet at Paxtang Cemetery is memorial to soldiers of the French and Indian War and the Revolution; dedicated in 1906 by Harrisburg Chapter, Daughters of the American Revolution. Fort Hunter, five miles from Harrisburg on Fort Hunter and Fishing Creek Road, was laid out about 1760, on a high bluff facing the Susquehanna River, colonial house, built in 1814 by Colonel Archibald McAllister, is on foundations of an English blockhouse known as Hunter's Fort.

XVII
LUZERNE COUNTY

FORMED September 25, 1786; named in honor of Anne Cæsar, Chevalier de la Luzerne, minister from France to the United States 1779-83. Ranks third in number of inhabitants of Pennsylvania counties. Along either bank of the Susquehanna, a broad and shallow river, lie rich, fertile, alluvial bottom lands, mostly well cultivated; bounding them are ranges of hills and mountains 1200-1600 feet above sea level; other mountains in the northwest of the county attain an altitude of 2200 feet. In the northeast lies the historic Wyoming Valley, Indian name, Maughwauwama, or large plains, a long, oval basin from Campbell's Ledge to Nanticoke Falls, some sixteen miles in length, with an average breadth of three miles.

Luzerne County lies within the limits of the Connecticut Charter, granted in 1662, and within the limits of the Pennsylvania Charter granted in 1681; this double ownership caused much contention in later years, finally the Susquehanna Company of Connecticut was victorious; settlers now came rapidly, and by 1778 were distributed in several villages, with schools, churches, and all the characteristics of New England orderliness and thrift, enthusiasm and devoted patriotism. The British leader, Colonel John Butler, saw that this settlement was exposed in position, and that they had sent the

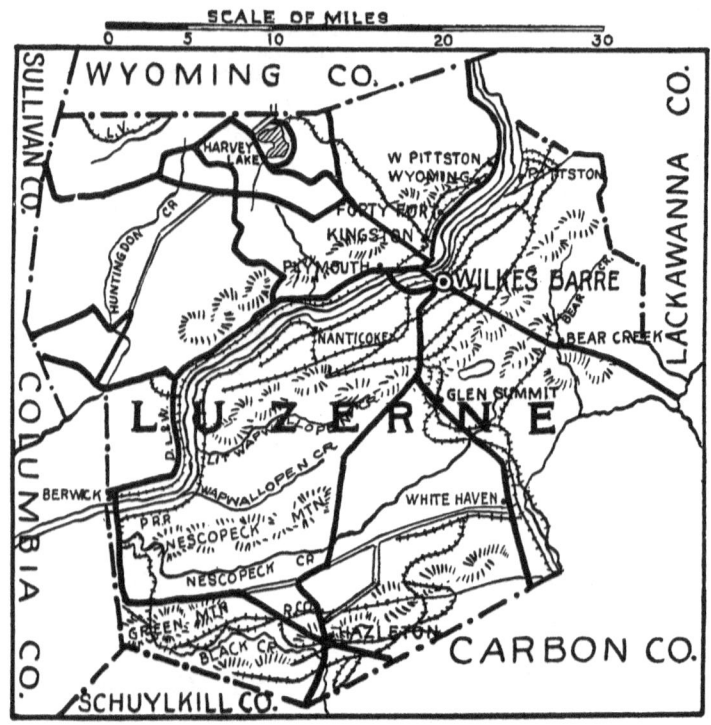

Luzerne County

LUZERNE COUNTY 279

best part of their militia to serve in Washington's army, so with a company of his own rangers, a regiment of Johnson's Greens, and a band of Indians, in all about 1200 men, he took the warpath from Niagara; they journeyed down the Susquehanna in bark canoes, landed above the settlement, and began their work of murder and plunder, harrowing incidents are made known by Campbell in his "Gertrude of Wyoming." The women and children were placed in the fort. At the junction of Fort and River Streets, in the borough of FORTY FORT; a conglomerate boulder with bronze tablet, marks the site of "Forty Fort," erected by the Connecticut settlers in 1772. From this fort, on July 3, 1778, the Wyoming Militia, numbering about 300, mostly old men and boys, marched forth to oppose the invading British troops and Indians, fight the Battle of Wyoming, and meet with complete defeat and atrocious massacre, in which the British officers were unable to set any bounds in the butchery of their savage allies; next day the fort was taken; the Indians burned all the houses; the inhabitants fled to the woods, and the valley was abandoned; a hundred women and children perished of fatigue and starvation. On Wyoming Avenue in the borough of Wyoming is the "Wyoming Monument," marking the burial place of many of the patriots who were slain in the battle and massacre; dedicated July, 1846.

On Susquehanna Avenue near Seventh Street is "Queen Esther's Rock," a half-breed queen of the Senecas, on which she tomahawked fourteen prisoners; marked by a tablet, placed by the Daughters of the American Revolution, bearing this inscription, "Upon this rock the Indian queen Esther slaughtered the brave patriots taken in the battle of July 3, 1778." On the bank of the river, near the Pittston Ferry bridge, in the borough of WEST PITTSTON, is a small monument marking site of Jenkins' Fort, destroyed by the British and Indians July, 1778. The Battle of Wyoming, with the subsequent massacre, was one of the important events of the Revolutionary War, as it led to the sending of the Sullivan Expedition in 1779 into the country of the Six Nations, whereby the power of their confederacy was forever broken. WHITE HAVEN Township was the place of Sullivan's army encampment, in 1779.

The oldest church in the county is in Forty Fort, not far from the site of the old fort, interior of the building remains as it was when erected in 1808; in the burial ground are many old graves, with headstones bearing quaint inscriptions. Other historic places marked by tablet or monument are, site of a bridge built by the engineers of General John Sullivan's army in the spring of 1779, on the banks of Ten Mile Run, northwest of Bear Creek Village, marked by boulder with tablet. Place where two commissioned officers, and three others of General Sullivan's army were ambushed and slain by Indians, April, 1779; marked by boulder with tablet. In the Public Square, WILKES-BARRE, is a monument marking site of Fort Wilkes-Barre, erected in 1776–77 by the inhabitants of the town; destroyed by the British and Indians July, 1778. On the river common, at the foot of Northampton Street, a boulder, with tablet, marks the site of Fort Wyoming, erected, 1771, demolished

LUZERNE COUNTY

in 1774 or 1775. And at the foot of South Street a boulder, with tablet, is erected near the site of Fort Durkee, built in 1769 by first settlers from Connecticut, named for their leader, Major John Durkee, who founded and named Wilkes-Barre in honor of John Wilkes and Colonel Barre; this fort fell into decay prior to 1776, it was located near site of a village occupied from 1758–63 by a band of Delaware Indians under "King" Tedyuscung.

WILKES-BARRE, county seat, was settled, 1772, population, 73,833. Places of modern interest, containing historical collections, portraits, and paintings, open free to the public, are the Courthouse, modified adaptation of classic, the façade, with Ionic porch, is very dignified, surmounted by a Gustavino dome; architects, Osterling, McCormick & French; said to be one of the handsomest and most elaborately decorated courthouses in this country; contains mural paintings by E. H. Blashfield, Kenyon Cox, Will H. Low, William T. Smedley, C. D. Hinton, and others. Irem Temple, Moorish design, with tall slender minarets at each corner. Osterhout Free Library, Gothic. Wyoming Historical and Geological Society. The Second National Bank, with interesting Ionic porch at entrance, steel frame, faced with brick and concrete, architects, McCormick & French. First Presbyterian Church and St. Stephen's Protestant Episcopal Church contain handsome memorial tablets and stained glass windows; a fine bronze relief, by J. Massey Rhind, is in St. Stephen's. In the Coal Exchange Building is the Atherton Atelier, T. H. Atherton, Jr., Superintendent, Architecture, in coöperation with Society of Beaux Arts. Particular care has been given to improving the public parks located in different parts of the city. Public square in center, and the river commons, stretching along the bank of the Susquehanna for a considerable distance, are attractive and noteworthy. Opposite the city, across the river, is Riverside Park, chiefly a natural grove of old trees.

The principal educational institution is Wyoming Seminary, co-ed, at KINGSTON, founded in 1844, conducted under auspices of the Wyoming Conference of the Methodist Episcopal Church, ranks high as a college preparatory school and has an academic art course. There are many places of scenic beauty; notably the Conyngham dairy and stock farms at Hillside, just outside Wyoming Valley, on the road from Kingston to Harvey's Lake, which is 1226 feet above sea level; one of the largest stock farms in the state, covering 651 acres. Sugarloaf Valley, not far from HAZLETON. The Hazleton Country Club. Glen Summit Springs and the neighboring country, Bear Creek Village, and Wyoming Valley, viewed either from Campbell's Ledge, Mount Lookout, or Prospect Rock.

The principal roads are maintained in good order, and there are no toll roads in the county. For many years the chief industry has been the mining of anthracite coal, discovered here in 1762; for a considerable period it stood first among the counties in annual output; first development of this coal for shipping to market from the Wyoming region was in 1776, when two Durham boats purchased cargoes from a

LUZERNE COUNTY

mine operated by R. Greer, near Wyoming. There are many large manufactories. Within a ten mile circle, having Wilkes-Barre public square as its center, there were, according to the United States census of 1910, thirty-three smaller municipalities, cities, boroughs, and hamlets, having a total population, including Wilkes-Barre, of 266,951. The other principal towns of this county are Hazleton, population 32,277; Nanticoke, 22,614; Plymouth, 16,500; Pittston, 18,497; West Pittston, 6968; Kingston, 8952. Peter Frederick Rothermel, prominent historical painter, was born in Nescopeck, this county, in 1817.

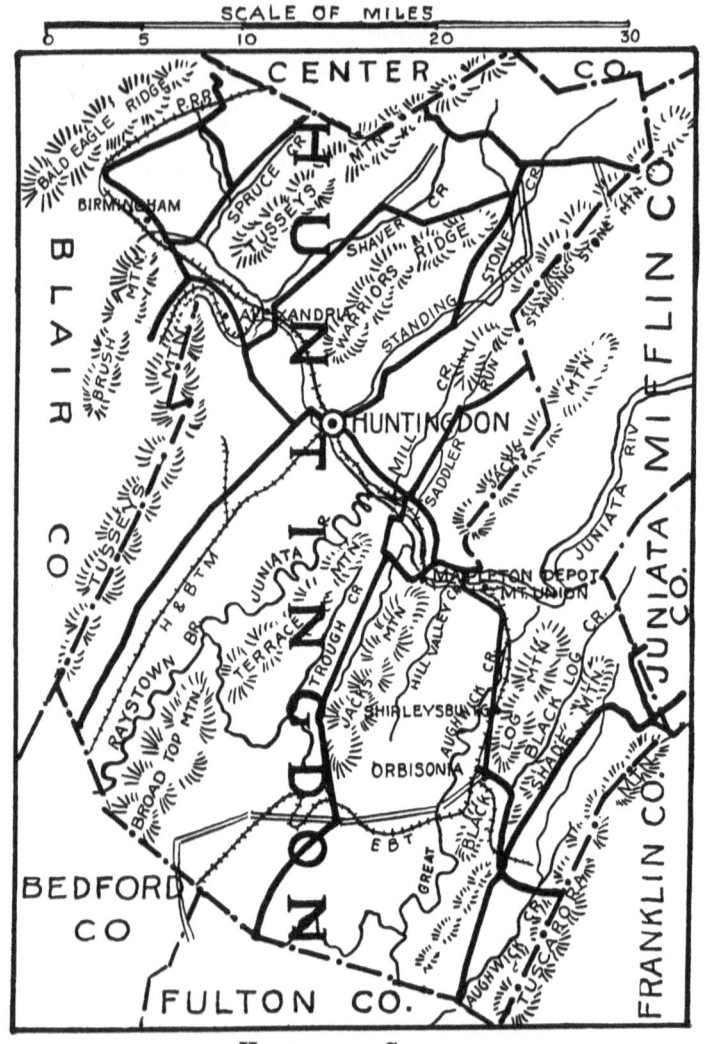

Huntingdon County

XVIII
HUNTINGDON COUNTY

FORMED September 20, 1787; named by Provost William Smith, of the University of Pennsylvania, in honor of Selina, Countess of Huntingdon, a benefactress of the University; lies within the central mountainous region, being drained by the Juniata. Many fine farms are on the rich soil of the river flats. Juniata iron early became famous, and numerous iron works were erected; the old Bedford Furnace was near Orbisonia. Abundance, variety, and value of the ores; rich and convenient deposits of limestone; contiguity of the Broad Top, Allegheny and Cumberland coal fields, combine to indicate the importance of this country. Other industries are coal-mining, lumber, agriculture, and manufactories. Large water-power dams of the Pennsylvania Central, and Raystown Water Power Companies generate electric light and power.

HUNTINGDON, county seat; population 7051, largest town on the Juniata. The first white visitors to this region were traders, in traffic with Indians, exchanging goods for furs and skins. On incursions, made before the middle of the eighteenth century, they found a tribe, a branch of the Six Nations, located on the now southeast portion of this borough, their wigwams circling around a pillar of stone, 14 feet high and 6 inches square, covered with hieroglyphics supposed to be a record of their history and achievements. This tribe, besides hunting and fishing, had cleared land and cultivated corn. This stone was regarded with great veneration by the natives; here they had assembled for centuries to hold their grand councils; its conspicuous position and appearance led the white visitors to name the locality, "Standing Stone," it stood above Second Street, on or near 208 Allegheny Street. Conrad Weiser, in 1748, and John Harris, in 1754, in accounts of their journeys to the Ohio River, both describe this stone.

The Proprietaries of this province, ever mindful of the rights of the Indians, would not grant lands, nor permit settlements to be made until the Indian title had been purchased; at a treaty held in Albany, in 1754, the Six Nations, consisting of the Mohawks, Oneidas, Onondagas, Cayugas, Senecas, and Tuscaroras, executed a deed to the Proprietaries for a large portion of the province, including the whole valley of the Juniata; soon after, the resident tribe migrated, and, it is supposed, carried the stone with them. The seal of the borough has, as its central figure, a Standing Stone. A second stone was erected by the settlers; and in 1896 a third, at Penn and Third Streets; as a memorial of the ancient standing stone of the Indians. Fort Standing Stone was built here at an early date; site about intersection of Penn and Second Streets, it was stockaded and provided with barracks, blockhouses, and magazines constructed of heavy hewn timber, and was the place of many important incidents during troublesome times following the defeat of General Braddock in 1755, and until peace was made with Great Britain in 1783.

Provost William Smith, D.D., obtained the land in 1766 from George Croghan, and numerous other tracts

HUNTINGDON COUNTY

in the vicinity, and in 1767 caused the town of Huntingdon to be laid out, now on the William Penn Highway; the proprietor donating plots of ground for a public school, cemetery, and to each of six prominent religious denominations. About 1797 a post office was established here, and John Cadwallader was appointed postmaster; a weekly mail was carried between Harrisburg and Huntingdon. The most important public buildings, architecturally, are Juniata College, nine buildings, erected 1878-1916; the older buildings are colonial; Library, Gothic, red brick with terra-cotta trimmings, built, 1907; contains memorial windows; the Church of the Brethren on the college campus, Gothic; McGee sandstone; erected, 1910; members of this sect settled in this county in 1775; and the J. C. Blair Memorial Hospital, Spanish mission style, light buff brick and Indiana limestone trimmings, on a commanding position overlooking the town. E. L. Tilton, New York, architect, also of the College Library and Church of the Brethren.

Among the places of historic interest in the county are Fort Shirley, built, 1755, on bluff near site of Indian town of Aughwick, now Shirleysburg. McAlevey's Fort, at the head of Standing Stone Creek Valley, named for Captain William McAlevey, afterwards general in the Revolutionary War. Warm Springs, five miles northeast of Huntingdon, known, in 1775, as a resort for invalids. Pulpit Rocks on the Warriors Ridge, on the old pike between Huntingdon and Alexandria. And Jack's Narrows, where the Juniata River cuts through Jack's Mountain, west of Mount Union. The Pennsylvania Canal extended through this county from Shaver's Aqueduct, below Mount Union, to line of Blair County, above Water Street; here in Indian times canoes came to receive supplies of lead. Two miles east is ALEXANDRIA, laid out, 1793; in 1800 the turnpike was completed to Alexandria, and stage service to Harrisburg began; fare charged travelers was six cents a mile; this town was the shipping point of grain for the rich Hart's Log and Shaver's Creek valleys.

XIX
ALLEGHENY COUNTY

FORMED September 24, 1788; named from Delaware Indian word signifying "Fair Water." Surface undulating, many elevations being precipitous. Is the center of one of the richest bituminous coal and natural gas districts in the world. Oil fields lie mainly in basins of Allegheny and Ohio Rivers. Staple manufactures are iron, steel and glass. The history of Allegheny County presents a greater variety of startling incidents than almost any other portion of the state. Mound builders were primeval inhabitants, site of ancient fortifications are on Chartier's Creek, eight miles from PITTSBURGH, county seat, second city in size in the state, on site of Shannopin's Town, chief of about twenty families of Delawares; he attended councils with the Governor; his name is signed on several state archives. By it ran the main Indian path from east to west.

Washington first came to "The Forks," in 1753, on way to Fort Le Boeuf. The French possessed it as Fort Duquesne 1754–58, when it was conquered by General Forbes; General Stanwix erected a stockade and named it Fort Pitt, for the British premier. In 1764, Colonel Bouquet built a redoubt on site of the Fort; old brick blockhouse is still standing, Penn Avenue near Second Street. First town of Pittsburgh built near the Fort in 1760, inhabitants enjoyed com-

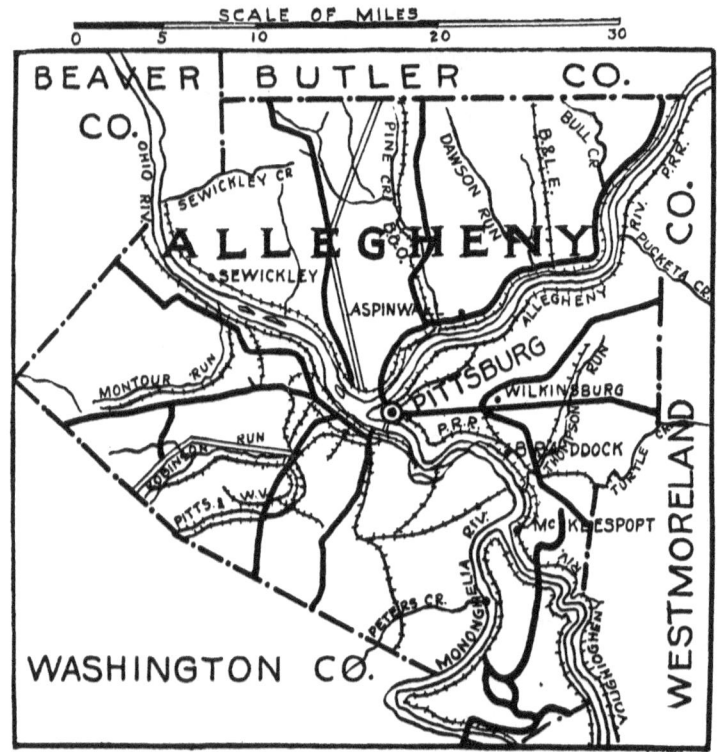

ALLEGHENY COUNTY

ALLEGHENY COUNTY 291

parative quiet until 1763, when Pontiac's War broke out and they were completely surrounded by savages, later rescued by Colonel Bouquet. In 1811 first steamboat ever run on western waters was launched at Pittsburgh, the "New Orleans." In 1839 first iron steamboat made in the United States, the "Valley Forge," was built here.

The sister city, ALLEGHENY, north side, was incorporated with Pittsburgh in 1907, combined population 588,343. An art commission was organized, 1911, for an improvement in public works of art in Pittsburgh, and to educate public sentiment for civic beautification; in 1915, E. H. Bennett, City Planning Architect of Chicago, was engaged to make a thorough economic and æsthetic analysis of "The Point," at junction of the Monongahela and Allegheny rivers.

Close to the business center is SCHENLEY PARK, 440 acres, acquired by gift to the city in 1889, contains the Carnegie Institute; Carnegie Institute of Technology; Phipps Conservatory and Hall of Botany, given by Mr. Phipps in memory of his mother, with one of the most beautiful bronze statues in the world, "Mother and Child," French sculptor; Hawkins Memorial, a bronze portrait figure, backed by wall of polished granite, base and floor marble, sculptor, Richard H. Couper, erected, 1904, in honor of Colonel Hawkins, Tenth Pennsylvania Regiment, in Spanish-American War; Panther Hollow, in which is an arch bridge, Beaver County sandstone, with panthers, sculptor, G. Moretti; and two other stone arch bridges built in 1892, architect, A. L. Schultz.

Near the Forbes Avenue entrance is the great central

building of the CARNEGIE INSTITUTE, established by Andrew Carnegie with large annual fund, in perpetuity, for purchase of objects of art and scientific collections; built 1892–95, Italian Renaissance, sandstone, architects, Alden & Harlow, enlarged in 1904–07, contains Library, Music Hall, Department of Fine Arts, and the Natural History Museum, in which are large collections of ancient pottery, Chinese glass, and porcelains representing various eras; jades and crystals; valuable collections of coins and medals; illuminated manuscripts and early printed books, cut and uncut gems; one of the largest collections of carved ivory in the United States; and art metal work. The Library operates more than one hundred and seventy agencies for free distribution of literature, within "Greater Pittsburgh."

On top of the building are four bronze groups, representing Science, Art, Literature, and Music. Bronze statues, Michelangelo and Galileo, are at entrance to Art Gallery. Entrance to Music Hall is through exquisitely designed bronze doors, wrought in relief, with bronze statues, Bach and Shakespeare, at either side. These bronzes were designed and modeled in the studio of J. Massey Rhind, and cast in Naples. Foyer to the Music Hall is considered the most beautiful portion of the Institute; here are twenty-four huge columns of Tinos marble, with gilded Corinthian capitals; and one of the finest organs in the world, on which the greatest organists obtainable give concerts of highly classical music, which are free, every Saturday night and Sunday afternoon. The great Archer, Queen Victoria's Jubilee organist, held this position for many

GALLERY OF THE SCULPTURE HALL, CARNEGIE INSTITUTE, PITTSBURGH

ALLEGHENY COUNTY 293

years. The Hall of Sculpture, designed on lines of the Parthenon, is two stories high, around the first story is a Greek Doric colonnade; above this is a row of Ionic columns, all of the most flawless, milk-white, Pantelicon marble, dug out of the quarries from which the marble of the Parthenon itself was obtained; collections of sculpture represent, chronologically, its history from early Egyptian to the Renaissance of the sixteenth century.

Among the artists represented in the permanent collection of paintings are Dagnan Bouveret, "Disciples at Emmaus"; Winslow Homer, "Wreck"; Whistler, "Sarasate"; E. A. Abbey, "The Penance of Eleanor"; George Innes, "The Clouded Sun"; also Anton Mauve, Bastien Le Page, Raffaelli, Gari Melchers, Jules Simon, and Childe Hassam. Annual exhibitions of international modern art are held in May and June, and many others by different art societies during the year. In the Entrance Hall are mural decorations by the late John W. Alexander, a native of Pittsburgh, typifying "The Apotheosis of Pittsburgh"; they surround the staircase and galleries to the third floor. Art societies holding annual exhibitions at the Carnegie Institute are, Associated Artists of Pittsburgh, organized, 1910; Art Society of Pittsburgh, organized, 1873, supported the Pittsburgh Orchestra for fifteen years, and gives excellent free exhibitions and lectures; Duquesne Ceramic Club, organized, 1891; Pittsburgh Architectural Club, Chapter Architectural League of America, organized, 1897. Pittsburgh Etching Club, organized, 1909, held exhibition of Whistler's etchings in 1914.

In the park, west of this building, is the Christopher Magee memorial fountain, made in 1907, granite, sculptor, Augustus Saint Gaudens. In front is Industry Statue, marble, after model in the Louvre, Paris. The Technical School, brick, built, 1905, architect, Henry Hornbostel, includes, in the art course, day and evening classes in applied design, and department of architecture. The Pittsburgh Athletic Association, architects, Janssen & Abbott, has interior decorations by Alfred Herter, and collection of paintings. Drinking fountain, Fifth Avenue, front of Montefiore Hall, placed in 1912, granite, with carved profile of an Indian; inscription, "Catahecassa, Black Hoof, war chief of the Shawnees," was present at Braddock's defeat in 1754, a friend and ally of the United States.

In SCHENLEY FARMS, directly opposite the entrance to Schenley Park, is the University of Pittsburgh, on a natural amphitheater. The buildings stand out very effectively against the sky line; founded in 1887, architect, Henry Hornbostel; landscape architect, Cass Gilbert; has departments of fine and industrial arts. Memorial Hall to Soldiers and Sailors of the Civil and Spanish Wars contains historic flags, statues, trophies and historical portraits.

Other parks are ALLEGHENY, north side, ninety acres, with monuments in honor of Washington, equestrian, made 1891, sculptor, Frederick Mayer; Baron von Humboldt, made 1869; Thomas A. Armstrong; and the Hampton Monument, made 1871, granite shaft, surmounted by bronze figure of a gunner, commemorates the bravery of Hampton's Battery in the Civil War. Within east entrance of Allegheny Cemetery

ALLEGHENY COUNTY 295

is the Arsenal Explosion Monument in honor of those who lost their lives September 17, 1862. Monument to General Alexander Hays, who was killed in the battle of the Wilderness, in 1864, by soldiers of his command. Gothic receiving vault. The Bindley mausoleum, replica of Napoleon's tomb in Paris, pure example of the Renaissance, has window by William and Annie Lee Willet. The Porter Angel and Cross, imported from Italy, fine example of marble carving. The Byers mausoleum, imitation of Temple of Minerva at Athens, white granite. Near by is the United States Arsenal, in ornamental grounds. RIVERSIDE PARK, on Perrysville Avenue, 217 acres purchased by popular subscription in 1894, has beautiful drives and footpaths; contains the observatory, connected with Allegheny University, in which the telescope was made by Mr. and Mrs. Tillinghast, in their home workshop opposite.

HIGHLAND PARK, 300 acres, northeast limit of city, acquired, 1872, has main water reservoirs and the Zoölogical Gardens; main gateway is 56 feet high with Doric columns, surmounted by bronze groups representing "Welcome," and bronze figures at base; Stanton Avenue entrance has two granite pedestals surmounted by equestrian statues, sculptor, G. Moretti, made 1897; in the park is Robert Burns statue, sculptor, J. Massey Rhind; and heroic bronze group, portrait statue, sculptor, G. Moretti, of Stephen C. Foster, 1826–64, standing pen in hand, beside a negro who is seated and playing a banjo; Foster wrote "Old Uncle Ned" and "Old Folks at Home"; was native of Pittsburgh; his grave is in Allegheny Cemetery. The view from Highland Park is very beautiful. Highland and Schenley Parks are connected by Highland Avenue and the Boulevard, making a continuous drive which forms the Carnegie promenade. The Soldiers' Monument is on Monument Hill, erected in 1871, to four thousand men of Allegheny County killed in the Civil War. Wayside Fountain, Fifth Avenue near Woodland Road.

Churches with notable architecture and windows: RODEF SHALOM Synagogue, Fifth Avenue and Morewood Street, architect, Henry Hornbostel, is said to have the finest tile dome in this country; windows, antique glass, from original drawings, made by William and Annie Lee Willet. ST. PAUL'S Roman Catholic Cathedral, Fifth Avenue, corner of Craig Street, stone, fourteenth century Gothic, built, 1907, architects, Egan & Prindeville; has beautiful altar of carved Carrara marble; pews and pulpit made of bog oak from Ireland; bronze stations, by Seibel, said to be largest and most artistic in the world; the great west window transepts, clerestories, ornamental and heraldic glass made by Willet, in the later delicate French Gothic spirit; also there is here much modern German and English glass. FIRST BAPTIST, Bellefield Avenue and Bayard Street, pure Gothic, fourteenth century, stone, built, 1902, architects, Cram, Goodhue & Ferguson.

THIRD PRESBYTERIAN, Fifth Avenue and South Negley Street, one of the most beautiful Gothic churches in the United States for spontaneity of design, warmth, and golden tints of stone; architect, Theophilus P. Chandler; windows by Willet are "The

THE CROWNING OF LABOR
Fragment from the Apotheosis of Pittsburgh, Mural in the Carnegie Institute, Pittsburgh

Painted by John W. Alexander

Ten Virgins," made, 1904, "The Holy City," 1905, of great beauty and color; and fine ornamental windows in clear glass with heraldic ornaments, in medieval hand-wrought lead; transept windows by Tiffany, American opalescent glass; east aisle window by Kenyon Cox; west aisle by McCausland, Toronto; this is an excellent church in which to study the different schools of glass.

CALVARY Protestant Episcopal, Shady Avenue and Walnut Street, Bedford limestone, thirteenth century Gothic, copy of Netley Abbey, architect, Ralph Adams Cram; the windows by William and Annie Lee Willet are among the most notable contributions to stained-glass art in this country, recalling those of the great Chartres Cathedral, with amount of painting reduced to a minimum, and lead treated as respectfully as the glass; also a Tiffany window, and some excellent English glass. EPIPHANY Roman Catholic, Washington and Franklin Streets, Romanesque, with Byzantine details, contains some beautiful art work, including "The Twelve Apostles," by Taber Sears. FIRST PRESBYTERIAN, Sixth Avenue and Wood Street, site deeded by John Penn in 1787; stone, French Gothic, erected in 1905, architect, T. P. Chandler, Philadelphia, has fine echo organ and chimes; windows by Tiffany, Lamb, and Clayton & Bell, London; medallion window and ornamental work by Willet. In LUTHERAN Church, Sixth Avenue, sanctuary window by Clayton & Bell, purely flat decoration, also window by Frederick Wilson. MOUNT ALVERNIA Chapel, Order of St. Francis, contains mural decorations by William Willet.

METHODIST, Beech Avenue, NORTH SIDE, stained glass window by Tiffany. Near by is the Carnegie Free Library, Federal and Ohio Streets, Romanesque; Fox Island granite with red granite trimmings; built, 1890; architect, H. H. Richardson; contains Library, Art Gallery, and Music Hall; in front is monument to Colonel James Anderson, red granite with bronze portrait bust, 1785–1861, sculptor, Daniel Chester French. Allegheny Post Office, French Renaissance, built, 1898, noted for gold dome; near by is colossal statue of "Labor."

Allegheny County Courthouse, Fifth Avenue and Grant Street, Romanesque, Worcester granite and marble, tower 425 feet high, built, 1888, the masterpiece of the great architect, H. H. Richardson; its interiors are equally imposing, the proportions of the corridors and especially the fan lancet, and convex-shaped ceiling, with its thousands of interlacing arches, twenty-one of which can be seen at one glance from the base of one of the stairways, excites the admiration of all beholders; it is without any other decoration but the beauty of its lines and shadows. Gaol is connected by facsimile of Bridge of Sighs. Frick building, built in 1902, Fifth Avenue and Grant Street, architects, D. H. Burnham & Co., a granite office structure twenty stories high, of the Greek Doric order; erected to express grace and beauty; batters from stylobate to cornice, three feet narrower at top than base; basement and entrance halls lined with Carrara marble; panels of Pavonazzo marble in ceiling; offices decorated with frescoes of the old Italian school; restaurant, medieval German; the Club story, Louis XIV style, is in stucco,

THE BLOCK HOUSE, PITTSBURGH

ALLEGHENY COUNTY 299

marble, bronze, and frescoes; two large bronze lions by Phimister Proctor are in entrance hall.

Bank of Pittsburgh, Fourth Avenue near Wood Street, classic, Alden & Harlow, architects, has mural decorations, allegorical of Pittsburgh, by Edwin H. Blashfield and the late Francis D. Millet. Iron City Bank, Westinghouse Building, mural decorations by William Willet. Farmer's Deposit Bank, sculptured frieze by J. Massey Rhind. Chamber of Commerce contains portraits of many prominent citizens. Friendship School, Friendship and Graham Streets, historical paintings of Penn, Washington, and Lincoln, by William Willet. View of the city seen from Mount Washington, with rivers and encircling hills, is more or less enveloped in smoke, excepting Sunday. Seventy-five per cent of the smoke nuisance in Pittsburgh has been abated.

BRADDOCK, population 20,879, on Monongahela River, twelve miles below Pittsburgh, famous, first as battle ground, General Braddock's defeat by French and Indians, 1754, when General Washington won his spurs, now is home of the Carnegie Steel Company. St. Mary's Protestant Episcopal Church, windows and mural decorations by William and Annie Lee Willet, Philadelphia. At mouth of the Youghiogheny River, so named by early explorers from hearing Indians calling to each other across its width, something that sounded like it, and meaning "Come again." McKEESPORT, home of the National Tube Company, producing more wrought iron pipes than any other plant in the world; St. Peter's Church, altar window by William and Annie Lee Willet.

Down the Ohio River, about six miles from Pittsburgh, begins Seven Mile Island, a garden spot, one time home of the famous Queen Alliquippa. Six miles farther is SEWICKLEY (Sweetwater), population 4955, named by Indians on account of its maple trees, on Lincoln Highway, a beautiful residence section with country estates which rival those about Philadelphia and New York. St. James' Church, window by William Willet. WILKINSBURG, population 24,403, within fifteen minutes of Carnegie Institute, has Wilkensburg Bank, classic, marble, built, 1909, architects, Moubly & Ussinger; and Rowland Theatre, built, 1912, Corinthian, architect, Hodgkinson.

XX
MIFFLIN COUNTY

FORMED September 19, 1789; named for General Thomas Mifflin, then President of the Supreme Executive Council of Pennsylvania, 1788-90, and first Governor under the Constitution of 1790. Scenery throughout is very beautiful; the twelve mile stretch of State highway through the famous long Lewistown Narrows gives glimpses of the Juniata, the peerless little river of more song and romance than any other in America, made famous by Mrs. Sullivan's song, "The Beautiful Blue Juniata," telling the love story of Alfarata, the roving Indian girl; the space between the mountains is barely wide enough to contain the highway, canal, river, and railroad. Mountains slope one thousand feet and are popular hunting grounds for bear and wild turkeys; quite a number of caves are found in the limestone formations of this county, though not easily accessible; Alexander's, in Kishacoquillas Valley, abounds in stalactites and stalagmites, preserving in midsummer ice formed in winter; Naginey's Cave, near Milroy, is most spacious; Hanawalt's Cave, near McVeytown, is of vast dimensions and contains calcareous concretions; crude saltpetre has been obtained here; McVeytown is birthplace of Joseph Trimble Rothrock, M.D.

Celebrated springs are Mifflin, near Painterville Station, has medicinal waters; and Logan's, six miles from Lewistown, near Reedsville, on left of the old

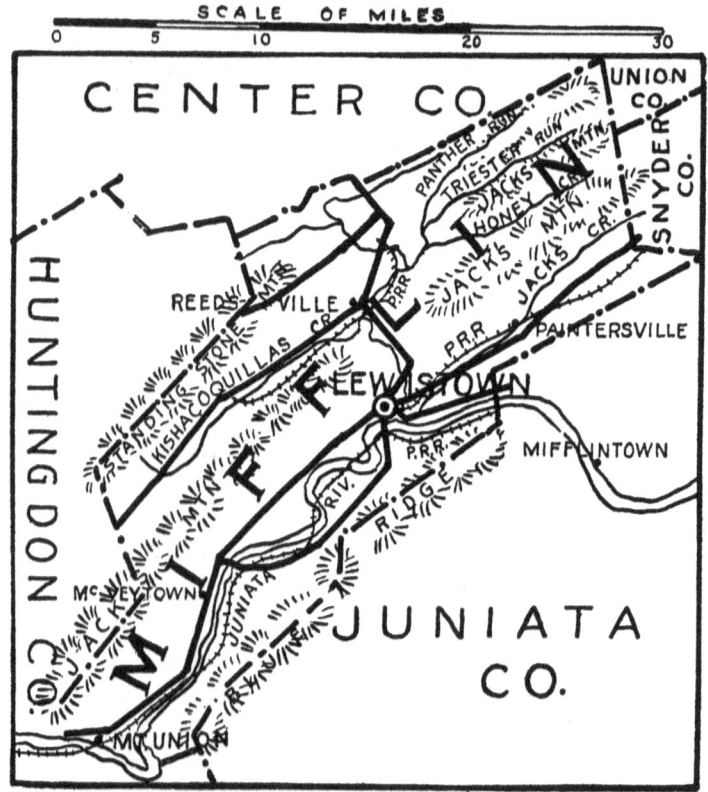

Mifflin County

MIFFLIN COUNTY

stage road between Lewistown and Bellefonte, Center County; here the Mingo Chief, Logan, friend of white man, Shikellimy's son, had his cabin, prior to 1771, when he left this region; he made the famous speech sent to Lord Dunmore in 1774, considered, among American classics, as a rare specimen of Indian oratory: "I appeal to any white man to say if ever he entered Logan's cabin hungry, and he gave him not meat; if he ever came cold and naked, and he clothed him not; during the course of the last long bloody war Logan remained idle in his cabin, an advocate for peace. Such was my love for the whites that my countrymen pointed at me as they passed, and said: 'Logan is the friend of white men.' I had even thought to have lived with you, but for the injuries of one man, Colonel Cresap, the last spring, in cold blood and unprovoked, murdered all the relations of Logan, not sparing even my women and children; there runs not a drop of my blood in the veins of any living creature; this called on me for revenge; I have sought it; I have killed many; I have glutted my vengeance; for my country, I rejoice at the beams of peace, but do not think that mine is the joy of fear; Logan never felt fear. Logan will not turn on his heel to save his life; who is there to mourn for Logan? Not one!" (Colonel Michael Cresap was not responsible for the murder of Logan's family; some white men, led by a liquor dealer, murdered them.)

First settlers, Scotch-Irish, in 1754, were not molested by Indians until 1756. Fort Granville was built, one mile northwest of Lewistown, on the old turnpike, site to be marked by the Pennsylvania

State Historical Society; it was destroyed when the canal was constructed. In 1829 the Pennsylvania Canal was opened and first packet boat run from Lewistown to Mifflintown. Chief industries are agriculture, and iron and steel works. Iron ore of the best quality abounds; two furnaces, belonging to the Glamorgan Iron Company, were destroyed in July, 1874, by a tornado that left scarcely a property without damage; the bridge over the Juniata was also destroyed, rebuilt, and again destroyed by ice freshets in December, 1874, and February, 1875. In Limestone Ridge, extending from Kishacoquillas Creek, is found hard, white sandstone, almost pure silicon, used in glass manufacture.

LEWISTOWN, population 9849, made county seat, 1790, was at first Kishacoquillas' Village, a chief of the Shawnees, with a population in 1731, of twenty families, located at the mouth of the stream. Courthouse, facing the square, brick, colonial with Ionic portico, and cupola, built, 1843, enlarged in the rear. Granite monument, dedicated, 1906, in honor of Mifflin County soldiers and sailors, is in the square. One block away on South Main Street is the Kishacoquillas Creek bridge, stone and concrete, built, 1902, a reconstruction of the old two-arch stone bridge built in 1807, the first was wood, in 1794; on the left is an old stone building, erected about 1794, a historic landmark that has served for many uses, once the "Seven Stars Inn," 1828-29; also a Masonic hall, 1830-39, it has two cellars, one beneath the other. At a point along the creek, just above the old building, is where Commodore David Conner, as a boy, made little boats and pitted

OLD STONE ARCH ON JACK'S CREEK
Built over one hundred years ago

them against each other in mimic warfare, thus foreshadowing his brilliant naval career in the War of 1812 and the Mexican War. Just above, on the high bank, fronting on Water and Brown Streets, is Lewistown's oldest burial grounds. Here are the graves of the Buchanan family, first settlers and owners of the land on which Lewistown is built. One mile east of Lewistown, on the oldest wagon and stage road running parallel with the present state highway, is an old stone arch bridge, over one hundred years old, a favorite subject for artists; it is near the bridge crossing Jacks Creek, on the state highway through Lewistown Narrows. MOUNT UNION, on southern boundary, lies at entrance to Jacks Narrows, made by the river forcing its way through Jacks Mountain.

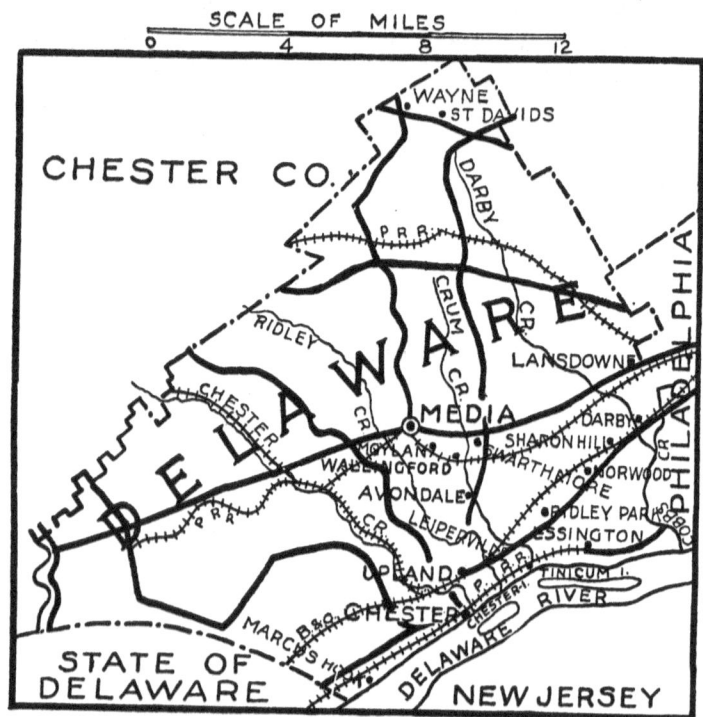

Delaware County

XXI

DELAWARE COUNTY

Formed from Chester County, September 26, 1789; named for Delaware River. Automobile Trip to Chester, return by Media and Swarthmore

FROM Thirty-second and Market Streets, Philadelphia, out Woodland Avenue (Darby Road), laid out in 1687, the old King's Road, pass UNIVERSITY OF PENNSYLVANIA buildings, to WOODLANDS CEMETERY, between Thirty-ninth to Forty-second Streets, seventy-five acres, acquired in 1840, contains colonial homestead, residence of William Hamilton, English Deputy Governor of Pennsylvania, under grant from William Penn, built, 1747–50, stone and brick; has portico, with pediment supported by six columns; considered by architects best specimen of colonial architecture in Philadelphia; many rare trees are there, sent by Mr. Hamilton in his trips abroad; to him Philadelphia owes the gingko tree of Japan and many varieties of magnolia.

BARTRAM'S GARDEN, 28 acres, open free to the public, one quarter mile south on Fifty-fourth Street, first botanical garden of international importance in United States; ground purchased by John Bartram, in 1728; from here he traveled long distances to Florida, the Adirondacks, everywhere collecting rare plants that he brought home in his saddlebags; he wrote down the results of his explorations, and sent to Europe botanical specimens of great interest, also painted sheets of illustrations, sending one set to the South Kensington Museum, London, which are still there in perfect condition; Linnæus proclaimed him the greatest natural botanist in the world, and sent him books and apparatus; his quaint old stone house is still standing, built by himself in 1731; his son, William Bartram, botanist and ornithologist, published the most complete list of American birds, previous to Alexander Wilson, whom he greatly assisted. Wilson lived at the corner of Fifty-first Street and Woodland Avenue, in a log house with an immense stone chimney. Near Bartram's Garden, on the Schuylkill River bank, at the western end of Gray's Ferry Bridge, is site of Gray's Garden, pleasure resort, time of Washington, reached from Philadelphia by a floating bridge, replaced by wooden telescope drawbridge built in 1808, by the P., W. & B. R. R.; stone monument, still standing, covered with most interesting and historically valuable inscriptions, marks opening of the first railroad to the South.

Sixty-fifth Street and Woodland Avenue, St. James' Protestant Episcopal Church, Kingsessing, built by the Swedes, 1762, building practically unchanged, has interesting burial ground. Sixty-ninth Street and Paschall Avenue is an old yellow mansion, built about 1723, home of the Paschalls, General Howe's headquarters after the Battle of Brandywine. Seventieth Street and Woodland Avenue, quaint old building, the Bannaker School, built in 1789, said to be oldest public-school building in Philadelphia, now used in connection with the school garden. Seventy-third

DELAWARE COUNTY

Street, Blue Bell Tavern, opposite, was terminus of the great trading path of the Minquas Indians leading from the Susquehanna; Island Road leads to "Cannon Ball" farmhouse, below Penrose Ferry, struck during bombardment of Fort Mifflin in 1777.

Crossing Cobb's Creek, the southern boundary of the city, and county of Philadelphia, we enter DELAWARE COUNTY, the oldest settled section of Pennsylvania. DARBY, an ancient town, birthplace of John Bartram, contains many old houses, and a Friends' meeting house, dating from the eighteenth century, with picturesque burying ground, where many colonial notables lie in unmarked graves; SHARON HILL, residential suburb, Convent of Holy Child Jesus, occupies buildings erected for John Jackson's Quaker School, famous in the middle of the last century; new decorated Gothic chapel of stone. Beyond NORWOOD is the old White Horse Hotel, now abandoned, built, 1720.

One and one-half miles to left, at ESSINGTON, on Tinicum Island, first permanent European settlement in Pennsylvania made by Swedes under Governor John Printz, 1643; fort built, named "New Gottenburg"; and government established. RIDLEY PARK, residential suburb; fine view to left, of Tinicum and the Delaware River, old quarantine station known as the Lazaretto; the Corinthian and Philadelphia Yacht Clubs are on the river front. LEIPERVILLE, McIlvain house, stone, opposite Colonial Hotel; Washington spent the night here after the Battle of Brandywine, and troops were encamped on slopes to the right. Hendrixson house, very ancient, built by Swedish settlers. Pass Baldwin Locomotive Works and great munition factories into

CHESTER, population 58,030, settled by Swedes about 1644, the oldest town in Pennsylvania, known as Upland until 1682, when Penn, landing here on October 28, named it Chester after the home of his companion, Pearson, in England. Penn convened here, in November, 1682, the first Assembly of the Province, at which was passed the "Great Law"; the Upland court was held here from 1668 to 1682; the courts of Chester County from 1682 until their removal to West Chester in 1786, and the courts of Delaware County from 1789 to 1851; Chester has grown from an ancient country town to a bustling industrial city, but many antiquities are preserved; principal among these are the old City Hall, stone, with pent roof projection and quaint clock tower, erected in 1724; the oldest public building in Pennsylvania, and one of the oldest in America; used as Chester County courthouse for sixty-two years, Delaware County courthouse for sixty-one years, and as hall of Chester borough and city since 1851; now being restored by the Pennsylvania Historical Commission and Honorable William C. Sproul, under contract that the city will maintain it for public uses forever.

Opposite on Market Street is the Washington House, erected and licensed as the "Pennsylvania Arms" in 1747, still maintained as a tavern; in this house, at midnight on September 11, 1777, Washington wrote his report to Congress of the Battle of Brandywine. Hope's Anchor Tavern, Fourth and Market Streets, built by David Cowpland prior to 1746. Group of old houses at Second and Edgmont Streets, Logan house, 1700, where Lafayette's wounds were dressed after the

ALFRED O. DESHING MEMORIAL ART GALLERY, CHESTER
Frazer and Robert, Architects

Battle of Brandywine, and Lloyd house, built in 1703 by David Lloyd, chief justice of Pennsylvania; here also stood the first courthouse, or "House of Defense," and first Quaker meeting.

Across Chester Creek, at the foot of Penn Street, is a memorial stone, erected on the two hundredth anniversary, to mark the spot where William Penn first landed in Pennsylvania; and near by, Lord Baltimore and William Markham, in 1681, took observations to determine the fortieth parallel of latitude, and location of boundary between Pennsylvania and Maryland; also site of Essex House, home of Robert Wade, wherein was held, in 1675, the first Friends meeting in Pennsylvania. Blue Anchor Tavern and Steamboat Hotel, near Second and Market Streets, bear marks of bombardment by the British frigate Augusta in 1777. Friends meeting house, erected, 1736, modernized in 1882; Friends Burying Ground formed, 1692, contains graves of Chief Justice David Lloyd, who died in 1731, and Grace Lloyd, his wife, who died in 1760, Justice Caleb Cowpland, Judge Henry Hale Graham, and, in unmarked tombs, many of the founders and pioneers of the commonwealth.

St. Paul's graveyard, Third and Market Streets; tomb of John Morton, a signer of the Declaration of Independence, who cast the deciding vote in the Pennsylvania delegation; also of D. Paul Jackson, Burgess of Chester, who was the first man to receive a degree from the University of Pennsylvania; and a quaint old memorial cut in sandstone with oddly carved figures and devices, dedicated to James Sandelands, who died, 1693, taken from the old church, erected in 1703. Chester Rural Cemetery, burial place of General Edward F. Beale, pioneer of California; has many interesting memorials.

Alfred O. Deshong Memorial Park of twenty-eight acres, in the heart of the city, with white marble art gallery, late Italian Renaissance, finished in 1916, designed by Brazer & Robb, New York, for Mr. Deshong's collection of about 200 paintings, bronzes, ivories, etc.; rare Japanese bronze lanterns and figures are in the grounds, and two remarkable bronze dogs with paws on cloisonné balls, at entrance; fine bronze doors and grills; also his old mansion, all given to the city of Chester with a large endowment, for public use forever. St. Paul's Protestant Episcopal Church, Broad and Madison Streets, founded in 1702, third building of this congregation, erected, 1900; twelfth century English Gothic, granite and limestone, architects, Nattress & Son; altar by Nattress, white marble; mosaic reredos, "The Supper at Emmaus," after Rembrandt; chancel window by Tiffany, "Conversion of St. Paul," after Doré; memorial to Rev. Henry Brown, rector for thirty years; clerestory windows, four Evangelists, by Nicola d'Ascenzo; chalice and salver given by Sir Jeffry Jeffrys in 1705, chalice and salver given by Queen Anne, in 1707, all of beautifully hammered silver, still in use; fine chime of ten bells; large folio Bible given at founding of the church by the Society in London, for the Propagation of the Gospel in Foreign Parts, to which St. Paul's owed much in its early years.

St. Michael's Roman Catholic Church, Edgmont Avenue above Seventh Street, granite, Gothic, fine altar and paintings. First Baptist Church, Seventh and Fulton Streets, stone, Gothic, founded, 1850, third edifice endowed by the Gartside and Crozer families. First Presbyterian Church, Fourth and Welsh Streets, brick, stuccoed, erected in 1852, fine memorial windows. Third Presbyterian Church, Broad and Potter Streets, stone, fine windows and carvings in wood. Madison Street Methodist Episcopal Church, Seventh and Madison Streets, organized in 1818 by John Kelly in his home; afterward services were held in the Courthouse for many years, where Bishop Asbury preached; present church erected, 1874, green serpentine. High school, stone, with commanding tower, West Ninth Street, modeled after Post Office Building at Washington.

Pennsylvania Military College, Fourteenth Street, handsome buildings with complete military and academic equipment; incorporated as a military university in 1862, by Colonel Theodore Hyatt; contributed many officers to the nation's service; present buildings erected in 1882, after a fire which destroyed the original structures. Chester Park and Crozer Park contain about 150 acres in valleys of Ridley and Chester creeks. Chester is a port of entry and contains large shipyards, steel, engineering, and textile industries.

UPLAND, founded by John P. Crozer in 1845 when he established cotton mills there on the site of the old Chester Mills, on Chester Creek, immediately adjoining the town of Chester; Chester Mills were built by Caleb Pusey in 1683, at the first water power above tide on Chester Creek; the mill, framed in England and brought over in the *Welcome*, was owned by Pusey, William Penn, and Samuel Carpenter; house, erected by Pusey in 1682, is probably the oldest structure in Pennsylvania. Crozer Theological Seminary, endowed by John P. Crozer, and sons, occupies buildings overlooking Chester, erected by John P. Crozer in 1858 for a normal school, used in Civil War as hospital, and occupied for a time by the Pennsylvania Military Academy; Pearl Hall, the seminary library, was built by William Bucknell, in memory of his wife; green serpentine in form of a cross; contains many rare books and the only known copies of many Baptist theological works; Crozer Hospital and Home for Incurables, fine stone buildings, were endowed by J. Lewis Crozer, who also left a large endowment for a free library in Chester. An old house on Upland Dairy Farm, now much distorted by modernization, built by Thomas Brazey in 1696, was for many years the home of the West family, collateral descendants of Benjamin West.

On Providence Road, first highway to be laid out in Pennsylvania, leading from Chester to the back townships, is LAPIDEA MANOR, residence of Governor William C. Sproul, colonial house, erected by Thomas Leiper, for his son James, enlarged in 1909 by Mr. Sproul, architect, W. L. Price; contains notable library with collection of Pennsylvania and local books and antiquities, paintings, and curios; interior wood carvings by Maene; on the fine grounds is a clock-tower, containing a bell cast in Bristol in 1741, for St. Paul's Church, Chester, and for 125 years was the only church bell in the town; across the grounds is to be seen the grade of the first railroad in America, built by Thomas Leiper in 1809, to carry stone from his quarries at Avondale to tidewater on Ridley Creek, where it was loaded in barges to be taken to the Delaware breakwater.

DELAWARE COUNTY 315

MOYLAN, south of Media, art colony, residence of Charles H. Stephens and Mrs. Charles H. Stephens (Alice Barber), contains valuable North American Indian collection, the old stone building, remodeled for art studios and dwellings, is among the most interesting in the county. Southwest of MEDIA is the Williamson free school of mechanical trades; generously endowed; built in 1888; includes twenty-four buildings on 230 acres; pupils between sixteen and eighteen years of age are received; they live as families, twenty-four in a cottage with a matron; preference to those born in Pennsylvania; benefits of school are entirely free, including boarding, instruction, and clothing during the entire course of three years.

MEDIA, county seat from 1851, population 4109; charter, with famous provision against sale of intoxicants, still intact, was granted, 1850: Courthouse with ample square, formed nucleus of the town; present building, modified colonial, Avondale marble, architects, Brazer & Robb. Old Providence Friends Meeting House, built, 1699; original Taylor log cabin is on State Street, and the old Rowland mansion. Christ Protestant Episcopal Church, stone, Gothic, has altar painting, "Murillo's Holy Family," copied by P. McIlhenny. Presbyterian Church, modified classic. Leiper Presbyterian Church, Gothic, Avondale marble, midway between Leiperville and Swarthmore, built in 1800, Andrew Jackson, James Buchanan, and Elisha Kent Kane, while guests of Judge George G. Leiper, worshiped here, slates on the roof were brought from Scotland; near is colonial residence of Perry Lukens on Fairview Road, hardware and other materials were brought from England, has original latch string lock. AVONDALE, old colonial residence of Thomas Leiper, near Crum Creek, built on plan of his Scotch home.

WALLINGFORD, residence of late Dr. Horace Howard Furness, America's greatest Shakespearean scholar. He left a working library of several thousand Shakespeare books, including "The Variorum" edited with his son. SWARTHMORE, college, founded, 1864, by members of the Hicksite Society of Friends, is located on a hill with a fine view of the Delaware River, campus over 200 acres, includes large tract of woodland and rocky valley of Crum Creek; buildings, mostly stone, French Renaissance, include the Sproul Astronomical Observatory, built in 1911, gift of William C. Sproul, contains one of the best telescopes in America; Library, English collegiate Gothic, built, 1907, local stone, with terra-cotta and Indiana limestone trimmings, architect, Edward L. Tilton, New York; the reading room is open through two stories, height twenty feet with gallery on three sides; Gothic beamed ceiling and leaded ceiling lights, interior finished with dark oak. In fireproof tower room is the Anson Lapham Friends' Historical Library, one of the largest collections of Quakeriana in America, contains original manuscripts of John Woolman's Journal.

Near the Library stands a house with gambrel roof, built in 1724, marked, with tablet, by Delaware County Historical Society, "Birthplace of Benjamin West, born in 1738, first great American painter, founder and second President of the Royal Academy, London"; exterior unchanged, now residence of college professors; the college owns, and is still collecting

//
DELAWARE COUNTY

original paintings and drawings by West. Meeting house built, 1881, follows the traditions of early colonial style. Parrish Hall, the main building, erected 1864–69, rebuilt after the fire in 1881, contains a portrait of George Fox by Sir Peter Lely, and other interesting portraits of early Friends and later benefactors of the college. Wharton Hall, men's dormitories, built in form of Oxford quadrangle, architects, Buntley & Sprigley. Stone gateway, north entrance, designed by Frederick B. Pyle.

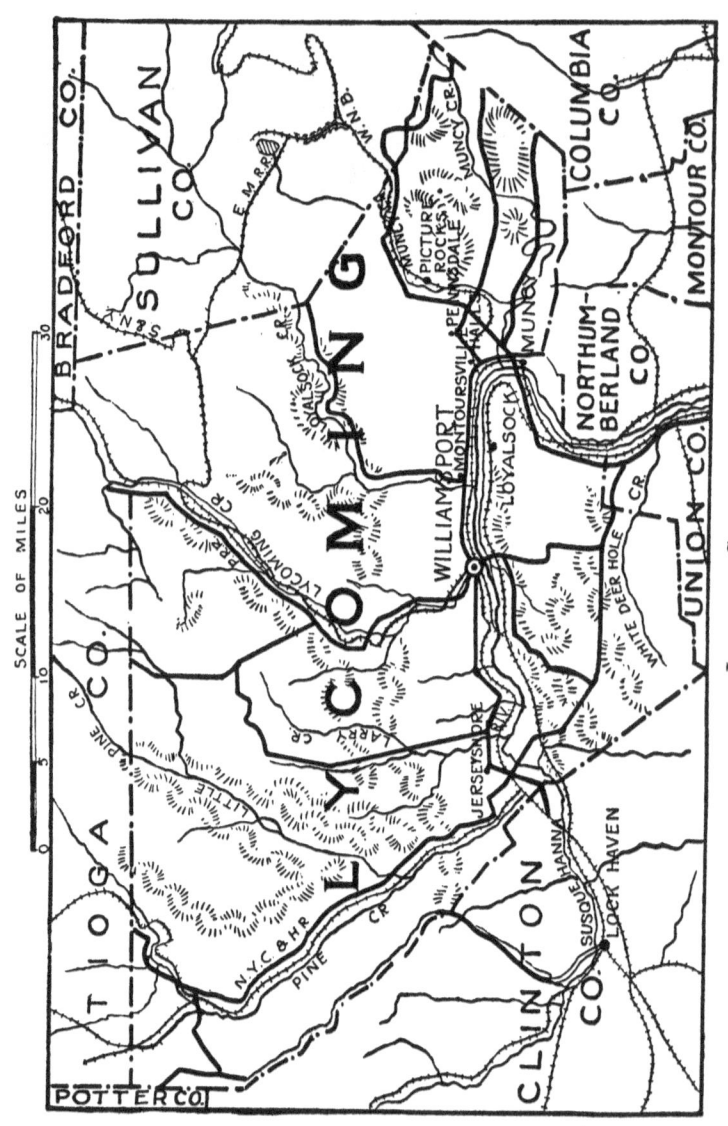

Lycoming County

XXII
LYCOMING COUNTY[1]

FORMED April 13, 1795; named for creek called by Delaware Indians Legani-hanna (Sandy Stream) or Lycaumic; mountainous with rolling hills; North Mountain, highest land, 2550 feet above sea level. Formerly a lumber region, now chief industries are agriculture and manufacturing. WILLIAMSPORT, county seat, founded, 1796, population 36,198, has a system of well kept roads; the Grampian and Vallamont drives wind over the hills north of the city, giving a view, over the West Branch Valley, that is remarkable for extent and beauty. Courthouse built in 1860, city hall, and post office are mid-Victorian. Masonic buildings include the Masonic Temple, Scottish Rites Building, Acacia Club, and Howard Club. Franklin School, Mulberry Street, North of East Fourth Street, has mural decorations of local scenery, "A Sweep of the Susquehanna Near Jersey Shore," artist, J. Wesley Little.

Christ Protestant Episcopal Church, East Fourth and Mulberry Streets, has windows from England, also by Tiffany and Lamb. "The James V. Brown Public Library," East Fourth Street, French Renaissance, Pennsylvania white marble, built in 1907, architect, Edgar V. Seeler, Philadelphia; contains a small permanent collection of paintings and an original portrait of Washington, by Rembrandt Peale, painted in 1795; art exhibitions are held here. Central Presbyterian Church, opposite Park Hotel, has windows by J. & R. Lamb. Covenant Presbyterian, West Fourth and Center Streets, has large windows by Tiffany and Lamb. Trinity Protestant Episcopal, West Fourth Street and Trinity Place, modern parish house, used as a community center. Opposite is Way's Garden, two and one-half acres, with fine old elm trees. Annunciation, Roman Catholic Church, West Fourth and Walnut Streets, Tiffany window, "The Ascension." St. John's Protestant Episcopal, architects, Duhring, Okie & Ziegler, windows by Nicola d'Ascenzo.

Brandon Park, beautiful with fine shrubbery, trees, and winding paths, has a band shell, playgrounds, swimming pool. Monument erected by Daughters of the American Revolution, Fourth and Cemetery Streets, on site of massacre of white settlers by Indians. Site of French Margaret's Village, niece of Madame Montour, noted on Scull's map, in 1759, is now within limits of the seventh ward; she was a notable character and enforced prohibition in her town; four miles east of Williamsport, on west side, mouth of Loyalsock Creek, near Montoursville, is site of Ostonwakin or Otsuagy, home of Madame Montour, famous French halfbreed, who lived there from 1727, and was still there in 1742, when Count Zinzendorf came to the village. The great Indian Trail from Muncy led up the Susquehanna River, on line of the present highway, through Ostonwakin, to East Third Street, Williamsport, then north of Third and Penn Streets to Park Street, there turned to West Fourth Street and to Lycoming Creek, French Margaret's town.

MUNCY, population 2054, on site of Fort Wallis, in

LYCOMING CREEK NEAR WILLIAMSPORT

LYCOMING COUNTY

1778, commanded by Colonel Thomas Hartley. St. James' Protestant Episcopal Church, built, 1859, English Gothic, architect, Richard Upjohn, New York, who first used principles of Gothic architecture in America; has Tiffany memorial window to Rev. Edwin Lightener. In Muncy Cemetery is monument to John Brady, famous Indian fighter, granite shaft of excellent proportions; his grave is in the old Hall's burial ground at Hall's Station. Site of Fort Brady; south side of Muncy, residence of Captain John Brady, fortified by stockade, was place of refuge, continuing so after his death; burned with Fort Muncy in 1779, when Muncy Valley was overrun. Another on the frontier was Fort Minigar, built, 1774, at White Deer Mills, north bank of White Deer Creek, probably stockade, included both fort and mills, burned, 1779. Picture Rocks village, founded, 1848, here Indian picture writings formerly decorated walls of rocks, rising from Big Muncy Creek. Studio of the late J. Wesley Little. Fort Antes, opposite Jersey Shore, marked by Daughters of the American Revolution.

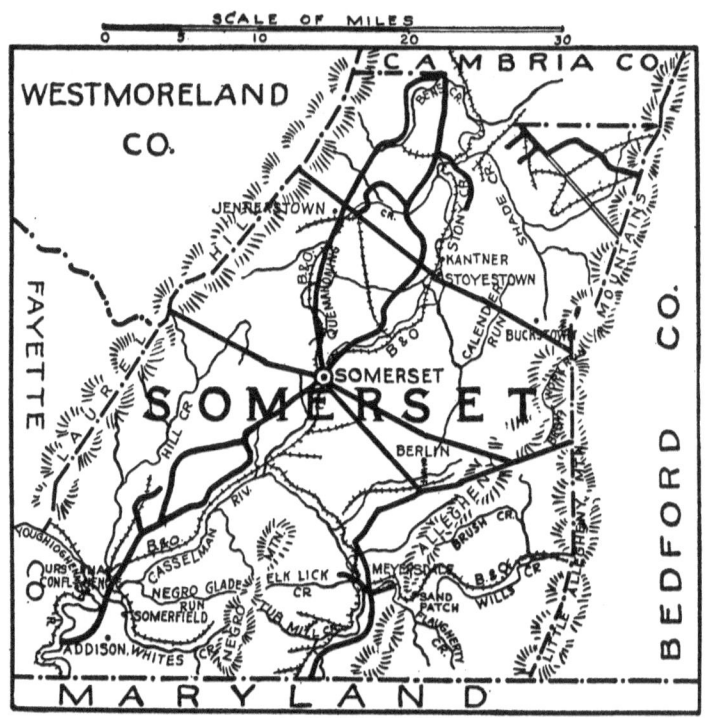

SOMERSET COUNTY

XXIII
SOMERSET COUNTY

FORMED April 17, 1795; named for Somerset, England. Chief industries are agriculture and mining. A mountain country of remarkable beauty, largely forests, although glades, or natural meadows, about the headwaters of streams are numerous and extensive enough to have the name, "The Glades," applied to the whole county; standing on the summit of either mountain range that bounds it, east and west, one gets a view of unsurpassed beauty; at distance of twenty miles the other stands out in bold outline, with intervening country of hill, valley, forest, glade, and numerous watercourses, which find their way to the Ohio, Susquehanna, and Potomac rivers; immortalized in James Whitcomb Riley's " 'Mongst the Hills of Somerset."

Nearly all this country, between the crests of the Allegheny Mountains and Laurel Hills, is one vast coal field, extending over the entire length, from Maryland to Cambria County, every vein of coal from the great Pittsburgh seam down being represented. Traditions of Indian villages are in the famous Turkey Foot, Casselman River forms middle toe at town of Confluence; also in Elk Lick township, Indian arrowheads and stone implements are found. In 1749, Christopher Gist, agent of the Ohio Company, was the first white man known to have crossed Somerset County; his route, along Nemacolin's trail, a Delaware Indian chief, led him through Addison Township and to the, later known, Great Crossing; again passing through in 1750, he kept a diary.

George Washington in 1753, crossed through Addison Township, with four frontiersmen, one as Indian interpreter, one French interpreter; every spot of earth that Washington trod in the line of duty is sacred soil for all true Americans; he passed through Somerset eleven times; on Braddock's ill-fated expedition in 1755, he lay for ten days at Great Crossing, on a bed of sickness, exempt by order of General Braddock. First road cut in 1754 was under Washington's direction, afterwards substantially the Braddock Road, following Nemacolin's trail, the chief who guided him; it began at Cumberland, Maryland, then a fort, and reached the Youghiogheny River, south of present village of Somerfield, at the Great Crossing; marked, only historic marker in the county.

The National Turnpike, commenced in 1811, has the same general course, occasionally using the same roadbed, crosses the Youghiogheny at Somerfield over a great stone bridge, still in good repair, completed July 4, 1818, and turned over to the United States on that day. President James Monroe and members of his Cabinet attended the opening of the bridge; this road became a great highway, over which passed a vast commerce, both east and west, wayside inns were nearly every mile, now none exist; the "Endsley," stone house, in Somerfield, built, 1818, long a noted tavern, is now a private residence.

Next great road in the county was the Forbes, or Bouquet Road, cut by Colonel Bouquet in 1758, it

STEPPING STONES, KIMBERLY RIVER

SOMERSET COUNTY 325

traversed the county from east to west, and like the Braddock Road, was purely military, constructed under protection of a strong army; over it passed the army of General Forbes on way to conquer Fort Duquesne; George Washington was with this expedition in command of the first Virginia regiment. The road started at Bedford and followed an Indian trail, it was improved between 1785-95 and became known as "The Great Road"; afterwards about 1806 as the Stoyestown and Bedford Turnpike; later taken by the State Highway Department, it is now a great speedway, "The Lincoln Highway," entering the county at BUCKSTOWN, crossing Stoney Creek at KANTNER, one mile west is Stoyestown over one hundred years old; six miles farther west is JENNERSTOWN, laid out in 1822 by General James Wells, who, in 1771, was wounded by Indians.

On Laurel Hills, three miles west of URSINA, is the Jersey Baptist Church, with ancient burial ground, has written record since 1775, first log church built, 1788, twice rebuilt; fine mountain scenery all along the route, and several places of historic interest, here, and in other parts of the county, sites of forts which date back to French and Indian wars and the Revolution, unmarked; few are now living who can point out the locality of these historic places with any degree of certainty. The Glades Road, laid out in 1772 from four miles west of Bedford to the Youghiogheny, via Stoney Creek, was made turnpike in 1816; along this road in 1810, on a farm nine miles east of Somerset, was born Judge Jeremiah Sullivan Black, Chief Justice of Pennsylvania; United States Attorney General; and Secretary of State. First railroad through Somerset county was the Pittsburgh division of the picturesque Baltimore & Ohio, opened in 1871, with its famous tunnels. At Mason & Dixon's line Negro Mount is about 2825 feet above sea.

SOMERSET, county seat, population 3121; laid out in 1795, elevation above sea level 2180 feet, has had three consuming fires, and has been rebuilt with greater beauty. Courthouse built, 1906, French Renaissance, Indiana limestone, architect, J. H. Fuller, Uniontown; Soldiers' Monument in grounds, pedestal with names of more than 400 Somerset County men who died in war for the Union, 1861–65; Somerset Trust Company, Indiana limestone, built, 1916, architects, Mowbray & Company, New York, Renaissance, beautiful proportions. Churches, built by E. H. Walker, Somerset; all with memorial windows, mostly made by Pittsburgh firms; are, Grace United Evangelical, brick, 1914; the Christian Church and parsonage, Doric, brick, 1910; St. Paul's Reformed, Gothic, brick, remodeled, 1915; also Trinity Lutheran, Corinthian, built, 1877, brick, architect, M. Simon, Harrisburg. Throughout the county are many churches; in some places where there is not even the semblance of a village there are churches that would be a credit to any town.

XXIV
GREENE COUNTY

FORMED February 9, 1796; named for General Nathanael Greene. Surface, fertile valleys, hills, and rolling uplands, making a region of natural beauty, well watered from the tributaries of the Monongahela River and Wheeling Creek. There are still a number of covered wooden bridges throughout the county, from fifty to a hundred years old, a very old double bridge crosses Ten Mile Creek, one mile east of Waynesburg; formerly an old forge and furnace were on this creek. Many Indian village sites that were occupied long before the advent of the whites are here; their age is indicated by large old trees growing on their mounds; three distinct forms of ancient burial are found here, showing that three waves of population swept over this land before the coming of the Europeans; the two principal Indian mounds now in the county, are at Crows Mills. Two great Indian trails crossed the southern part of the state, the Warrior Branch passing through this county to the Ohio River. A chain of forts crossed Greene Co., ending at Fort Zane, now Wheeling; three are especially well known—Fort Ryserson and Block House at western end of county; Fort Jackson west of Waynesburg; and Fort Garard on Whitely Creek; seven miles west of GREENSBORO, the birthplace of Robert J. Burdette, and his eminent sister Mary G. Burdette.

GREENE COUNTY

GREENE COUNTY

The earliest glass works were established by Albert Gallatin, on the Monongahela in 1785; they were the forerunner of the vast business at Pittsburgh and vicinity. First settlers were Scotch-Irish. Chief industries, agriculture and the mining of bituminous coal; the Pittsburgh vein of rich depth and highest coking value, and three other veins, almost as rich, namely, the Waynesburg, Freeport, and Mapletown. Oil and gas production is very valuable, there are a number of gas-pumping stations within the county. The Philadelphia Gas Company has one at Brave, said to be the largest in the world; near Brave is JOLLYTOWN, with a monument to Jesse Taylor, first Greene County soldier to fall in the Civil War.

County seat, WAYNESBURG, population 3332; laid out in 1796; named for General Anthony Wayne, who with his troops proved most successful in ridding this section of the Indians. A chain of parks with formal gardening goes through the center of the town, divided by streets; in the center of one is the Soldiers' Monument; erected in 1899; Waynesburg College, empowered by the Legislature to confer honorary degrees, faces College Park; portrait of Dr. A. B. Miller, a former president, is in Alumni Hall. Courthouse, colonial, with cupola, surmounted by wooden statue of General Greene; was erected in 1852; brick, painted gray, has six lofty Corinthian columns supporting the front porch. Jail on same ground.

First Methodist Church, Romanesque, Cleveland stone, has memorial windows. The public schools are liberally provided with the Elson photogravures, reproductions of great masterpieces, mostly in sepia. Five miles southeast of Waynesburg is Gordon Ridge; Nettle Hill sixteen miles southwest, both notable places of particularly beautiful scenery. CARMICHAELS, originally New Lisbon, one of the oldest towns, beautifully located, has Greene Academy, incorporated, 1810; Senator Albert Cummins was born near here.

XXV
WAYNE COUNTY

FORMED March 21, 1798; named for General Anthony Wayne. A picturesque, mountainous section, possessing more lakes than any other county in the state, some over 2000 feet above sea, ranging in area from 3 to 358 acres, many of them well stocked with bass, perch, pickerel, and other fish, while the whole county abounds in trout streams. From north to south is a wonderful expanse of scenery; FARVIEW, altitude, 1500 feet, on the Moosic Mountain, near Waymart, includes, in its panorama, the distant Catskills; from the southern roads, extended views are also enjoyed. A beautiful drive follows the Wallenpaupack Creek (slow water) passing the Falls at Hawley, meeting place of the Paupack Indians; good roads continue to Milford and the Water Gap, or to Gouldsboro, Scranton and Wilkes-Barre. On the road from Honesdale to Carbondale the path of the old Delaware & Hudson Gravity Railroad may still be traced.

Early industries were hunting, lumbering, and tanning; now the modern creamery is an important factor, also stock raising and agriculture. One hundred years ago a small colony of Germans settled a half mile west of Bethany and started a glass factory, utilizing native sand and clay; from 1847 to 1861 window glass was manufactured at Tracyville; in 1865, Christian Dorflinger built large factories for manufacturing and cutting glass, at White Mills, five miles south of

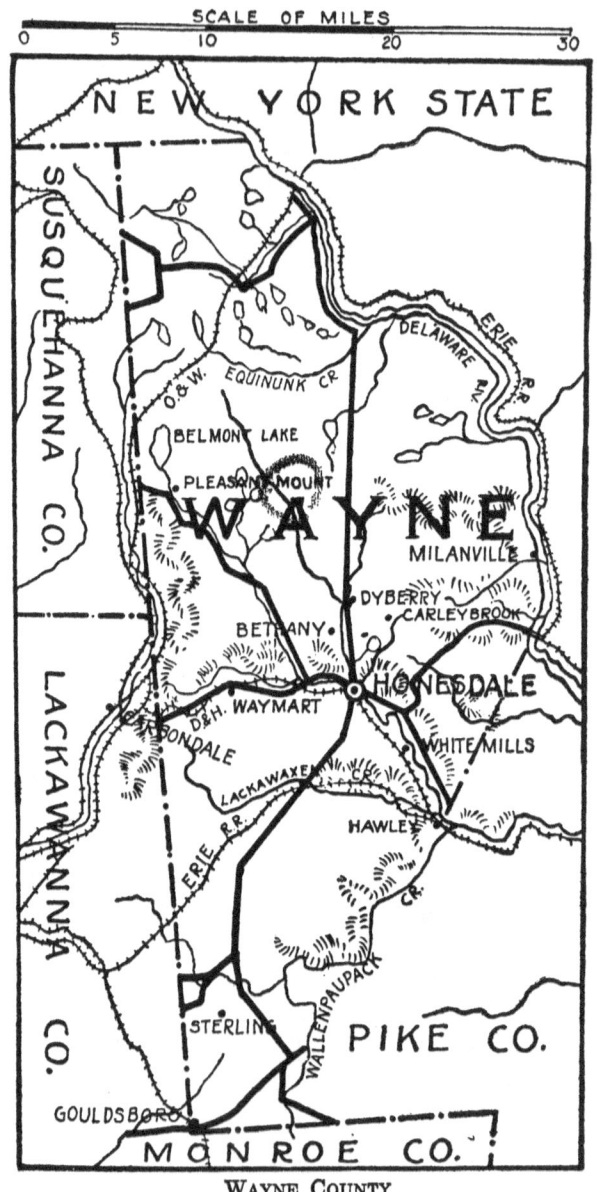

WAYNE COUNTY

WAYNE COUNTY

Honesdale; glass-cutting factories are now numerous in the county, and gold decorating of glass has been introduced among Wayne's industries.

HONESDALE, made the county seat in 1841; population 2756; altitude, 1000 feet; named for Philip Hone, president of the Delaware and Hudson Canal Company, which started here for tidewater at Rondout on the Hudson, built 1826-28, abandoned, 1898; Honesdale owes its growth and prosperity to the canal; it was one of the anthracite stepping stones to a waiting market. Three locomotives were purchased by the canal company to draw coal from the mines in Carbondale and vicinity to the canal at Honesdale; the first one, the Stourbridge Lion, was brought by canal boat to Honesdale in 1829 and a trial trip was made; the wooden rails, then used for the railroad, were not firm enough for the strain of the engine, and it was never run again; however, Wayne County takes precedence in having had the first locomotive ever run in America make its trial and only trip at Honesdale; it is now at the Smithsonian Institute, Washington. The New York & Erie Railroad follows the course of the old canal through the town.

Courthouse built, 1880; brick with stone trimmings; contains portrait of General Anthony Wayne, copied from original in Wayne family, Philadelphia, by Miss Jennie Brownscombe, native of Wayne County; two large Parrott guns in front are relics of the Civil War. It faces Central Park, where stands a Soldiers' Monument, dedicated in 1869 by Govenor John W. Geary; pedestal with bronze plates inscribed with names of nearly 350 Wayne County men lost in Civil War; also fountain in center of park, memorial of the National Centennial, both placed by the women of Honesdale who are said to be the first in the state to organize a Village Improvement Society; they, aided by the town council, have done much for the beautifying of the town; the parks have received special attention; besides Central Park are North Park, and on either side of the Main Street bridge lie Torrey Park, West, and Riverside Park, East, overshadowed by Irving Cliff, 300 feet high, named in honor of Washington Irving, who, while in Honesdale in 1841 with Philip Hone, climbed to the summit of the ledge overlooking the town.

Grace Protestant Episcopal Church, Gothic, stone, contains white marble font, good design, gift of Philip Hone, in 1848. Baptist Church, wood, classic, with Ionic columns supporting the porch, built 1843–45. Glen Dyberry Cemetery contains grave of Attorney General Samuel E. Dimmick, died, 1875, marked by granite shaft; his residence, brick, is south of courthouse. North of Honesdale is stone arched bridge over Carley Brook, made in 1909; builder, Samuel Brown from England.

BETHANY, first county seat in 1800, was staked out in the primeval forest. Courthouse, built, 1800, is now used as a store; new courthouse and brick offices were built 1820–23, the office building still standing; courthouse was abandoned in 1842, after it was remodeled it became the University of Northern Pennsylvania, with the public square as campus, and was burned in 1857. Between the old cemetery and the street stands the first Presbyterian

RIVERSIDE PARK, IRVING CLIFF, HONESDALE

WAYNE COUNTY 335

church erected in the county, in 1822. Several old dwellings have beautiful colonial doorways. An old tavern, built by Henry Drinker, in 1802, still stands. PLEASANT MOUNT, altitude, 1600 feet, sixteen miles north of Honesdale, residence of General Samuel Meredith, officer in the Revolutionary War, and United States Treasurer under Washington, commission dated September 11, 1789; he lived near, on manor lands, from 1803-17, said to have been visited by Thomas Jefferson; the house was burned; granite monument in his honor was erected by the state, unveiled, 1904, represents a Continental general, from a design by Miss Clara Keen; architect, Martin Caufield, both of Honesdale.

The Delaware River forms the eastern boundary; a woodland road follows the river. At MILANVILLE, is the old Skinner house, oldest, still in use in Wayne County, loopholes near the roof were made for defense against Indians; many Indian relics were found around here. Wayne County's only battlefield, unmarked, is in Sterling township, called "Little Meadows," near it passed an old Indian trail, from Delaware River to Wyoming Valley; on July 4, 1778, the day after the Wyoming Massacre, Indians attacked a few white people, with loss on both sides. On the Eastern and Belmont Highway is a nine-sided, stone schoolhouse of early construction. Three others are found in the county.

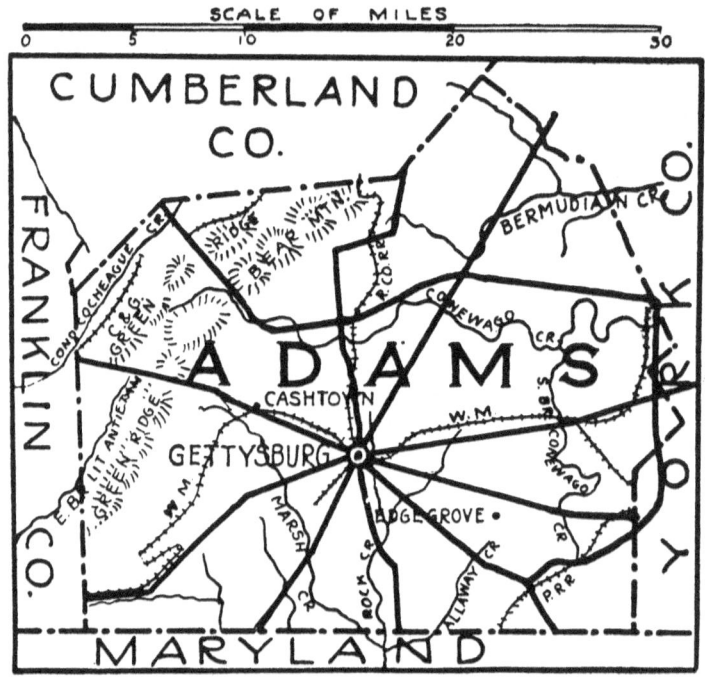

Adams County

XXVI
ADAMS COUNTY

FORMED January 22, 1800. Named for John Adams, then President of the United States; notable for the Battle of Gettysburg; chief industry, agriculture. County seat, GETTYSBURG, founded in 1786, population 4439. First court held in residence of General James Gettys; present courthouse contains portraits of Justices Marshall and Gibson. Federal Building, the post office, marble, Corinthian, architect, J. Knox Taylor, Washington, D. C., contains interesting battle-field museum, maps, and miniature reproductions. The United States Battle Field Commission has offices here. The Wills Building, at the corner of Center Square and Lincoln Highway, is where President Lincoln stayed November, 1863, before his famous address. Presbyterian Church, nearly 176 years old, where President Lincoln worshipped November 19, 1863; the pew he occupied has a bronze plate; church used as hospital during the battle.

Lutheran Theological Seminary, west of town, on Seminary Ridge, contains large copy of Leonardo da Vinci's "Last Supper," painted by the late James B. Sward, Philadelphia; also used as hospital by Union soldiers; it is said that General Lee took observations from its tower; near, in Reynolds Grove, General John F. Reynolds was killed, place marked by bronze equestrian statue, sculptor, H. K. Bush-Brown. In the Dobbin House, stone, on Steinwehr Avenue, built, 1776, was conducted first classical school in Pennsylvania, west of the Susquehanna. Southeast corner of Washington and High Streets was the first home of Pennsylvania College, established in 1832; now northwest of the town on a beautiful campus; main building, "Old Dorm," is fine colonial architecture. Jennie Wade War Museum near cemetery, shows bullet marks, home of only citizen killed during the battle, has collection of relics and curios. Artists of note born here are Charles Morris Young and Lytton Buehler.

The BATTLE FIELD covered 16,000 acres, not including cavalry field four miles east; Union Army was commanded by General George G. Meade, 80,000 to 90,000 men; Confederate Army, commanded by General Robert E. Lee, about 80,000 to 85,000 men; desperate charges were made in hand-to-hand conflicts. The cyclorama, "Battle of Gettysburg," painted by Paul Philippoteaux, is on exhibition. The Gettysburg Battle Field Memorial Association was incorporated by the Legislature of Pennsylvania to hold and preserve the battle ground, with natural and artificial defenses, as at time of battle, and to mark definitely lines of battle of all troops. It is now a national park and cemetery, in charge of a commission, appointed by the Secretary of War, including over 7000 acres with fifty miles of macadam roads amid most beautiful scenery.

Here we have the greatest number of memorials in Pennsylvania, erected by the various states. Among the 404 monuments and 894 markers are, The National Monument, white granite, four figures at base, representing War, History, Peace, Plenty; shaft supports

OLD PITTSBURGH AND PHILADELPHIA PIKE
This pike, in Adams County, was used by both armies during the Civil War

ADAMS COUNTY

Statue of Liberty; all figures are of Italian marble, carved in Italy, sculptor, Randolph Rogers; bronze equestrian statue, General George Gordon Meade, near center of line of battle, sculptor H. K. Bush-Brown; bronze equestrian statue, General John Sedgwick, north of Little Round Top, sculptor H. K. Bush-Brown; bronze equestrian statue, General Winfield Scott Hancock, east Cemetery Hill, sculptor, F. Ellwell; bronze equestrian statue, General Henry W. Slocum, on Steven's Knoll, near Culp's Hill, sculptor, E. C. Potter; bronze statue, General John F. Reynolds, at entrance to National Cemetery, sculptor, J. Q. A. Ward; bronze statue, General Alexander Stewart Webb, sculptor, J. Massey Rhind, placed at the Bloody Angle where Pickett's charge was halted and beaten back; General Webb was the officer in command at this spot; bronze statue, General Warren, on Little Round Top, sculptor, Gerhart.

Pennsylvania State Monument, double arch, 110 feet high, 80 feet square at base, crowned with dome surmounted by a bronze Victory, eight bronze statues at base of Ionic columns, Lincoln, sculptor, J. Otto Schweizer; Curtin, sculptor, W. Clarke Nobel; Meade, sculptor, Lee O. Lawrie; Hancock, sculptor, Cryus P. Dallin; Pleasanton, sculptor, J. Otto Schweizer; Reynolds, sculptor, Lee O. Lawrie; D. McM. Gregg, sculptor, J. Otto Schweizer; Birney, sculptor, Lee O. Lawrie; bronze tablets around base contain names of every soldier of Pennsylvania in Battle at Gettysburg, 34,530. New York State Monument, tall granite shaft, supporting bronze statue of liberty, with four bronze battle reliefs in pedestal; bronze trophy, state shield and corps badges at base of shaft, sculptor, Casper Buberl. Vermont State Monument, fluted shaft surmounted by statue of General George J. Stannard. Irish Brigade Monument, Celtic cross, with Irish hound at base, sculptor, Rudolph O'Donovan.

In the National Cemetery are buried 3589 Union soldiers; it was dedicated November, 1863, when President Lincoln delivered his immortal address, ending, "This nation, under God, shall have a new birth of freedom—and that government of the people, by the people, and for the people, shall not perish from the earth." Fiftieth anniversary of the battle, fought July 1-2-3, 1863, was celebrated here in 1913 by reunion of veterans.

The Russell Tavern, now a residence on old Shippensburg Road, three miles north of Gettysburg, is where Washington stopped in 1794, after quelling the Whiskey Rebellion. In Cashtown, the Civic League has formed a recreation park, using the old tavern for a Library; west of this town is the old Pittsburgh and Philadelphia Pike, used by both armies during Civil War. Conewago Mission at Edgegrove was established in 1741 by two Jesuit missionaries; present church, colonial, stone, was built in 1787; enlarged, 1851; paintings over the altar and in the transepts were made by Francis Stecker; Roman Catholic missions were established within a radius of twenty miles from this mother house.

XXVII
CENTER COUNTY

FORMED February 13, 1800; named for its position in center of state; notable for the State College. Chief industry, agriculture; formerly mining and manufacture of iron; limestone is extensively quarried; coal is mined about Philipsburg and Snow Shoe. The state owns 21,000 acres of forest reserve, through which several of the state highways pass; "Fireline" cuts made by the state foresters may be seen.

For a wonderful mountain ride, take the State Road from Tyrone, Blair County, to Bellefonte, following Bald Eagle Valley, and passing several small towns named for women, where remains of iron furnaces may be seen; near Snow Shoe Intersection, a state highway leads up the mountain, with unsurpassed views, to Snow Shoe; follow this road to Philipsburg, then to Bald Eagle Valley. Another beautiful ride is on the state road from Mifflinburg, Union County, across the mountain, through Millheim and Spring Mills to the Old Fort. From Spring Mills a short trip may be made to Penn's Cave; this is "Penn's Grandest Cavern"; the trip through the cave is 1400 feet in length, made in motor boats carring torches or acetylene lights, the water is a transparent greenish color, greatest depth 35 or 40 feet.

A road from Lewistown, Mifflin County, to Lock Haven via Bellefonte, crosses the Seven Mountains

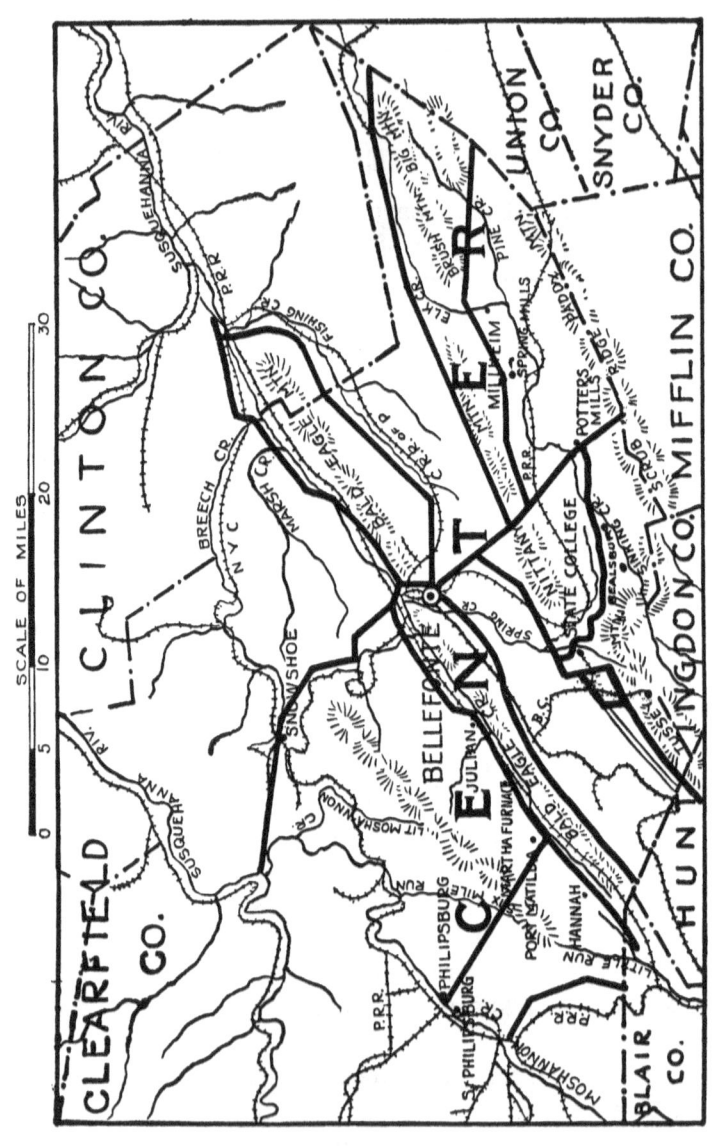

Centre County

CENTER COUNTY 343

with wonderful views; at Potter's Mills is an old furnace and mill. Near the "Old Fort Tavern" is marker, on site of stockade built in 1768 against Indians, placed by Bellefonte Chapter of Daughters American Revolution. Leaving Penn Valley, the road crosses Nittany Mountain, Bald Eagle Mountains may be seen beyond, with crest of Alleghenies in the background.

From Pleasant Gap a detour may be made to STATE COLLEGE; population 2405; Pennsylvania State College was founded by the United States Government; in 1862 Congress passed the Land Grant Act, offering to each state and territory in the Union a gift of public lands, the proceeds from the sales to provide for the maintenance of a college to promote the liberal and practical education of the industrial classes, in the several pursuits and professions of life. The offer was accepted by the Legislature of this state in 1863, and the institution, then known as the Agricultural College of Pennsylvania, designated to receive the Land Grant. There are thirty-four buildings on a campus of 1500 acres; "Old Main," built in 1857 as the Agricultural College of Pennsylvania, native limestone, is fine specimen of early architecture; the chemistry and liberal arts buildings are Classic style; mining and agricultural groups, Italian Renaissance.

The college maintains departments of study in industrial and fine arts, architecture, art history, and engineering; architectural exhibitions show many specimens of students' work, some of them prize winners in the Beaux Arts contests; the ornamental gateway, a gift of the class of 1916, was designed by the students. College Museum contains, among the portraits, those of the seven Presidents of the college, and Governor Beaver, also other paintings, marbles and metal work. Art is being emphasized in the summer school. Auditorium presented by Charles Schwab, Esq., has in the lobby, heroic statue, "The Hewer," by George Gray Barnard. Opposite on the campus is the Carnegie Library; architects, Seymour Davis and Paul A. Davis.

Near State College is a picturesque village, BOALSBURG, laid out with a small formal center square, from which streets radiate toward the distant mountains. Colonel Theodore Boal, architect, who raised and equipped a machine gun company for the World War, has created a museum for his warfare collections, curious old armor, dating back to the Crusaders, and a large amount of World War relics, German airplanes, helmets, gas masks, etc.; there is also a Napoleon Room; and he has erected a chapel, old Spanish model, which houses rare wall hangings, vestments, church furnishings, and manuscripts in Spanish, dating from the time of Columbus; they were inherited by Mrs. Boal, a direct descendant from Columbus. Colonel Boal also keeps up, on his property, a reservation or captain's camp, for the Twenty-eighth Division, the Iron Division.

BELLEFONTE, county seat, population 3996, was founded, 1795, by James Harris and Colonel James Dunlop, who gave the ground for the courthouse and academy; and certain lots, to be sold, to provide for the erection of said buildings. Name said to have been suggested by Talleyrand, who visited James Harris at his home "Marlbrook," now the Bellefonte Poor House;

COURT HOUSE AND GOVERNOR CURTIN MEMORIAL, BELLEFONTE

CENTER COUNTY

being asked by Mrs. Harris to suggest a name for the town he said, "Bellefonte, for this beautiful spring"; the spring is computed to flow 14,600 gallons per minute, and scarcely varies, entire supply being conveyed to the borough. It is a conservative and aristocratic old town, with residences of Governors Curtin, Beaver, and Hastings, whose homes may still be seen; and fine old colonial doorways; the library of Judge Ellis L. Orvis is noted for its rare first editions, one of the best in Pennsylvania.

Courthouse is in the Public Square, built, 1805, Greco-colonial, with Ionic columns, architect, probably Ezra Ale, has been twice enlarged without changing the front; entrance to the east addition harmonizes with the main west front; architects, Newman & Harris, Philadelphia, for enlargement in 1911. Contains portraits of past judges of the county. In the diamond, in front of courthouse, is state memorial to Pennsylvania's War Governor and United States Ambassador to Russia, Andrew G. Curtin; bronze, heroic, portrait statue on granite pedestal, sculptor, W. Clark Noble; on either side are bronze panels giving names of Center County's soldiers in wars of the Republic. The Bellefonte Academy, founded in 1805, burned 1905, was rebuilt, classic, architect, Robert Cole of Bellefonte.

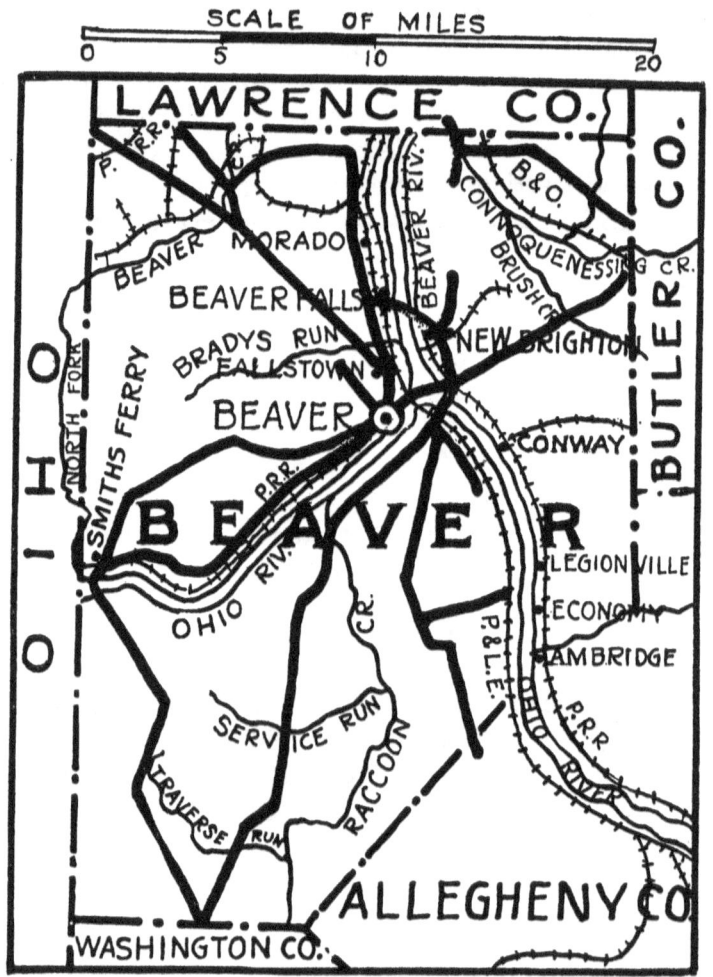

Beaver County

XXVIII
BEAVER COUNTY

FORMED March 12, 1800; named for one of our most industrious little animals; was in the track of earliest of French and English explorers of the Mississippi Valley, to which the Ohio River Valley forms an integral part. It was the scene of heroic labors of Moravian and Jesuit missionaries, who built their stations on the borders of the Beaver River. The Indian villages were the homes of some of the most noted warriors of the aboriginal tribes, and sites of important treaty conferences between them and the colonial governments of Pennsylvania and Virginia. Chief industries are coal and steel. Yards of the Pennsylvania Railroad at Conway, said to be the largest in the world; the famous glass factories of Rochester and Monaca, are at junction of the Ohio and Beaver rivers. Four bridges are here, including that of the Pittsburgh and Lake Erie Railroad, a massive structure of fine engineering skill, 90 feet above the river.

BEAVER, county seat (Indian, Shingoes Town), population 4135, was laid out in 1791, on a high level plateau overlooking the Ohio River, by the Surveyor General of the state. Five streets, 100 feet wide, following direction of river, were planned, with five of same width crossing at right angles, and each square divided again by streets 25 feet in width; eight squares were reserved for use of the town, one at each corner, north, east, south and west, and four in the center, which, with a wide strip fronting the river, constitute the parks; all beautifully laid out, they have large trees, and are planted with ornamental shrubbery. The present added territory, east and west, makes the town twice the original size. Courthouse, brick with stone trimmings, is on one of the center squares; the jail, a quaint old stone building, faces on opposite square; in center stands the Soldiers' and Sailors' Monument. At foot of Market Street is a tall flagstaff marking site of Fort McIntosh, built, 1778, by General McIntosh, on earlier site of a French town built in 1754.

BEAVER FALLS, population 12,802, oldest and largest manufacturing town, consequent on the great water power of Beaver River and Falls, has Geneva College and a fine Carnegie Library. The residence section is on a bluff 200 feet high, with fine view. NEW BRIGHTON, population 9361, connected with Beaver Falls by bridges, has the Merrick Art Galleries, acquired by gift to the city, with collection of paintings of merit and value, and liberal endowment for purpose of adding to the collection, library, museum, and to employ teachers in the future. Armory is headquarters of the famous Tenth Regiment. Near the town is a ravine, through which flows Brady's Run, scene of many thrilling events in life of the famous Indian fighter, Captain Samuel Brady. Morado has a beautiful park on the Beaver River. At Rock Point, on the Connoquenessing Creek, is wild and tumultuous scenery.

LEGIONVILLE, General Anthony Wayne wintered his soldiers here in 1792; the trenches and position of

BEAVER COUNTY 349

some of the redoubts are still discernible; marked by flagstaff, erected by the Fort McIntosh Chapter, Daughters of the American Revolution. Farther east is quaint old town of ECONOMY, home of the Harmony Society, disciples of Doctor Rapp; thrifty, industrious people of the past, almost effaced by the town of Ambridge, of the American Bridge Company, who purchased a large tract of their land.

Near Smith's Ferry, on the north bank of the Ohio, is large group of interesting Indian picture carvings, cut into the surface of the Piedmont sandstone, exposed in the river at a three foot stage of water; they are scattered over the surface of the rock ledge, for a space about forty feet in width, and 700 feet in length, and represent a great variety of the forms of men and animals, birds, fish, and reptiles, including the beaver, bear, wolf, turtle, snake, and eagle, human footprints and the tracks of various beasts; as well as inanimate objects, scalphoop, bows, and arrows; there is also a picture of a bison chasing a dog; another large collection of similar pictures, on the Susquehanna River at Safe Harbor, Lancaster County, contains the same forms of the wolf and the turtle, from which well-known tribes of the Delaware Indians were named, which would seem to connect them with that tribe; casts and photographs of these carvings may be seen at the Carnegie Museum, Pittsburgh.

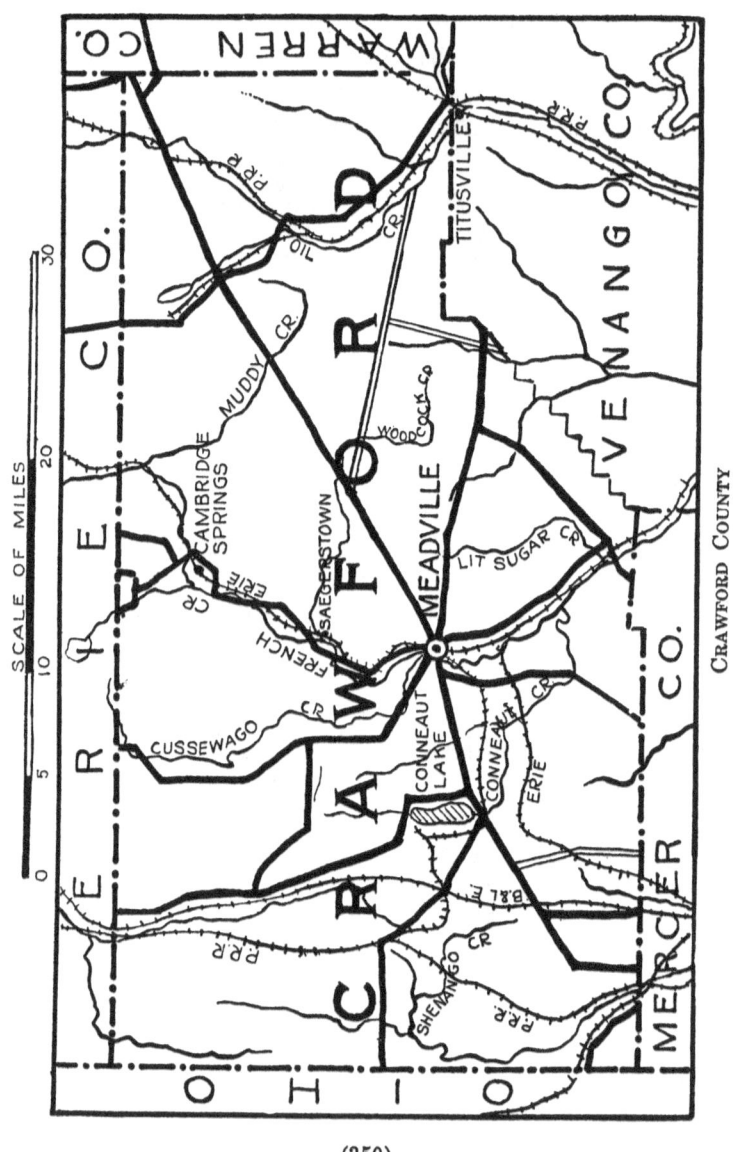

Crawford County

XXIX
CRAWFORD COUNTY

FORMED March 20, 1800; named for Colonel William Crawford. First well in the world drilled for petroleum, was completed here in 1859; valley of Oil Creek, south of Titusville, once most productive of oil in United States. Land peculiarly suited to grazing, stock raising, and general farming. French Creek was followed by Washington, 1753, from Franklin, Venango County, to Fort Le Breuf, Erie County. He returned, descending it in canoe; on French Creek, north of Meadville, are Saegerstown and Cambridge Springs, with famous health-giving waters. Conneaut Lake, three and one-half miles by one mile, is largest lake in Pennsylvania, covering about 1200 acres.

MEADVILLE, county seat, population 14,568, settled in 1788 by David Mead; his house still stands on Randolph Street, with modern outer walls; at roots of a maple tree, planted by him, is granite marker, inscription, "This house, erected May, 1797, by General David Mead, founder of Meadville; Ensign in the War of American Revolution; Major-General, 14th and 15th Division, Pennsylvania Militia; rendered signal service in the war of 1812, and an associate Judge at the time of his death. Placed by the Colonel Crawford Chapter, D. A. R., 1902." In Diamond Park, center of city, five acres, set in huge granite boulder found there, is bronze tablet, inscription, "In commemoration of Colonel William Crawford, born in Virginia 1732, burned at the stake by Delaware Indians near Sandusky, Ohio, June 11, 1782. Revolutionary soldier, friend and companion of Washington, brave and distinguished frontiersman of Western Pennsylvania; this county is named in his honor. Erected by Colonel Crawford Chapter, D. A. R., 1912"; also Pioneer's Monument, erected May 12, 1888, to mark one hundredth anniversary of Meadville; and the Soldiers' Monument, erected, 1890. Parrott guns, relics of the Civil War, are at the base; inscription, "Crawford County's tribute to her loyal sons, 1861–1865."

Courthouse faces the park, Renaissance, architect, E. T. Roberts, built in 1870. On a house west of the park is a tablet, inscription, "Site of first Court House and Gaol, north of Pittsburgh, 1804–25; placed by Colonel Crawford Chapter, D. A. R., 1909"; also facing the park are the post office, built by the government, 1910, Georgian architecture, red brick and white marble; and the Unitarian Church, built in 1835, red brick, classic, Doric architecture. On the terrace, at Locust Street, is a small stone tablet, marking an old Indian trail, along which Washington passed to Fort Le Boeuf; The "Terrace," an attractive residence street, is the sloping ground following the old canal.

Meadville Free Library contains a complete file of the "Crawford Weekly Messenger," published by Thomas Atkinson at Meadville, first newspaper northwest of the Allegheny Mountains; annual exhibitions of paintings by American artists are held here; an excellent permanent collection is being accumulated by the art association, among the artists represented

CRAWFORD COUNTY 353

are Charles C. Curran, Charles Bittinger, and Charlotte B. Coman.

Allegheny College founded in 1815, co-ed, is well equipped as to instructors, apparatus, and buildings, campus twenty acres, nearly one million dollars endowment; Bentley Hall, the oldest building, erected in 1820, is of fine colonial architecture; Library, classic architecture, contains autograph letters from Thomas Jefferson, James Madison, James Monroe, John Wesley, Commissions to Timothy Alden, first President, descended from Longfellow's John Alden; portraits of all the Presidents of the college, President Clark by Inman, also Hon. James Winthrop, and of Rev. William Bentley of Salem, Massachusetts, who bequeathed here his library, one of the rarest in the country.

The Pennsylvania College of Music, chartered, 1887, is complete in its faculty and curriculum, for study in every department of music and allied arts. Meadville Theological School, chartered 1846, contains a fine library; in the chapel is a portrait, by John Neagle, Philadelphia, painted in 1848, of Harm Jan Huidekoper, founder of the school; he was the first representative of the Holland Land Company in Meadville in 1802. Lafayette Hotel is on site of "The Gibson Tavern," where Lafayette dined in 1825. A house on Water Street, corner of Steers Alley, is site of blockhouse built, 1794; and North Ward School is on site of the State Arsenal, 1816-58; all three marked with tablets by Colonel Crawford Chapter, Daughters American Revolution.

TITUSVILLE, chartered as a city in 1866; population 8432; named for Jonathan Titus, first settler in 1796.

Here in 1859, Colonel Edwin L. Drake, by drilling, gave to the world rock oil; first oil well half mile southeast of center of town, is marked by a boulder monument, with large tablet, showing replica of photograph of oil derrick and surrounding trees, taken when oil was discovered; inscription, "This native boulder marks the spot where, through the foresight, energy and perseverance of Edwin L. Drake, the first well was drilled for oil, August 27, 1859; oil was found at a depth of sixty-nine feet; this great discovery inaugurated the Petroleum Industry. Erected by the Canadohta Chapter, D. A. R., Aug. 27, 1914"; Drake Monument, entrance to Woodlawn Cemetery, emblematic figure of a driller, bronze, heroic size, curving architectural background, granite; sculptor, Charles Niehaus; tomb of Drake faces the monument; Drake Museum, west of Titusville, brick, architect, Edwin Bell, contains collections of interest relating to early history of the oil industry.

Benson Memorial Library, Franklin Street, near Main Street, colonial, brick and Indiana sandstone, built, 1902, architects, Jackson & Rosencrans, New York. St. James Protestant Episcopal Church, built, 1863, Gothic, native stone, has fine Tiffany window. Presbyterian Church, built, 1887, Romanesque, Medina sandstone, is on site of log church built in 1815; stained glass window by the Montague Pastle-London Co. of New York. Presbyterian Chapel, 1907, Romanesque, stained glass window by Lamb, New York. The Commercial Bank has a portrait of John L. McKinney, former president, by John C. Johanson.

DRAKE MONUMENT WITH STATUE OF THE DRILLER, TITUSVILLE
Charles H. Niehaus, Sculptor

XXX
ERIE COUNTY

FORMED March 12, 1800; named for Lake Erie, the name Erie from a tribe of Indians, Eries, conquered by the Iroquois Confederacy in 1653, their identity and language is lost; curious mounds and circular embankments, still found in several places, show traces of a race superior to the Indians; human bones in large quantities have been unearthed on line of the Pennsylvania and Erie Railroad, indicating huge physical development, one was nine feet in height. The triangle north of Pennsylvania and west of New York was purchased, by authority of Governor Mifflin, in 1791, from the United States, to obtain a lake port for the state; conveyance being signed by President Washington and Thomas Jefferson, Secretary of State; afterwards the Indian title was purchased from the Six Nations, through the diplomacy of Cornplanter (Gyantwachia), the Seneca chief, for which the state gave him a reservation in Warren County; later the Indians resolved to prevent the settlement of Presque Isle by Americans, but General Wayne gained a decisive and final victory against them in the battle of "Fallen Timbers" on Maumee Road in 1794.

The Shore belt, for ten miles in width, is noted for grape and fruit raising; back of this is a productive agricultural section. Iron and steel industries predominate. Principal roads are along the south shore of Lake Erie, called the East and West Lake Roads,

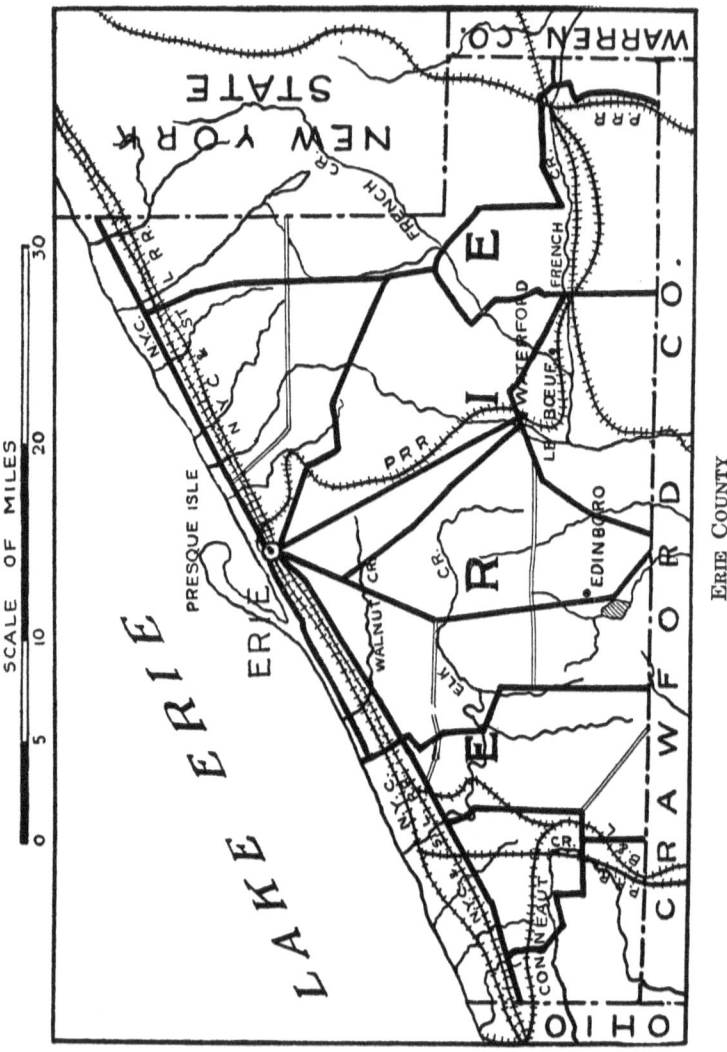

Erie County

ERIE COUNTY 357

that form a fifty-mile section of the international touring route across the continent. The old French Road from Erie southeast to Waterford, 18 miles, was originally part of the stage route between Pittsburgh and Erie, and also the old portage route from Lake Erie, for military and commercial purposes, to the head waters of the Allegheny River navigation, at Fort Le Boeuf, Waterford, on Lake Le Boeuf.

In 1753, Major George Washington, twenty-one years old, first caught the attention of mankind; he came with a message from Governor Dinwiddie of Virginia, to notify the French to discontinue fortifying Presque Isle and Le Boeuf, claiming them to be British territory. Captain Riparti came from Presque Isle for the conference. Washington was accompanied by Christopher Gist (White) and an Indian interpreter. They were in Fort Le Boeuf from December 11-16, and treated courteously by the French officers, who stated they would communicate with their superior officer, Marquis Du Quesne, but at present must refuse to comply.

ERIE, county seat, population 93,372, on site of Presque Isle Fort, built by the Marquis Du Quesne in 1753; one of the chain of thirteen French forts extending from Quebec to Fort Du Quesne; is 35 feet above the lake, 573 feet above sea level. Surveyed by Andrew Ellicott, in 1795, first Surveyor General of the United States, three public parks of five acres each were in the original plan, along Sixth street, one mile apart. Perry Square, Sixth and State Streets, on original plan, is focus of public life, it contains memorial monuments to Captain Charles V. Gridley, bronze statue, erected in 1913, commander of the flagship of Admiral Dewey's Squadron, in Manila Bay; Eben Brewer, bronze statue, first American postmaster in Cuba; General Anthony Wayne, large granite boulder surmounted by two cannon, erected, 1902; and bronze statue to Civil War soldiers, erected, 1872.

Courthouse, facing Perry Square, classic, Corinthian columns, native stone, erected in 1852, the bell is a trophy of war, from the British battleship *Queen Charlotte*, in 1813; court room contains complete representation of portraits of Erie County judges. Public Library, South Perry Square, Italian Renaissance, granite, built in 1897, architects, Alden & Harlow, Pittsburgh, contains portraits of Commodore Perry, General Anthony Wayne, Captain Charles V. Gridley, President Lincoln; in the Art Gallery is a small permanent collection of works by American artists, among those represented are Childe Hassam, R. M. Shurtleff, F. S. Church, George R. Barse, Arthur Parton, H. Bolton Jones, Charles A. Hulbert, and Henry Mosler; annual art exhibitions are held here by the Erie Art Club.

The Library also has a museum, with relics of the French and Indian, the Revolutionary War, the War of 1812, and later wars. Erie has a conservatory of music, with an organized symphony orchestra, and glee club. The old Custom House, State Street, north of Perry Square, built in 1837. classic, brick with white marble steps and Doric columns, was first used as a United States bank, now in possession of the Grand Army of the Republic. Erie has fifty-five churches, eighteen missions, and

WASHINGTON STATUE
Site of Fort De Boeuf, Waterford
Mr. and Mrs. E. C. Kilpatrick, Sculptors

other religious societies, also two cathedrals. St. Paul's, Protestant Episcopal, West Sixth Street, Gothic, stone, built, 1866, architect, St. John of Detroit, rose window by Tiffany, who also made some of the memorial windows; St. Peter's Roman Catholic, Tenth and Sassafras Streets, Gothic; Medina New York red sandstone, trimmed with white sandstone from Amherst, Ohio, and Mercer County, Pennsylvania, built in 1893, architect, C. C. Keely, New York; contains statues of St. Peter and St. Paul, Carrara marble, made in Italy; stations and stained glass windows from Munich, Germany; other windows made in this country. Memorial windows are also in the First Presbyterian Church; St. Mary's and St. John Kanty (Polish).

The State Soldiers and Sailors' Home and Marine Hospital, built, 1867–68, brick and stone, is located on the lake front; on the grounds is a replica of the original blockhouse fort, where General Anthony Wayne died in 1796, after his conquest of the Northwest in 1795; he was buried here, until his body was removed in 1809 to St. David's burial ground, Radnor. The blockhouse, showing plan of construction, was built in 1880, as memorial to General Wayne, it contains relics, and part of coffin lid with his inscription; these grounds were the reservation, on old City Plan of 1795, set apart for fortifications, in the most commanding position, for protection to entrance of harbor. Most of the military history of Erie is interwoven with the location between Parade and Wayne Streets, north of Fifth Street; here was the first white settlement, Presque Isle Village, and French fort in 1753. On bluff near Parade Street, blockhouses were erected, 1753–96–1813.

Parade Street formed part of the old French road to Fort Le Boeuf, French garrison, 1753-59; English 1760-63, and in 1785 American 1795-1806, also 1812-13. Here in 1763 took place the hard fought two days' battle of Presque Isle, with Pontiac, chief of the Ottawas, who, with a vast force, simultaneously attacked all thirteen forts, and captured nine of them, including Presque Isle and Le Boeuf, and again this was the objective point of the Indians in 1794, when they were finally conquered by General Wayne.

Here Thomas Rees, first justice of peace, entertained in his tent at the mouth of Mill Creek, a French exile, the Duke de Chartres, subsequently Louis Philippe, king of France. At the foot of Peach and of Cascade Streets, granite blocks, with brass markers, note approximate positions where Commodore Oliver Hazard Perry's ships were built, on which he won the victory of the "Battle of Lake Erie," in 1813. The powder used to fight that battle was made at Du Pont's, Wilmington, Delaware, and brought through Pennsylvania in Conestoga wagons. The second flagship of his fleet, the *Niagara*, is in Erie Harbor, having been raised from the sand of Misery Bay, where it lay for nearly a century; it was rebuilt by the state at a cost of $75,000 for the Perry Centennial in 1913; the first flagship, *Lawrence*, was raised and rebuilt for the Centennial Exposition in Philadelphia, in 1876; also in Erie harbor is the United States warship *Michigan*, now named *Wolverine* and used as a naval militia training ship; built in 1844, it was the first iron warship, and brought to Erie in sections from Pittsburgh; the original engine

ERIE COUNTY

is still intact and seaworthy; now oldest ironclad vessel in the world.

At foot of French Street, Commodore Perry's fleet landed with the captured British squadron. This place was camping ground of the Pennsylvania militia; in War of 1812-13, the British fleet was drawn up in front of the harbor, to destroy Perry's vessels while under construction; Captain Daniel Dobbins of Erie, commander of the *Ohio*, was the guiding spirit in building the fleet; 2500 soldiers encamped here, with cannon mounted, and such military preparedness as to forebode disaster to an enemy attempting entrance to the harbor. General Lafayette visited Erie in 1825, and a banquet was given him.

The Presque Isle peninsula, surrounding Erie harbor, has a state park, of more than 1500 acres, which is free to all; it gives Erie a large and thoroughly protected harbor; 100 acres were reserved for United States fortifications and dockyards; a life-saving station here, established in 1876, is place of interest. Presque Isle Bay is the finest natural harbor on the Great Lakes, four and one-half miles long, one and one-half miles wide. Lakeside Park, an irregular and sloping strip of land along the water front, from Mill Creek on east, to City line west, sixty-five acres, was laid out in 1888 by John L. Cully, landscape engineer; other open spaces are the Waterworks Park; the Reservoir; Erie, Trinty and Lakeside Cemeteries. Present city planner is John Nolan, of Massachusetts. Erie has also twenty smaller parks, of these the largest are Glenwood, between Sassafras and Cherry Streets, purchased by Erie Public Park Association in 1903, 114 acres, a natural forest with large stream of clear water and swimming pool; the Fish Hatchery, Twenty-third and Sassafras Streets, one of the most important in the state; Waldamere, four miles west on Lake Erie, and the State Normal School Grounds at Edinboro, sixteen miles south of Erie.

XXXI
VENANGO COUNTY

FORMED March 12, 1800, territory then recently acquired by treaties from the Indians, named from In-nan-ga-eh (a rude figure cut in a tree), Seneca language. A well-watered country, the Allegheny River meandering through rugged hills, about 400 feet high, presents places of rare scenic grandeur; into it flow several streams of considerable volume, among them Oil Creek, French Creek, and Big Sandy. For a number of years after the discovery of petroleum, in 1859, it continued to be the principal oil-producing field; now chief industries are manufacturing, refining of petroleum, lumbering, and agriculture.

FRANKLIN, county seat, population 9970, named for Benjamin Franklin, was laid out by William Irvine and Andrew Ellicott, state commissioners, in 1795, on a plateau where a few Seneca Indians were living in comparative security, with a lookout on the highest point of the highest hill, giving views up and down the two beautiful rivers. Being a conservative town, the original city plan has been closely followed, descendants of the early white settlers are living on their own lands from original surveys. Courthouse, Renaissance, brick, in center of a fine wide park, contains portrait of John Morrison, first town crier; near by is Soldiers' Monument, marble shaft surmounted by an eagle; on the pedestal are carved names of Venango County soldiers killed in the Civil War; opposite is the *Franklin News* office, Renaissance, good modern construction.

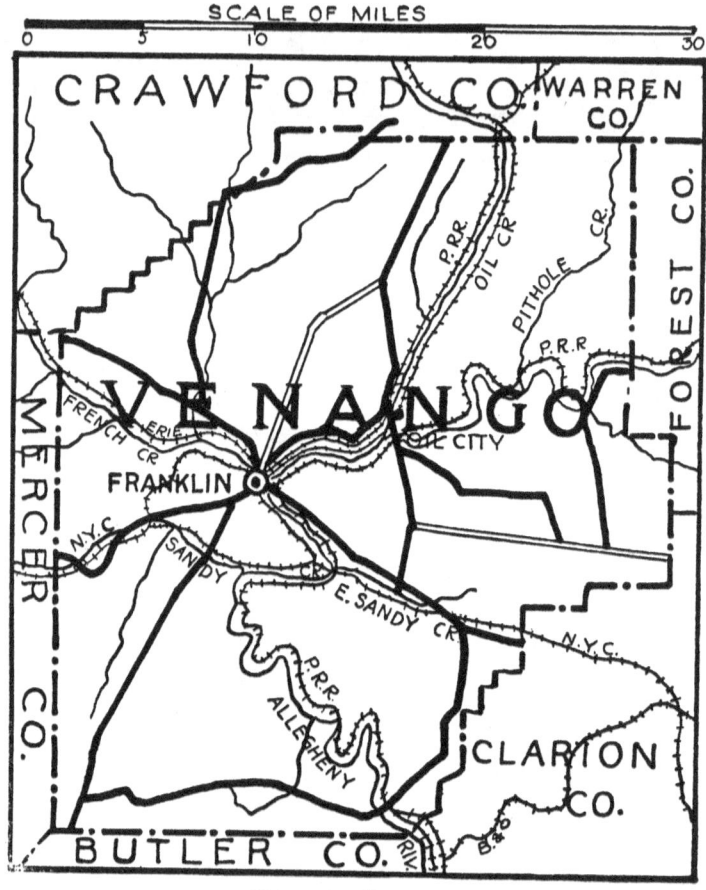

Venango County

VENANGO COUNTY 365

St. John's Protestant Episcopal Church has fine Tiffany windows; the Presbyterian, Baptist, and Roman Catholic churches all have good architecture and stained glass windows. Fine Armory Building. Original lock and dam are preserved intact, in an early canal extended to Franklin, from the "Feeder" Canal several miles below Meadville, on French Creek, its course is plainly seen at many places along the creek; five old bridges that were swept away by fire and ice have been replaced by modern structures; one is called the "Washington," concrete, handsome design.

Three early frontier forts were here, sites marked by monuments and tablets, Fort Machault, French, Elk Street near Sixth Street, 1753-59; Washington came here on way to Fort Le Boeuf, 1753; this fort had a share in the maneuvers that precipitated "the great seven years war" and dissipated the dreams of an extended French empire; the expedition which brought on actual hostilities was organized and received its impetus at Fort Machault. French troops passed through, and often a thousand Indians lingered here. Fort Venango, Elk Street at Eighth Street, English, 1760-63, captured and burned by the Indians during Pontiac's war; and Fort Franklin, on Franklin Avenue west of Thirteenth Street, built by United States 1787-96, later abandoned; also the Old Garrison, on bank of French Creek near junction with Allegheny River, erected by the United States after Fort Franklin. This city has never failed in a military crisis; during the war of 1848, George C. McClellan led the "forlorn hope" which captured the fortified buildings at Chepultepec, making the taking of the palace possible.

Six miles down the river is "Indian God Rock," on

which are still seen Indian picture writings; near this rock, Celeron, a Frenchman, under orders from the governor of Canada, is said to have buried one of the engraved leaden plates, placed at various points from Lake Erie to the Mississippi River, as marks of renewal of French possession. Opposite is a bald mountain, from which are fine views of river scenery; among the hills are numerous caves and ravines, a lovely ravine is Glen Fern south of Franklin; Monarch Park, halfway to Oil City, is a well-equipped pleasure ground. OIL CITY, on Oil Creek, population 21,274, so named because it was the center of the oil industry after discovery of petroleum in 1859. In early days, "Seneca Oil" was obtained from the Indians, who gathered it by spreading their blankets in Oil Creek, the surface of which was covered with oil.

Hasson Park, with forty acres of natural wooded area, has rustic, stone, arch gateway at Bissell Avenue entrance. In Christ Protestant Episcopal Church are memorial windows by Lamb, New York. United States Post Office at the corner of Seneca and Clifford Streets, built by the Government in 1906, Romanesque, gray brick and stone. Carnegie Library, built, 1904, modified Romanesque, gray brick and stone; architect, Charles D. Bollon, Philadelphia. Five bridges over the Allegheny River include the original suspension bridge and "The Petroleum," said to be finest in strength and dimension north of Pittsburgh; in 1892 a large petroleum tank caught fire and burning oil spread over the water in the creek it also set fire to the buildings, and many lives were lost. From Franklin and Oil City, public highways, now under state control, lead along streams and over uplands of great beauty.

IRON FURNACE—OIL CITY AND VICINITY

When the iron and steel industry started, iron furnaces such as the above were built near deposits of bog ore, and the product shipped by the river to Pittsburgh long before railroads arrived or cities appeared

XXXII
WARREN COUNTY

FORMED March 12, 1800; named for General Joseph Warren, who fell at the Battle of Bunker Hill in 1775; land is varied, with mountains, plains, and narrow valleys; the Allegheny River flows through, with tributaries large enough for floating rafts or propelling machinery. The beautiful Kinzua Hills, east, are nearly 2200 feet above tidewater, over them is the famous Kinzua Viaduct, said to be the highest in the world. Early industries were lumber and oil, now they are chiefly agriculture and manufacturing.

WARREN, made county seat in 1819, was first laid out by General William Irving and Andrew Elliott, state commissioners in 1795; population 14,272; in 1800, first sawmill in the county was started which is said to have made the first raft of lumber ever floated down the Allegheny; it also sawed lumber in 1805 for Jackson's Tavern, in which George W. Fenton, afterwards governor of New York, in 1806, taught school, until the schoolhouse of round logs with openings covered by oiled paper for windows, was ready. Courthouse, built, 1825, was first brick building in the county. A suspension bridge crosses the Allegheny here, built about 1871; near entrance to bridge is the Soldiers' Monument, granite, erected in 1909, on which are inscribed the battles of Warren County men in Civil War. Bronze monument to General Warren and his soldiers is in the west park, dedicated, 1910, placed by the

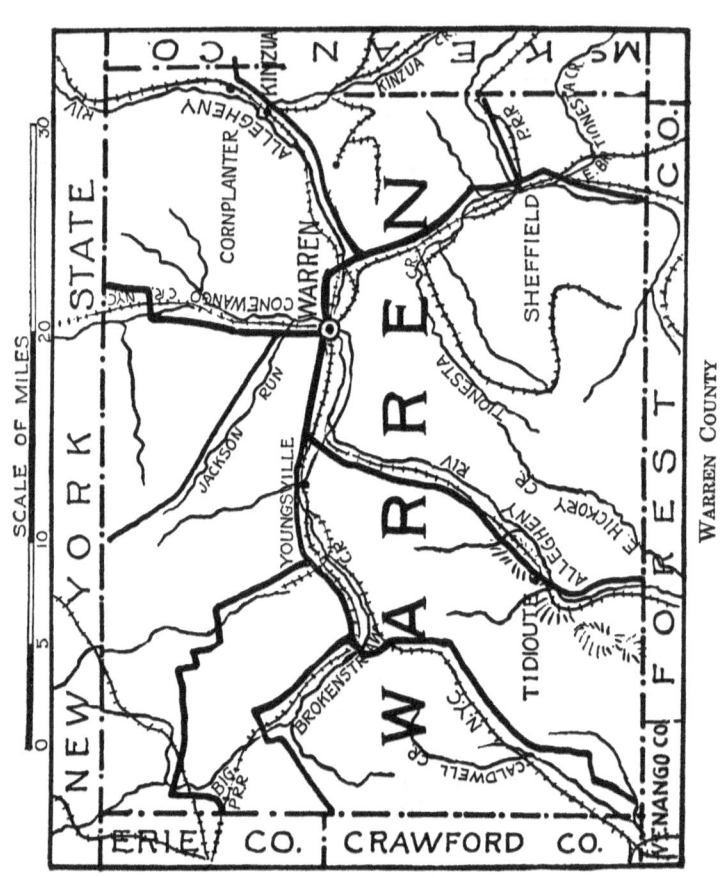

WARREN COUNTY

WARREN COUNTY 369

Joseph Warren Chapter, Daughters of the American Revolution. Memorial Library, classic, Doric; architect, Wetmore, New York, is on site of residence of Francis Henry, Esq.

TIDIOUTE, population 1065, in midst of most picturesque surroundings, hills 500 to 700 feet high, covered thickly with forests, where the Allegheny River makes a beautiful curve, crossed here by a suspension bridge built between 1860-70, was famous as an oil-producing community, and the center of a large and excited population, now a quiet residence of wealth and refinement. Also on banks of the Allegheny is the Cornplanter Reservation, given to the great Seneca chief and his heirs for ever, as a reward for military service and influence during the War of 1812; in 1866, the State Legislature authorized the erection of a monument here, inscription, "Gyantwahia, The Cornplanter, Died at Cornplanter Town, Feb. 18, 1836, aged about 100 years."

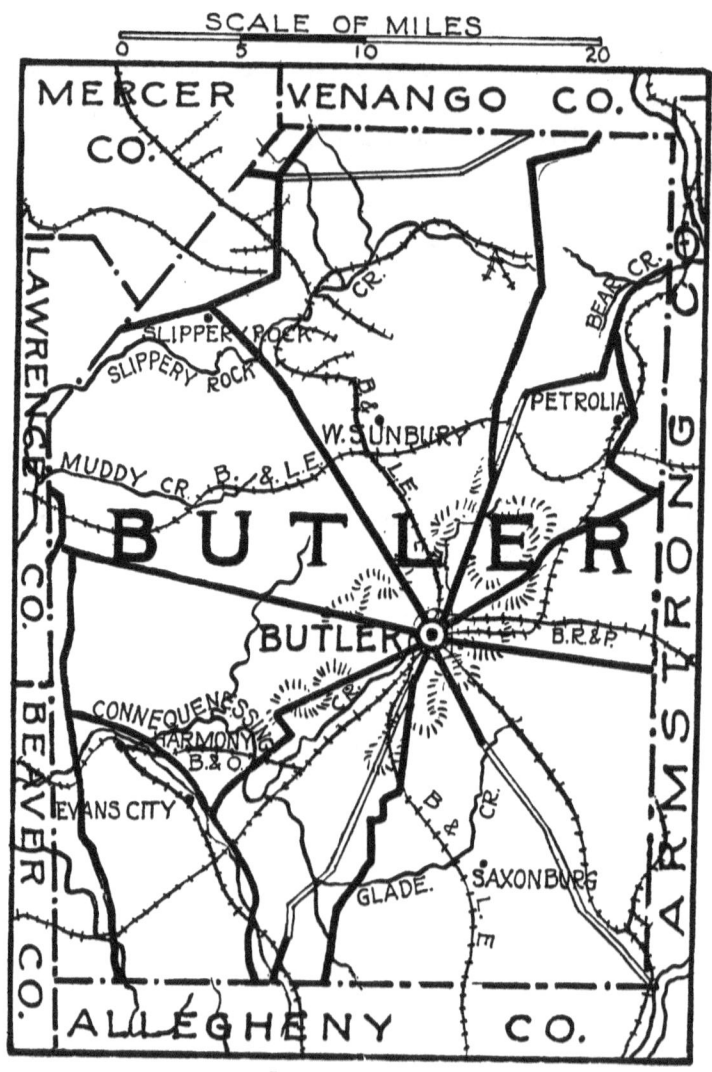

Butler County

XXXIII
BUTLER COUNTY

FORMED March 12, 1800; named in honor of General Richard Butler, born in York County; natural scenery is varied, with hills, knolls, and ridges, intervening valleys and broad, fertile fields, while many streams dash over rocky bottoms in all directions and flash their clear waters in the sunlight. The county is rich in old traditions. In 1753, Washington passed through over the Indian trail extending from site of Pittsburgh to Franklin, Venango County; Lafayette stopped here overnight, and many stories of hairbreadth escapes from Indians are related, among them that of Massy Harbison and her baby, who after seeing two of her children killed and scalped, almost starved for days, but finally escaped; the descendants of that baby still reside in the county. Robert Morris owned about 100,000 acres of land in this region. Chief industries, notably its large output of oil and gas, also manufactories; the Standard Steel Car Works, one of the largest plants in the United States, and the Standard Plate Glass Works.

BUTLER, county seat, population 23,778; laid out in 1803; rectangular, sheltered on all sides by hills; on the top of a small knoll is the public square, with fountain, walks, grass plots, and flower beds; it contains the Soldiers' Monument, dedicated in 1894 to "Our Silent Defenders"; facing the park is the Courthouse, Gothic French style, with a high tower, stone, built in 1885; architect, James P. Bailey, Pittsburgh; remodeled in 1908 by J. C. Fulton, of Uniontown; interior has mural paintings, representing historic scenes in Butler County; the Woman's Club furnished a rest room for women here in the basement. Two interurban street railway lines from Pittsburgh have their terminus near this point. Within two squares is the Post Office, built, 1914, Grecian; light brick with granite Ionic columns; architect, Oscar Wenderoth. Opposite is St. Paul's Roman Catholic Church, English-Gothic, with stone tower 180 feet high; constructed of beautifully colored local sandstone in the rough, trimmed with the same stone dressed smooth; roof, variegated shingle tile; architect, John T. Comes, Pittsburgh; interior has mural decorations by the Christian Art Guild; the altars are known as "Tryptich," said to be the only ones of their kind in America; the sanctuary is considered among the richest and most complete in this country; stained glass windows from George Boos, Munich, Bavaria. St. Peter's German Catholic Church has stained glass windows from Munich, made by Meyer & Company, who also made windows for St. Peter's Protestant Episcopal Church.

The county has numerous fine, concrete bridges; Butler Viaduct is the largest, 1060 feet between the approaches connecting East Wayne Street with Center Avenue across a deep ravine, built in 1915 by the Fort Pitt Bridge Works. Two miles northeast of town is a pleasure park of natural beauty in a wooded valley, well equipped with dining rooms, ball grounds, lake for boating, etc. Five miles from Butler on the heights above Herman Station is ST. MARY'S MONASTERY,

BUTLER COUNTY

Gothic, built by the Capuchin Fathers, of which St. Fiedelis College forms a part. SAXONBURG was laid out in 1832 by John Roebling, here he lived and manufactured the first wire cable, which he used in constructing suspension bridges that made him famous, notably the Brooklyn Bridge across East River, New York. At EVANS CITY, on a grassy knoll in the cemetery, is the Soldiers' Monument; Quincy granite shaft, surmounted by an eagle standing on a globe, the names of forty-five soldiers are inscribed on it; dedicated, 1894.

On the same road is HARMONY, an old historic settlement, founded by George Rapp of Germany; who organized a society known as Harmonites, they purchased 5000 acres of best farm land along the Connoquenessing Creek, amid beautiful scenery, and formed a communistic colony; all money and goods went into a common fund; all worked together in harmony and concord; the quaint old cemetery is surrounded by a wall four feet thick; at the entrance is a gate consisting of one large stone which turns on a pivot; more than one hundred of the sect are buried here; high up on the bank, above the creek, is a curious stone formation called "Rapp's Seat," here, tradition relates, "Father Rapp" used to sit and oversee the work carried on by the community; the tourist is well repaid for the climb by the beautiful view from that high point. Another historic place is known as the "Old Stone House" on Mercer Turnpike, ten miles north of Butler, used as a tavern in the eighteenth century; here in 1843, an Indian named "Mohawk" killed Mrs. Wigton and her four children.

A State Normal School with fine large buildings and wide, shady campus is at SLIPPERY ROCK. About 1792, numerous depredations by Indians were quieted for some time by General Brodhead's expedition to the head waters of the Allegheny River with Captain Samuel Brady's help, a notable Indian fighter; his leap of 23 feet over the waters at Slippery Rock, 20 feet deep, with Indians back and front, gained the praise of the Indian chief, who said, "Blady make good jump." At WEST SUNBURY an agricultural school has lately been established.

VINEYARD HILL.
Harmony Rapp's seat is back of the tree. The path leads to it

XXXIV
MERCER COUNTY

FORMED March 12, 1800; named for General Hugh Mercer of the Revolutionary War, who was killed in the Battle of Princeton; rolling land, well watered with springs and creeks; coal underlying one-fourth of land in the county; chief industries are iron, steel, and agriculture; early settlers were Scotch-Irish. In 1812, Mercer County people were frequently called upon to aid in defense of Erie; the whole county would be aroused in a day by runners; in a few hours most of the men, whether militia or volunteers, would be on the march; one call came on Sunday, while service was being held in the courthouse; the sermon was suspended, news announced, benediction given, and immediate preparation for march commenced; at another time, news of threatened invasion came in the middle of grain harvest; the response was immediate, only one old man was left in the town.

MERCER, county seat, population 1932; was once an Indian village of seventy lodges; no settlement was made here until after Wayne's victory over the Indians in 1795; it was laid out in 1803, on two hundred acres of land given by John Hoge of Washington County. The courthouse, built, 1909, colonial; brick, stone, and concrete; is in center of the public square of three acres; interior finished in white marble; mural painting in dome by Edward Everett Simmons, represents Power, Innocence, Guilt, and Justice; in the court

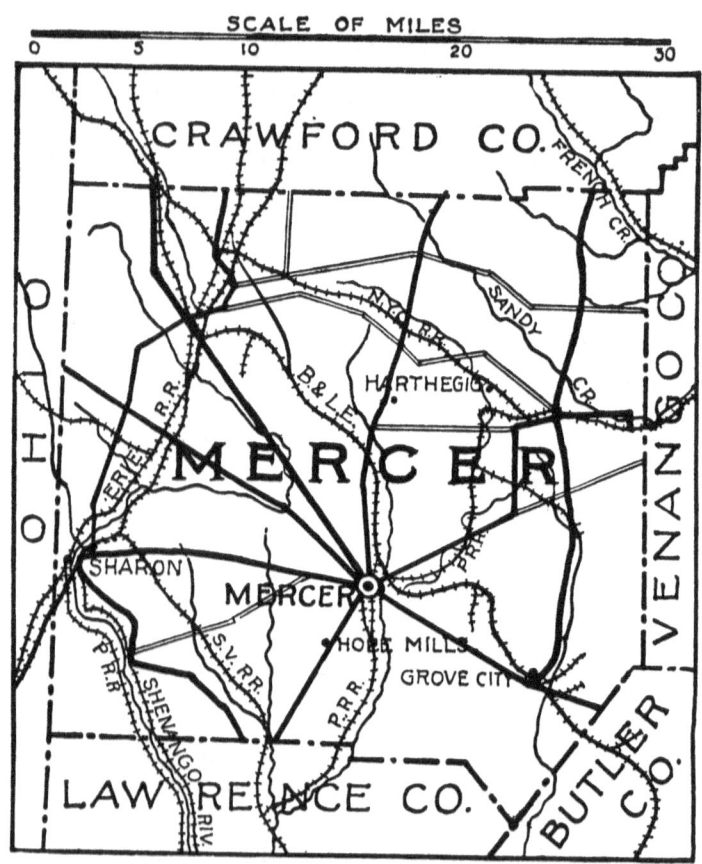

Mercer County

MURAL PAINTING IN THE DOME OF MERCER COUNTY
COURT HOUSE

Painted by Edward Everett Simmons

rooms on second floor are symbolic mural paintings, "Criminal Law," by Vincent Aderente, and "Civil Law," by Arthur Foringer, made in 1911; panels 11 by 12 feet; in the judges' chambers is a portrait of Honorable Henry Baldwin, former member of the Mercer County bar, and Justice of the Supreme Court of the United States, 1830-44. On courthouse grounds is the monument, granite and bronze, to soldiers of Mercer County in the war of 1861-65.

The Humes Hotel, at the northeast corner of the Public Square, built, 1817, then known as "The Hackney House," oldest hostelry in the county, had as guests Marquis de Lafayette in 1824; his room, No. 12, is open to guests; President Taylor and Buchanan, and General John B. Gordon of Georgia also visited here. The celebrated Harthegig healing springs, named after an Indian chief, is near Mercer; Indians claimed it healed them of many diseases. HOPE MILLS was the birthplace and the early home of George Junkin, D.D., who was father-in-law of General Stonewall Jackson; his father was a captain in the War of 1812. GROVE CITY is a picturesque college town, being the home of Grove City College, founded by Dr. Isaac C. Kettler. Buhl farm, near SHARON, is a recreation park for citizens of Shenango Valley and has club house, swimming pool, golf, tennis, and baseball grounds.

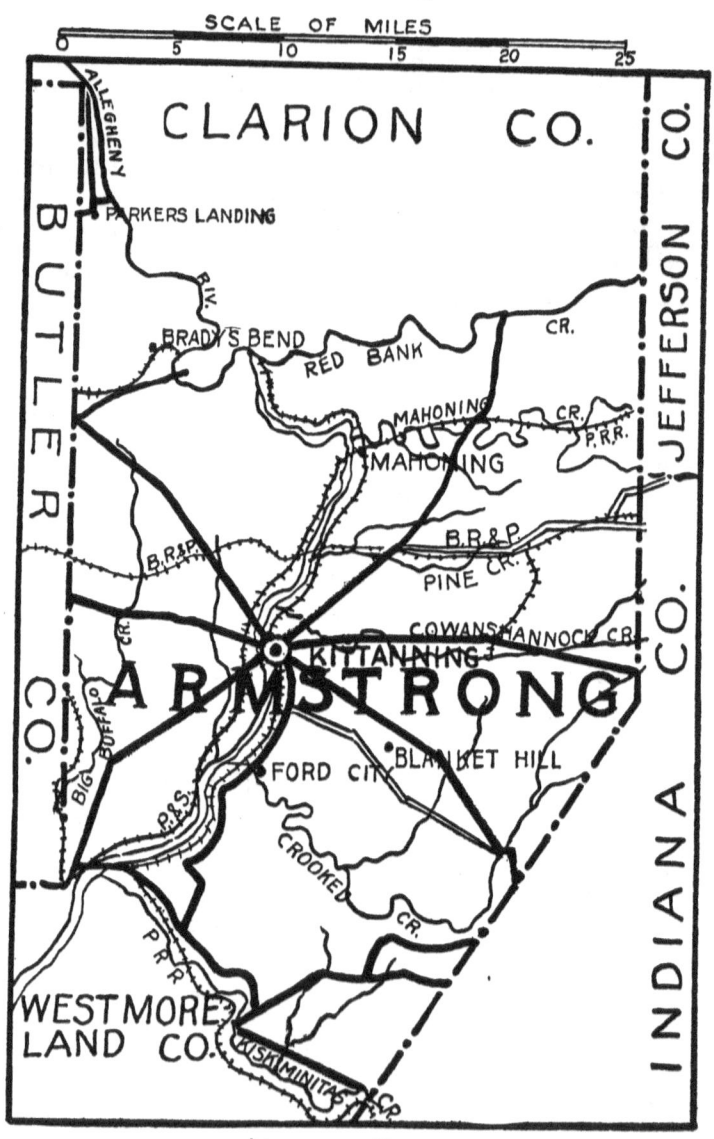

ARMSTRONG COUNTY
(378)

XXXV
ARMSTRONG COUNTY

FORMED March 12, 1800, and named for General John Armstrong, who commanded the expedition against the Indians at Kittanning in 1756, and destroyed their town; a hilly and well-watered region with fine farming lands on bottoms and hills. Bituminous coal and limestone are found in all parts of the county; cannel coal of excellent quality, oil, gas, and iron ore; the plate-glass industry at Ford City is said to be the largest in the world. Historic places are, site of Fort Jacob; Battle of Blanket Hill; and point where Washington and Gist crossed the river, not marked.

KITTANNING, county seat, settled in 1804; population 7153; on site of an Indian village of same name; later it was one of the French and Indian forts, extending via Venango and Fort Le Boeuf to Erie. An Indian trail left Horse Shoe Bend at Kittanning Point, Blair County, and came through Cambria County to Cherry Tree, Canoe Point, Indiana County, crossing from there to Kittanning. The courthouse, jail, and sheriff's house are built together, of fine cut stone from Catfish Quarry, Clarion County, cupola, 108 feet from the ground, foundations, 7 feet wide, sunk in solid rock 24 feet below the surface; architect, James McCullough, Jr., Kittanning, built, 1870-73.

At MAHONING, in 1780, was a fierce encounter with the Indians by General Brodhead, commander of Fort

Pitt, and Captain Samuel Brady, and another encounter at Brady's Bend. Captain Brady fought in the Revolution, at siege of Boston, in the massacre at Paoli, and in 1779 was ordered to Fort Pitt. FORD CITY, population 5605, has statue of Colonel J. B. Ford, father of plate-glass industry. Several fine churches are here.

XXXVI
INDIANA COUNTY

FORMED March 30, 1803. Named for Indians; early settlers, mostly Scotch-Irish, who not only had the Indians to contend with, but also venomous reptiles and beasts of prey, with which the country abounded; near the cabin door one would hear the quick snap of the viselike jaws of the wolf, one could see the panther crouching in a tree, or the catamount glaring from a thicket. Chief industries, agriculture and coal mining; entire county is underlaid with bituminous coal of finest quality; glass and brick-making are important; electricity and natural gas solve the heating and lighting problems.

INDIANA, county seat, laid out in 1805; population 7043; courthouse, in center of town, brick and gray stone, Renaissance, built, 1871, jail in same style joins it, built, 1888. Town hall, brick with Cleveland limestone trimmings, Renaissance, built, 1913, architect, H. King Conklin, Newark, New Jersey. Savings and Trust Company, white brick, Renaissance. Presbyterian Church, semi-Gothic, Hummelstone, has fine windows, one by Dodge, New York, formerly with Tiffany. United Presbyterian Church, Moorish, brick, built, 1851. State Normal School, northeast of town on high ground beautifully kept, buildings all of stone or brick, modern school construction, contains good reproductions of famous paintings and replicas of celebrated sculpture, distributed throughout the build-

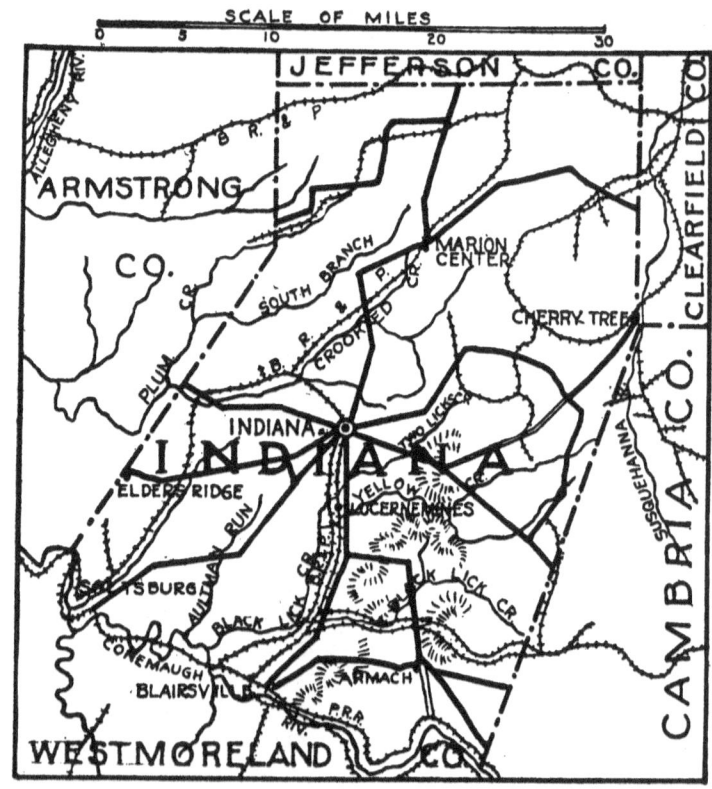

Indiana County

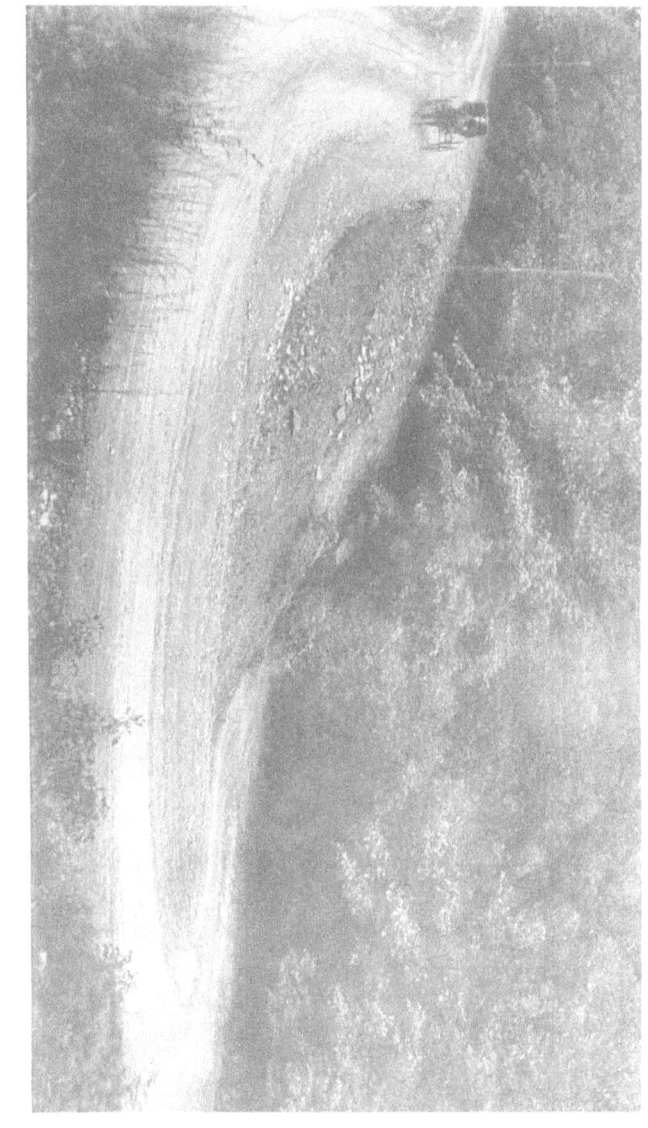

THE DEVIL'S ELBOW, EAST OF INDIANA
One of the most picturesque spots in the county
Illustration loaned by "The Indiana Progress," Indiana

INDIANA COUNTY 383

ings as a decorative and educational element; portrait of Jane E. Leonard, principal since opening in 1875, artist, H. S. Stevenson, Pittsburgh, was given by the alumni; and interesting class windows in Leonard Hall, given by three separate graduate classes, makers, Rudy Brothers, Pittsburgh; near the borough is Devil's Elbow, one of nature's beauty spots.

Armstrong Spring, an old Indian camping ground, on Indian Trail, "Kittanning Path," which passed north of the Rice Hill, west to this spring, in private property, and through normal school grounds to Kittanning, Armstrong County; over this trail Lieut. Colonel John Armstrong was sent with seven companies against Indians, at the battle of Blanket Hill, Kittanning, in 1756. Two miles west on Kittanning Pike is site of Clark's blockhouse, first building in the county, the spring and part of old stone fort are still there, not marked.

CHERRY TREE, on Susquehanna River prominent point on old purchase line, in treaty of William Penn with the Indians at Fort Stanwix, 1768, also called "Canoe Point"; from here, the Indians carried their canoes to the Allegheny River at Kittanning, sixty miles away; a direct line between these two points formed part of the boundary of lands acquired from the Six Nations. Where original Cherry Tree stood is the meeting point of Indiana, Cambria, and Clearfield counties, monument erected by county commissioners; designed by E. F. Carr & Company, Quincy, Massachusetts, unveiled 1894; Governor Beaver made the address; inscription, "This monument is erected to mark Canoe Place, the corner of the Proprietaries Purchase from the Indians by Treaty at Fort Stanwix, New York, November 5, 1768." In the southeast is a tunnel, part of old portage railroad through spur of Alleghenies, where the Conemaugh makes a bend of two and one-half miles. Near are Aurora Falls, for sixty feet over rock and through a picturesque gorge to the Conemaugh River (Kiskiminetas) which forms southern boundary, tributary streams fall twenty to thirty feet to the mile.

Near ARMAGH is the old Buena Vista Furnace, one of three operated in southeast section in the early forties, relic of the early iron industry when ore was taken from the hills, melted into pig metal, and transported to the markets over the old Pennsylvania Canal. BLAIRSVILLE, on proposed William Penn highway, settled, 1819, population 4391, named for John Blair of Blair's Gap. First United Presbyterian Church, Tudor Gothic. LUZERNE is said to have largest electrically equipped coal (bituminous) operations in the world, and develops power to other operations within a radius of twenty-five miles. SALTZBURG, settled in 1817 by Andrew Boggs, is near site of an Indian village, beautiful Kiski Falls are here; several wells producing salt of excellent quality were put down from 1813 and later. ELDER'S RIDGE, academy, stone, built in 1816, was the first state vocational school in Pennsylvania. The underground railway was in active operation in Indiana County during the latter days of slavery.

XXXVII
CAMBRIA COUNTY

FORMED March 26, 1804; named by early Welsh settlers for the Cambria Hills in Wales; has been called the Switzerland of America. Here are many places of historic and scenic interest. The old Kittanning Trail crossed the country in the north through Ashville, where there is an Indian burial ground. Near Carrollton is Hart's Sleeping Place; he was a signer of the Declaration of Independence; the British made special exertion to take him a prisoner, so he wandered through the woods, sleeping in caves, being constantly hunted by the enemy. South is LORETTO, a quaint old mountain town with one street, and an almost entirely Roman Catholic community, founded by Prince Demetrius Gallitzin, who brought a colony of settlers into the Allegheny Mountains about 1796, and labored as a missionary in this district for forty years; he died in 1840; the church he built here has been rebuilt in a costly manner by Charles Schwab in honor of his birthplace. St. Francis College has the tomb and monument of Prince Gallitzin in grounds. Southeast is GALLITZIN at western end of a tunnel two-thirds of a mile long on the Pennsylvania Railroad, 2160 feet above sea; a bronze statue of the prince is here. PRINCE GALLITZIN SPRING, with a monument near by, is along the State Highway near Summit, on top of the Alleghenies.

Beyond is CRESSON, a noted and beautiful summer

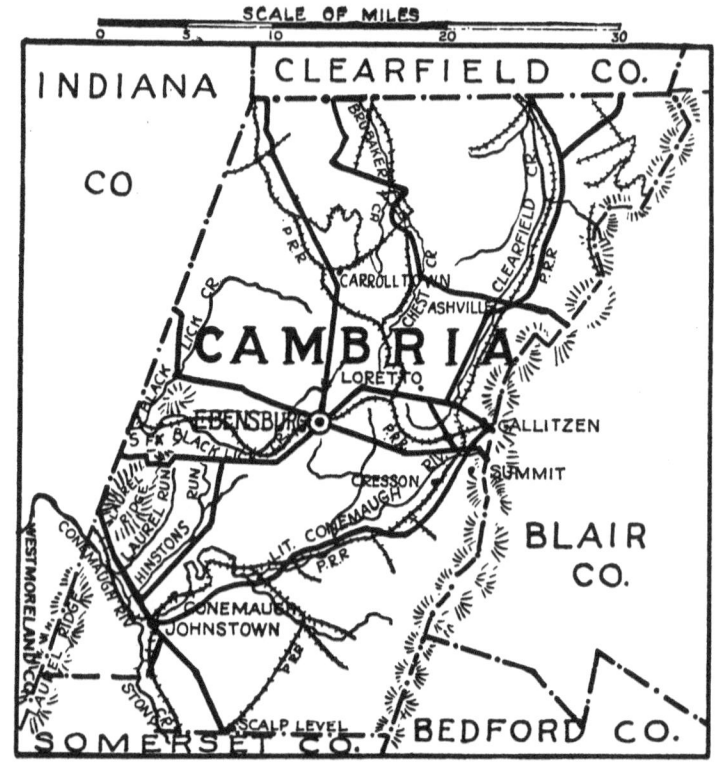

CAMBRIA COUNTY

MONUMENT TO THE UNKNOWN DEAD OF THE JOHNSTOWN FLOOD

CAMBRIA COUNTY

resort; here is Mount Aloysius Academy and the State Tuberculosis Sanatorium No. 2. EBENSBURG, county seat, laid out in 1805; population 2179, is also a summer resort; through the woods and around the lakes of this region the rhododendrons grow as tall as trees and are gorgeous in their bloom. Descending along the upper waters of the Conemaugh, numerous vestiges are seen of the old Portage Railroad, a series of inclined planes, connecting the State Canal at Hollidaysburg east and Johnstown on the west. Dickens wrote of the scenery along the canal, "Sometimes the way wound through some lonely gorge like a mountain pass in Scotland." Many dams, which are really lakes, have been built by manufacturers, the largest is three and one-half miles long, surrounded by wooded hills with here and there a waterfall.

JOHNSTOWN, population 67,327, at confluence of the Conemaugh River and Stony Creek, was founded in 1800 by a Swiss Mennonite, Joseph Schantz (Johns). A glance at the deep, narrow valleys, with their high inclosing walls, goes far to explain the possibility of so tremendous a catastrophe as that which overwhelmed Johnstown on May 31, 1889. Conemaugh Lake, two and one-half miles long, one and one-half miles wide, was reserved as a fishing ground by a club of Pittsburgh engineers, its waters were restrained by a dam 1000 feet long, built by the state as a reservoir to store water for the state canal during the dry seasons; a continuance of violent rains filled the lake to overflowing; the break occurred at three o'clock in the afternoon, a gap of 300 feet being formed at once. The water that burst through swept down the valley in a mass one-half mile wide, forty feet high, carrying everything in its way, completely destroying Johnstown and other towns and villages in its track, going 18 miles in seven minutes, the distance between Johnstown and the lake. The mass of houses, trees, machinery, railway iron and human bodies was checked by the railway bridge below Johnstown, which soon caught fire, probably burning to death hundreds of persons imprisoned in the wreckage. About 2205 lives were lost; in the Grandview Cemetery a large space is dedicated to the "Unidentified Dead," with a Westerly granite monument, having heroic size statues of Faith, Hope, and Charity; sculptor, F. Barnicoat, Quincy, Massachusetts; there are 778 individual markers for the bodies, largely unidentified, laid out geometrically, so that from whatever angle the plot is seen, they are in curved rows.

Johnstown was an important shipping station on the canal connecting Philadelphia and Pittsburgh. An interesting feature now remaining is the canal tunnel at bend of the Conemaugh, four miles east of Johnstown; second such tunnel built in America; constructed by the state about 1828 or 1830; the first is in Lebanon County, made in 1827. The Carnegie Library received by bequest from James M. Swank, historian and iron and steel statistician, his books and historical relics. Franklin Street Methodist Episcopal Church, Gothic, gray sandstone; the sills under the windows of the auditorium are dressed stones from the abandoned Pennsylvania Canal Locks, near site of the present Pennsylvania Railroad station; architect, George Fritz. First Presbyterian Church, at the corner of Walnut and Lincoln Streets, dedicated, 1913; modified English

THE GAP BELOW JOHNSTOWN

CAMBRIA COUNTY

Gothic, Cleveland gray sandstone and green tile, architects, Badgley & Nicholas, Cleveland.

The Cambria Steel Company began in 1840, when George S. King and David Stewart discovered a vein of iron ore about fifteen inches thick, on the Laurel Run, west of Johnstown; they built the first blast furnace in Cambria County in 1842, calling it the Cambria Furnace; in 1843 Dr. Peter Shoenberger bought out David Stewart's interest; he was the great ironmaster of his time, conducting a chain of furnaces, forges and rolling mills, stretching almost 500 miles, from the old Marietta furnace in Lancaster to the Wheeling, West Virginia, iron works. The Cambria Iron Works were completed in 1853, and sold to a syndicate of Philadelphians who selected Matthew Newkirk as president; in 1854 they rolled the first iron rails; the first steel rails in America were rolled here in 1867 from blooms imported from England. Iron is the county's chief industry.

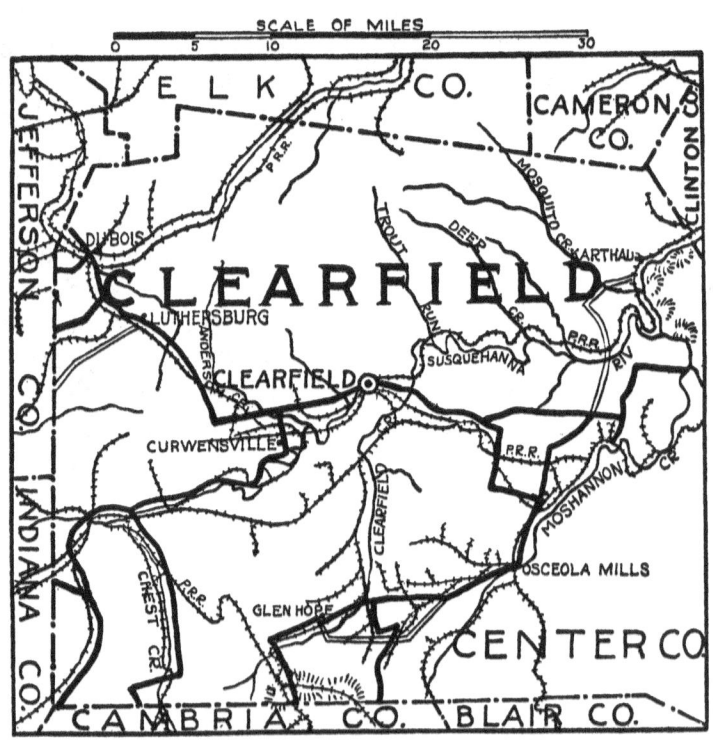

CLEARFIELD COUNTY

XXXVIII
CLEARFIELD COUNTY

FORMED March 26, 1804; named by the first settlers from a cleared field in the forest made by the Indians, site of "Chingleclamouche's old Town," said to have been the most considerable Indian village on the upper West Branch of the Susquehanna, now Clearfield Borough. The whole county is a continuous prospect of intensely picturesque scenery; surface mountainous, with ranges broken into innumerable, irregular spurs, indented by streams; from many hilltops views of the greater part of the county may be seen; the "Knobs," its loftiest summit, is constantly in view, and the intermediate country, a panorama of natural beauty, ever changing in atmospheric effects; all the creeks, tributaries of the West Branch of the Susquehanna, have scenery which beggars description, a veritable feast for the painter, poet, and romancer; Moshannon and Clearfield Creeks had their beaver dams.

Up Anderson's Creek, on the old Milesburg and Le Boeuf road, opened prior to 1802, a detachment of regulars marched against the British at Lake Erie in the War of 1812. Important Indian trails traversed this county, crossing the head waters of Clearfield Creek, Chest Creek, near "Hart's Sleeping Place," and the West Branch at Canoe Place. Another ran from Bald Eagle Creek where Marsh Creek empties, in Blair County, going west crossed Moshannon and

Clearfield Creeks to Chingleclamouche; this was also called the Trader's Path; none of the present roads are made upon the Indian trails. A mortar-shaped stone has been located about five miles east of Clearfield, on the State Highway, and has been marked by local Daughters of the American Revolution as site of an Indian mill for grinding corn.

Early settlers were mostly from older Eastern counties; these were followed by Germans, Irish, Scotch-Irish, and French. Chief industry, the mining of bituminous coal. In 1828 Peter Karthaus arrived in Harrisburg with six arks, laden with bituminous coal from his mines in this county, it was exhibited in front of the Capitol; not until about 1870 did the industry begin to assume any great magnitude; today the yearly output aggregates millions of tons, and the lower measures are not yet developed. Peter Karthaus also started the iron industry, near KARTHAUS, but it was short-lived; here, it is said, the first successful attempt was made in Pennsylvania to smelt iron by means of bituminous coal. Other important industries are vitrified brick, drain tile, and tanning.

CLEARFIELD, county seat; population 8529; on land owned by Abraham Witmer, laid out, 1805, in regular squares like Philadelphia; streets running east and west are named, those north and south numbered. Two small parks were reserved along the West Branch. Principal buildings are scattered. Courthouse, brick, Romanesque, built in 1860, architects, Cleveland & Bachus, contains portraits of former judges, among them Honorable John Holden Orvis; it is located in center of the original plan of the borough. Near are

CLEARFIELD COUNTY

most of the churches, of which the Trinity Methodist Episcopal, Romanesque, and St. Francis' Roman Catholic, Gothic, may be mentioned for architecture. The high school is well lighted and of best school construction; each of the principal towns of this county has its high school. Prominent men of Clearfield were, Honorable William Bigler, State Governor, and Honorable William A. Wallace, United States Senator; they are buried in Hillcrest Cemetery; a monument to Govenor Bigler was erected by the state.

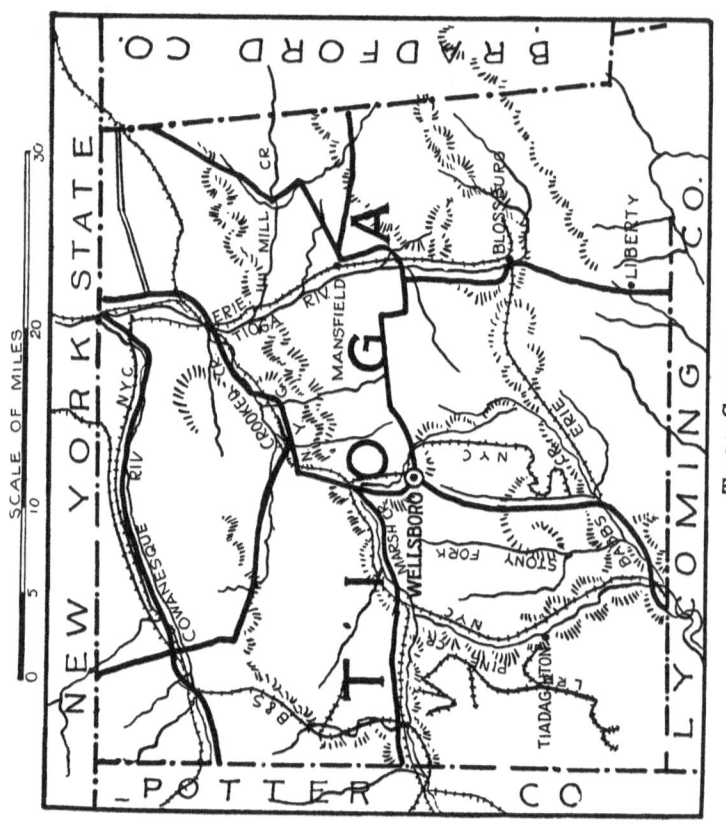

Tioga County

XXXIX
TIOGA COUNTY

FORMED March 26, 1804; name, corruption of the Iroquois word "Tiagoa" (gateway); noted for its high altitude and wonderful views; part of Allegheny plateau, where it breaks into parallel flat-topped mountains, supporting, in shallow basins, several isolated bituminous coal fields. Heritage of timber is being dissipated; the State Tree Nursery at Asaph is trying to replace the great waste. Chief industry, agriculture, land for dairy purposes is among the finest in the state, several extensive milk condenseries. Indian trails crossed the county from Big Tree on the Genesee, among the Senecas, to the frontier at Northumberland. First great road was built by Charles Williamson of New York in 1792, agent for Sir William Poulteney, who had received a large grant of land in New York State, adjoining Pennsylvania, in the "Genesee Country," home of the Seneca Indians; the road, commencing at Loyalsock, passed through what is now Williamsport, up Lycoming Creek to Trout Run, over Laurel Hill to "Block House," now Liberty; here Williamson built a blockhouse of logs 20 by 40 feet, as place of refuge; to Peter's Camp, now Blossburg, where coal was discovered in 1792; ending near Bath, New York, it opened up to settlers 15,000,000 acres of land in Pennsylvania north of Williamsport; this road is still used from Williamsport to Tioga County.

TIOGA COUNTY

County seat, WELLSBORO, population 3452, named for William Hill Wells, United States Senator 1799–1814, laid out March 21, 1806, in a primeval wilderness. Courthouse, center of group of county buildings facing the public green, colonial with cupola, built in 1835, native sandstone and conglomerate, which was hauled on ox sleds for several miles over poor roads; high on the southwest wall is carved the outline of an eagle, insignia of one of the stonecutters from the neighboring Welsh settlement. Opposite, across the green, is the brick office of the Bingham Estate, built in 1855, and still occupied by the agent, patent of 1,000,000 acres, land mostly in northern tier, included site of Binghamton, New York. William Bingham, lived 1751–1804, was a Philadelphia merchant, member of Continental Congress, and of the United States Senate. Facing the courthouse is a Soldiers' Monument to Civil War heroes, dedicated, 1886; also on the green is a monument to the late John Magee, who developed the coal fields and railroads of the county, a colossal portrait bust on polished granite pedestal; sculptor, Samuel Conkey, New York.

Best modern buildings are, The Presbyterian Church, Gothic, Ohio sandstone, erected in 1894, architects, Culver & Hudson, Williamsport, contains, among memorial windows, one to George Dwight Smith, killed in the battle of Smith Mountain; also Tiffany tablet to Mrs. A. C. Shaw, white marble, framed in mosaic of favrile glass. St. Paul's Protestant Episcopal Church, fronting the green, is a choice example of Norman Romanesque, the last ecclesiastical work of the late Halsey Wood, New York, built in 1897,

ANTIQUE CAPITAL, CHESTER PLACE, WELLSBORO
Used as a sun dial

From Stanford White collection

TIOGA COUNTY 397

native sandstone, windows furnished by Tiffany, are quiet and pleasing in tone, of unusual harmony with the masonry; pulpit and altar are also from the Tiffany studios; the church contains many fine memorials. St. Peter's Roman Catholic Church was remodeled from the old academy, locally an important and historic institution; standing on a hill the church raises aloft a gilded cross, impressive and beautiful above the surrounding foliage.

The broad main street is paved with brick, around a central strip of green grass, and shaded with fine old elms and maples. The Wellsboro Cemetery, purchased in 1855, was laid out by B. F. Hathaway, landscape gardener, of Flushing, Long Island; stone arch gateway, Romanesque, of local conglomerate, is memorial to Honorable Henry Warren Williams, Justice of Supreme Court, buried here; architect, J. H. Considine, Elmira; on summit of the knoll is the grave of George W. Sears, poet of outdoor life and wood lore, monument has bas-relief bronze portrait, set in granite; Honorable John J. Mitchell, Judge of Pennsylvania Supreme Court and United States Senator, is also buried here. Woodland Park, twenty-six acres, is owned by Leonard Harrison, Esq., who generously maintains it for public use; has surface of hill and dell, stretches of natural forest, and fine views from its higher outlooks.

Several citizens have grounds formally laid out, and planted under professional advice; of these, designed by Bryant Fleming, of Townsend & Fleming, Buffalo, is Chester Place, left to the borough by bequest, for a public library; the garden has an Italian roofed pergola ending with a marble bust and seats, on top of the terrace which divides the upper and lower gardens; a sundial, fastened to an old Spanish Renaissance capital, which came from the collection of garden marbles made by the late Stanford White, is on a rectangular plot of green, and forms the center of one garden room, surrounded by a brick walk, in turn framed by a broad border of shubbery; into the brick pavement are set little marble panels, carved with designs of roses, birds, etc., other insets contain quotations appropriate to gardens; set into the wall outside at right and left of entrance, are tiles with trees in bas-relief, inside, correspondingly placed, are reliefs showing old Italian garden decorations, Socrates and Hercules.

Just outside of Wellsboro is an old covered wooden bridge, in Pine Creek Gorge, through which the Tyadaghton (River of Pines) runs, mountains rise perpendicularly on either side for 1000 feet; the gorge is sixteen miles long, filled with trout stream tributaries, where also bear, deer, and other game abound.

In MANSFIELD is a state normal school, on beautifully terraced hill, five buildings, brick with marble or brownstone and terra-cotta trimmings, built 1889–1909, later buildings, modified classic; contains many fine carbon prints of famous paintings and buildings, also plaster replicas of noted pieces of sculpture. Carnegie Free Library, classic architecture, built, 1912, light-pressed brick; architects for school and library, Pierce & Bickford, Elmira, New York.

XL
McKEAN COUNTY

FORMED March 26, 1804; named for Thomas McKean, second Governor of Pennsylvania; mean altitude 1700 feet. Mount Jewett is one of the high points in the state; half a mile from Mount Jewett is the great Kinzua Viaduct on the Erie Railroad, said to be the highest bridge in the state across a ravine. The electric line to Olean, New York, eighteen miles, through Red Rock, reveals great scenic grandeur. Chief industry, producing and refining petroleum.

SMETHPORT, county seat; was incorporated in 1807; population, 1568. In the courthouse grounds is a granite monument to the Civil War soldiers of this county; it was shown in the Centennial Exposition, Philadelphia. St. Luke's Protestant Episcopal Church, a gift from Hon. Henry Hamlin; consecrated 1892; is pure fourteenth century English Gothic; architect, Halsey Wood. Altar and reredos of Caen stone, surmouted by a very beautiful, delicately carved canopy; memorial font, Caen stone; all memorials were designed by the architect; organ from Johnson & Sons, Westfield, Massachusetts. In the public school grounds is a tablet marking the route of General Brodhead's expedition. On the highway, near Lafayette, is a tablet marking place where General Brodhead passed across the county from Allegheny River, when he came from Pittsburgh against the Indians; placed by Smethport Daughters of the American Revolution.

BRADFORD, chief city; population, 15,525; is said to contain the only plant in America for the manufacture

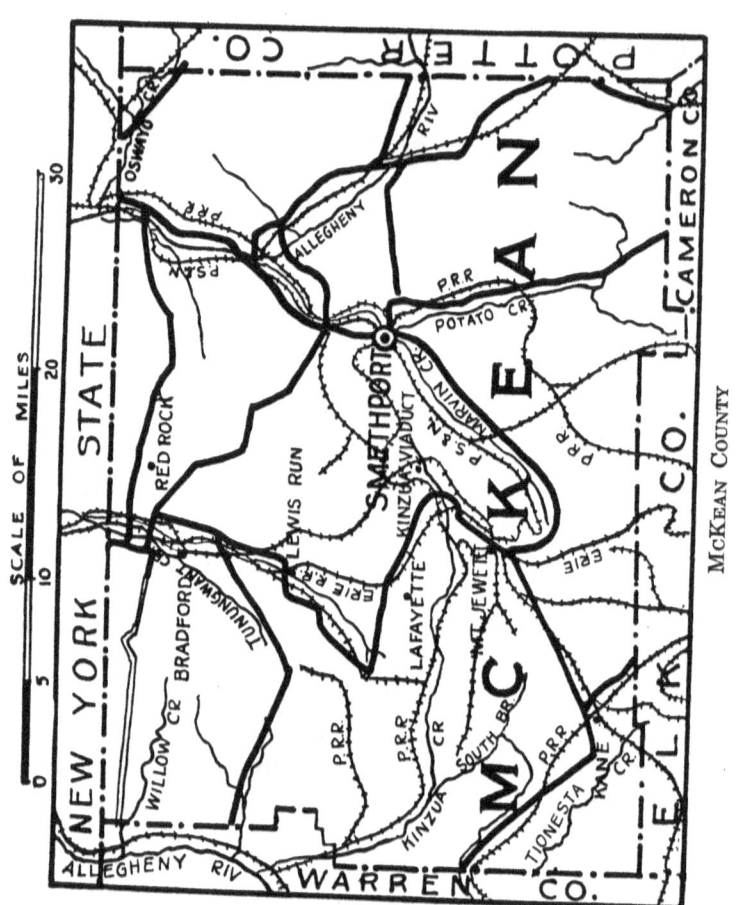

McKean County

KINZUA BRIDGE
The highest bridge in the world

of oxalic acid, it produces 10,000 pounds daily. The City Hall, Post Office, and Carnegie Library are fine buildings. The McKean County Historical Society has rooms in the Carnegie Library; among their collections are valuable historical papers and autographs, photographs, and samples of products relating to the oil industry, portraits of distinguished Pennsylvanians, and busts of General Kane and of Abraham Lincoln; the latter, by Theophilus Mills, is said to be one of the only two living masks ever made of Lincoln; it was made six weeks before the assassination, and after many years it was purchased from the son of the sculptor by Mr. R. B. Stone, and placed in the Bradford Library. The Museum and Art Gallery, owned by Lewis Emery, Jr., Esq., is at times open to the public. On the public square is a boulder, in honor of Governor McKean, from a tract of land in Annin Township, deeded to Thomas McKean by John Bull, a patriot of the Revolution. A tablet commemorating the Spanish War soldiers was erected by Spanish War veterans.

KANE, a beautiful mountain resort, has Evergreen Park, a native forest, given to the town by the Erie Railroad, through their agent, General Thomas L. Kane; a path through the forest is named for General Grant, who frequently enjoyed trout fishing here with General Kane. Facing this park is the high school; classic style, architects, Davis & Davis, Philadelphia; contains good collection of photographic reproductions of famous paintings and architecture. The Presbyterian Church is memorial to General Kane, commander of the Bucktail Regiment, erected by his family. At LEWIS RUN the great Indian hunter, Jim Jacobs, lived.

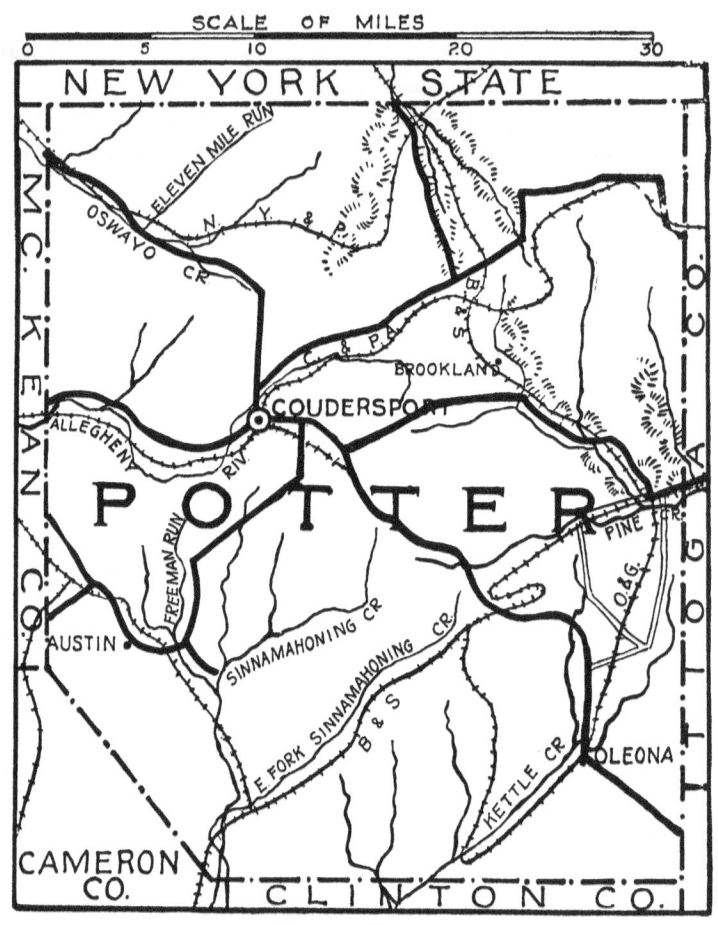

Potter County

XLI
POTTER COUNTY

FORMED March 26, 1804; named for General James Potter, an officer of the Revolution, is an almost trackless wilderness covered with dense growth of pine and hemlock, the haunt of bear, deer, wolf, panther, fox, and other wild game. Mean elevation is about 1900 feet above sea. At head waters of the West Branch, Genesee and Allegheny rivers, in the north, the ground is rolling, with beautiful farms; the southern part is broken by deep valleys and lofty mountains, with most picturesque scenery, especially in the Kettle Creek and Sinnemahoning valleys. Probably the first white man to cross the county was David Zeisberger, who passed down the Allegheny River to mouth of the Tionesta, Forest County, in 1767; his journal, now on file in the Moravian Library at Bethlehem, tells of the wild beauty of the county. Farming and stock raising are gaining, but the main industry is still lumbering, with second growth of hardwoods, maple, beech, and birch, which will in time be a great nucleus of wealth.

Earliest important road is the Jersey Shore Turnpike, running from Jersey Shore at the mouth of Pine Creek, Lycoming County, through most wonderful scenery to Coudersport and on to Buffalo; an effort is being made to have this historic highway improved, as it is the most direct way from the West Branch Valley to Buffalo. On this road is the site of Oleona.

Ole Bull, the famous violinist, attempted the settlement of a colony of Norwegians; in 1852, he purchased 11,144 acres on Kettle Creek, in the then almost unbroken forests; and laid out four villages, New Norway, New Bergen, Oleona, and Walhalla; this proved a sad failure, and the land is now included in the State Forest Reserve. Ole Bull's Castle, with a great stone wall, still partly standing, was built about a mile below Oleona, on the crest of a bluff. Travel is generally good in summer, during the winter the heavy snowdrifts are often too deep for passage, temperature often falling to 40° below zero.

COUDERSPORT, county seat, settled in 1807; population 2836; courthouse, substantial, colonial building in the square, on the main street; in the grounds is the Soldiers' Monument, a granite shaft, pedestal has names of Potter County men who fell in war for the Union. The famous Bucktail Regiment was recruited largely from Potter County, noted marksmen, many had been famous hunters, and because of their wonderful skill with the rifle were made sharpshooters in the Civil War. Christ Protestant Episcopal Church, incorporated, 1833, present stone building, Gothic, built in 1885, on ground given by Miss Katharine Dent. The beautiful little church, "All Saints," at Brookland, near the old Dent Homestead, memorial to Henry Hatch Dent, by his children, maintained by endowment, is native stone, with stained glass windows, marble memorial altar, and other artistic furnishings, open by appointments of the Bishop, it stands, as old "St. Martins-in-the-Field," a solitary witness for Christianity and the Church.

First Presbyterian, oldest church organization in

ON THE SINNEMAHONING CREEK

POTTER COUNTY

Coudersport, established 1832, first building made in 1849, on ground given by John Keating, Esq., present building, Fourth and Main Streets, dedicated in 1903, Italian Renaissance; other denominations have good church buildings. The Pennsylvania Historical Commission has made an appropriation for the placing of a monument to David Ziesberger at Coudersport; they will also place tablets at site of Ole Bull's Castle and near the Austin disaster; the Austin flood, in 1911, when the town was almost blotted out, and many lives were lost and property destroyed, was perhaps the worst calamity which has ever visited the county. Three miles east of Coudersport is "The Sweden Valley Ice Mine," in a shaft about six feet square and twelve feet deep; during the hot summer weather ice is formed here in large quantities; the Smithsonian Institution has published a number of articles concerning these ice caves.

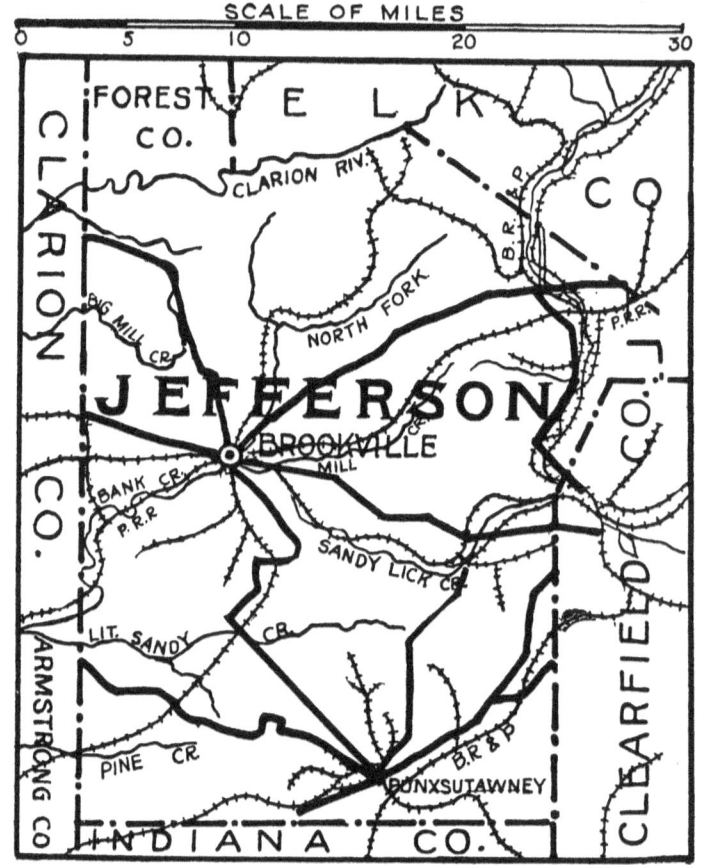

Jefferson County

XLII
JEFFERSON COUNTY

FORMED March 26, 1804; named for Thomas Jefferson; steep and rugged hills line the watercourses of every stream, alternating with fine valley land, traversed by good roads through most picturesque scenery; the views are a continual delight. In early days large tracts of this land were held by rich proprietors who would neither improve nor sell at a fair price. The pioneer hewed his canoes out of pine trees, large enough to receive a barrel of flour crosswise; a homemade rope of flax was attached to the front to pull them over the ripples. The county is wonderfully rich in coal and an abundance of natural gas, and has developed more along commercial than it has along artistic lines. Chief industries: stock raising, coal, iron, glass, and silk.

County seat, BROOKVILLE, laid out in 1830; population 3272. Hunts Point, now Carrier's addition of Brookville, was once an Indian village. Main Street runs east and west. Pickering Street crosses at right angles. Courthouse, at the corner of Main and Pickering Streets; Renaissance, brick; contains portraits. The Brookville Park Association is making great civic improvements; a park of ten acres is in the center of the town and a fine new park building or auditorium is being erected; the organization being truly altruistic, to the intent that no dividends shall be paid to the subscribers, but all profits applied to municipal improvements. There are several churches, among them may be mentioned the Presbyterian and Methodist for architecture; both Romanesque; stone. The Presbyterian has good stained glass windows. The Daughters of the American Revolution have placed a small monument to Joseph Barnett in the old cemetery. Fort Barnett was one mile east of Brookville, on the old turnpike (Mead's Trail); his cabin in 1799 is said to have been the only one within seventy-five miles.

PUNXSUTAWNEY, population 10,311, was an Indian village; during the eighteenth century, Moravian missionaries labored here among the Delaware tribes of the Algonquin Indians; Brother Ettewein kept a faithful record of his travels and work, describing his journey along Mahoning Creek, then named by the Indians "Mohulbucteetam," or place where canoes are abandoned. Rev. David Barkley and his son-in-law, Dr. John W. Jenks, from Newtown, Bucks County, a graduate of the University of Pennsylvania in 1816, later made an associate judge, owned the land and laid out the town in 1820 in squares, including one for the public, which in this century has been made into a beautiful park by Frederick Olmstead, landscape gardener, of Brookline, Massachusetts; on each corner are old cannon from the Civil War. A fine brick post office with Ionic portico is here, built by the United States Government, and many beautiful churches. Christ Episcopal Church is built with stone taken from the creek bed and laid without any cutting; the soft brown color was caused by the mineral in the water, and is permanent.

XLIII
SUSQUEHANNA COUNTY

FORMED February 21, 1810; named for situation, at head waters of the Susquehanna River, which completely drains the county, every stream flowing into it as it flows around a spur of the Alleghenies with the highest outline of two mountains; original Indian names, Onaquaga and Miantinomah. The scenery is beautifully diversified; there are numerous lakes, the largest, Crystal Lake, is over a mile long; from Elk Mountain, with its three peaks, sixteen lakes are visible, and the Water Gap is plainly seen on a clear day; from Ararat, 2040 feet above the sea level, is also an extended view. A panorama of great beauty is seen from the heights of Gibson Township; the slopes furnish unsurpassed grazing and abound in orchards and gardens; named for Chief Justice Gibson, the town was first settled in 1792 by Joseph Potter.

The most beautiful auto ride through the county is from Montrose to SUSQUEHANNA, incorporated in 1853, called the City of Stairs; Erie Railroad shops are here, the buildings, covering eight acres, include a Library and Lecture Hall. Martin's Creek Viaduct, 1600 feet long with eleven spans, on the Lackawanna Railroad, is said to be, next to the Tunkhannock Viaduct on same road, the largest concrete bridge in the world; this road is known as the shortest route between New York and Buffalo; owing to its high elevation through this county, the views are of extraordinary

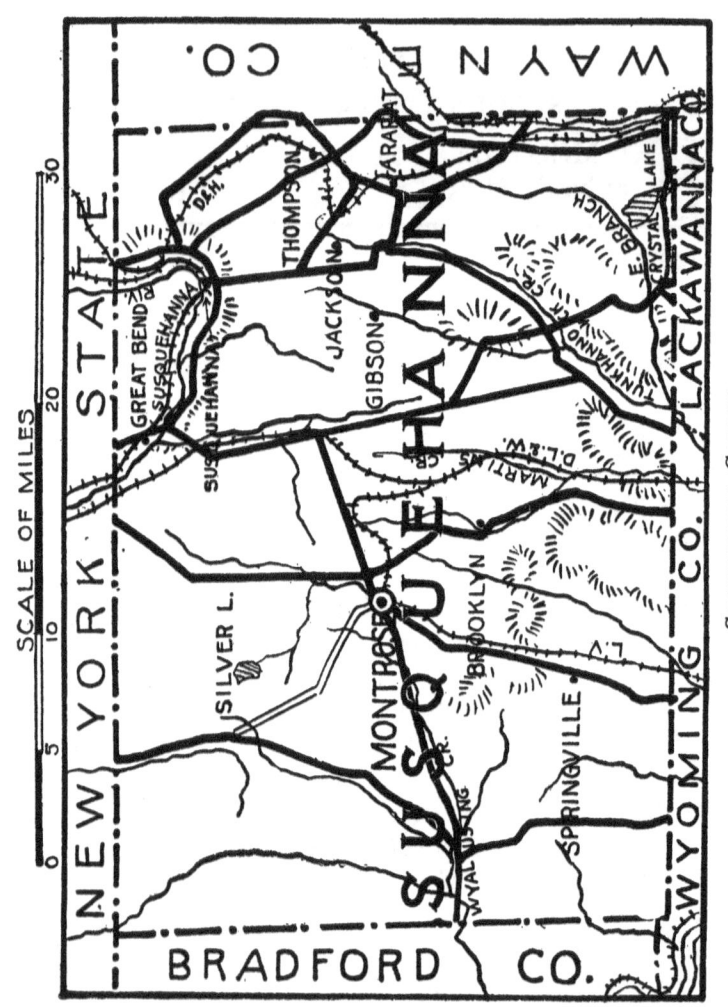

Susquehanna County

SUSQUEHANNA COUNTY

beauty. Earliest white settlement was at Great Bend; General James Clinton, with 1600 men, encamped here in 1799, *en route* to join General Sullivan at Chemung against the Indians. Chief industry, agriculture and butter making.

MONTROSE, population 1661; made county seat in 1811, first settled by Stephen Wilson of Vermont in 1799, is a notable health resort because of its altitude; it was developed through the liberality of Dr. R. H. Rose and Isaac Post, the latter was first postmaster in 1808. Dr. Rose purchased 100,000 acres in 1807, partly in Silver Lake Township, and developed the resources of the county. Public buildings face the square, in which is the monument to Civil War soldiers. Courthouse, a fine structure, colonial architecture, built in 1842, contains a portrait of Honorable Galusha A. Grow, who was sent to Congress from this county. The conference building seats 3000; here The Bible Institute is held each summer. At SPRINGVILLE was farm of Zophar Blakeslee, whose daughter, Sarah, was married to Honorable Asa Packer. BROOKLYN was early residence of George Catlin, who became noted as a painter of Indians. JACKSON started as a beaver meadow. When THOMSON was first settled, in 1820, an unbroken forest of beech wood stretched eastward for fifty miles.

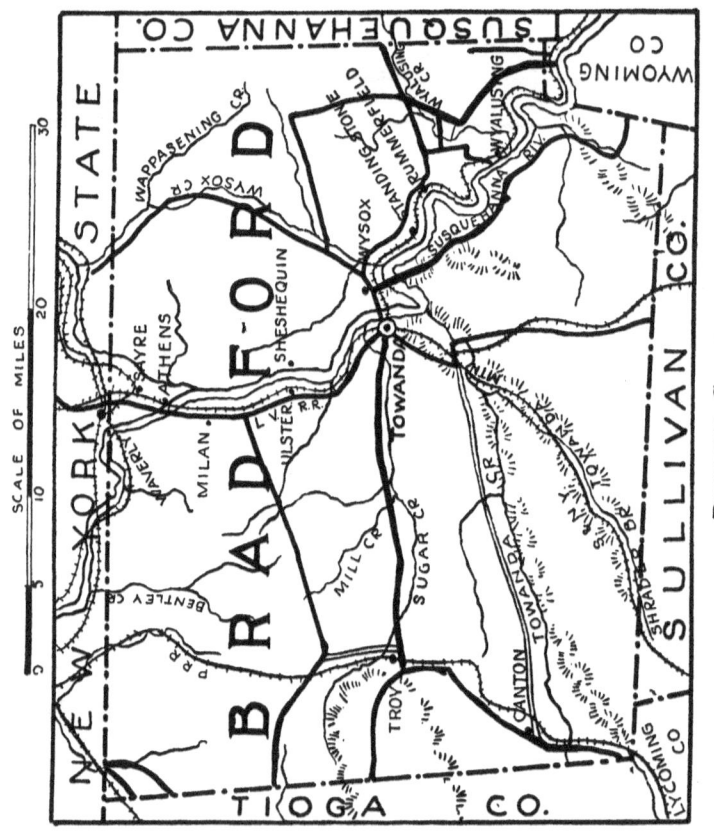

BRADFORD COUNTY

XLIV
BRADFORD COUNTY

FORMED February 21, 1810, as Ontario; on March 24, 1812, named in honor of William Bradford, an attorney general in the cabinet of Washington; surface hilly or rolling. Chief industries are dairying and breeding of fine cattle and thoroughbred horses. Said to be first place on record visited by a white man in Pennsylvania; in 1615 Stephen Bruhle, explorer and interpreter for Samuel Champlain, with twelve Huron Indians, came to Carouantian, a palisaded village of the Carouantiannais, on Spanish Hill, just above present towns of Sayre and Athens; he found here 800 warriors, 500 of whom went with him to aid Champlain against the Onondaga stronghold in New York. Bruhle returned to Carouantian, remained during the winter of 1615–16, and explored the Susquehanna River to the sea, making report to Champlain.

First road was the great Indian warpath along the Susquehanna, used by General Sullivan and his Continental Army in expedition against the Indians in 1779; the state road, from Wilkes-Barre, up the river, through Wyoming and Bradford counties, is substantially on this old trail; historic places along the road are well marked, a monument thirteen feet high, native stone, from Campbell's Ledge above Pittston; erected by the Moravian Historical Society in 1871 near Wyalusing, marks location of the Moravian mission, inscription, "To mark site of Friedenshutten (Machwilusing), a settlement of Moravian Indians between 1765–1772"; this mission was removed to Beaver County in 1772. Farther west, near the Presbyterian church, is a large boulder with bronze tablet, inscription, "Near this site from August 5–8, 1779, camped the army of Maj. Gen'l Sullivan, on their expedition against the Six Nations, erected by Machwilusing Chapter, D. A. R. 1914"; this road after leaving Wyalusing, leads over the hill a distance from the river, to which it returns again at Rummerfield, near where Mrs. Roswell Franklin was killed by Indians; her family was rescued.

Farther up the river is the county's oldest historic landmark on west bank of the Susquehanna, "Standing Stone," 25 feet high, 21 feet at base, tapers from 4 to 3 feet in thickness, rising out of the water; a landmark even in early Indian history; plainly visible from the road; General Sullivan's army of 3500 men camped on the plain opposite; three miles east of Towanda is Wysox village and creek, in front of an old brick church is where Major Henry van Campen, with two other captives, succeeded in releasing themselves, under guard by twice their number of Indians, killing all except one. Near is a large boulder of Barclay sandstone, with bronze tablet; inscription: "This stone commemorates the passing through Wesauking, Aug. 9 and Oct. 4, 1779, of Maj. Gen'l John Sullivan and his troops against the Six Nations. Erected, 1908, by the George Clymer Chapter, D. A. R., Towanda, Pennsylvania"; on the level plain between this creek and the river General Sullivan's army camped.

From Wysox the road diverges west from the old trail, continues over a modern steel bridge, built in 1915, replacing an old covered wooden one made in 1834, to Towanda. Eight miles northwest is Ulster; passing on the way: near mouth of Sugar Creek is site of an important palisaded Indian village called "Ogehage," later "Oscalui," still later, in 1779, "Newtychanning," marked; at junction of this great warpath along the Susquehanna, with one leading from this point to head waters of Towanda Creek near Canton; thence to head waters of Lycoming Creek, down that stream to West Branch of the Susquehanna near Williamsport. At Ulster (old Sheshequin) was a Moravian mission, removed at time of migration to Beaver in 1772; a steel bridge crosses the river here. Next is Milan village, near which was Indian Queen Esther's Town, destroyed by Colonel Hartley in 1778.

Proceeding on General Sullivan's road, one crosses the Chemung (Tioga) River on a modern steel bridge and enters Athens, formerly Tioga Point; here was Fort Sullivan, base of supplies for the army; destroyed by themselves in October, 1779, on their departure for Wyoming; marked by boulder with bronze tablet, inscription: "In Sullivan's expedition, the march that destroyed savagery and opened the Keystone and Empire States to civilization, four brigades, furnished by the States of Pennsylvania, New York, New Jersey, and New Hampshire, with Proctor's Artillery, and Farr's Riflemen took part; at Tioga Point, long the southern door of the Indian Confederacy, 5000 troops encamped; here stood Fort Sullivan, with four blockhouses, from August 11 to October 3, 1779; tablet erected by Tioga Chapter, Daughters of the American Revolution." Below the plate is embedded a ball from one of General Sullivan's guns; the road separates here, one following the Susquehanna to Owego, the other following the Chemung to Elmira (Newtown), New York; near the latter road is the "Battlefield of Newtown," where General Sullivan fought the Tories and Indians in 1779.

A soldiers' monument is on the campus in front of the old ATHENS Academy, designed by McKim, Mead & White, New York; ground foundation twenty-five feet square, inclosed in granite curbing with polished globes at each corner; pedestal, eleven feet high, rising from the center, polished granite, on unpolished granite coping, surmounted by a bronze group, "The Protection of the Flag," a barefoot drummer boy with a flag over his shoulder and a tall, fearless soldier, holding a musket which points to the ground, sculptor, George T. Brewster; inscription, in bronze letters, fitted to the face of the granite: "*Pro patria et gloria.* Erected to the memory of our soldiers who fought in defense of the flag"; presented by Joseph Whipple and Charlotte Snell Stickler. Spaulding Library and Museum, classic Renaissance with Ionic porch, open to the public, contains paintings, portraits, and relics. In 1688 a Spanish fort was near the present borough of Athens; population 4384.

TOWANDA, county seat, laid out in 1812; population 4269; courthouse native sandstone, classic Renaissance, built in 1897; in front is the soldiers' monument, at base are bronze tablets inscribed with names of battles of Bradford County men in war for the Union;

DEFENSE OF THE FLAG

McKim, Mead & White Pedestal
George T. Brewster, Sculptor

Pickett's charge at Gettysburg; and the battle scene at Antietam; dedicated in 1901. Towanda Free Library, French Renaissance, brick, built, 1897, was given and endowed by Francis R. Welles of Paris, France; architects, Barney & Chapman, New York; contains a special set of art books, "L'Art."

In Christ Protestant Episcopal Church, native sandstone, is memorial window to William Ulysses Mercur, Chief Justice of Pennsylvania, 1882–87; makers, Cox Sons & Buckley, London. The Methodist Episcopal Church, also, has memorial windows. Historical Society of Bradford County, fireproof building open to the public; contains Indian and Civil War relics, curios, and portraits of pioneer men and women, a reproduction of a pioneer log house, and specimens of all native woods in the county. In Riverside Cemetery is the grave of David Wilmot, who made the famous proviso, engraved on his monument, against slavery. There are many borough and township high schools in Bradford County.

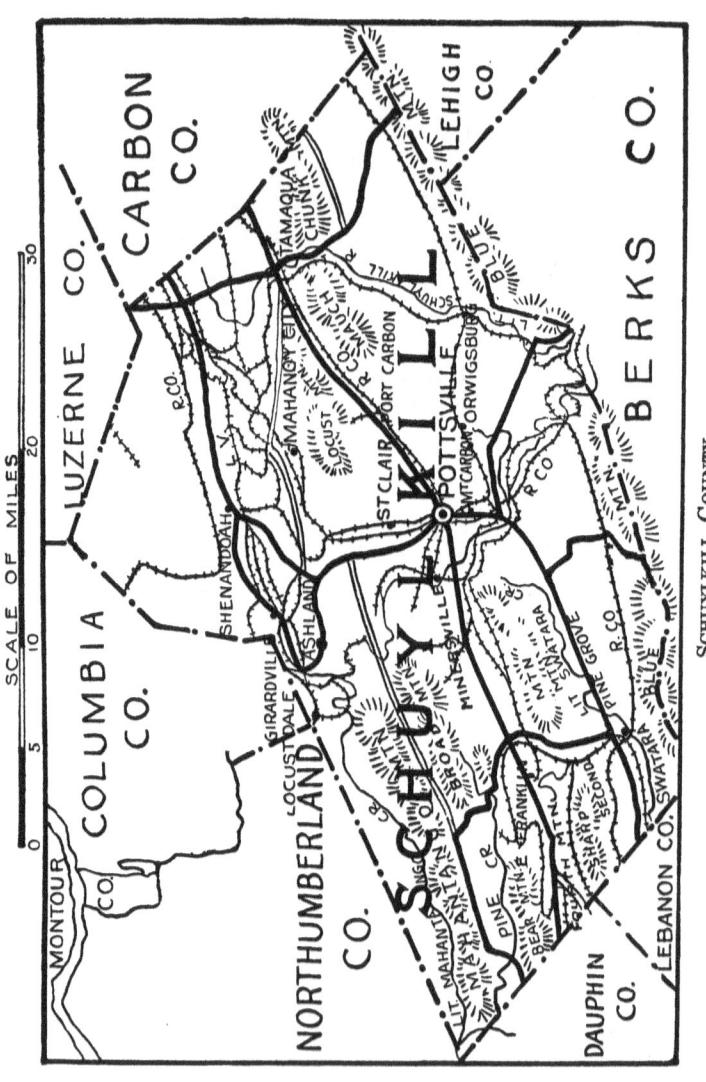

Schuylkill County

XLV
SCHUYLKILL COUNTY

FORMED March 1, 1811, named for the Schuylkill River; was purchased from the Six Nations in 1749. George Godfried Orwig, first settler, in 1747, lived at Sculp Hill; he was followed by other Germans. ORWIGSBURG, first county seat, in 1811, was founded in 1796, by Peter Orwig, son of George; old courthouse still standing, is used as a factory; extensive views from here of mountains and agricultural valleys. In chain of frontier forts, were Franklin, built, 1756, by order of Benjamin Franklin; Fort Henry, south of Pinegrove; and Fort Lebanon, later known as Fort William, the most important, its site near Auburn, is marked by boulder with bronze tablet, inscription, "On this site stood Fort Lebanon, built, 1775, by Colonel Jacob Morgan, for protection of early settlers against Indians, erected in 1913 by Mahantongo Chapter, Daughters of the American Revolution, Pottsville, Pa." Indian warriors came down from the mountains and made savage forays on the peaceful farms, in which many people were massacred, and mills and houses were burned; the old oak tree is standing near, from which sentinels took observations; in this fort the first religious services in the county were held.

One mile from Fort Lebanon is the old Red Church, built in 1755, destroyed by Indians, 1756, rebuilt, 1776, celebrated its sesquicentennial in 1905. This county revels in picturesque scenery; excellent roads curve through valleys of surpassing richness and fertility, or wander along a ridge with glorious views on either side; in the north, the sky line of a mountain range is often broken by a weird coal breaker; in every direction there is beauty and interest. Laurel may be seen by the acre, and much rhododendron. Great cliffs of various colored conglomerate rock are found throughout the county.

This is the southern limit of the ANTHRACITE COAL fields in east central Pennsylvania, the only ones of importance in the United States; divided into three well-known trade regions, Wyoming; Lehigh; and Schuylkill; comprising an area of 480 square miles, in the counties of Carbon, Columbia, Lackawanna, Northumberland, Luzerne, Susquehanna, and Schuylkill. Discovered in Schuylkill County by Nicho Allen in 1790; while camping out overnight, he built a fire among some rocks, under shelter of the trees; during the night, being awakened by unusual heat he saw the rocks a mass of glowing fire, he having ignited the outcrop of a bed of coal. The birth of this great productive industry may be dated from 1820, when 365 tons were sent to Philadelphia from the head waters of the Lehigh River. 80,000,000 tons per annum are now produced; location of coal was shown in William Scull's map of Pennsylvania published in 1770; three places marked.

In 1795 it was used successfully for smithing by a blacksmith named Whitestone, but not generally for this purpose until 1806. In 1812, Colonel George Shoemaker produced coal from a shaft on land he owned, now known as the Centreville Tract; loaded nine wagons and drove to Philadelphia, where he was

SCHUYLKILL COUNTY 421

accused of being an impostor, attempting to sell stone for coal; he sold two loads for cost of transportation, and gave the rest away to those who promised to try to use it; he induced Messrs. Mellon & Bishop to try it in their rolling mill in Delaware County, where it was found to be a complete success; iron was heated in much less time than usual, and the workmen said, "It passed through the rolls like lead."

From 1830, rapid improvements were made in methods of mining and transporting coal. First breaker in this county was erected by Gideon Bast on Wolf Creek, near Minersville. The St. Clair shaft was sunk in 1845, by Alfred Lawton, to Primrose vein, 122 feet; in 1851, E. W. McGinness continued the depth of shaft to the Mammoth vein, 438 feet. At Wadesville a shaft was sunk 619½ feet. A shaft located by General Henry Pleasants is deepest coal shaft in the United States, 1584 feet. The collieries of the Philadelphia & Reading Coal Company are the most extensive. Property in Schuylkill and Columbia counties 18,333 acres, one third coal, devised by Stephen Girard to the City of Philadelphia in trust, comprises some of the most valuable tracts in the anthracite region; Girard was largely instrumental in building the Schuylkill Canal to Philadelphia, connecting with this was a railroad and a series of gravity planes between Girardville and Mount Carbon, head of the canal; the Girard Railroad, opened in 1834, was one of the greatest engineering feats of the time, attracting international comment; much of the masonry is still to be seen.

In 1690, William Penn called attention to the feasibility of passage by water between the Susquehanna

River and Tulpehocken Creek, a branch of the Schuylkill; in 1762 David Rittenhouse and Dr. William Smith surveyed a route for a canal, to connect waters of the Susquehanna and Schuylkill, via Swatara and Tulpehocken Creeks; and actually traced a line between the Delaware and Ohio Rivers at Fort Pitt, thence to Erie. The Union Canal connecting the Schuylkill and Susquehanna Rivers was completed in 1826 by the Schuylkill Navigation Company; they did great work in their day; years of greatest prosperity were from 1835–41.

In 1800, Reese & Thomas located an iron furnace on the site of Pottsville. In 1807 Greenwood furnace and forge were erected by John Pott. In 1839, Pioneer furnace at Pottsville, under Burd Patterson, was blown in with anthracite coal, by Benjamin Perry, and ran for about three months, among the first to use successfully anthracite coal in the blast furnace in United States. POTTSVILLE, county seat, 1395 feet above sea; population 21,876, laid out in 1816, has not one level street; flights of steps are frequently used to get to various heights; fine views from every point. A commission for city planning has lately been appointed.

Courthouse erected in 1892, architect, Mr. Taylor, stands on a hill in a terraced square, has portraits of judges; in the old courthouse, to the rear, now torn down, the Mollie Maguires were tried and convicted in 1876. Soldiers' Monument erected in 1891 is in Garfield Square, on a pedestal are names of battles fought by Schuylkill County men in Civil War; the Washington Artillery and National Light Infantry of Pottsville, 246 men, were part of the 530 Pennsyl-

HENRY CLAY IRON MONUMENT, POTTSVILLE

vanians who first arrived at our national Capital for its defense in 1861; Schuylkill County sent 13,000 volunteers; there are also soldiers' monuments at Port Carbon, St. Clair, and Mahanoy City. A statue of John Pott is in the playground of Center Street public school, formerly a cemetery.

Pennsylvania, the coal-producing state of the Union, has every reason to be grateful to Henry Clay for advocating a protective tariff on her principal product; Pottsville's enthusiasm culminated in the Henry Clay Monument, completed in 1855, soon after his death, west of South Center Street, an iron Doric column, surmounted by an iron statue of Henry Clay, after the painting by P. F. Rothermel, "Senate of 1850"; first colossal iron casting of its kind made in the United States; from sidewalk to top of statue, 205 feet. Pottsville Cemetery contains grave of Joseph Elison, member of Greely Arctic expedition, who died at Port Haven, Greenland, in 1884, soon after being rescued by the late Rear Admiral Schley; a diary, kept until his hands were frozen stiff, will soon be published by the Pottsville Historical Society. Parks in Schuylkill County are, "Lakeside," above Mahony City; "Marlin," near Pottsville; "Manilla," east of Tamaqua; "Woodland," between Ashland and Girardville;"Washington," between Ashland and Locust Dale; they are combinations of formal gardening with natural beauty; "Tumbling Run Dam," near Pottsville, is beautiful in its setting. SHENANDOAH, population 24,726, contains a mixed mining population; twenty-six languages and dialects are spoken here.

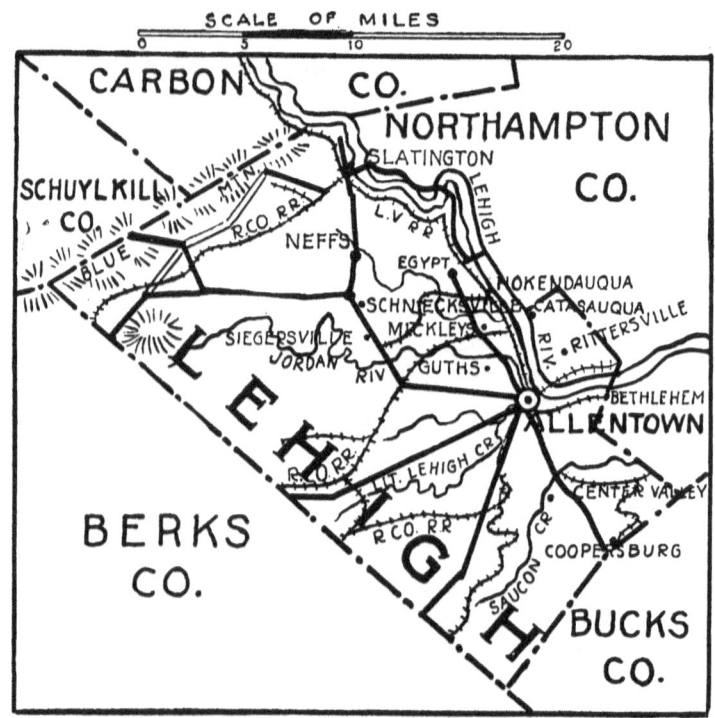

Lehigh County

XLVI
LEHIGH COUNTY

FORMED March 6, 1812; named for Lehigh River, from an Indian name, Lechauwekink (where there are forks); Indian trails forked in various directions below Bethlehem. The Blue Mountains are north and the Lehigh Hills south, containing large deposits of slate and cement. Chief industries, agriculture and manufacturing.

ALLENTOWN, county seat, at junction of Jordan and Little Lehigh Creeks; population 73,502; was settled in 1751 by Chief Justice William Allen, a friend of the Penns; is entered from the south by, it is said, the largest concrete bridge in the world, erected by a trolley company, 2650 feet long and 120 feet high; built in 1913. The city has an abundant supply of pure water, pumped direct from the spring to the residences; daily flow, 12,000,000 gallons. Courthouse, colonial, with cupola, Fifth and Hamilton Streets. First Presbyterian Church, North Fifth Street, near Hamilton, Renaissance. Jail, North Fourth Street, near Linden, feudal architecture, with tower 100 feet high, brown sandstone. Architect G. A. Aschbach.

Allen Park, Fourth and Walnut Streets, contains "Trout Hall," stone, built, 1770, by James Allen, son of the founder, which will be occupied by the Lehigh County Historical Society; West Park and River Park are also in Allentown; west of the city is Dorney's Park, along Cedar Creek. In Center Square is the

Soldiers' Monument to the men of Lehigh County in the Civil War; on the pedestal are bronze bas-reliefs depicting scenes of war and reconciliation, and medallion busts of Generals Meade, McClellan, Hancock, and Hartranft. United States post office, at the corner of Sixth and Turner Streets, classic, built in 1906; brick and Indiana limestone; architect, George B. Page, Philadelphia. Several fine churches of brick or stone show Italian and Gothic architecture. The Zion Reformed, Gothic, stone, built, 1840, Hamilton Street between Sixth and Seventh, is notable for having sheltered the Liberty Bell and the Christ Church bells, during British occupation of Philadelphia, in 1777; marked by tablet, placed by the Liberty Bell Chapter, Daughters of the American Revolution. The Rhoads House, 107–109 North Seventh Street, built, 1762, by a Revolutionary patriot, is the oldest building in the city.

MUHLENBERG COLLEGE with preparatory school, is beautifully located at Twenty-sixth and Chew Streets, on campus of seventy-two acres; the buildings, brick and stone, were built from 1903 to 1915; administration building, English Renaissance, architects, Ruhl & Lange; contains portraits, including one of Dr. Muhlenberg, by Gilbert Stuart; the late Peter A. Gross, in 1914, provided by will for the founding of an art school in Muhlenberg College, and an art museum in Allentown. Allentown College for Women, Walnut Street between Thirtieth and Thirty-first Streets, classic; and the new high school, North Seventeenth Street, classic Ionic, are fine buildings. At Seventeenth and Chew Streets are the State Hospi-

ZION REFORMED CHURCH, ALLENTOWN
Guardian of the Liberty Bell and Christ Church Bells during the Revolution

LEHIGH COUNTY 427

tal, Georgian; brick and Indiana limestone; and the Nurses' Home, memorial to Judge Edward Harvey; said to be the best equipped for the purpose in the United States, architects, Ruhl & Lange.

Road from Rittersville to Bethlehem passes Central Park, overlooking Lehigh River, and the historic Geissinger farm, where Solomon Jennings settled in 1736; he was a participant in the Indian Walk of 1737. BETHLEHEM (see Northampton County). State road from Allentown to Slatington passes through WERNERSVILLE, near where Lynford Lardner built, in 1740, a hunting lodge, "Grouse Hall," and where the Jordan Reformed Church was founded in 1752, present stone building erected, 1808. Through GUTHSVILLE, Guth homestead still standing, built, 1745, through SIEGERSVILLE, on left is Colonel H. C. Trexler's game preserve of 2000 acres, containing buffalo, elk, deer, and trout hatchery. To SCHNECKSVILLE, former home of Professor Rudy, founder of the Rudy School, Paris, in 1865, an International Association of Professors; he was a Fellow of the French Academy. Here is Land Spring Park.

The next village, NEFFS, has an ancient graveyard, burial place of many Revolutionary patriots. Then to SLATINGTON, heart of the slate region. A chain bridge built over the Lehigh River in 1826 leads to LEHIGH GAP. Another state road from Allentown goes through CATASAUQUA; here, in 1914, was celebrated the seventy-fifth anniversary of the successful uniting of the state's two chief resources, the use of ANTHRACITE COAL in the IRON FURNACES, by David Thomas from Wales. Coke has since replaced anthracite, but the furnaces and the general method are much as Thomas left them; these were the mother furnaces of the Bethlehem Steel Works, Cambria Iron Works, Thomas Iron Works at Hockendauqua, and the stupendous development of the iron trade in this country. A private art collection owned by D. G. Dery, Esq., comprises an important collection of paintings, statuary, bronzes, ivories, Chinese porcelains, and jades. Continue on state road through Mickley's to EGYPT. Union Church, Lutheran and Reformed, founded, 1734, in log church; present brick building erected, 1785. Near by is Deshler's Fort, built, 1760, and the Troxell-Steckel House, stone, built, 1756. A mile north is tablet, placed by Lehigh County Historical Society, marking place where occurred the last Indian massacre in this county, of three families in 1763.

XLVII
LEBANON COUNTY

FORMED February 16, 1813; Scriptural name, from the cedar trees covering the range of mountains on northern boundary, "Cedars of Lebanon"; settled by Germans in the east, by the Scotch-Irish in the west. Leading industries, agriculture, iron, tobacco. Three solid hills of rich, magnetic iron ore have been worked for over 170 years, and still seem inexhaustible; they require no mining, simply to be quarried; down to the present these mines have produced more iron ore than any other single iron ore property in the United States. In 1737, Peter Grubb became sole owner of these ore hills; he built Hopewell forge on Hammer Creek, and the large blast furnace was named for Cornwall, his ancestral home in England. The property was inherited by his two sons, who were colonels in the Revolutionary War; cannon balls and stoves were cast here for the Continental Army. In 1798, Robert Coleman purchased five-sixths of these ore banks; they were near the old road between Harris Ferry and Philadelphia, known as the Berks and Dauphin Road. Later his grandsons, Robert and G. Dawson Coleman, built furnaces on the Union Canal, then the great means of transportation; by that time charcoal furnaces were going out.

The construction and operation of the Union Canal through this county, connecting the Schuylkill River at Reading with the Susquehanna at Middletown, was a

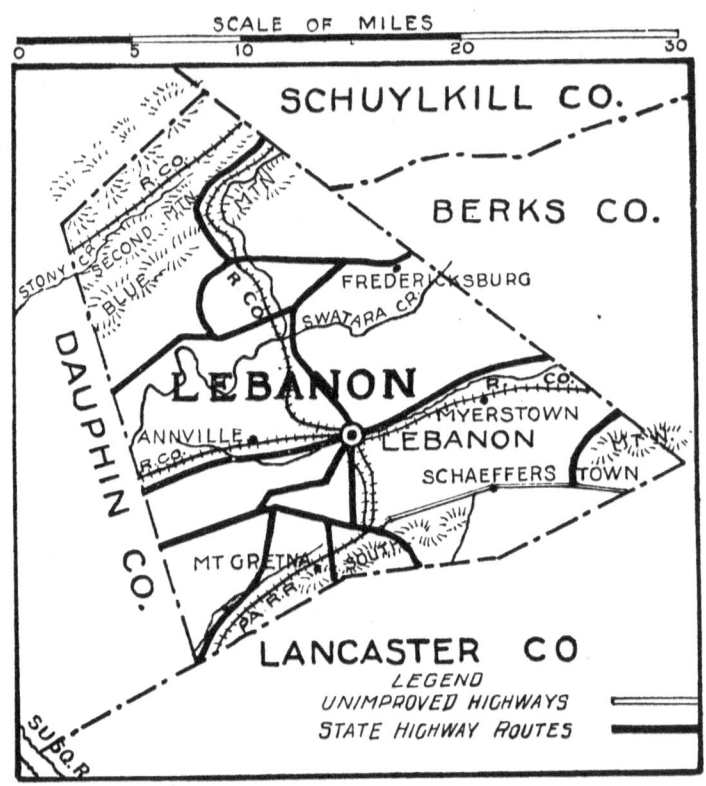

Lebanon County

THE OLDEST CANAL TUNNEL IN THE UNITED STATES
North Lebanon

LEBANON COUNTY

momentous event, with its tunnel 767 feet long, first in the United States. Extract: "Lebanon, June 15, 1827. Last Monday evening, June 11th, the citizens of this town and vicinity had the privilege of seeing the first boat, the *Alpha* from Tulpehocken, come up the Union Canal and remain at North Lebanon for the night; the next morning it continued its journey westward and passed through the tunnel; this was the first boat to pass through a tract of ground upon which corn and potatoes were being grown."

County seat, LEBANON, population 24,643, on the William Penn Highway; settled in 1750. Streets run north and south, east and west. Courthouse, at the corner of Eighth and Cumberland Streets, colonial, brick. United States post office, classic, with Doric columns. A historic inn, the St. Eitz, built in 1752, was occupied by George Washington. Hill Church, colonial, brick; in the yard is a monument to Rev. John Casper Stoever, first Lutheran minister in Lebanon County, in 1733. St. Luke's Protestant Episcopal Church, Gothic, stone, built without a nail, has three memorial windows, "The Nativity," by Lamb; others made in England; also fine collection of altar cloths, chasubles, and credence cloth made abroad, in filet, of fifteenth century design. Soldiers and sailors' monument in Monument Park; tall, fluted column with Ionic capital. Lebanon Historical Society has collections of local interest. ANNVILLE is seat of Lebanon Valley College, founded by the United Brethren in 1865; a school of high grade under supervision of that church.

MT. GRETNA, a camp ground of 1000 or more acres, 1000 feet above sea level, was purchased by the state for mobilization of the state's National Guard. It will accommodate 20,000 men, and has been used for this purpose since 1885. The War Department considers Mt. Gretna an ideal military camp, sanitary and well drained. SCHAEFFERSTOWN, one of the earliest and most historic places in this county, laid out in 1744, had the first waterworks system in the United States, in 1753. Franklin House built in 1750; in the cellar there is a remarkable series of carved arches; it served as a place of refuge from Indians. Fountain Hill Park is here. MYERSTOWN is the seat of Albright College. FREDERICKSBURG has the Lick Monument, erected, in 1881, by James Lick, in memory of his grandfather's services at Valley Forge, and of John Lick, founder of Lick Observatory on Mount Hamilton, California.

XLVIII
UNION COUNTY

FORMED March 22, 1813, named for the Union; chiefly agricultural, is divided by spurs of the Alleghenies, known as White Deer, Nittany, Buffalo, Paddy's, and Jack's mountains, into three valleys; the center, Buffalo Valley, is one of the garden spots in Pennsylvania, formerly home of many Amish and Dunkards, good farmers and citizens.

LEWISBURG, county seat, laid out in 1785; population 3204; named for Ludwig (Lewis) Doerr, who purchased the land from Richard Peters of Philadelphia. A rare specimen of conveyancing is deed, lot 51, in plan of Lewisburg, tracing title from the Creator, down through Adam and Eve, to one Flavel Roan, recorded at Sunbury, in deed book F, 1793. Finely located at mouth of Buffalo Creek, West Branch of the Susquehanna, on the great Indian path from Sunbury to Muncy, now main highway from Harrisburg to Williamsport, and on line of turnpikes leading from Erie through Waterford, Meadville, and Franklin to Susquehanna River. Seat of Bucknell University, incorporated in 1846, co-ed, with courses in arts, science, philosophy, and engineering; the Library and Museum have the Jeremiah Gernerd collection of Indian relics, open to the public; from the top of the astronomical observatory is a fine view. In Lewisburg Cemetery is the grave of Colonel John Kelly, distinguished in Indian warfare and the Revolution; he died in 1832; his

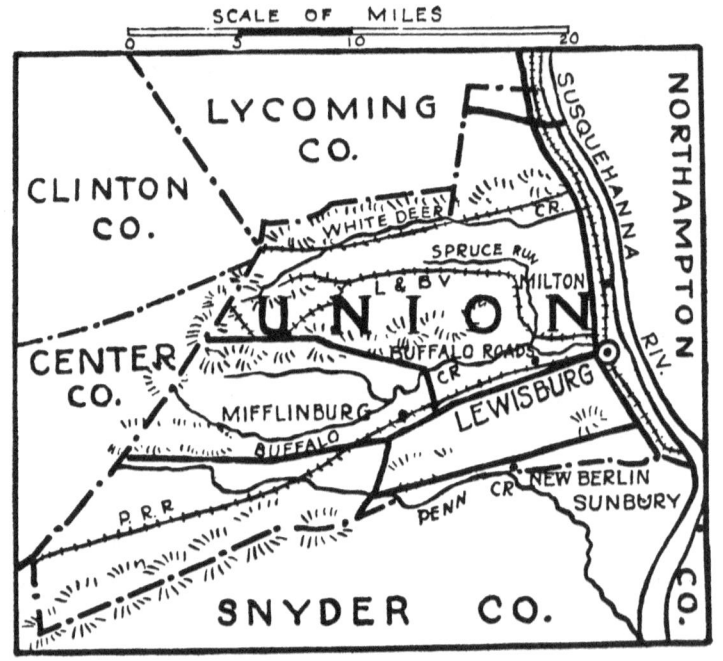

Union County

UNION COUNTY 435

monument, with military emblems, was erected in 1835, sculptor, W. Hubbard; also the grave of Mary, widow of Captain John Brady, the great Indian fighter, who was massacred by Indians and buried near where he fell, in Lycoming County.

One mile west of Lewisburg, from the top of Smoketown Hill, is a fine view of Buffalo Valley across the Susquehanna to Muncy Hills and North Mountain. Historic places, site of Shikellimy's old town, a wooded crest opposite Milton, four miles north of Lewisburg; he was chief of the Oneidas, and father of Logan the Mingo chief, place now called Oak Heights. DRIESBACH, five miles west of Lewisburg, German Reformed and Lutheran Church, first log building built, 1788, on site of present brick church; in burial ground is the grave and monument to Samuel Maclay, born, 1741, brother of William Maclay; inscription, "Samuel Maclay, United States Senator 1803–09, Surveyor, Farmer, Soldier, Legislator, Statesman. Erected by State of Pennsylvania, 1908." Buffalo X Roads, Presbyterian Church, first built, 1775, present brick building about 1846.

MIFFLINBURG, the neatest town you ever saw, with uniform curbing and walks, population 1744, in heart of Buffalo Valley (named for Governor Mifflin); ten miles west of Lewisburg, laid out 1792, by Elias Youngman. NEW BERLIN, laid out, 1792, by George Long, delightfully situated on north bank of Penn's Creek; first county seat; at one time home of Union Seminary, Central Pennsylvania College.

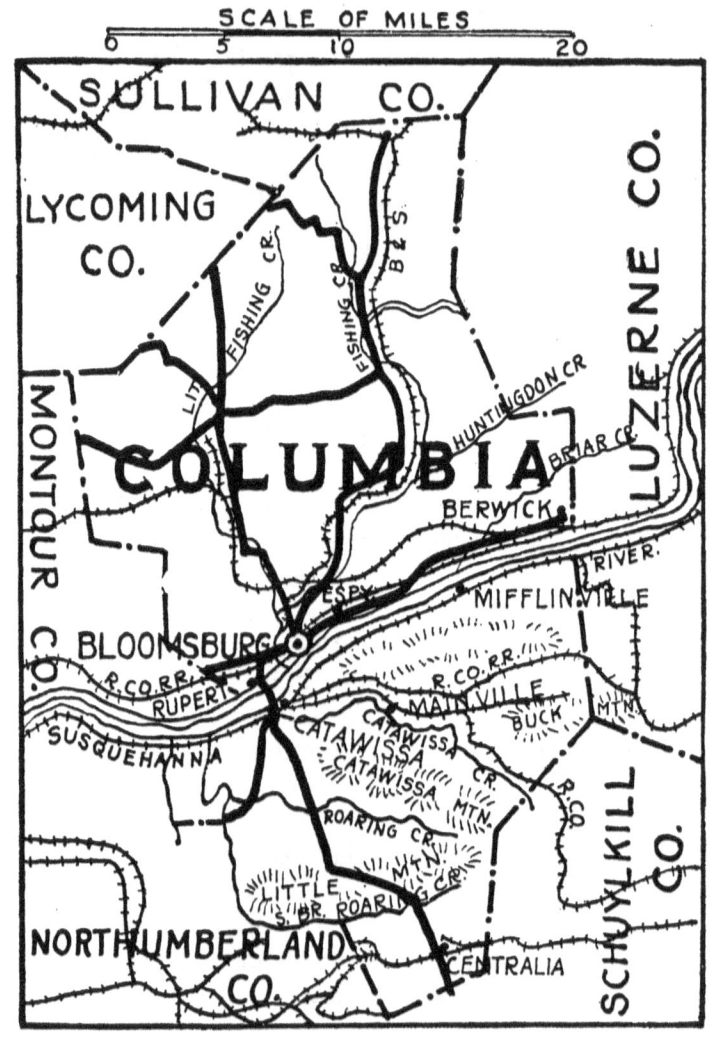

COLUMBIA COUNTY

XLIX
COLUMBIA COUNTY

FORMED March 22, 1813, name explains itself; is in Appalachian Mountain belt; surface quite broken, with wonderfully beautiful drives. The Catawissa Railroad, noted for its remarkable trestle bridges, first one at Mainville, runs through this county, crossing the Susquehanna River at Rupert. Arable land, mostly red shale and limestone, with deposits of iron ore at Bloomsburg, and the anthracite coal basin at Centralia. Chief industries, manufacturing; the carpet mill here is said to be the second largest in the United States. Earliest historical bands of Indians, in this county, were the Shawnees and Delawares, vassals to the Six Nations; Wyoming Path, their route of travel for hunting or war, left Muncy on the West Branch, ran up Glade Run, through a gap to Fishing Creek and on to Luzerne County, through Nescopec Gap, and up North Branch to Wyoming.

BLOOMSBURG, population 7819, laid out in 1802 by Ludwig Eyre, on a bluff on Fishing Creek, became county seat in 1846. In 1772, the Shawnee Indians had a village between the mouth of the creek and the town. James McClure located his farm near the same point in 1781; a fort was erected there, built by Major Moses VanCampen, now marked, from which he led scouting parties. In 1779, VanCampen, as quartermaster, accompanied General Sullivan's expedition against Indian towns on the Genessee. There is much discussion here about city planning. The town lies due north and south, named streets; east and west numbered; Second Street being the main street, and also forms part of state highway leading from Harrisburg to Wilkes-Barre. Courthouse on Main Street, Renaissance; contains, it is said, "a very beautiful piece of tapestry." Jail, stone, feudal architecture. Soldiers and Sailors' Monument at the intersection of Main and Market Streets, erected in 1908.

The Methodist Church, Gothic, stone, has a Tiffany window, "Christ Blessing Little Children"; other churches that may be mentioned for architecture are St. Paul's Protestant Episcopal and First Presbyterian, both Gothic; St. Matthew's, Evangelical Lutheran, Trinty Reformed, and St. Columba's Roman Catholic, colonial. In 1869, this was made the educational center of northeast Pennsylvania, with the State Normal School, corner-stone laid by Governor Geary in 1868. Normal auditorium, colonial; and other extensive buildings. CATAWISSA, originally a Quaker settlement; scenery fine and picturesque; was laid out in 1787 by William Hughes from Berks County; has an old Friends' meeting house. John Hanch was one of the first to build an iron furnace here on the Catawissa in 1816; earlier the Piscatawese or Gangawese (Kenhawas) had wigwams here. Fort Jenkins, near mouth of Briar Creek, on the Susquehanna, was attacked and burned by Indians, 1779–80; a house is now on the site of the fort. BERWICK was settled by Evan Owen in 1783. Here in 1826 the steamboat *Susquehanna* blew up while ascending the Nescopec Falls. Also ground was broken here for the North Branch Canal.

L
PIKE COUNTY

FORMED March 26, 1814, named for General Zebulon Pike, killed in Canada, 1813. When the chronicler takes up his pen to write of the glories of Pike County in works of art, architecture, and monuments to the departed "Great," in peace or war, he is somewhat appalled at the dearth of them; the landmarks are what God made, softened and beautified by time.

MILFORD, county seat, population 768, was laid out by John Biddis, 1793, in squares, after pattern of Philadelphia; it rests high above the Delaware River, overlooking a valley of myriad hues that have made the town notable for its quaint, umbrageous beauty and repose. Pioneer settlers were substantial people whose descendants still reside here. It is a popular resort for trout fishing in the spring, vacationists in the summer, and for deer and bird hunting in the fall. Courthouse, brick, French design, built in 1873, in center of town, facing the public square; two mortars from the Civil War are in the front lawn; opposite is the jail, built in 1815 as courthouse and jail, made of native boulders carefully selected for shades and tints; some are opalescent and show brilliantly in certain lights; a wooden trout, five foot long, pointing the way of the wind, is as old as the building.

Forestry building, probably handsomest village structure of its kind in the United States, erected in 1900 by the late James Wallace Pinchot, Normandy

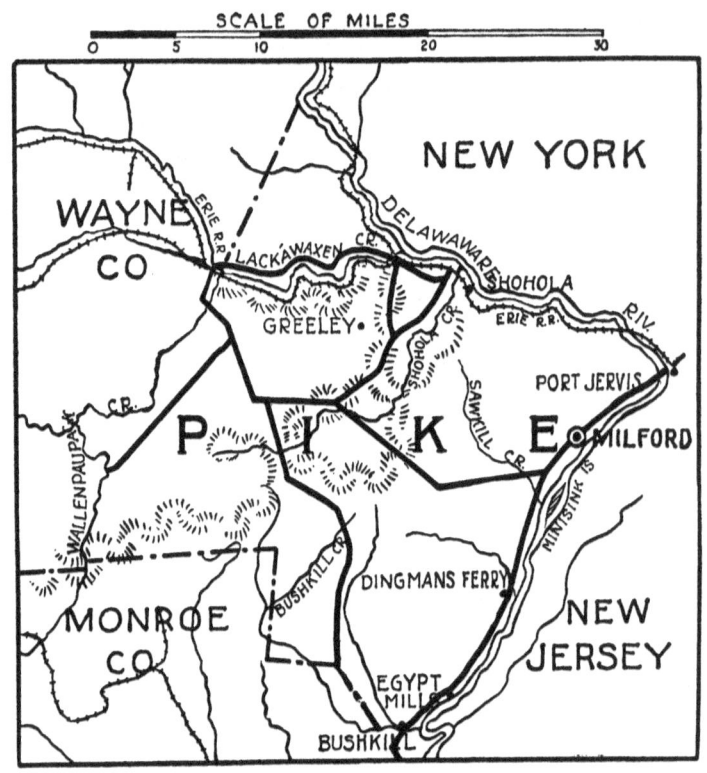

Pike County

PIKE COUNTY 441

design; native stone; architects, Hunt & Hunt; in niches are busts of Washington and Franklin; mortised in alternately are bas-reliefs of F. A. Michaux, 1746–1802, author of "Flora Boreali Americana"; General Lafayette in 1777; and Bernard Palissy, 1506–89, potter, and writer on botany and forestry; sculptor, J. F. Weir. The Homestead Library, formerly home of Cyrille Pinchot, pure colonial, is in center of town; to the rear is Normandie Cottage, an architectural gem, replica of a peasant's home cottage.

Gray Towers, the Pinchot estate, native stone, reproduction of a baronial castle in the Scottish Highlands, crowns the hill about 1000 feet above Milford; the old Scotch garden, with high stone wall, is of rare beauty; Yale School of Forestry is on the Pinchot estate, within echo of the Sawkill Falls. Monument to Tom Quick, the avenger of the Delaware, is on his birthplace; he killed ninety-nine Indians to avenge the death of his father, who was the first settler in Milford, in 1733. The principal denominations are represented in the churches. Old inns are, the Crissman House, built, 1810; the Sawkill House, 1823, southern colonial; the Dimmick House, 1828, Horace Greeley stopped here in 1840 and later; one of his fondest hopes was the coöperative, community of interest settlement, known as the "Sylvania Society," which he, with others, organized in 1842 at Greeley; founded on the "Sacredness of toil," but the young men, sons of affluent parents, who had been sent there by New Yorkers who bought stock, did not know how to work, nor did they wish to learn, and so they deserted.

The Bluff House on the banks of the Delaware, built, 1876, commands a fine view; lawn of Milford Inn is planted with rare shrubs and trees from all parts of the world; the Hermitage has three unique bronze sundials, sculptor, Louis F. Ragot; the one depicting Father Time with upraised reaper, is beautiful. The Hermit's Glen, so a legend goes, is where an old French hermit of profound knowledge and benevolence found the water of life after a world-wide search; these waters now flow into the lake through two bronze masques; two cement giants hold up the dam that feeds the lake. Wells Glen lies along the Sawkill Brook; rhododendrons, wood flowers, and giant hemlocks make it beautiful. Childs Park, back of DINGMAN'S FERRY, given in perpetuity for use of the public by Mrs. G. W. Childs, is a rugged mountain stretch, woodland and meadow; cataracts and deep pools are in the trout stream that comes through it.

BUSHKILL, another haunt for nature lovers, and SHOHOLA, all remarkable for beautiful falls, glens, caves. In writing of the Delaware Valley, Edmund Clarence Stedman says: "But here there is no swooning of the languid air, and no seeming always afternoon; it is a morning land with every cliff facing the rising sun; the mist and languor are in the grain fields far below; the hills themselves are of the richest, darkest green; the skies are blue and fiery; the air crisp, oxygenated, American; it is no place for lotus eating, but for drinking water of the fountain of youth, till one feels the zest and thrill of a new life that is not unrestful, yet as far as may be from the lethargy of mere repose." Among the artists who have painted here are, William M. Chase, J. Alden Weir, Swayne Gifford, Carroll Beckwith, Henry Satterlee, Charles C. Curran, W. A. Rogers, and Benjamin Constant, France.

SAWKILL FALLS, MILFORD

LI
PERRY COUNTY

FORMED March 12, 1820; named for Commodore Oliver Hazard Perry; lying between the Tuscarora and the Blue Mountains, it abounds in beautiful scenery, low hills, rich valleys, and abundant streams. Chief industry, agriculture.

NEW BLOOMFIELD, county seat, settled in 1820; streets run due east and west, north and south. Courthouse faces the center square; colonial with cupola, brick; built in 1868; fireproof annex, built, 1892. Soldiers' Monument in the square, memorial to soldiers and sailors of Perry County. Among the good church buildings may be noted the Methodist; architect, M. A. Kast, Harrisburg. SHERMANSDALE was in 1720 an Indian village. At MARYSVILLE a long stone arch bridge on the Pennsylvania Railroad line crosses over the Susquehanna River from Rockville, Dauphin County. The Marysville Civic Club has done much for the improvement of the town, and has beautified the town square and schoolyard.

Beyond DUNCANNON, where an immense traffic in coal and iron is carried on, one goes through the valley of the beautiful Juniata; the scenery along this river, as one crosses ridge after ridge of the Alleghenies is most picturesque, and the region traversed is full of historical reminiscences of the struggles of the early Scotch-Irish colonists with the Indians, and of the enterprise of David Brainard and other missionaries. At MILLERSTOWN one threads the Tuscarora Gap, where the railway, river, road, and canal squeeze their way through a narrow defile; this lay in the land of the Tuscarora Indians.

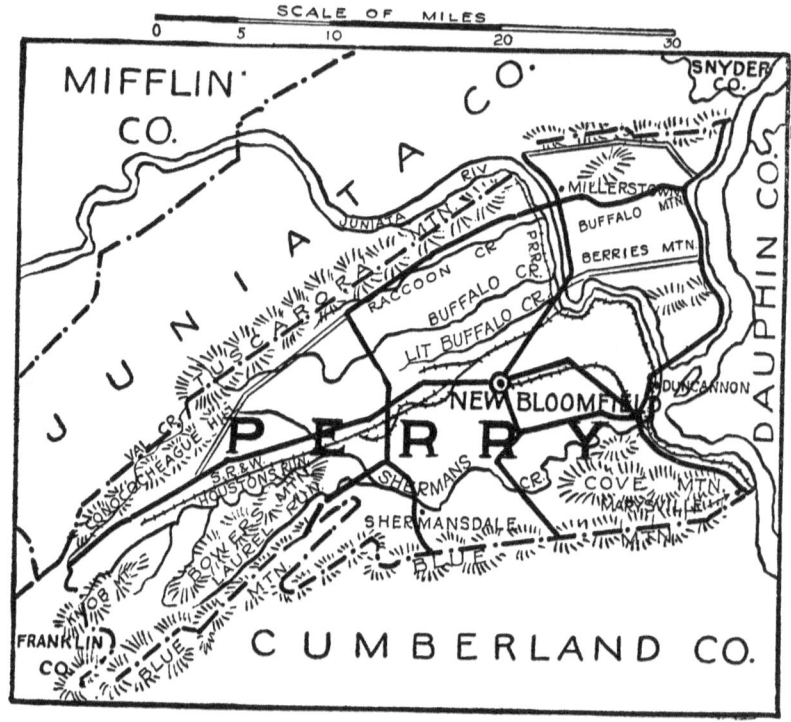

Perry County

JUNIATA COUNTY
LII

FORMED March 2, 1831; name, from the Juniata River, was given by the original people who lived in this region, and who were obliterated by the Iroquois; root of word means "a stone." "Standing Stone" may be regarded as translation of "Onojutta-Haga" or the Juniata people. A mountainous country with many fertile valleys, situated between the Tuscarora and Blue Ridge Mountains, famous for its scenery, with the blue Juniata making a wide sweep. The old Pennsylvania canal followed its banks throughout its whole course. First settlers were mostly Scotch-Irish.

The old homestead of Francis Innis, one and a half stories, stone, east of McCoysville, is still in possession of descendants, now used as a spring house; his two children, captured by the Indians, were recovered among those delivered to Colonel Bouquet in 1764. Another old landmark, eight miles away, is the D. B. Esh house, on east Waterford Road, built by Mr. Graham in 1802; has an open stairway carved by hand. First road laid out in 1768, was from Sherman's Valley to Kishecoquelas Valley. The historic road between Harrisburg and Pittsburgh, through the famous Jack's Narrows, over which stage coaches traveled, is now part of the William Penn Highway. Sites of Forts Bingham and Patterson will soon be marked by the General Thomas Mifflin Chapter,

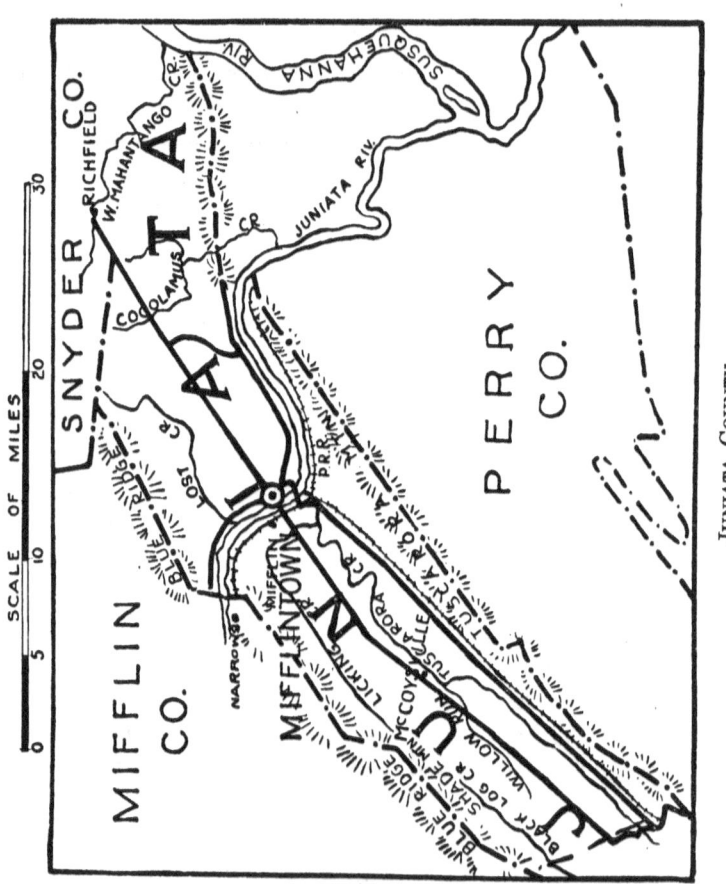

JUNIATA COUNTY

Daughters of the American Revolution. Chief industries, agriculture and manufactories.

MIFFLINTOWN, county seat, population 1083, joined with its twin borough, MIFFLIN, on Pennsylvania Railroad main line, by bridge over the Juniata, was laid out in 1791 by John Harris, and named in honor of the governor of the state, General Mifflin. Courthouse in center of town on Main Street, built, 1874, brick, Georgian, with Ionic porch and cupola; in the yard is a monument, surmounted by a spread eagle, to Civil War soldiers from Juniata County, erected in 1870. The churches are of good architecture, and the graded high school is said to be the best between Harrisburg and Huntingdon.

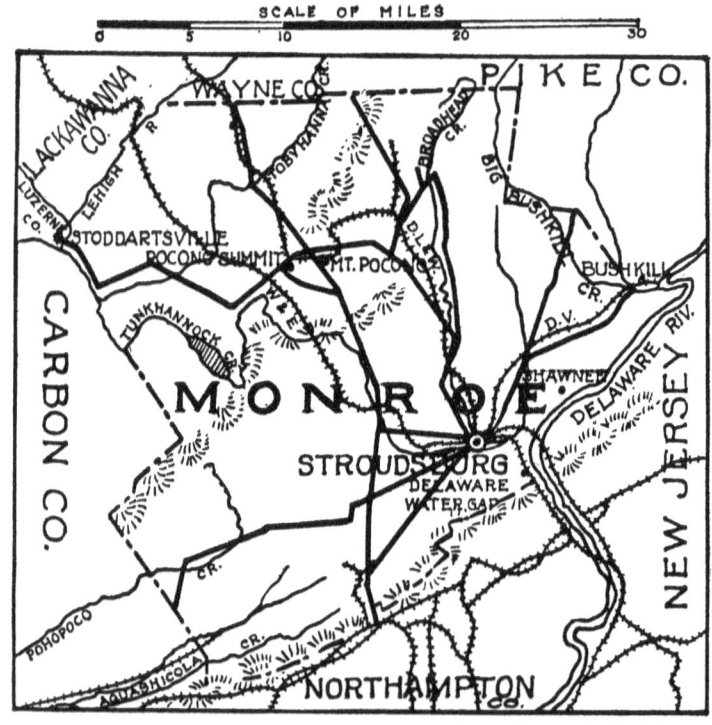

MONROE COUNTY

LIII
MONROE COUNTY

FORMED April 1, 1836; named in honor of President James Monroe. The Pocono Mountains and long, fertile valleys cover the surface. Chief industries, farming, lumber, and manufacturing. In the southeast, where the Delaware River turns suddenly at Mount Kittatinny, towering 1600 feet above it, is the Delaware Water Gap, with views of great distance from the highest point; near are the Wind Gap and Smith's Gap; William Penn's famous Walking Land Purchase ended near here. The Milford Road, laid out about 1800, from Easton, leaves Delaware River at Water Gap village, thence four miles to Stroudsburg, then to Bushkill and beyond.

STROUDSBURG, county seat; population 5278; first settled by Jacob Stroud, laid out at right angles, with a liberal plan of broad avenues, and houses set back thirty feet from the sidewalk, resembles a New England village. Courthouse, built, 1890, of rough stone, with high chimneys and belfry, contains portraits of judges; with jail and county house forms group facing the public square. Churches are of all principal denominations. The National Bank and other buildings are chiefly by Lacy & Son, architects. A fine stone and iron bridge, built by the state, over Broadhead Creek, connects the two boroughs of Stroudsburg and East Stroudsburg; it replaced a wooden one, over one hundred years old, carried away by the freshet in 1862. In 1755, Indians crossed over the old bridge, burned Dansbury Mission and other buildings, leaving Stroudsburg without a house or resident. Ephraim Collver, who had a grist mill there, escaped with his family to the Moravians at Bethlehem.

About 1756, a line of forts were erected to protect the frontier settlements; sites are unmarked; Fort Norris at Greensweigo, Eldred Township, on road toward the Minisinks, eighty feet square, was completely stockaded. Fort Hyndshaw, at the mouth of Bushkill Creek, was built for the Revolutionary War. Fort Hamilton was built in 1757, some one hundred feet beyond the Lutheran Church in western part of the town. Fort Penn, center of town, was residence of Jacob Stroud, who died in 1806; here in 1778, he cared for thirty or more persons, fugitives from the Wyoming massacre, who crossed the Pocono plateau with great toil and distress, later proceeding to their former homes in Connecticut. At Locust Ridge in Wyoming Valley, a battle was fought called the Pennamite War, between Connecticut claimants and Pennsylvanians. General Sullivan and his troops, in 1779, laid out a road through this county, from Wind Gap to Stoddartsville, Wilkes-Barre, and on, continuing an expedition from Easton to Genessee Valley, against the Indians; it may still be traced almost the entire way. General Daniel Brodhead and most of his male relatives from Monroe County, were in the Revolutionary War.

Monroe County was a portion of the lands of the Minisinks; there were several Indian villages; the Delaware chief, Tedyuscung, born on the Pocono Mountains, resided here. It is said that the first white

MONROE COUNTY 451

settlement in Pennsylvania was at Shawnee, by the Low Dutch or Hollanders, in "Meenesink," many years before William Penn's charter. When Nicholas Scull surveyed the land for the province, Samuel Depui was here; he purchased land in 1727 from the Minsi Indians, now site of Shawnee, an attractive village, five miles east of Stroudsburg; and the same property later from William Allen, 1733, for whom the oldest survey in the county was made.

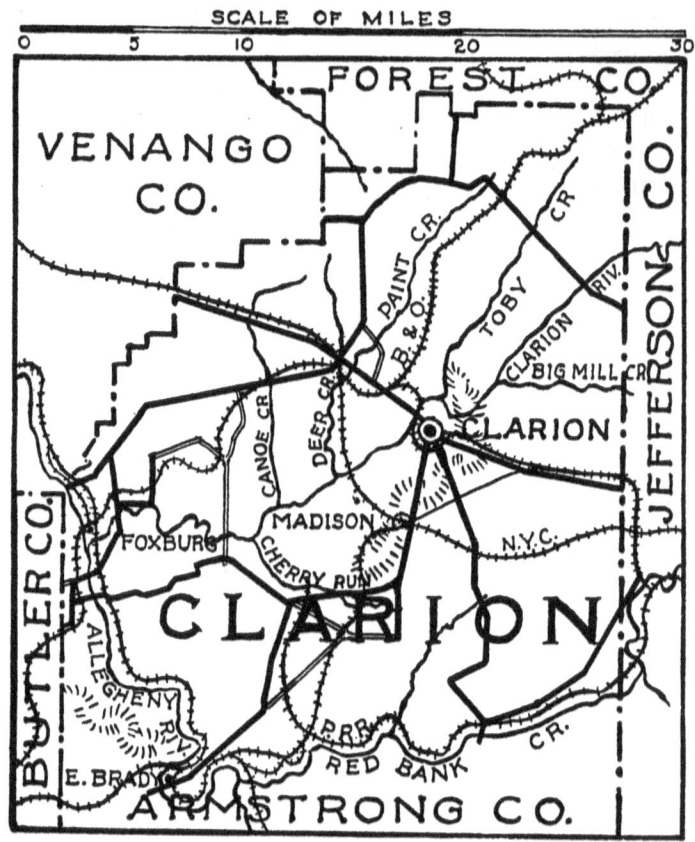

Clarion County

LIV
CLARION COUNTY

FORMED March 11, 1839; named from Clarion River. The scenery is beautiful and diversified; at the highest point, over 1600 feet above sea level, a flagstaff has been erected; from here, on a clear day, may be seen the bridge at East Brady and four villages in the far distance. Hills and valleys are dotted here and there with oil and gas wells. There are beautiful views along the Clarion and Allegheny rivers and Redbank Creek; the scenery at East Brady is notable on account of the precipitous hills and winding streams. First white settler was Captain Samuel Brady of Revolutionary fame; his parents having been killed by Indians, he swore vengeance against them. He conducted an expedition in 1779 under General Brodhead, who had started with a large force from Fort Pitt. The Indians had become troublesome along the Allegheny River; Brady, in advance with scouts, discovered them on a flat rock at a place which is now East Brady; he took possession of a narrow pass, and when the Indians arrived, he opened fire, with the main army in the rear; escape was impossible, and nearly all were killed or taken prisoners.

In early days this region was called "The Iron City," on account of its many furnaces; forty were in operation at one time, they are now cinders and banks of earth. The oil production in this county has been wonderful;

5000 oil wells were drilled in Clarion after 1870, and there is still much wealth in it; other industries are gas, coal, and agriculture. Two long tunnels are at Madison Furnace on the railroad between Clarion and Franklin; it is said there are but two longer ones in the world. The first bridge was built across Clarion River in 1834. The present one, which is of fine construction, is the third.

CLARION, population, 2,793, made county seat in 1840; is finely located on a hill 1500 feet above sea level, on the Bellefonte and Meadville Turnpike. Public buildings face the park; Courthouse, third reconstruction, completed in 1882, Georgian; architect, Mr. Betts; contains portraits of judges. Jail, Norman architecture, stone with brick front, was built in 1874. Connected with the State Normal School is a stone chapel containing busts of Abraham Lincoln and Henry W. Longfellow; also Navaree Hall, Spanish architecture, stone, brick, and concrete; architects, Allison & Allison, Pittsburgh.

Among the six churches are the Methodist and Presbyterian, stone, Roman architecture. The Woman's Club has accomplished much for civic improvement, changing the cemetery from an unsightly spot to a place of beauty, planting the park with shrubbery and flower beds, and starting a free public library; in the park is a monument to Civil War soldiers. At FOXBURG is a fine free, memorial library; colonial; native sandstone; architect, Arthur H. Brockie, Philadelphia. In the "Memorial Church of Our Father," native sandstone; architect, James Sims, Philadelphia; is a painting by Edwin Howland Blashfield, "The Angel of the Resurrection."

LV
CLINTON COUNTY

FORMED June 21, 1839; named for DeWitt Clinton. Has superb scenic beauty; lofty mountains, rolling hills, and highly productive valleys border the West Branch of the Susquehanna River. About one-fourth is State Forest Reserve of mountainous wilderness, where large and small game, trout, and other fish abound. Chief industries are in vast deposit of commercial clay, from which is made fire, building and paving brick, tile sewer pipe, and concrete blocks; and a large chemical plant, very important in war chemicals; agriculture, including tobacco growing; several creameries and a large milk condensery.

LOCK HAVEN, with advance road signs, county seat; population 8559. Through the efforts of the city government, Board of Trade, and Women's Civic Club, John Nolen, of Cambridge, Massachusetts, was engaged to prepare a formal "City Plan" for the future growth and development of the city. This plan includes no radical changes or extravagant improvements, but conforms to the requirements of a small community. Embraces simple, but definite plans for the esthetic improvement of the fronts of the Susquehanna and Bald Eagle Rivers, between which Lock Haven is situated. The proper location and grouping of future public buildings, with a civic center at Monument Place, the intersection of the two main thoroughfares.

Clinton County

THE SUSQUEHANNA TRAIL
River front of Lock Haven

CLINTON COUNTY

The installation of modern street lighting systems with underground wires. And the gradual improvements in store fronts and business places.

It calls for the establishment of drives, playgrounds, and parks; the acquiring of a woodland reservation, adjoining Highland Cemetery, at the edge of the town, for a public park; and purchase of an outlying mountain top for future recreation. Much of the plan has been carried out. A unique and beautiful parkway has been made by utilizing the abandoned basin of the old canal, which cut through the heart of Lock Haven;

it had become a dump heap, but under the Nolen plan was filled, and has blossomed into one of the show places of the city, with flower beds, lawn, trees, and special landscape garden effect at each end. The river front has been made into a park, at entrance to the bridge, over the Susquehanna, a modern structure built by the state, which replaced a picturesque, covered bridge built, 1855, about 800 feet long; it includes the old toll house, pronounced by Mr. Nolen a valuable asset for the city. A smaller, quaint, old covered wood bridge, same period, about four miles from Lock Haven, spans Bald Eagle stream, on Bald Eagle Valley Road; near is the Clinton "Country Club" house, artistically built of cobblestones, architect, Lester Kintzing, New York.

The Courthouse, red brick and brownstone, surmounted by two dome-shaped towers, built in 1869, on site of an earlier one built, 1842, is on Water Street facing the river. On the river front is a stone marker, inscription, "Located in the stockade of Fort Reed, built, 1775, for defense against the Indians." On the river road, leading to Williamsport, near McElhattan, is site of Fort Horn, stone marker, both placed by the Hugh White Chapter, D. A. R., to mark the last two, of the trail of stockade fortifications, built along the river in defense of the pioneer settlers. Where Lock Haven stands was original site of several Indian villages; burial places; and marked one of their great thoroughfares from the north to the coast. Granite monument to 1938 soldiers of Clinton County in the Civil War is in center of city.

St. Paul's Protestant Episcopal Church, stone, Gothic, with spire, built, 1852, on Main Street, has memorial windows by Tiffany and Lamb, New York, and chancel window from England. The Immaculate Conception, Roman Catholic Church, built, 1905, and rectory, 1915, Gothic, with two towers, Hummelstone brownstone, architect, J. A. Dempwolf, York, Pa., corner of Water and Third Streets, is on site of an earlier church, built in 1857, dedicated by Rev. John C. Gilligan, pioneer missionary. Central State Normal School, on ground given by Philip Price of Philadelphia, founded, 1871, includes twelve buildings, on thirty-two acres of land, commanding extended view; the main building was erected in 1890, architect, A. S. Wagner, Williamsport; art course includes the theory and practice of teaching art; industrial art and lectures on art history; reproductions of paintings, and European architecture, also replicas of sculpture, are placed about the buildings.

CLINTON COUNTY

Ross Memorial Free Library, on Main Street, opened, 1910, further endowed by the late Wilson Kistler, sends traveling libraries to rural schools; contains painting by E. H. Shearer, "Ole Bull's Castle in Potter Co."; a noteworthy collection of North American Indian relics, 10,000 pieces, owned by Dr. T. B. Stewart, has been offered as a loan to this library, the collection is especially rich in local relics of domestic life and implements of war. "The Fallon House," built in 1855, still in excellent condition, is said to have been built with funds of Queen Isabella II, of Spain, who invested largely of her private fortune in Pennsylvania, for a retreat in case of revolution. In Highland Cemetery is an exact reproduction of the St. Martin's Cross, 16 feet 8 inches high, on the Island of Iona, off the coast of Scotland, erected in 1914, in memory of Samuel Richard Peale.

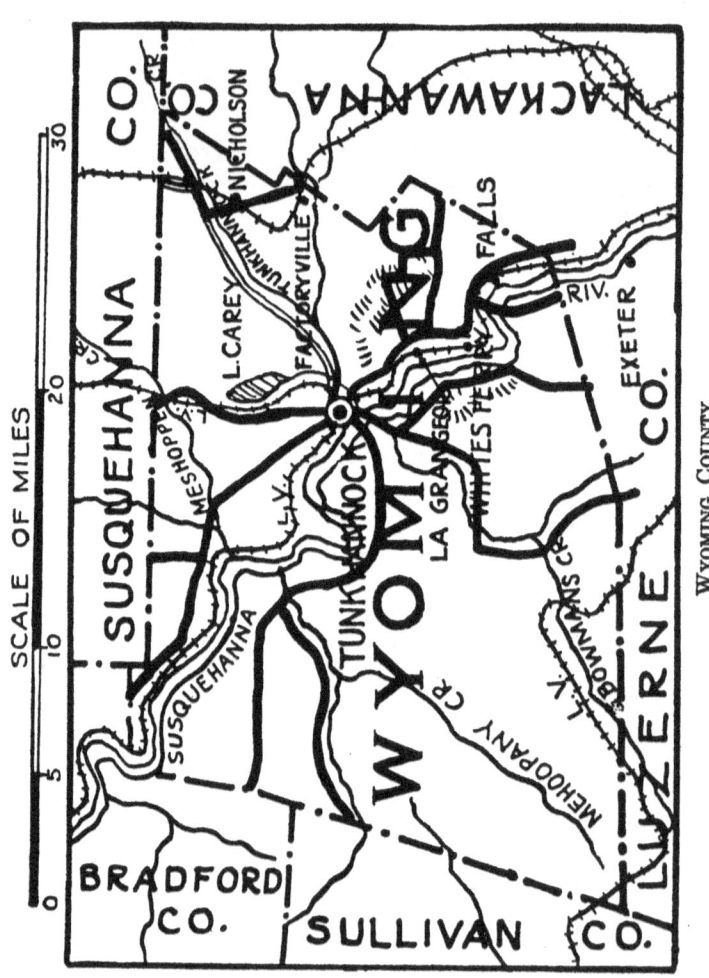
Wyoming County

LVI
WYOMING COUNTY

FORMED April 4, 1842; named from the Wyoming tribe of Indians who occupied the land when the white settlers came; name signifies extensive flats.

Lies in the northern opening of the wonderful Wyoming Valley, celebrated for its fertility and beauty; surface diversified by numerous spurs of the Appalachian system, which tower into lofty peaks; Mount Solecca, 1000 feet above the river; Mount Chodano, nearly opposite, about the same height; Mount Metchasaung, still higher, at La Grange. Several lakes are well stocked with fish; the largest, Lake Cary, three miles long, one mile wide, is surrounded by lofty pines and hemlocks. Glen Moneypenny, six miles below Tunkhannock, is a wildly picturesque location; many such are to be found among the mountains of this country.

This beautiful setting was the scene of Indian plottings that culminated in the Wyoming Massacre in 1778 (see Luzerne County). The following year General Sullivan's army passed through this region, on march to subdue the Six Nations, and encamped on the shore of the Susquehanna River at Tunkhannock, where the tannery now stands. Forty years ago passenger pigeons were so plentiful that when they flew across a town in dense flocks, they obscured the sun; one colony occupied a strip of woodland in

Wyoming County, seven miles long by three miles wide; Alexander Wilson wrote of counting ninety nests in a single tree. Chief industries, agriculture and manufacturing.

TUNKHANNOCK, county seat; population 1736, first called Putnam, after General Israel Putnam of Revolutionary War; settled, 1790; was incorporated 1841. Lies due north and south, east and west. Courthouse on Courthouse Square has two marble tablets in the corridor, with names of Revolutionary War soldiers buried within the limits of Wyoming County, placed by Tunkhannock Chapter, Daughters of the American Revolution. The Soldiers' Monument is on the same grounds. Among the churches of different denominations, the Methodist may be mentioned for Gothic architecture. At FACTORYVILLE is the Keystone Academy. Crossing Tunkhannock Creek, near Nicholson, is the Tunkhannock Viaduct, said to be the largest concrete bridge in the world, 2375 feet long, 240 feet high, above water level; height from bedrock 300 feet; carries the double tracks of the main line of the Lackawanna Railroad from mountain to mountain across the valley.

LVII
CARBON COUNTY

FORMED March 13, 1843; named for its coal deposits; coal was first discovered by Philip Ginter in 1791, on top of Sharp Mountain, now town of Summit Hill, nine miles southwest of Mauch Chunk. In 1818 the Lehigh Navigation Company and the Lehigh Coal Company were formed; under skilful management the almost insuperable obstacles in the way of transportation were overcome; boats 18 feet wide by 25 feet long, two or more hinged together, were floated by artificial freshets on the Lehigh; owing to the great fall in the river and consequent rapidity of its motion, dams were constructed near Mauch Chunk, with sluice gates, invented by Josiah White, a manager of the Navigation Company; they were the first on record used permanently; Lehigh coal is the hardest known anthracite in the world. Other mineral productions are iron, slate, and mineral paint. Wire rope was first invented in Mauch Chunk.

The first settlers were Moravian missionaries who, in 1746, purchased 200 acres on the north side of Mahoning Creek above its mouth, for converted Mohican Indians; each Indian family possessed their own lot of ground and Gnadenhütten became a town; the church stood in the valley, with the Indian houses forming a crescent on one side, on the other side was the missionary's house and burial ground. The road to Wyoming lay through the settlement, being the

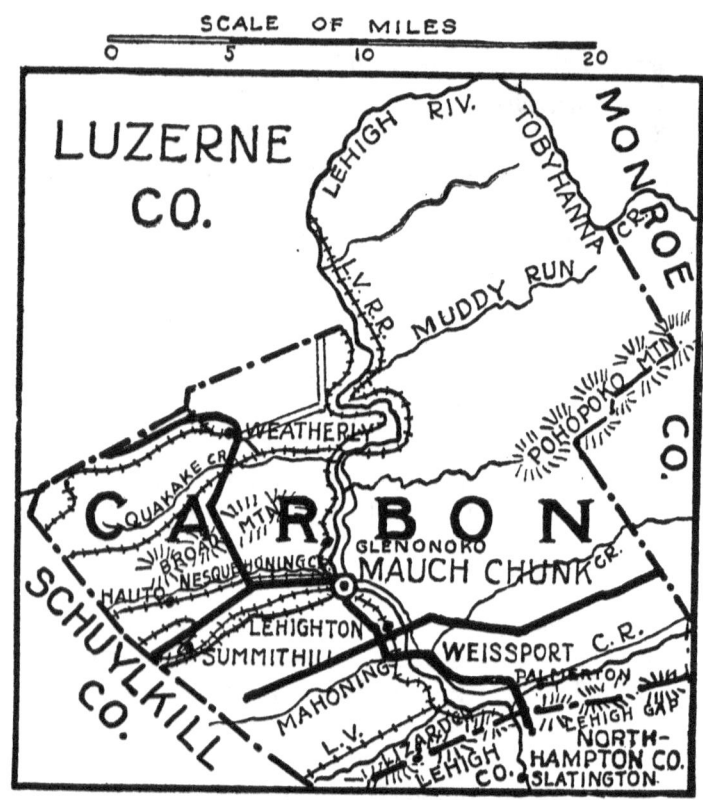

CARBON COUNTY

CARBON COUNTY

famous Warrior's Path over Nescopec Mountain. In August all partook of their own first fruits in a love feast. Christian Ranch and Martin Mack were the first missionaries residing here; several parts of Scripture had been translated into the Mohican language; the Holy Communion was administered every month, the Indians calling that "The Great Day." In 1749 Bishop (Baron) John de Watterville went to Gnadenhütten and laid the foundation of a large church; Indian congregation 500 persons. After Braddock's defeat in 1755 the whole frontier was open to the savage foe; suddenly in 1757, the mission house on the Mahoning was attacked and burnt by French and Indians, and many inhabitants were murdered; a broad marble slab, placed there in 1788, near LEHIGHTON, marks the grave of those massacred.

In 1756 Benjamin Franklin was authorized by the Provincial Government to erect forts on the Lehigh; one opposite Gnadenhütten was named Fort Allen, for William Allen, the Chief Justice. At WEISSPORT, in the rear of the "Fort Allen House" may be seen the well dug under Franklin's supervision; it was within the inclosure of the fort and supplied the soldiers with water. Weissport was settled by Colonel Jacob Weiss, Quartermaster General in the Revolutionary Army, on site of Fort Allen. Municipal parks are at Lehighton and Weissport, given by Jacob Weiss. Also at Lehighton is All Saints' Chapel, early English Gothic.

In 1780 Andrew Montour, leader of an Indian party, captured the Gilbert family, twelve persons, and took them over Mauch Chunk and Broad Mountains into the Nescopec path, across Quakake Creek to Mahoning Mountain and over wild and rugged country to Canada; eventually they were all redeemed at Montreal, in 1782, and returned to Byberry. A view of great scenic beauty is from Prospect Rock, over the Nescopec Valley; Cloud Point, frequently covered by vapor, may be seen; near is Glen Thomas with a picturesque Amber Cascade, named for David Thomas, pioneer in the iron trade. GLEN ONOKO, two miles above Mauch Chunk, with its wild beauty, total ascent over 900 feet, forms the channel for the clear stream which flows over innumerable cascades to the Lehigh; the most noticeable are "Chameleon Falls," fifty feet high, and "Onoko Falls," ninety feet high, with overhanging rocks, covered with moss and ferns.

MAUCH CHUNK, county seat, population 3666; Indian name means Bear Mountain; first settled in 1815; has one principal street, following the tortuous course of Mauch Chunk Creek as it winds through a narrow gorge between three high, steep, and rocky mountains, averaging 850 feet above the town. The important buildings are directly on this street. Courthouse, Norman, brownstone, quarried at Rockport, Carbon County; built in 1894. Jail, where some of the Molly Maguires were executed. The Dimmick Memorial Library, built in 1890, brick. Churches here and in East Mauch Chunk are unusually handsome. St. Mark's Protestant Episcopal, Gothic, stone, has memorial windows by J. & R. Lamb; the reredos is very beautiful. First Presbyterian, colonial, brick, has a memorial window by John LaFarge, and one by Tiffany. The Immaculate Conception, Roman

CARBON COUNTY

Catholic, also has fine stained-glass windows. St. Paul's Methodist Episcopal is the oldest church in the town.

The Woman's Clubs are seeking to improve conditions, sanitary and scenic; to widen the life of the town and in every way make it more in unison with its natural surroundings. In the limited space of the narrow valley, land is too precious to be used except for buildings, but the hills are so magnificent that they look to them for the necessary beauty; Flagstaff Park has natural effect. The first railroad in Carbon County and one of the oldest in the United States, is the famous SWITCHBACK, a gravity road, extending from Mauch Chunk to SUMMIT HILL, opened in 1832, for bringing coal from the mines to the canal; used now only for pleasure; a double track is laid to the summit of Mount Pisgah, 2322 feet distant from the foot, at an angle of twenty degrees, with elevation about 900 feet above the river. Scene from the top is superb, with a succession of mountain ridges rising, range after range, with distant view of Lehigh Water Gap, and farther to Schooley's Mountain in New Jersey. The principal attraction at Summit Hill is the burning mine, discovered to be on fire in 1859. General Craig of Revolutionary fame resided here.

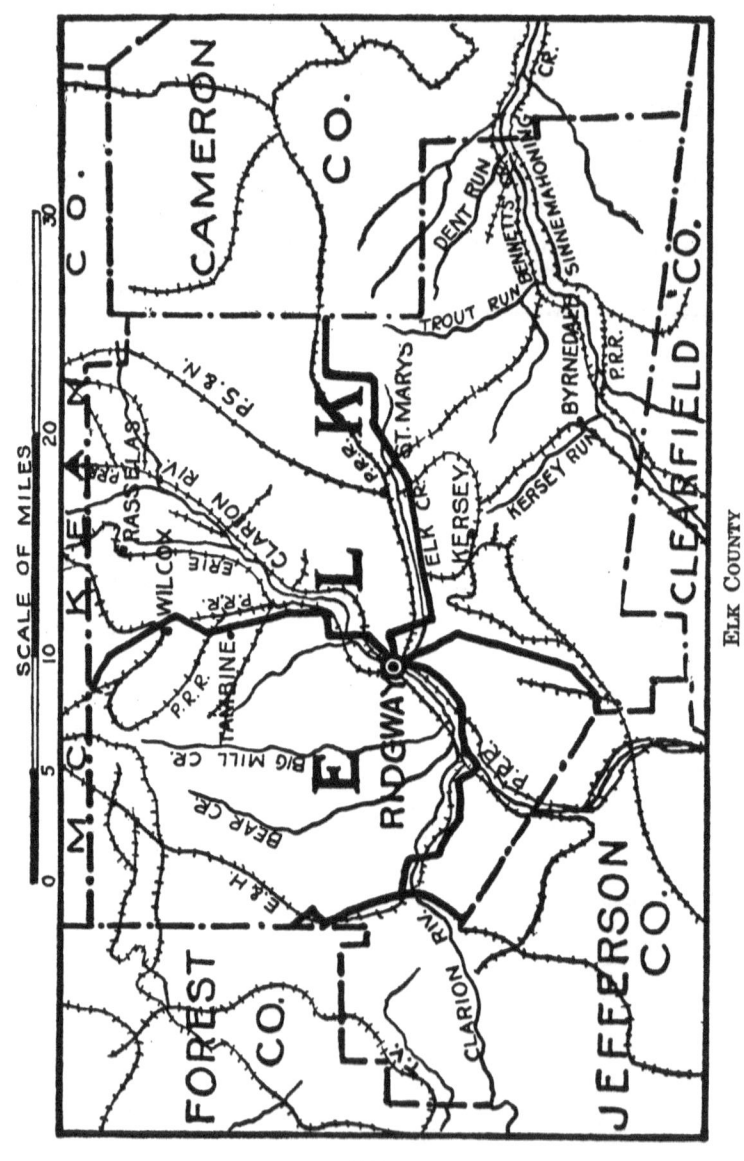

ST. MARK'S P. E. CHURCH, MAUCH CHUNK
This church is built on solid rock

LVIII
ELK COUNTY

FORMED April 18, 1843; possesses everywhere great scenic beauty; a large herd of elk, last-known herd of the Black Forest, still existed, for which the county was named; the last elk was killed in 1857. The Black Forest formerly covered a vast area of northwest Pennsylvania, the deep green of the hemlock giving a mystery of blackness; here many varieties of large and small animals abounded. Climate and geological formation differ from surrounding counties in ratio of altitude; the growing season is usually two or three weeks later on account of late frosts; agriculture is now chief industry. Bituminous coal was discovered by "Blind Mike" on Priest's Land at St. Mary's in 1853, and is continuously worked. Natural gas, oil, high-grade clays, and shale are other mineral resources. Jimanandy Park, 3600 acres of almost virgin forest, stocked with deer; through which a trout run flows, is the property of heirs of Senator James K. P. Hall, and Honorable Andrew Kaul; permission to inspect the park may be obtained at office of J. R. P. Hall at St. Mary's.

RIDGWAY, county seat, laid out in 1843 and named for Jacob Ridgway, Philadelphia, who was United States Consul at Antwerp; population 6037. Courthouse, center of town, built in 1872, brick, with clock tower, surmounted by a large statue of Justice; stands in a well-kept park with jail in the rear. Main Street, very wide, paved with brick, has many fine residences. Forest Lawn Cemetery contains the Hall and Hyde family mausoleums and a large community mausoleum built in 1912. ST. MARY'S, ten miles from Ridgway, along the state road through beautiful scenery, is largest town in the county, population 6967; known as the Summit City, on a high plateau, altitude 1660 to 1950 feet. Has wide streets paved with brick, and is surrounded by a fertile farming country. The Charles A. Luke Memorial Park, four acres, acquired by gift in 1873 for the public, was laid out by George C. Miller, landscape gardener of Boston, Massachusetts, in 1914, through St. Mary's Village Association.

St. Mary's Roman Catholic Church, oldest and largest in the county, built in the fifties by the German Catholic colonists, from plans made by the late Ignatius Garner, native undressed sandstone, recently dressed with cement, spoiling its rusticity. In St. Mary's Cemetery are buried Baron Van Essel and many war veterans. Large German Benedictine College and Convent conducted by the Sisters of St. Benedict, established, 1862, is one of the three schools in America which teach the Della Sade system of voice culture, introduced by the venerable Sister Marie who learned the system of the great Italian master. In the Convent is said to be an original Van Dyke painting. Sacred Heart Church, native sandstone, Gothic. The Shiloh Presbyterian Church is an ecclesiastical building of native sandstone. At St. Mary's and Kersey Road is a small chapel, wood, old German design, built in 1870 by the late George Decker, in fulfillment of a vow; prayer service is held here at stated times.

ELK COUNTY

Going east from Kersey, road leads through "The Barrens," a sandy rocky stretch of land denuded of vegetation by forest fires, on the old Bellefonte Pike. Scenery is wonderful toward MOUNT ZION, where there is a typical country church and burial ground. At Mount Zion corner, the road takes three courses; left leads to BYRNEDALE with its fifty coke ovens, coal tipples, and washer plant. WILCOX, in northern part of county, lying in the famous gas belt of Elk County, has large glass factory. A few miles back is TAMBINE; near here President Grant, guest of General Thomas Kane, spent a day fishing for trout. From Wilcox, along the Big Level Road, is Rasselas; here Captain (later General) Kane pinned a buck's tail on the hat of Hiram Woodruff, first member recruited for the Bucktail Regiment. On the old Milesburg and Clermont Pike, William C. Walsh carried the first mail through this section in 1828.

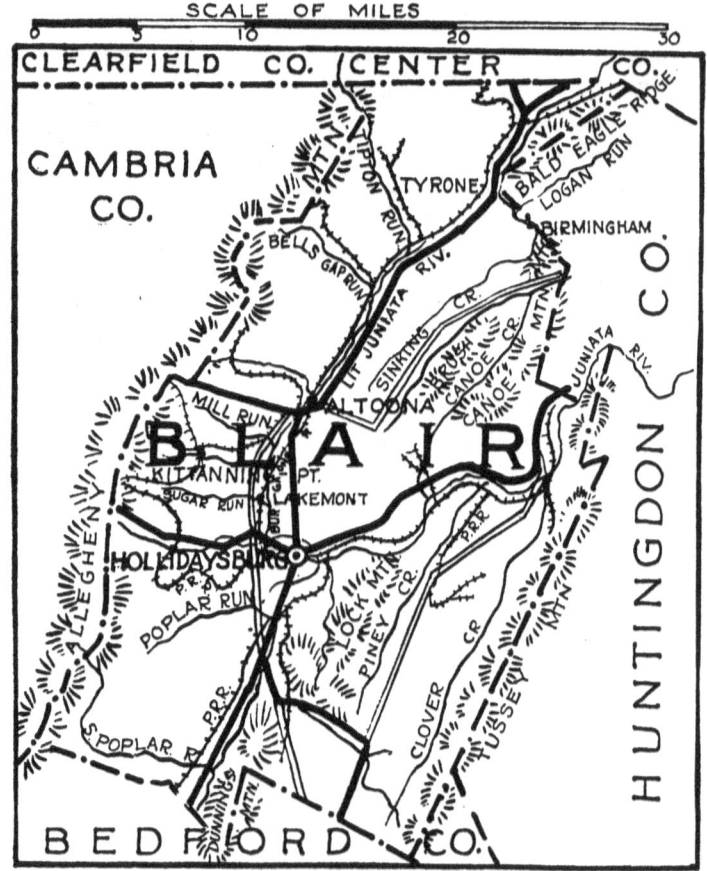

Blair County

LIX
BLAIR COUNTY

FORMED February 26, 1846; named for Honorable John Blair, native of this county, and public-spirited citizen; in 1820, he laid out, and was President of the Huntingdon, Cambria and Indiana Turnpike, first in this section. Blair County lies in the beautiful Juniata Valley, settled by Scotch-Irish, English, and Germans; much of the soil is very fertile. Chief industries, agriculture, coal mining, and manufacturing. It is the center of a network of roads, mostly built as turnpikes from 1830-50; now state roads.

TYRONE, altitude 692 feet above sea level, population 9084; outlet for important bituminous coal products; lies in a basin formed by the base line of old Tussey, a famous mountain, and the bold ridge known as Bald Eagle. The home of Captain John Logan, eldest son of Shikellamy, was at mouth of Bald Eagle Creek; second son, James Logan, the Mingo chief, named for Secretary Logan of Germantown, went west to the Ohio; his son (Tod-kah-dohs) married a daughter of Chief Cornplanter. About three miles east from Tyrone is the Sinking Valley, named from the Sinking Creek, an underground watercourse; near is BIRMINGHAM, with a pleasure ground, where there are one hundred springs and a large cave; a school for girls is here.

ALTOONA, population 60,331; altitude 1171 feet above sea level; founded by the Pennsylvania Railroad in 1850, consists almost entirely of their shops and workmen's houses. St. Luke's Protestant Episcopal Church, native stone, first built in 1858; second building in 1881, using the same stone; Gothic, F. C. Withers, New York, architect; has an English window, also one by Tiffany, "The Resurrection," exhibited in Paris in 1900; memorial to Almet E. Read, Esq.; brick rectory and school, gift of General John Watts De Peyster, as memorial to his daughter, first school for advanced education in Altoona.

In the Logan House, built, 1854, by the Pennsylvania Railroad, was held the conference of the loyal war governors in 1862, namely, A. G. Curtin, Pennsylvania; John A. Andrew, Massachusetts; Richard Yates, Illinois; Israel Washburn, Jr., Maine; Edward Solomon, Wisconsin; Samuel J. Kirkwood, Iowa; O. P. Morton (by D. G. Ross, his representative), Indiana; William Sprague, Rhode Island; F. H. Pierpont, Virginia; David Tod, Ohio; N. S. Berry, New Hampshire; Austin Blair, Michigan; to devise ways and means for coöperating with President Lincoln in suppressing the Rebellion. King Edward VII, as Prince of Wales, stopped here. On the William Penn Highway, formerly an old portage road, is site of an early historic hotel, "Fountain Inn," mentioned by Dickens in "American Notes"; here William Henry Harrison stopped overnight on his way to Washington in 1841, to be inaugurated President of the United States; Henry Clay and Jenny Lind also stopped here.

Near junction of Sugar Run with Burgoon's Run, three miles south of Altoona, in 1781, Indians killed a number of militiamen from Fetter's Fort, built in

BLAIR COUNTY

1775, by firing on them from ambush. A monument dedicated in 1909, marks the place where the wife of Matthew Dean and three of their children were killed by Indians in 1788, while he and the other children were working in the fields. In Blair County are also sites of Fort Roberdeau, built, 1778, and Fort Lowry, 1779, unmarked. Magnificent views from Nopsononock, at summit of the Alleghenies, Prospect Hill, and Kittanning Point, where the Pennsylvania Railroad is carried around the famous Horseshoe Curve. A little farther, the Pennsylvania Railroad passes through a tunnel two-thirds of a mile long, 2160 feet above sea level.

Lakemont Park is a noted place of scenic beauty near HOLLIDAYSBURG, population 4071, county seat, laid out in 1820; named for James Adam Holliday, who lived here prior to the Revolution. Courthouse, Romanesque; built 1876–77; remodeled and enlarged in 1906; on grounds are jail, feudal style, architect, John Haviland, and a Soldiers' Monument. Highland Hall, stone, colonial doorway, with beautiful grounds, is now Miss Cowles' school for girls. Entrance to old Presbyterian Cemetery is a Norman gate, designed by Price J. McLanahan, Philadelphia, hewn timbers, held in place by bolts of wood, supporting a red tiled roof. Main street is part of the old turnpike between Philadelphia and Pittsburgh, shaded by beautiful old trees; here in days of the canal, in 1834, boats met the Portage Railroad at foot of the Alleghenies; freight and passengers were carried over the mountain by inclined planes and stationary engines; by this means travel from eastern Pennsylvania was continued through the Ohio River to the Mississippi. Charles Dickens took the trip over the mountain in 1842; the Allegheny Portage Railroad in boldness of design and difficulty of execution compared well with the passes of the Simplon and Mont Cenis. "Ant Hill" woods, almost within town limits, were said to be the only hills of the kind in this country; they were written up in the *Century* magazine by Dr. McCook; a hill was taken to the Academy of Natural Sciences, Philadelphia; they are now level with the ground, through vibration of the trolley. Less than a mile from town are "Chimney Rocks," famous council chamber of the Indians; with view of unsurpassed beauty of the Juniata Valley, old Portage Road, and Allegheny Mountains. On western slope, much of the Portage Road is used for the highway; the Monumental Arch is still standing.

LX

SULLIVAN COUNTY

FORMED March 15, 1847, named for General John Sullivan; is noted for picturesque scenery, mountains, valleys, lakes, streams and waterfalls, forests, and distant views. Either the scenic Williamsport and North Branch Railroad or the state highway, that parallel each other and enter the county near Muncy Valley, lead to beautiful Eaglesmere, 1900 feet above sea; on Lewis Lake, one and a half miles long, one-half mile wide; depth never definitely determined, fed by subterranean waters. About the shore, tree bound, with luxuriant growth of rhododendron and laurel, and rock faced to deep water, there are lovely nooks, and a bathing beach of white sand at the northern end. Passing from Eaglesmere through "Celestia," where the lands were deeded in 1864, by Peter E. Armstrong and wife, to "Almighty God"—the deed may be seen at the county courthouse— one comes to LAPORTE, population 175; highest and smallest county seat in Pennsylvania, 2000 feet above sea level, with its natural beauties, including "Lake Mokoma," is also an attractive summer resort. It was laid out in 1850, by Michael Meylert, who owned the land and built the first courthouse; present building, facing the park, is Romanesque; brick; beautiful Lombardy poplar trees are in the yard. Within the last twelve years advanced civilization has penetrated into Sullivan County in good state highways, rural mail

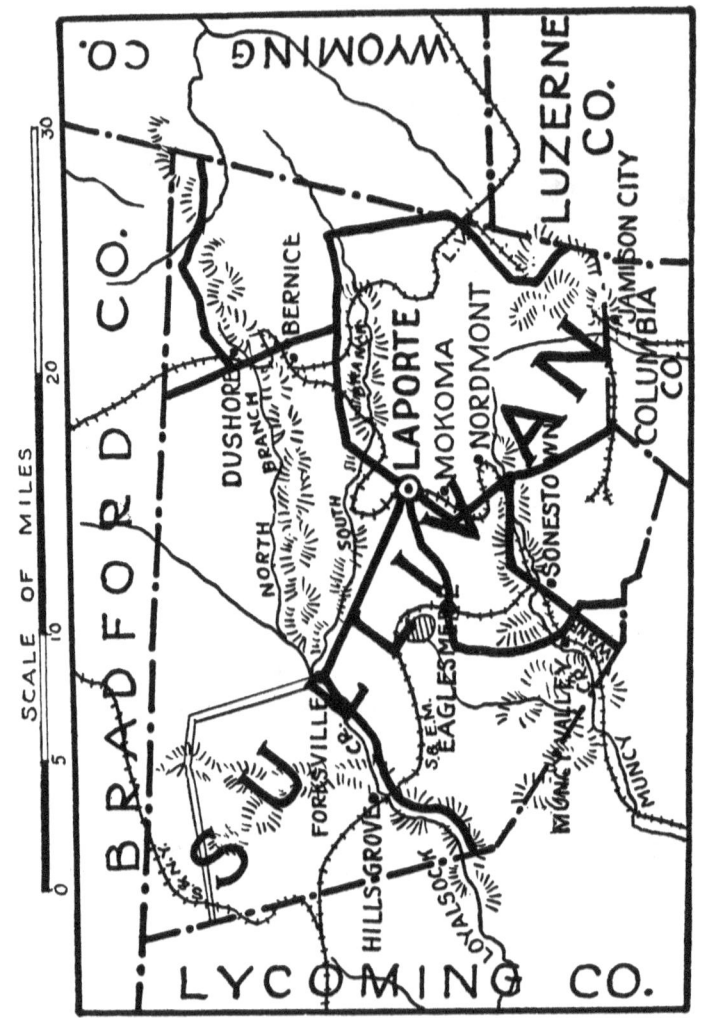

Sullivan County

routes, telephones, and several borough and township high schools. The streets of LaPorte are wide and well kept, and the park is in care of the Ladies' Village Improvement Society.

At the top of the mountain, on the road toward Sonestown, is "Fiester's View," where the deep valley of Muncy Creek, walled on the east by the towering North Mountain, 3000 feet above tide, near Nordmont, is beautiful beyond description. At the junction of the Big and Little Loyalsock Creeks is the pretty little town of FORKSVILLE. Dr. Priestly purchased a large tract of land about here, laid out roads, and made many improvements. Four miles distant, on the state highway toward Hillsgrove, on Kings Creek, is Lincoln Falls, a waterfall about 30 feet in height at the head of a gorge with perpendicular walls of rock, varying from 50 to 80 feet in height. A few deer, quite a number of bear, foxes, rabbits, and squirrels are in this county; a state game preserve is in the southeast near Jamison City. There are some good trout streams, and the lakes are well stocked with fish. The most valuable industry is coal from the Bernice coal fields in the east. The production of hemlock tanned sole leather is important. Farm products and dairying are general.

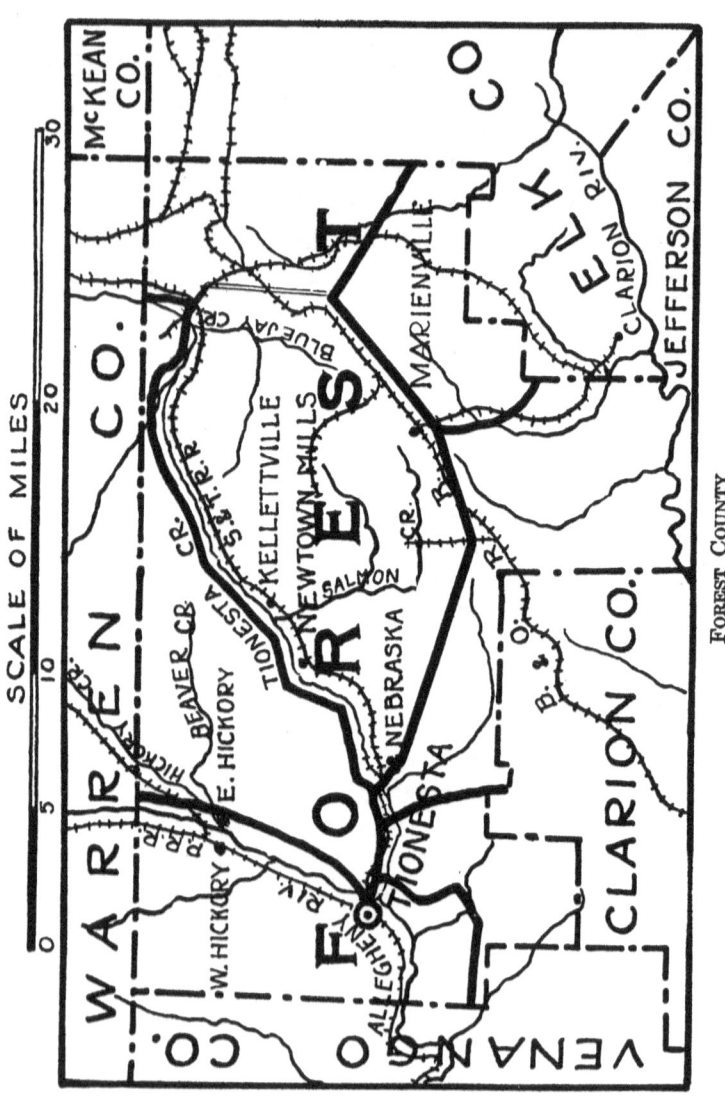

Forest County

LXI
FOREST COUNTY

FORMED April 11, 1848; named for its great variety of timber; hemlock and pine, east; dense forests of deciduous trees west along the Allegheny River. Game large and small abounds; streams are full of brook trout. Atmosphere is fragrant with health-giving ozone, strengthening the weak and restoring those affected with lung trouble. Chief industry is lumbering; in western part agriculture, and the growing of fine apples.

David Zeisberger, first white man in Forest County, came in 1767, Moravian missionary to the Monseys, a wild and warlike tribe; he stayed two years in their three villages, Goshgoshunk (Holeman's Flats), Sa-que-lin-get, Place of Council (Tionesta) and La-hun-ichannock, Meeting of the Waters (East Hickory), and migrated with them to Fort Pitt. After Monseys, came the Senecas under Cornplanter, in 1770. First settler Cyrus Blood, surveyor, who cleared land for Marienville, first county seat, and improved it. "The Big Level," name of old state road, 1728 feet above sea, follows northeast from Marienville to Mount Jewett, McKean County, roadbed compact and solid, 100 feet wide, was first made in Cyrus Blood's time. On this road is Beaver Meadows, formerly a dam built by beavers, which backed water over an area one and one-quarter miles long by one-eighth mile wide; dam four and one-half feet high.

Along the Guitonville road toward Marienville, on a high plateau with two miles of straight, natural, firm roadbed, is Job's Pinnacle, from which is a fine distant view of Tionesta Valley; a mile farther, Pisgah, also a pinnacle, is on Salmon Creek Hill; the whole hill is composed of magnetic iron ore, on a sandstone foundation, above shale and slate stratification; in surveying, the magnetic attraction is so great the needle is paralyzed; it is a mass of rocks; another magnetic iron ore hill is Bald Bluff, where lightning strikes freely. Stony Point, back of Salmon Creek Hill, near Newtown Mills, is the highest land; scenery about here is so beautiful at the mouth of Salmon Creek, that Erion Williams, the early surveyor, called it Eden revived. Beautiful scenery is along the State road parallel with the Sheffield & Tionesta Railroad, crossing a large iron bridge over Tionesta Creek at Nebraska, two miles farther, over another iron bridge, and three miles to Ross Run. This land produces oil and gas in good quantities.

At Kellettville, on the Tionesta, pieces of ancient pottery have been exhumed, showing that this was the home of a race older than the Indians, who had not made pottery in this section; three miles above Kellettville is a long sloping rock in the bed of Tionesta Creek, "Panther Rock," where Ebenezer Kingsley, a pioneer hunter, shot many cougars; state paid twenty dollars bounty for a panther, twelve dollars for a wolf. Picturesque falls are on Blue Jay Creek; near its mouth is Rocky City, on Tionesta Creek, a vast aggregation of rocks like tall towers, with grand scenery, nearly opposite is a prehistoric square hole forty feet deep, no record of its formation.

FOREST COUNTY

TIONESTA, population 642, county seat, incorporated, 1852. Principal buildings, Courthouse on high ground in public square of two acres, brick, built 1870, architect, Keene Vaughn, contains proof copy of "Zeisberger preaching to the Indians in Forest County in 1677," engraved by John Sartain, with a volume of Zeisberger's Life and Notes, a gift from the Pennsylvania Historical Society, Philadelphia; and a receipt signed by David Zeisberger, framed in wood of the wild cherry tree under which, legend says, he originally preached; also portraits of prominent men of Forest County. Jail, brick and stone, in courthouse ground, built by Van Dorn Prison Company, Cleveland, Ohio, in 1895. The Forest County National Bank, native stone, Romanesque, built, 1899, architect, C. M. Robinson, Altoona. Presbyterian Church, brick, 1910, on site of old wooden church, built, 1851; and Methodist Church, brownstone, built, 1909; both contain memorial windows.

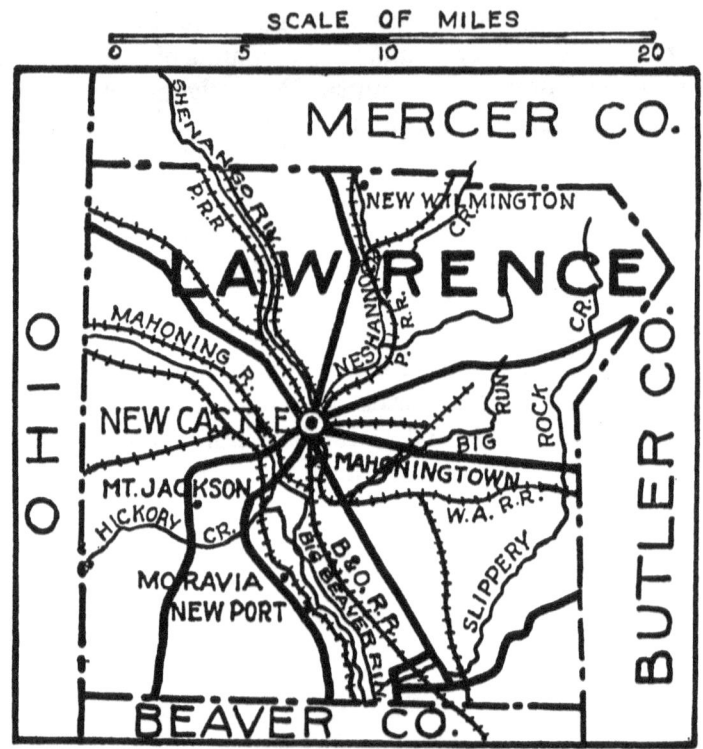

Lawrence County

LXII

LAWRENCE COUNTY

FORMED March 20, 1849; named for Perry's flagship, in the Battle of Lake Erie, which was named in honor of Captain James Lawrence, United States Navy. Lawrence was mortally wounded in the War of 1812, on the frigate *Chesapeake*, against the British ship *Shannon;* as he was carried below he said: "Don't give up the ship." Chiefly settled by Scotch-Irish. The old canal to Lake Erie, built in 1833, went through center of the county, and did much to develop the resources—bituminous coal, iron ore, and limestone. Chief industries, manufactories and agriculture. Many beautiful drives are all through the county in every direction.

The Moravian missionaries, David Zeisberger and Gottlob Senseman, were the first white men who dwelt here, long before the county was formed; they migrated with the Indians from Bradford County, through Forest County, and were the greatest missionary power to them. They were visited by Glikkikin, a renowned warrior of great eloquence, who with his escort, purposely tried to refute the doctrines of Christianity; they were received by Anthony, a native convert, who treated them courteously and made such an impressive speech on Christian doctrine that he astonished the visitors; Zeisberger, coming in then, confirmed his words, and Glikkikin, instead of delivering his speech, replied: "I have nothing to say. I believe your words."

On return to his town, he advised the savages to go hear the Gospel; he made them another visit, informed them that he had determined to embrace Christianity, and invited them, in the name of his chief, Packauke, to settle on land on Beaver River, near his town Kaskaskünk, now New Castle; this land was to be for the exclusive use of the mission. The offer was accepted, and on April 17, 1770, they left Oil Creek in fifteen canoes; in three days they reached Fort Pitt, proceeded down the Ohio to Beaver River, and ascended that river to the locality given, now Moravia, passing an Indian village, near present Newport, of women, all single and pledged never to marry.

When encamped, they sent an embassy, Zeisberger, and Abraham, a native, to Packauke, who were received by the chief at his own house; he gave them welcome and pledged protection; they built houses, cleared land, planted, and prepared for winter. The Indians began to visit them, the Monseys from Goshgoshünk were the first to cast their lot with the Christian Indians; Glikkikin soon came and became a Christian force. Finally the Monseys adopted Zeisberger into their tribe; the ceremony took place at Kaskaskünk; they invested him with all the rights and privileges of a Monsey; this proved a complete triumph and was the source of much good influence among Indians. White settlers began to come after Wayne's Treaty of Greenville, in 1795.

NEW CASTLE, county seat, incorporated as a city in 1869, population 44,938, was laid out, at the junction of the Shenango, Neshannock, and Mahoning Rivers, where they form the Beaver River, in 1798, by John

LAWRENCE COUNTY 487

C. Stewart from New Castle, Delaware. It has natural gas, fine churches, schools, public buildings, bridges, and many beautiful residences, including that of Ex-Lieutenant Governor William M. Brown, on the North Hill. Courthouse, colonial, built in 1852, in spacious grounds, on a hill in east part of the city. The first Methodist Episcopal Church has a memorial window to Ira D. Sankey, the singing evangelist, who was born and lived here; subject, "Ninety and Nine"; maker, Sellars, New York; also Hofmann's "Christ" in stained glass. High school, brick, of best school construction, well lighted; has reproductions on the walls of fine works of art. The Oak Park Cemetery has some beautiful memorials.

This is one of the manufacturing communities of western Pennsylvania, which form the greatest industrial district in the world; within a radius of sixty miles of New Castle, the annual tonnage is over 200,000,000, while the combined annual tonnage in and out of Liverpool, London, Hamburg, Suez Canal, and New York is 116,000,000. The American Sheet and Tin Plate Mill is said to be the largest in the world; they constructed a miniature playground for the only exhibit sent from New Castle to the Panama-Pacific Exposition in 1915; it showed the kind of humanitarian work done by the company, and was representative of this city, where the playground has done a vast amount of good among the foreign population employed in the immense furnaces; engineering works; and the great cement plants making 5000 barrels of Portland cement daily. The United States Steel Corporation, Carnegie Steel Company, maintains children's playgrounds, with a moving picture theatre, average attendance 1800 children daily; The "Rosena" blast furnace yard is kept like a park in grass, flower beds, and neatness.

Cascade Park has great natural beauty. A part of the beautiful Slippery Rock is in the southeast of this county. At Mount Jackson is Battery B Monument in honor of the Round Head Regiment. NEW WILMINGTON, population 8861, has Westminster College, under United Presbyterian administration; near here was the McKinley blast furnace, owned and operated by President McKinley's father. His son worked here as a boy.

LXIII
FULTON COUNTY

FORMED April 19, 1850, named for Robert Fulton. The Tuscarora Mountains rise like a huge barrier on the eastern boundary, with numerous other ridges and peaks. Streams that flow into the Potomac River are largely fed by splendid limestone springs. From the Susquehanna to the Ohio River the scenery cannot be surpassed for picturesque beauty; far sweeping valleys, rugged mountains, grand forests, form a constantly changing panorama. It is both beautiful and historic. The Chambersburg and Pittsburgh Turnpike, built in 1814–15, now the Lincoln Highway, was first an old Indian trail from Harrisburg, through Fort Louden, Clinton County, and westward to Bedford, crossing the center of the county.

In the days following Braddock's defeat in 1755, this region became the arena in which the red warrior of the forests and the white frontiersman fought to the death. Not a valley, creek, nor mountain range, site of modern city or town, but what was the scene of thrilling events, some of which influence the world for all time. Early settlers were Scotch-Irish, on the Aughwick, and in the great cove. Chief industries, iron ore, bituminous coal, and agriculture. Dickey's Mountain, in the southeast, is rich in hematite and fossil ores.

McCONNELLSBURG, county seat; population 689; land granted to William and Daniel McConnell by

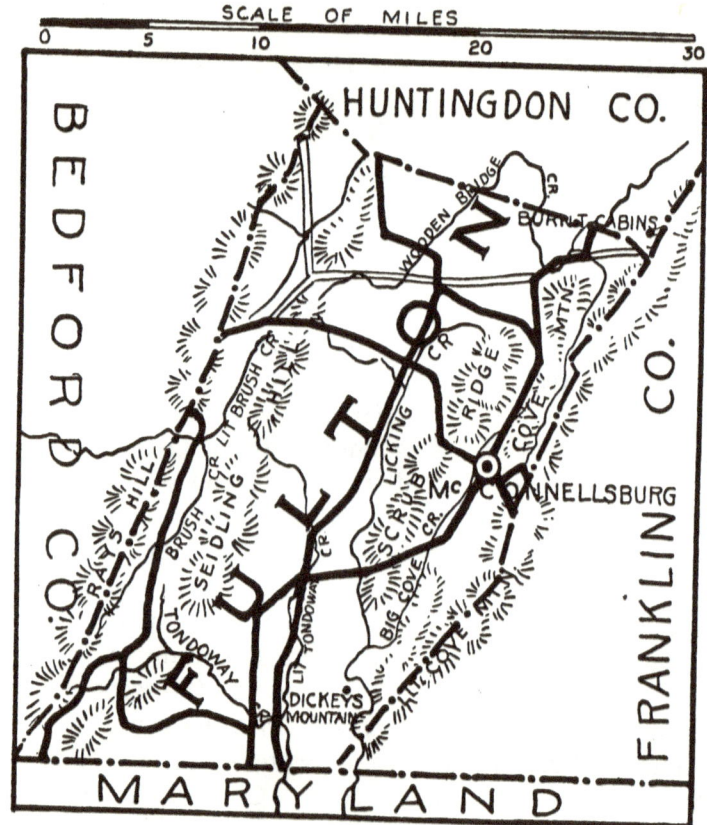

Fulton County

warrant in 1762, is in the heart of the great cove; it was laid out in 1786, and in 1830 was one of the most important stopping places on the old turnpike. Here, from 1827-47 were the Hanover Iron Works, two furnaces, and two forges, that used hematite ore, mined from Lowry's Knob, one mile distant. It is said that no territory of equal extent in this state is so rich in iron ore as is Fulton County. Fort Littleton in the north was one of a chain of government forts from the east to Fort Pitt. BURNT CABINS, on the old state road, was named because of the burning of the cabins of early settlers near here by the provincial authorities. It is said that Fulton County contributed more men to the Civil War, in proportion, than any other county in Pennsylvania.

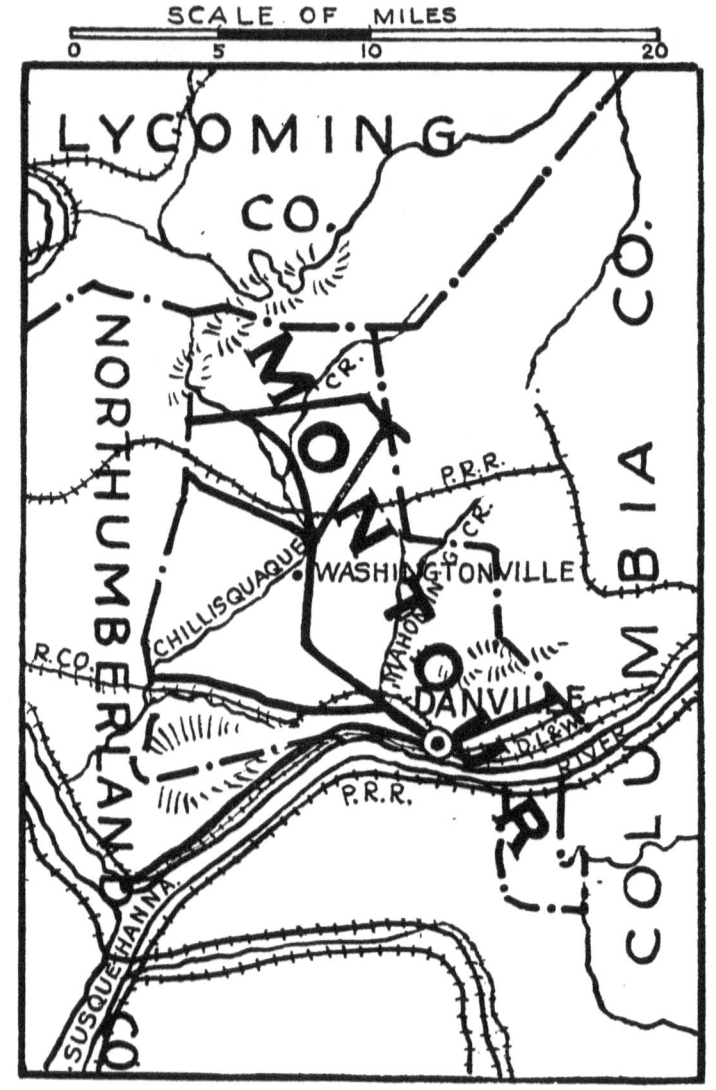

Montour County

LXIV
MONTOUR COUNTY

FORMED May 3, 1850; named for Catharine Montour; surface hilly; traversed by several barren ridges. Muncy Hills lie along the northwest border, while down the river for miles stretches the Montour Ridge, furnishing quantities of best iron ore; there is also finest limestone; and much fertile land, drained by the Chillisquaque and Mahoning creeks. Chief industries are iron and steel production, and manufactories. Here, it is said, the first "T" rail was made, in 1844, and the first cannon in the United States, made of anthracite iron, was cast at the foundry in 1842.

DANVILLE, county seat; population 6952; was settled in 1790; beautifully located, it nestles between Bald Top and Blue Hill. Mahoning Creek, named after a tribe of Indians who peopled this part of the country, flows through the town, which is built on part of the tract of land surveyed on warrant of John Penn to John Lukens, Surveyor General of the United States, dated, January 31, 1769. A bridge built by the state in 1904 is one-quarter mile long and connects Montour with Northumberland County; at its entrance is River Front Park, laid out in 1912, with concrete walks, flower beds, and fountain. Market Street Park, center of town, has an electrically lighted fountain. Memorial Park, a beautiful knoll, was formerly the burial ground of the Presbyterian Church; in 1908 it was laid out as a park with flower beds, and is kept up by the council and public-spirited citizens; the Soldiers' Monument is here, with two cannon of the Civil War near.

Courthouse, Georgian, built in 1871. Jail built, 1892, architect, J. H. Brugler, has modern equipment, and for months at a time is empty. Among the fifteen churches, the most notable in architecture is Christ Memorial, Protestant Episcopal, fourteenth century, English Gothic; massive architecture, native limestone of varied tints, with Ohio stone for the traceried windows. The Thomas Beaver Free Library. Young Men's Christian Association with gymnasium and swimming pool; George F. Geisinger Memorial Hospital; and State Hospital for the Insane, constructed by S. S. Schultz, M.D., corner-stone laid by Governor Geary in 1869, are all important buildings, among the best equipped and most modern in the state. WASHINGTONVILLE is site of Fort Bossley, on the Chillisquaque Creek.

LXV
SNYDER COUNTY

FORMED March 2, 1855, named for Hon. Simon Snyder, Governor of Pennsylvania, 1808-17; three terms; noted as the first governor to urge legislation for free public schools; he was the great war governor of 1812; served in the Assembly from 1789-1808, and was speaker of the House from 1802-08; he lived at Selinsgrove. From end of Northumberland Bridge, built by Theodore Burr in 1814, on West Branch of the Susquehanna; the road leading south to Selinsgrove passes Blue Hill, noted for beautiful scenery. On top was formerly Hotel Shikellimy, burned in 1895; on one of the rocks overhanging is a natural profile named for Shikellimy, who sauntered about here. Farther on is a single arch stone bridge; for half a mile, beginning at this bridge, is a state road built by the Commonwealth of Pennsylvania. Governor Pennypacker handled the first shovel of dirt in 1904; it was laid out first by James F. Linn in 1829, has since been extended.

SELINSGROVE, first settlers, in 1755, were all killed by Indians, laid out by and named for Anthony Selin in 1827, population 1937; Governor Snyder mansion, built by himself in 1816, is near center of town, colonial, massive stone walls, with arched door ten feet high and large side porch, in well kept grounds. Due west from Selinsgrove, towards Middleburg, is Susquehanna University, formerly Missionary Insti-

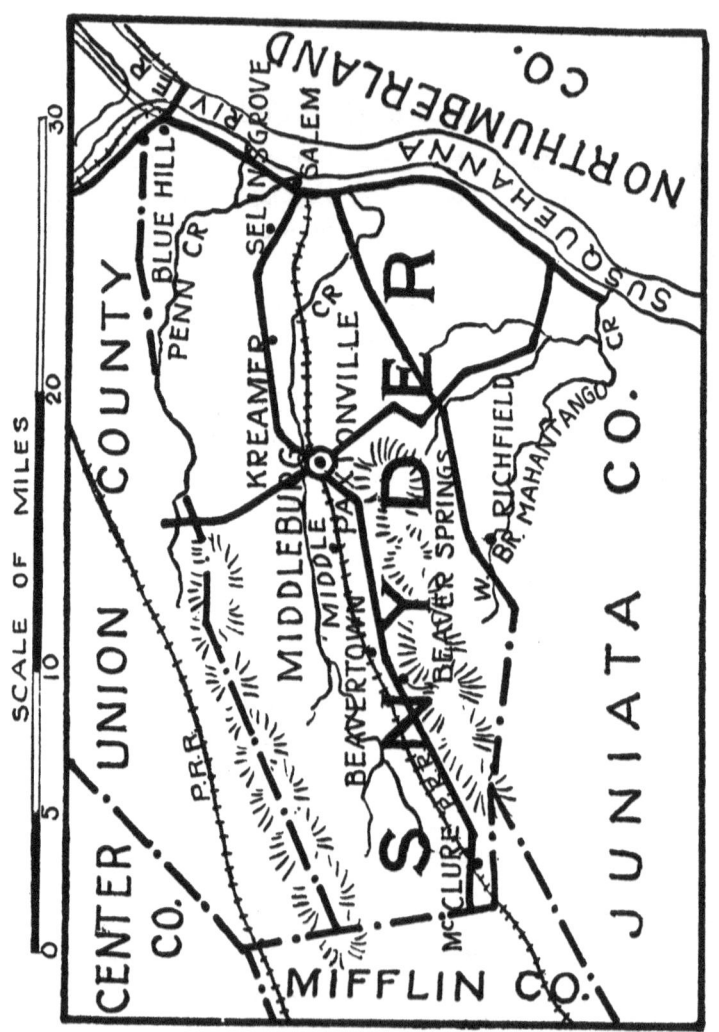

SNYDER COUNTY

tute; collegiate and theological courses, six large and several small buildings; main building, Selinsgrove Hall, was built in 1859, Gustavus Adolphus Hall in 1895, contains collection of forty-two pictures of Gustavus Adolphus, also brass memorial tablet to the men appointed in 1856, by the Evangelical Lutheran Synod of Maryland, to organize the Missionary Institute; the buildings contain portraits of Governor Simon Snyder, members of the faculty, and other Lutheran clergymen; on the campus is a granite Celtic cross, marking grave of the founder, Benjamin Kurtz, D.D., LL.D.; in the old Lutheran Cemetery is grave of Governor Snyder, Quincy granite monument, surmounted with his bust, life size, erected by the state in 1885.

Two miles west is SALEM; Row's Church, log, built, 1780, modernized in 1897. In KREAMER is the old brick hotel used for special sessions of court before 1855, for cases in immediate neighborhood; a short distance in the field stands the old block house, erected before 1781, where white settlers gathered in defense against Indians. One mile farther west, in 1781, Indians killed five members of the Stock family. Ten miles west from Selinsgrove is MIDDLEBURG, county seat; 498 feet above sea level; population 984; laid out in 1800. In Glendale Cemetery is grave of Hon. George Kreamer, nephew of Governor Snyder, and member of the Legislature, 1812–13; member of Congress, 1823–27; also grave of Captain Federick Evans, member of State Legislature, 1810–11, a defender of Fort McHenry, Baltimore, where, in 1814, the "Star-Spangled Banner" was written by Francis Scott Key.

On the banks of Stump's Run is shaft monument to soldiers and sailors of this country who fought in the different wars; erected in 1904, by county commissioners; Soldiers' Memorial Building, open to the public, is near the Lutheran Church; it was dedicated 1908; interior lined with marble, names of all soldiers and sailors of Snyder County are preserved within its walls, John F. Stetler, architect. Wooden bridge across Middle Creek, in good repair, is said to have been built in 1808 by John Aurand. Two miles west of town are the Hassinger Lutheran Churches, General Council east, present building erected in 1871, third on original site, first building in 1785; a split occurred, and the General Synod members built, in 1782, a quarter mile west; present church, in 1915.

Almost due south is Paxtonville, 510 feet above sea level; has wooden bridge over Middle Creek, built in 1851, John Bilger, builder; and ruins of Beaver blast furnace, once busiest industry in Middle Creek Valley, erected by Hon. Ner Middleswarth, the Kern Brothers and John C. Wilson, 1848–56; it was operated until 1866, power secured from a 200-foot head of water, running over two overshot wheels, one over the other. Westward is farm of Ner Feese on which gold and silver were discovered. BEAVERTOWN; population 525; 651 feet; originally Swifttown, named for John Swift, who had the land patented in 1760; was residence of Hon. Ner Middleswarth from 1792; he was reëlected thirteen times member of Legislature, twice speaker of the House —in 1828 and 1836; member of Congress, 1853–55; his last public service was that of associate judge.

BEAVER SPRINGS, elevation 591 feet, laid out in 1806, early chief industry, ore mines. Scenic beauty from Shade Mountain, a long ridge, summit near Beaver Springs, 1672 feet above sea level. McCLURE, six miles west, is where folding houses are manufactured; the largest ever made was produced here, and shipped to South America.

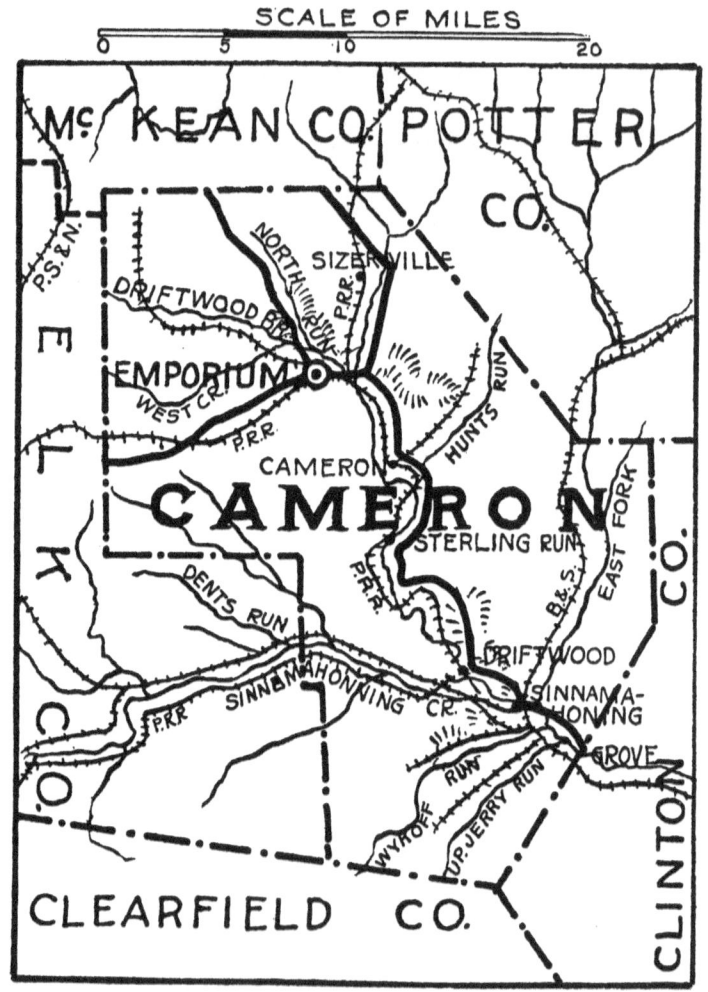

CAMERON COUNTY

LXVI
CAMERON COUNTY

FORMED March 29, 1860; named in honor of Hon. Simon Cameron, state senator at that time. Situated among the spurs of the Alleghenies, altitude varies from 794 feet to 2100 feet above sea level. The Sinnemahoning Creek and its tributaries drain three quarters of the county into the Susquehanna; along these waters, roads were cut and towns built for the extensive early lumbering and tanning operations; primeval forests of hemlock, oak, cherry, elm, and some of the finest white pine in the state. Beds of coal and fire clay still await development. Salt spring and a mineral spring of rare medicinal value are near SIZERVILLE. The county is now largely given up to the manufacture of high explosives, nitro-gelatine, smokeless powder, gun cotton, picric acid; in 1915 there was a merger of four powder companies who created a plant of vast proportions, over one hundred buildings, extending from the edge of Emporium, for over a mile, along the banks of Driftwood Creek.

EMPORIUM, county seat; population 3036; incorporated 1861; altitude 1031 feet above sea level; first settled in 1811, as Shippen, name changed through deference to an old tradition; in 1785, an agent of the Holland Land Company, owning large territories in Pennsylvania and New York, removed the bark from a tree where the town now stands, and carved the word, "Emporium." A typical mountain town, the streets follow the winding way of Driftwood Stream, or climb the mountain side where magnificent views of scenic grandeur await the beholder. Best architecture, the Episcopal Church, brown stone, English chapel design, Cram & Ferguson, of Boston, architects, built in 1901; other denominations have modern brick buildings. The large brick courthouse, built, 1890, is in a park on the hillside, overlooking the town; in the grounds is monument to soldiers of the Civil War.

CAMERON, in 1889, one hundred coke ovens, "beehive" design, were built here to coke the coal in the near-by hills, for the blast furnace at Emporium; now abandoned, and today mountain wild flowers blossom along the row of silent hearths. STERLING RUN; in this quaint village belongs the honor of the first church in the county, Presbyterian, "The Pine Street Church," erected in 1826, so-called in consequence of the old Pine Street Church, Philadelphia, contributing funds to pay the workmen and buy the windows; the lumber and much of the construction being donated by the pioneers; built of hewn pine logs, chinked with plaster of moss and mud, and fastened with hand-wrought nails, this little chapel endures, while those who shaped it sleep in the little churchyard at its threshold.

DRIFTWOOD, near the "Crescent," a half moon shaped mountain forming sides of the valley for nearly three points of the compass; claims the first settlement by white man within the county, in 1804; in the center of the village, facing the Sinnemahoning Creek, is the "Bucktail" Monument, in memory of Cameron's sons who fought for the Union, erected by the state in

CAMERON COUNTY 503

1908, inscription, "From this town, on April 27, 1861, the Cameron, Elk and McKean County Rifles, under leadership of Thomas L. Kane, afterwards Commanding Officer of the Regiment, later a Major-General, embarked on four rafts for Harrisburg, where they were mustered into the service of the State, and formed the nucleus, about which the Bucktail Regiment of the Pennsylvania Reserve Corps was organized; which during its time of service, was almost continuously attached to the army of the Potomac."

SINNEMAHONING (Stony-lick), site of an Indian village called "The Lodge," the battle ground of Peter Grove, famous Indian fighter, a picturesquely beautiful spot. Here were born the beautiful Clafflin sisters, Lady Cook (Tennesee Clafflin), and Mrs. Martin Woodhull (Victoria Clafflin), now a wealthy philanthropist in England; their father, Buckman Clafflin, a pioneer, opened the first store in the county in 1829.

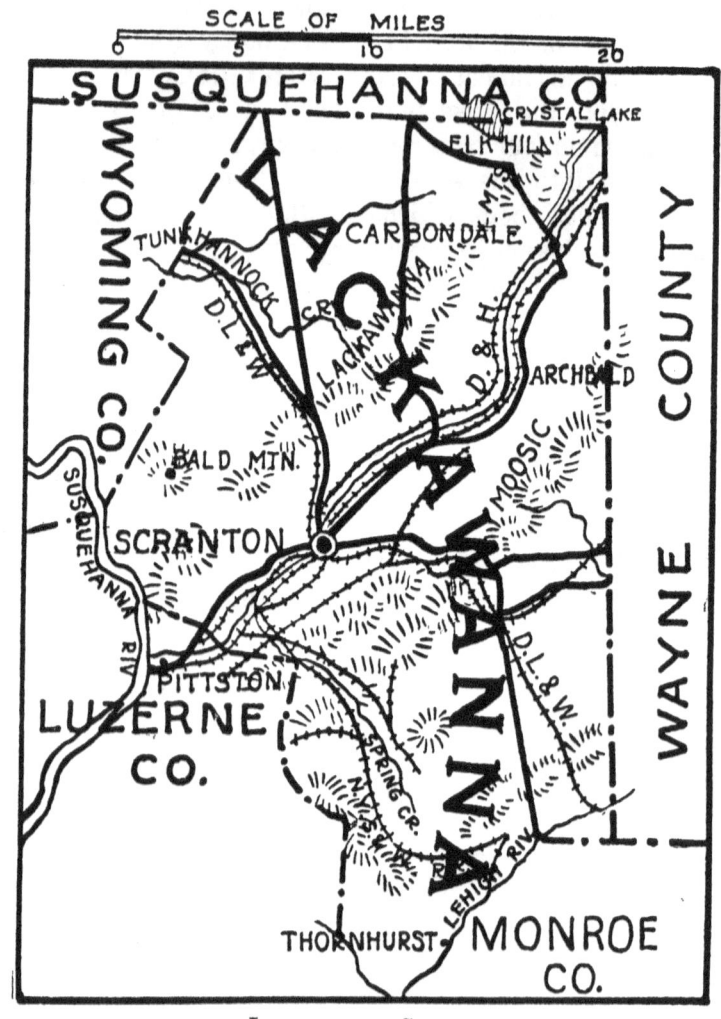

Lackawanna County

LXVII
LACKAWANNA COUNTY

FORMED August 13, 1878; named for the great Lackawanna coal basin; an Indian word, signifying "The Forks of a Stream." Chief industry, anthracite coal mining, confined to the long-depressed trough forming the Lackawanna Valley and to the mountains bordering it on both sides, with Bald Mountain, in Lackawanna Range, 2250 feet high, and Big Stoney among the Moosic Mountains, 2230 feet. Originally settled by Connecticut people who disputed the right of Pennsylvania to jurisdiction; life and growth have been the result of the coal-mining industry, which brought into it large numbers of Welsh, Irish, German, English, and Scotch, whose descendants dominate the region; latterly have come Polish, Slavs, Italians, and Lithuanians, a heterogeneous but rapidly assimilating mining population.

The mining of anthracite coal began at Carbondale in the early twenties; the old No. 1 plane is marked with monument and tablets; coal was taken over the Moosic Mountains to Honesdale, Wayne County, by steep inclined planes, up which the loaded cars were drawn by ropes or cables, and the empty cars let down; thence by canal to Roundout, on the Hudson; on the levels, between planes, cars were drawn by horses; later a descending grade was given to the tracks over which the cars ran by gravity; a similar gravity railroad near Scranton, carried coal to the Delaware &

Hudson Canal at Hawley, below Honesdale, both now abandoned for steam roads.

The country northwest has well-cultivated farm lands; that, southeast, blends with the Pocono Highlands, is wild and picturesque; an almost unbroken wilderness for thirty miles, excepting along the line of the Delaware, Lackawanna & Western Railroad; on both sides of this road are good highways; the main road, the whole length of the valley, is exceptionally fine. The road from Gouldsboro Station was built by Jay Gould, 1855, when he was interested with Mr. Pratt in a tannery at Gouldsboro (now Thornhurst).

At Carbondale, crossing Moosic Mountains, is road to Honesdale, following the line of the old Delaware & Hudson gravity road; at Dundaff, about five miles north of Carbondale, this road runs along the edge of Crystal Lake, near are the Twin Knobs of Elk Hill, about 2500 feet high. A point of geologic interest is the Archbald Pot Hole, said to be largest of the kind in this country; a cylindrical hole twenty feet deep, by thirty feet wide, eroded in the ice age through the overlying rocks down to the coal measures.

SCRANTON, county seat, population 137,783; laid out on site of an Indian village, Muncy Tribe; began as an iron town; iron in large quantities was found in the hills three miles south of the city, and a suitable quality of limestone was also supposed to exist there; but the coal business superseded; the old ore mine, and abandoned road to furnaces at Scranton, are of historic and picturesque interest.

The courthouse, on Washington Avenue near center of town, stands in a square of ground, Romanesque,

West Mountain stone, built 1881-84, architect, S. G, Perry. St. Luke's Protestant Episcopal Church. Wyoming Avenue near Linden Street, Gothic, West Mountain stone, built 1866-71, architect, R. M. Udjohn, New York; contains Tiffany mosaic panel, back of font, "Baptism of Christ," also Tiffany window in chancel, "The Ascension." St. Peter's Cathedral, at corner of Wyoming Avenue and Linden, Italian Renaissance, brick, built, 1866, architect, Joel Amsden; remodeled 1883 by Durand, Philadelphia. Administration Building of the International Correspondence Schools, Wyoming Avenue between Vine and Mulberry Streets, Gothic, West Mountain stone, built in 1898; architect, W. Scott Collins; window by Kenyon Cox, made in 1898, "Science Instructing Industry."

The Scranton Public Library (Albright Memorial) is placed as an accent of beauty, corner of Washington Avenue and Vine Street, French chateau style, fifteenth and sixteenth centuries, after Cluny Museum, Paris; gray Indiana limestone and brown Madina stone laid in coursed ashlar, built in 1893; architects, Green & Wicks, Buffalo, New York; contains portraits of Joseph J. Albright, painted in 1902, artist, Bayard Henry Tyler; and of John J. Albright, artist, Chartrain, France; stained glass windows are illustrative of celebrated book bindings in the past; a marble mosaic floor is in the entrance hall.

Second Presbyterian Church, Jefferson Avenue between Vine and Mulberry Streets, Romanesque; West, Mountain stone, built 1885; has Tiffany windows, "Charity" and "Hope." Madison Avenue Synagogue, near Vine Street; Byzantine, West Mountain stone, built 1902, architect, George W. Kramer, New York. First Presbyterian Church, corner of Madison Avenue and Olive Street, perpendicular Gothic, Indiana limestone; built 1903, architect, Holden, New York; windows by John La Farge, "The Woman at the Well"; and by Tiffany, "The Ascension"; Tiffany mosaic, "Pentecost." Immanuel Baptist Church, corner of Jefferson Avenue and Mulberry Street, Gothic, Hummelstown redstone, built 1909, architect, Edward Langley, Scranton. Elm Park Church, corner of Linden and Jefferson Streets, Romanesque, West Mountain stone, built 1892, architect, George W. Kramer.

Lackawanna Railroad Station, Lackawanna and Jefferson Avenues, Renaissance, Indiana limestone, granite base, built 1909, architects, Kenneth Murchison, New York, and Edward Langley; has interior finishings of Grueby tiles; and mosaic mural panels of views along the Lackawanna Railroad. The Everhart Museum of Natural History, Science and Art, in Nay Aug Park, south end of Milberry Street, given by the late Dr. I. F. Everhart, and sustained by generous endowment; Renaissance, terra-cotta, built 1908, architects, Blackwood & Nelson; contains also the Hollister collection of Indian curios. Much natural beauty centers about the water supply system of the Scranton Gas and Water Company, which has over ten miles of fine driveways, including the road to top of Mount Anonymous, overlooking the lake; and Long Swamp Drive and roads up about Scrub Oak Mountain.

BOOKS USED AS REFERENCE, AND CONTRIBUTED ARTICLES

American Art Annual..........F. N. Levy
Annals......................J. F. Watson
Automobile..................Blue Book
Colonial Doorways.............A. H. Wharton
Early Pietists................J. Sachse
Fairmount Park...............C. S. Keyser
Forges and Furnaces..........Colonial Dames
Guide Book to Historic Germantown......................C. F. Jenkins
Hikes for Boy Scouts of America.Charles D. Hart
Historic Excursions............J. Campbell
History of Pennsylvania........Egle
Indian Trails..................G. P. Donehoo
List of Sites..................William J. Campbell
Music........................F. I. Brock
Our Philadelphia..............J. and E. R. Pennell
Pennsylvania Primer...........Barr Ferree
Philadelphia.................Sharf & Westcott
Philadelphia Firsts............W. I. Rutter, Jr.
Philadelphia Streets...........J. Jackson
Population....................U. S. Census for 1920
Story of Philadelphia..........L. J. Rhoads
The Keystone.................Pennypacker
United States................Baedeker
Washington's Itinerary.........William S. Baker
Many County Histories and Historic Reports.

www.ingramcontent.com/pod-product-compliance
Lightning Source LLC
Chambersburg PA
CBHW031538300426
44111CB00006BA/98